Story and Art by Arina Tanemura

SAKURA HIME
Princess Sakura

3

SAKURA HIME
The Legend of Princess Sakura

CONTENTS

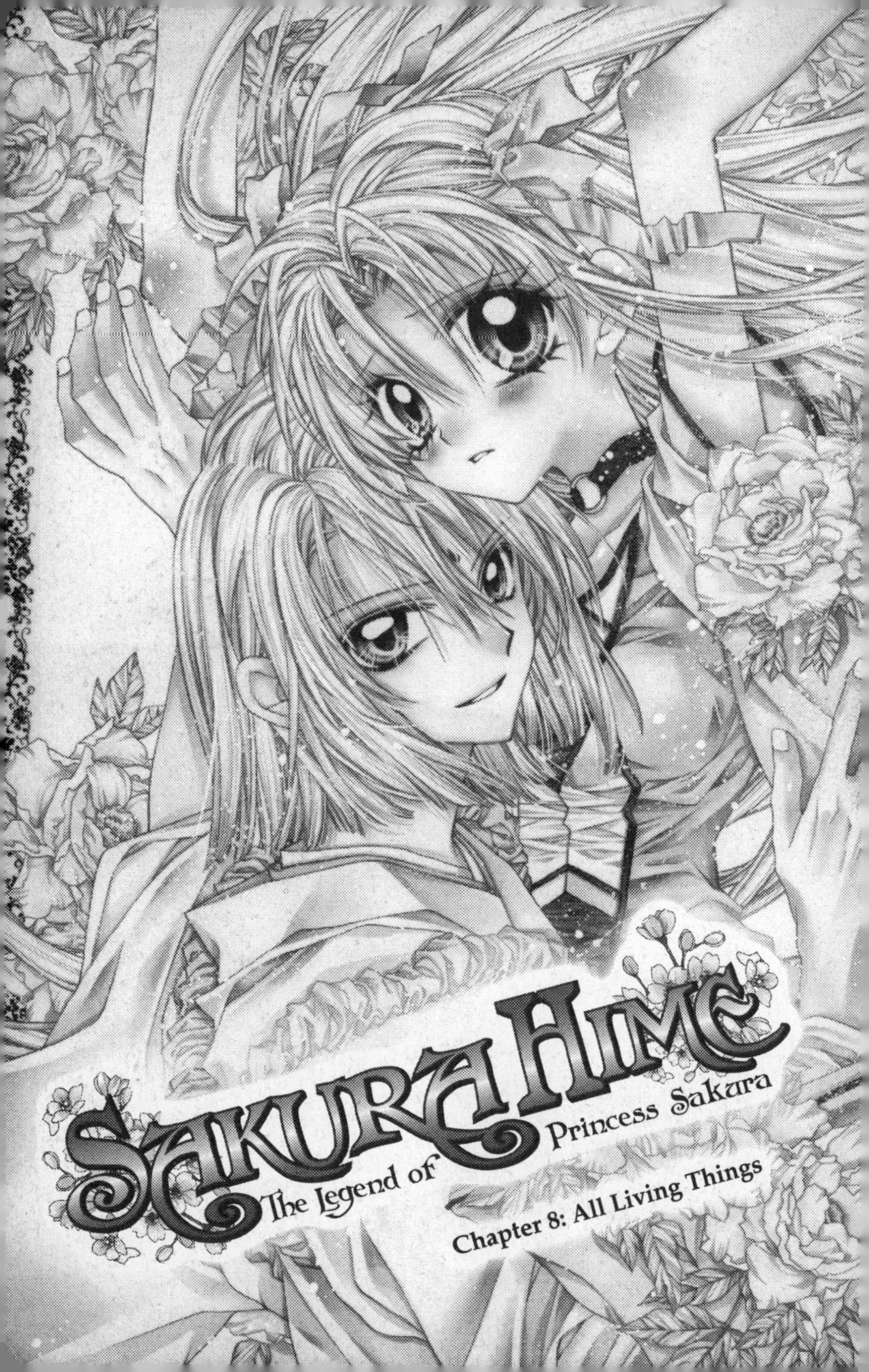
SAKURA HIME
The Legend of Princess Sakura
Chapter 8: All Living Things

Characters
PRINCESS SAKURA
Princess Kaguya's granddaughter who has the power to defeat youko. She is Aoba's betrothed.
AOBA
Prince Oura, the emperor's son. He hates Princess Sakura...?!
BYAKUYA
A priestess who knows Princess Sakura's secret.
KOHAKU
A ninja. Klutz.
FUJIMURASAKI
Aoba's uncle and the Togu.
ENJU
A mysterious man.
ASAGIRI
Princess Sakura's friend.
HAYATE
Kohaku's childhood friend. He used to be human.
OUMI
Princess Sakura's lady-in-waiting. She hates the youko.
COUNCILOR
Aoba's Adviser

SAKURA HIME
The Legend of Princess Sakura

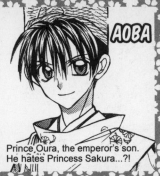

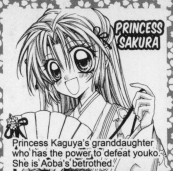

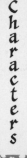

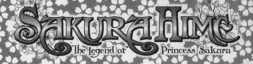

Story Thus Far

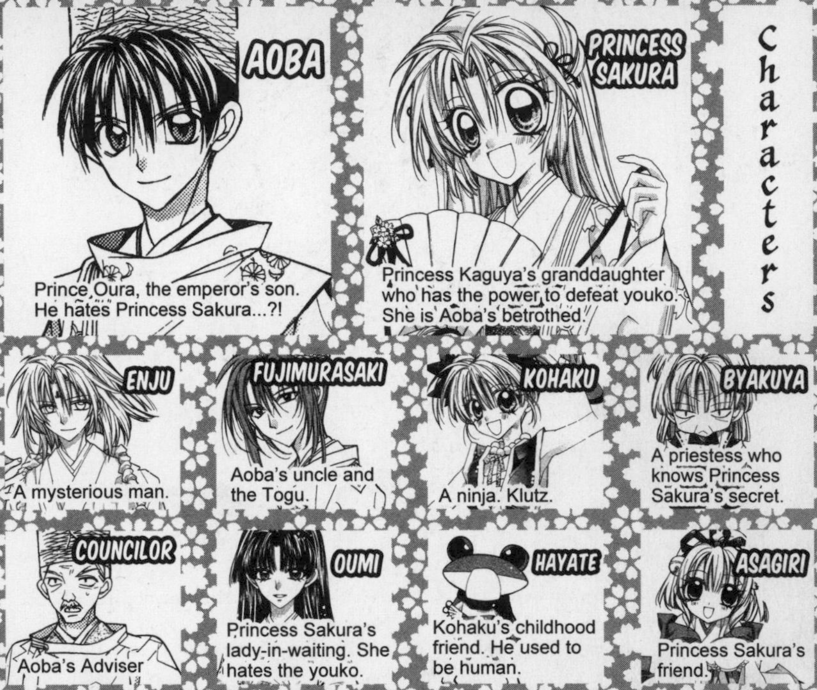

Heian era. Princess Sakura is 14 years old. She is suddenly ordered by Aoba to come to the capital. She runs away, but circumstances take a sharp turn when she looks up at the full moon that night.

Sakura learns that she is actually Princess Kaguya's granddaughter and the only one who can wield the mystic sword Chizakura to defeat the youko. She also finds out that her soul symbol, which reveals her fate, is "destroy"...

When Aoba learns of it, he captures Sakura, intending to kill her. But Fujimurasaki arrives and gives Sakura orders from the emperor to officially hunt down a youko.

Sakura heads for Uji where she is taken outside by her lady-in-waiting, Oumi, who wishes to speak with her. Sakura is happy, thinking Oumi wants to be friends again, but Oumi suddenly turns into a youko and attacks! Sakura is told she she must use Chizakura, but she is unable to make the decision to kill Oumi.

Then the man who turned Oumi into a youko appears before Sakura...

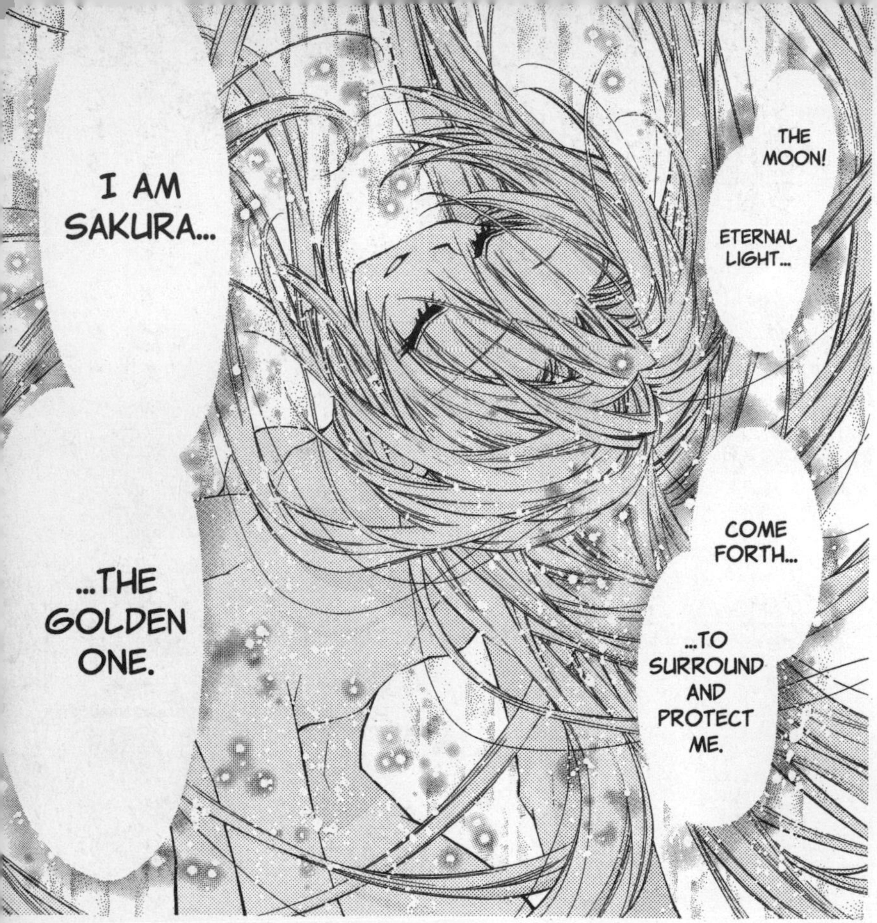
THE MOON!
ETERNAL LIGHT...
COME FORTH...
...TO SURROUND AND PROTECT ME.
I AM SAKURA...
...THE GOLDEN ONE.

Chapter 8: All Living Things

Lead-in What lies at the end of love and hatred?

※ I'm giving away the story, so please read this after you read the chapter.

We're in the midst of things, so I'm sorry I can't really talk a lot about this chapter either... This was when there was a huge councilor fad going on among the staff members. (My assistants and the editor.) "Middle-aged men" and "curvy girls" are characters that not many shojo mangaka create, but I like those kinds of characters, so I draw them. I want to create another older male character again...

"What is your favorite panel?!"...

My favorite panel is (Sorry... This is a request from a fan letter I received). Hmm... The panel that shows the transformation effect, I think. I took a very long time drawing it, so I guess that's why I've developed strong feelings for the scene.

I draw my youko with a feeling of frustration, thinking, "Hmm... I'm terrible at drawing them..." but I've received fan letters that say the youko are scary, so I've realized that the readers are about 30% more pure-hearted than I imagined. But I'd still like to work harder in drawing them.

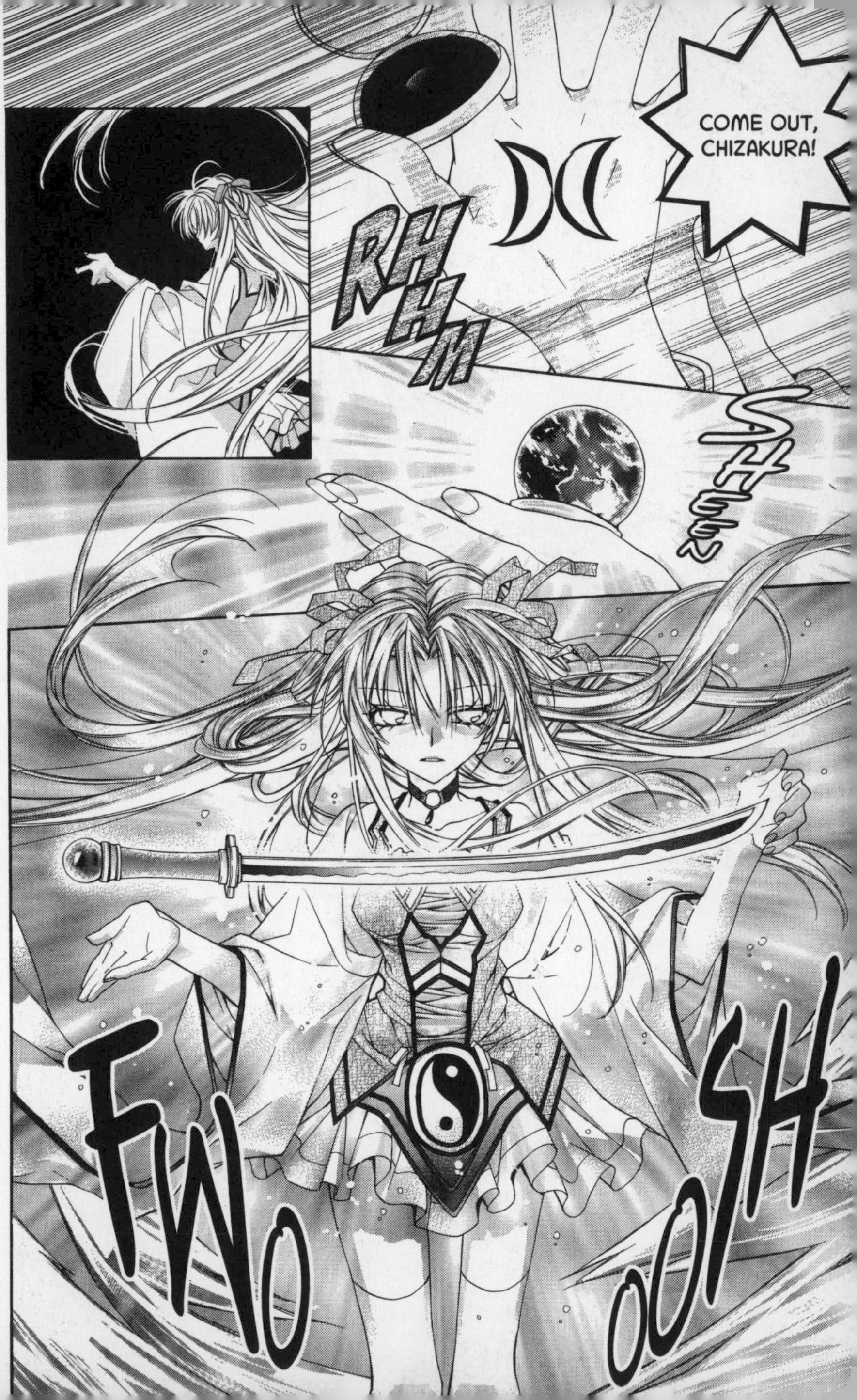
COME OUT, CHIZAKURA!
RHHM
SHEEN
FWOOSH

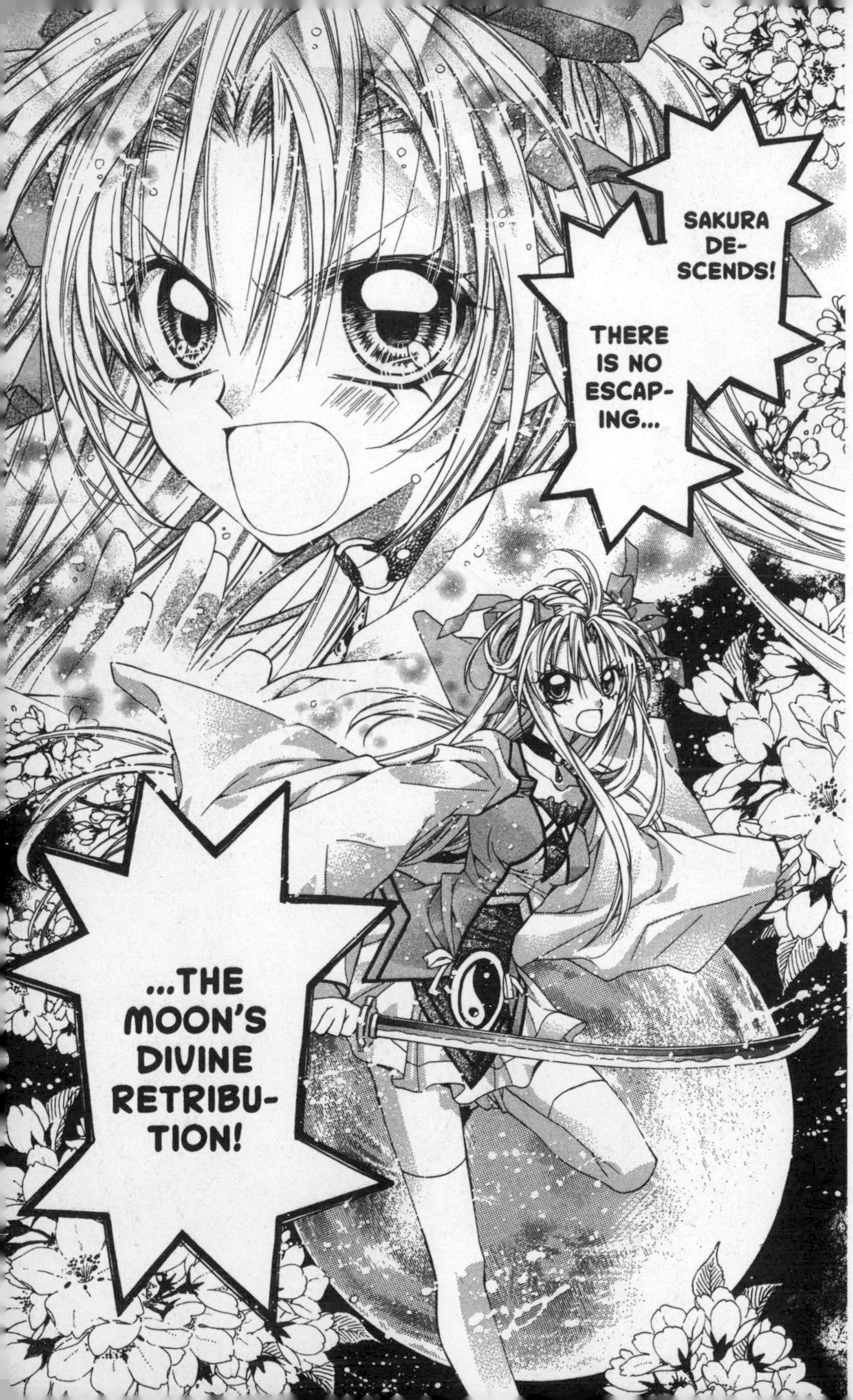
SAKURA DE-SCENDS!
THERE IS NO ESCAP-ING...
...THE MOON'S DIVINE RETRIBU-TION!

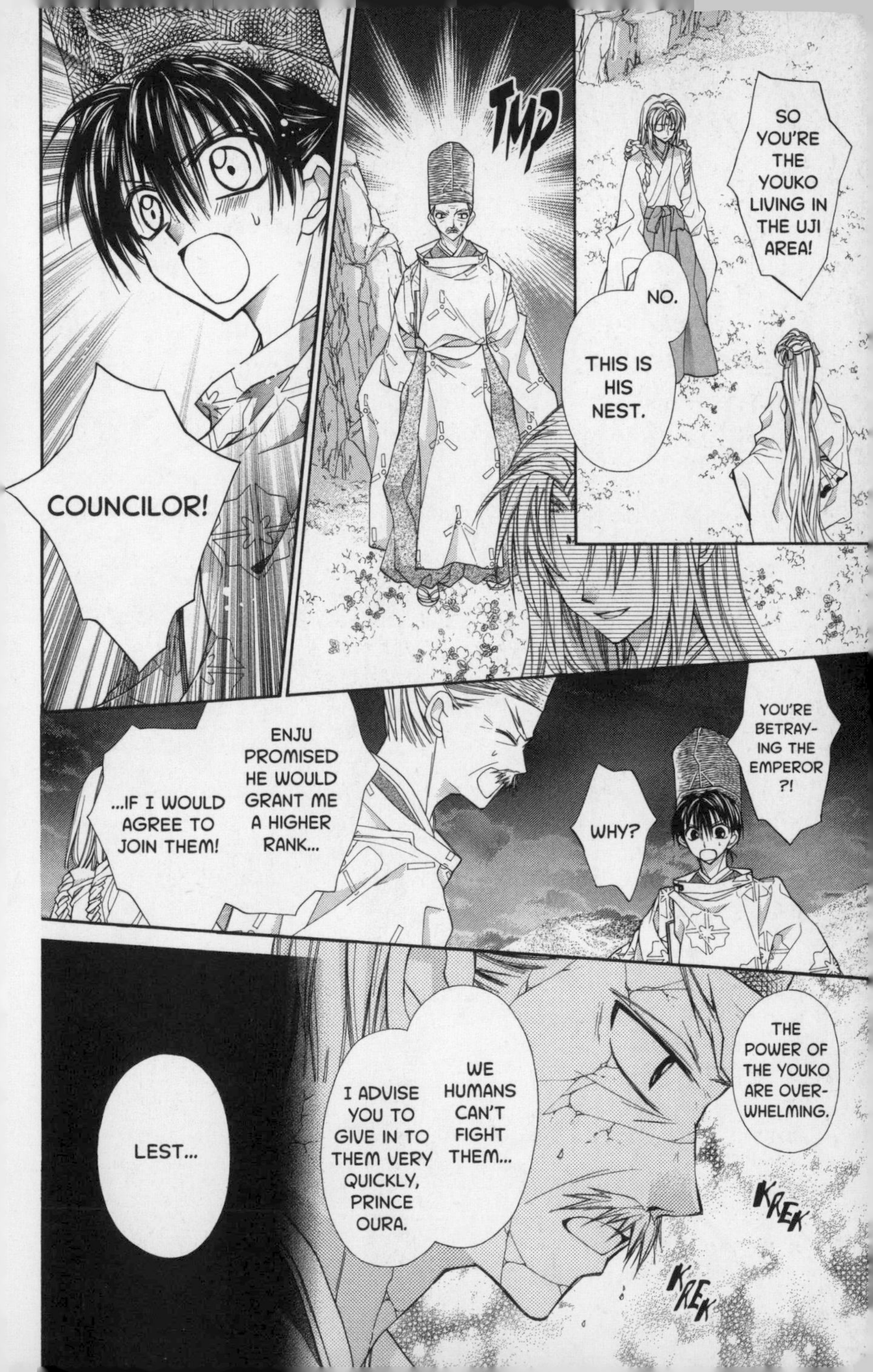
SO YOU'RE THE YOUKO LIVING IN THE UJI AREA!
NO.
THIS IS HIS NEST.
TMP
COUNCILOR!
YOU'RE BETRAY-ING THE EMPEROR?!
WHY?
ENJU PROMISED HE WOULD GRANT ME A HIGHER RANK...
...IF I WOULD AGREE TO JOIN THEM!
THE POWER OF THE YOUKO ARE OVER-WHELMING.
KREK
KREK
WE HUMANS CAN'T FIGHT THEM...
I ADVISE YOU TO GIVE IN TO THEM VERY QUICKLY, PRINCE OURA.
LEST...

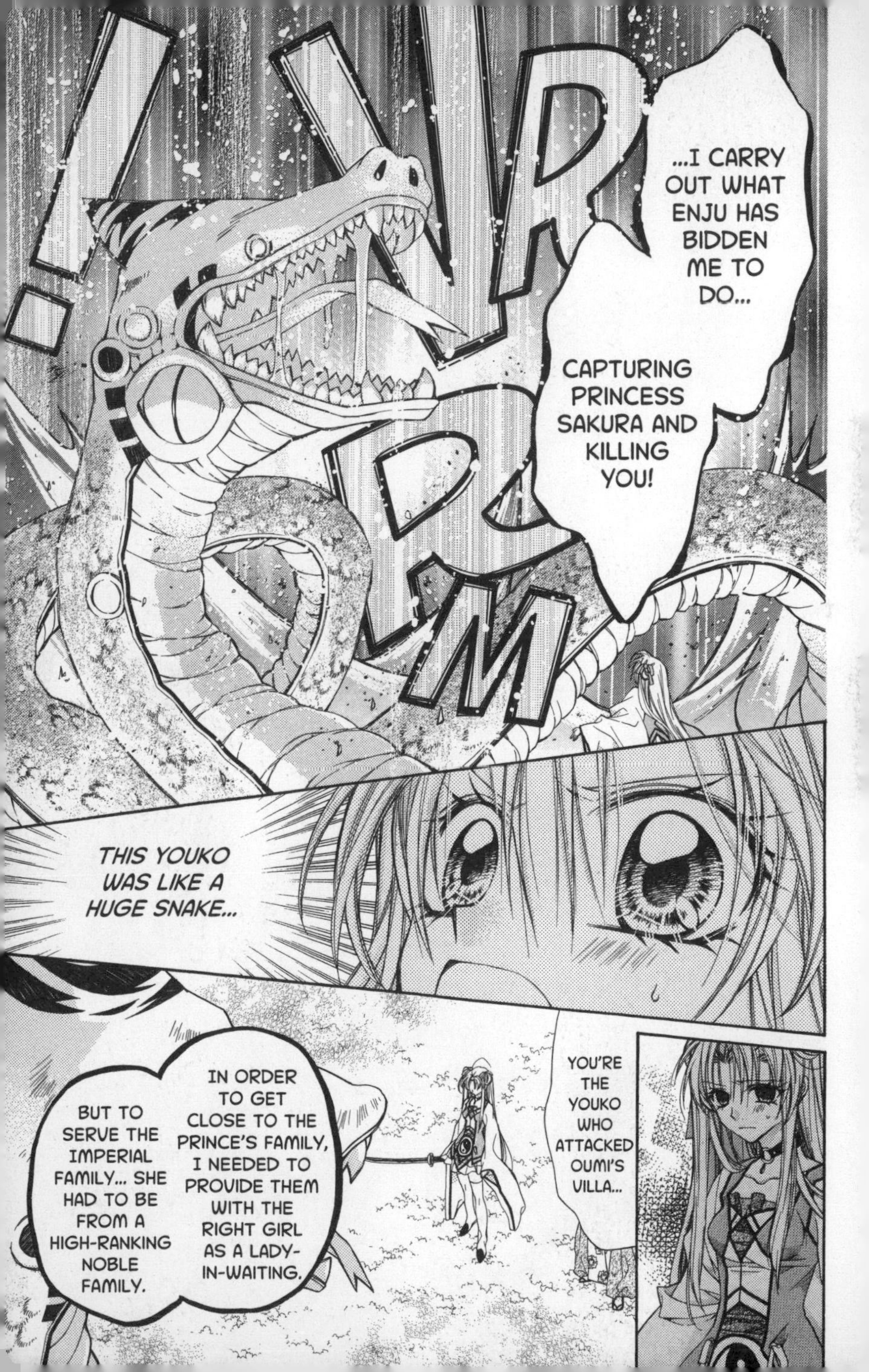
...I CARRY OUT WHAT ENJU HAS BIDDEN ME TO DO...
CAPTURING PRINCESS SAKURA AND KILLING YOU!
THIS YOUKO WAS LIKE A HUGE SNAKE...
YOU'RE THE YOUKO WHO ATTACKED OUMI'S VILLA...
IN ORDER TO GET CLOSE TO THE PRINCE'S FAMILY, I NEEDED TO PROVIDE THEM WITH THE RIGHT GIRL AS A LADY-IN-WAITING.
BUT TO SERVE THE IMPERIAL FAMILY... SHE HAD TO BE FROM A HIGH-RANKING NOBLE FAMILY.

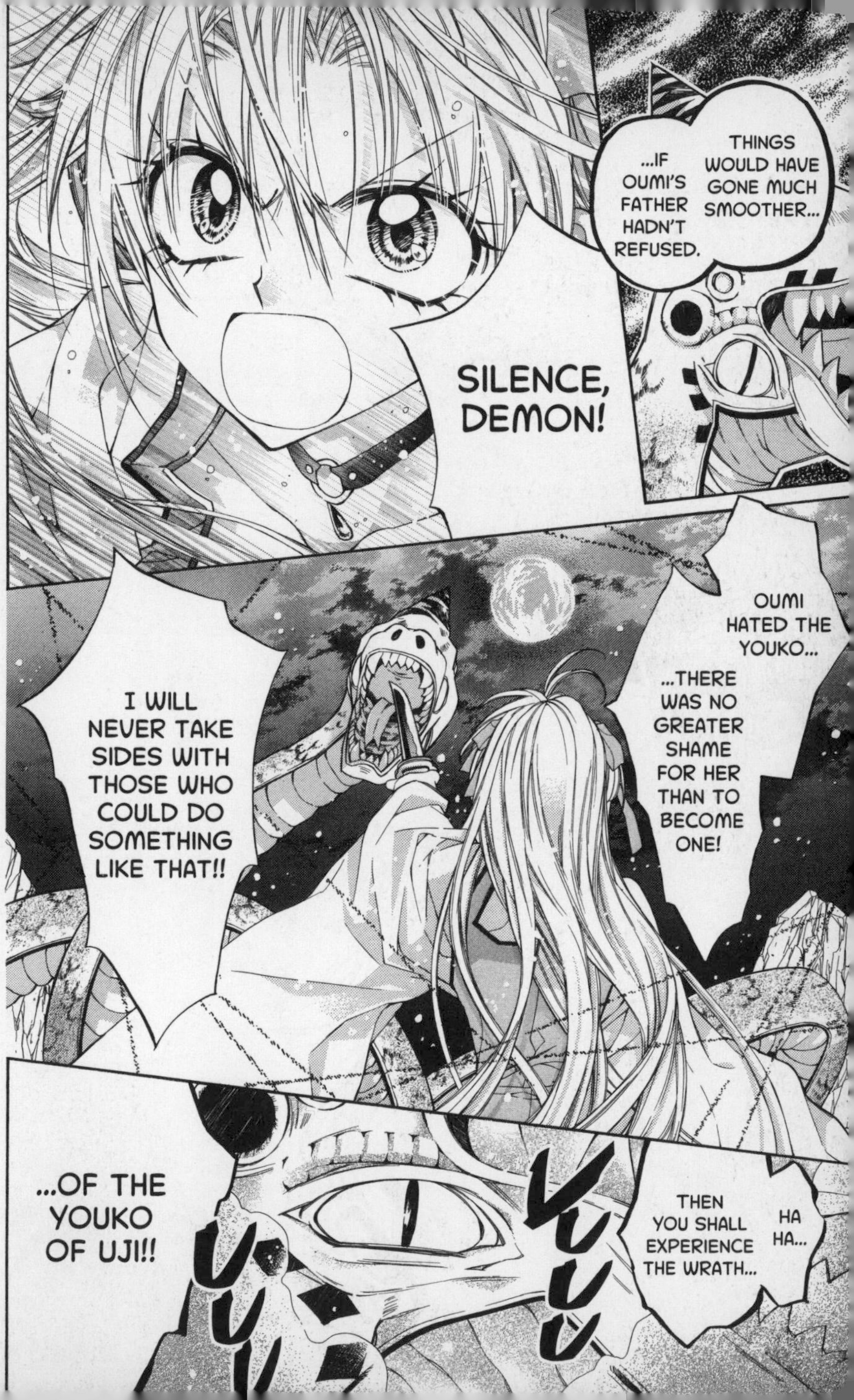
THINGS WOULD HAVE GONE MUCH SMOOTHER...
...IF OUMI'S FATHER HADN'T REFUSED.
SILENCE, DEMON!
OUMI HATED THE YOUKO...
...THERE WAS NO GREATER SHAME FOR HER THAN TO BECOME ONE!
I WILL NEVER TAKE SIDES WITH THOSE WHO COULD DO SOMETHING LIKE THAT!!
HA HA...
THEN YOU SHALL EXPERIENCE THE WRATH...
...OF THE YOUKO OF UJI!!

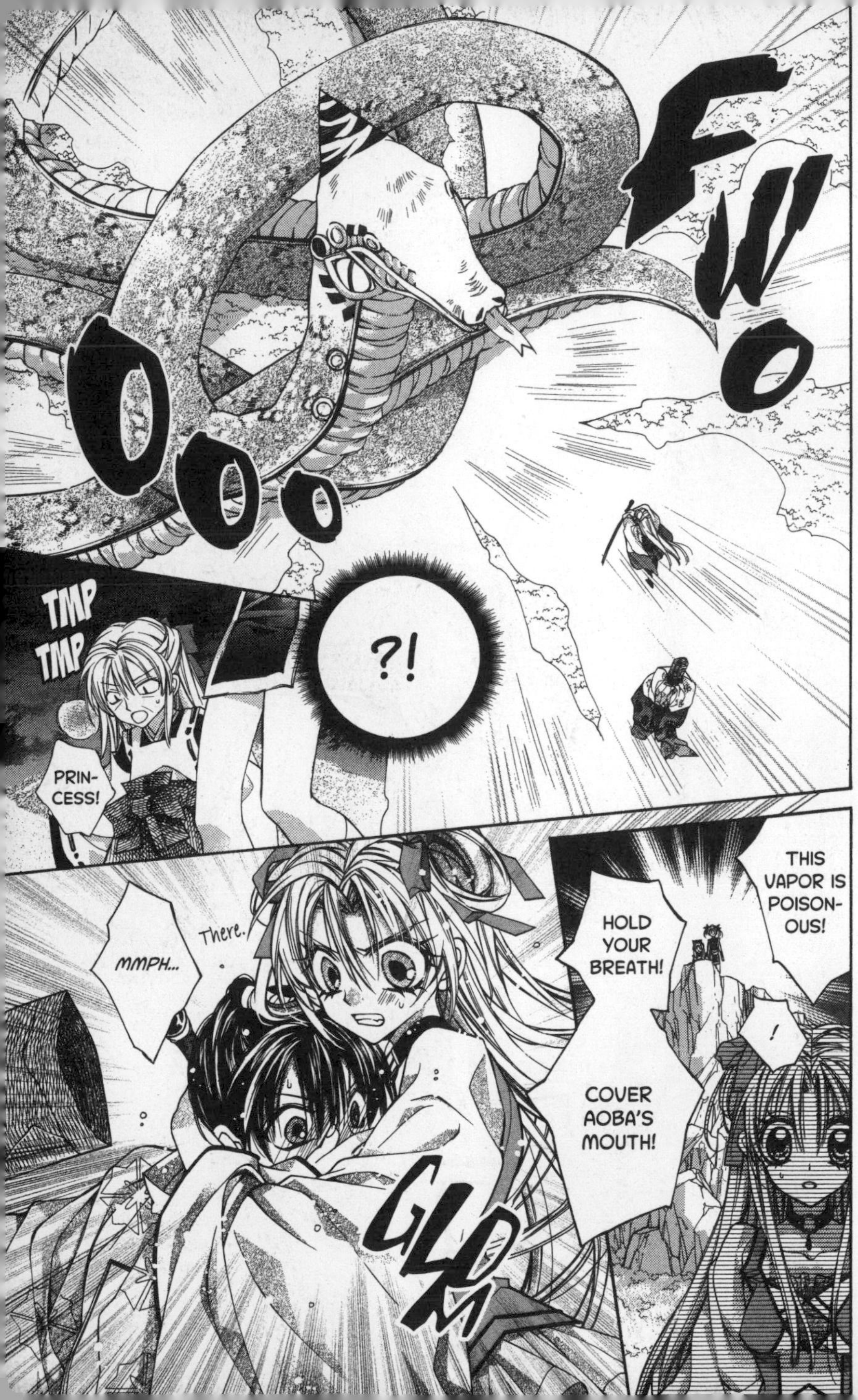
FWO
OOOO
?!
TMP
TMP
PRIN-CESS!
THIS VAPOR IS POISON-OUS!
HOLD YOUR BREATH!
!
COVER AOBA'S MOUTH!
GLR
There.
MMPH...

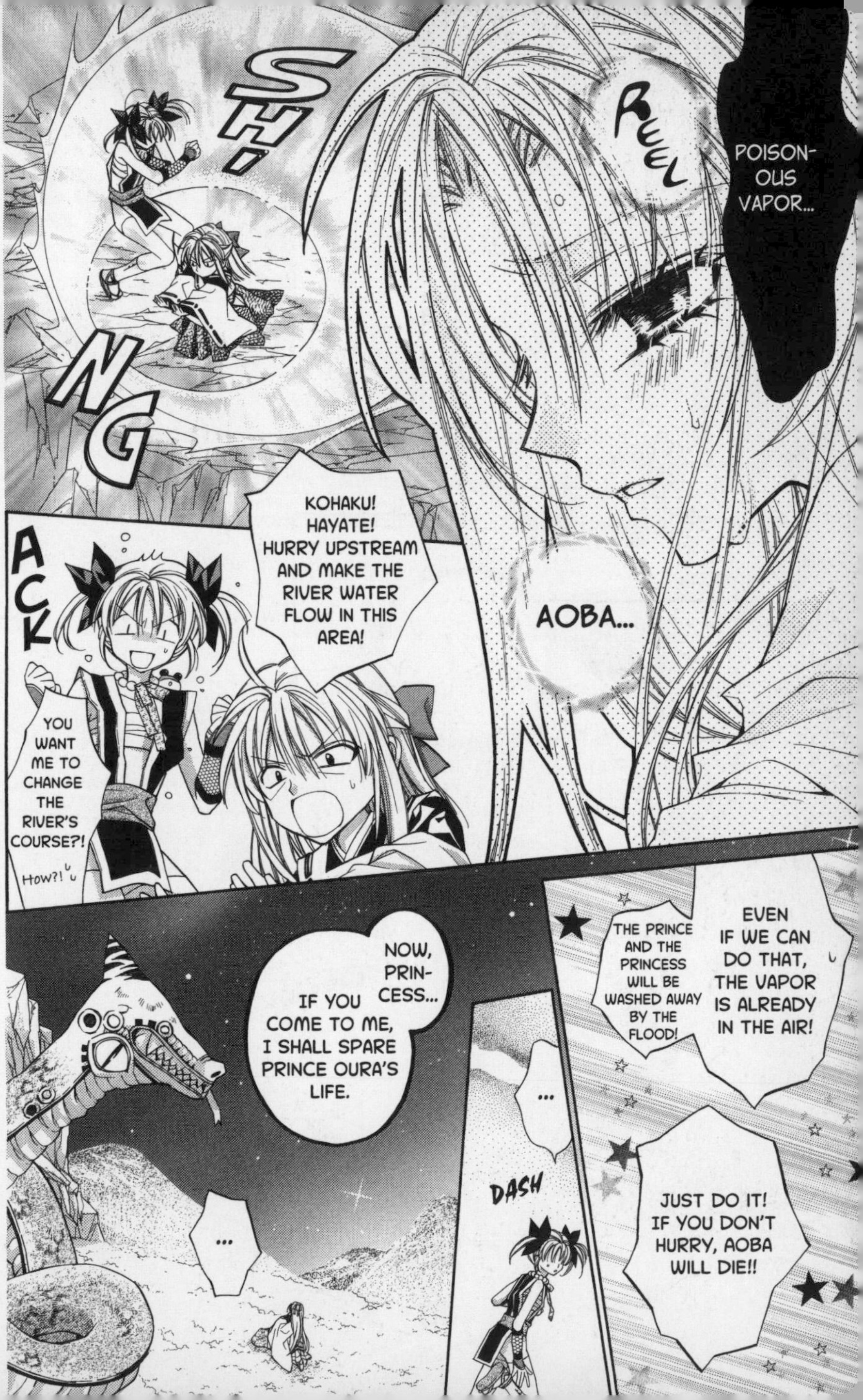
REEL
POISON-OUS VAPOR...
AOBA...
SHING
KOHAKU! HAYATE! HURRY UPSTREAM AND MAKE THE RIVER WATER FLOW IN THIS AREA!
ACK
YOU WANT ME TO CHANGE THE RIVER'S COURSE?!
How?!
EVEN IF WE CAN DO THAT, THE VAPOR IS ALREADY IN THE AIR!
THE PRINCE AND THE PRINCESS WILL BE WASHED AWAY BY THE FLOOD!
...
JUST DO IT! IF YOU DON'T HURRY, AOBA WILL DIE!!
DASH
NOW, PRIN-CESS...
IF YOU COME TO ME, I SHALL SPARE PRINCE OURA'S LIFE.
...

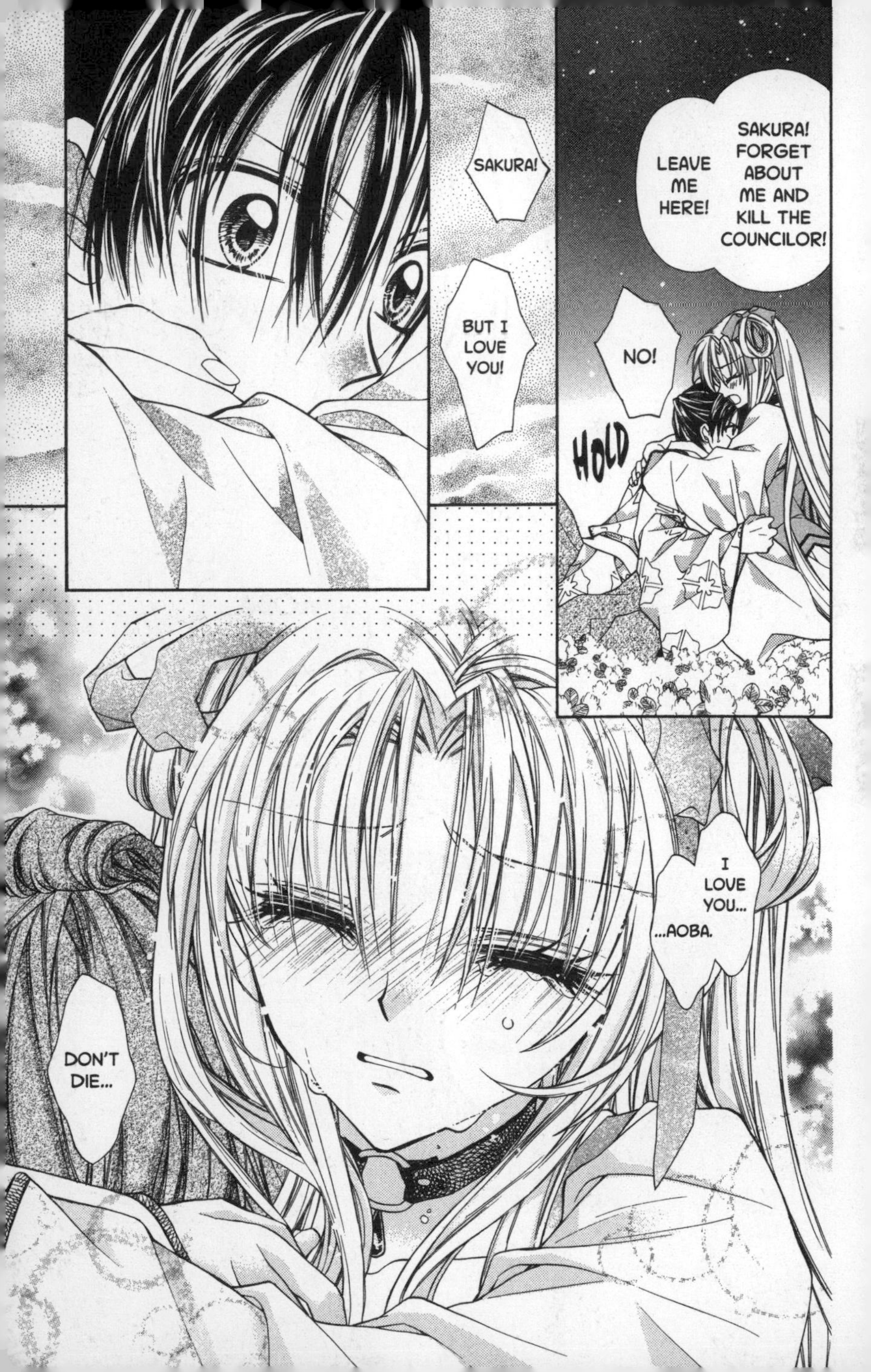
SAKURA! FORGET ABOUT ME AND KILL THE COUNCILOR!
LEAVE ME HERE!
NO!
HOLD
SAKURA!
BUT I LOVE YOU!
I LOVE YOU...
...AOBA.
DON'T DIE...

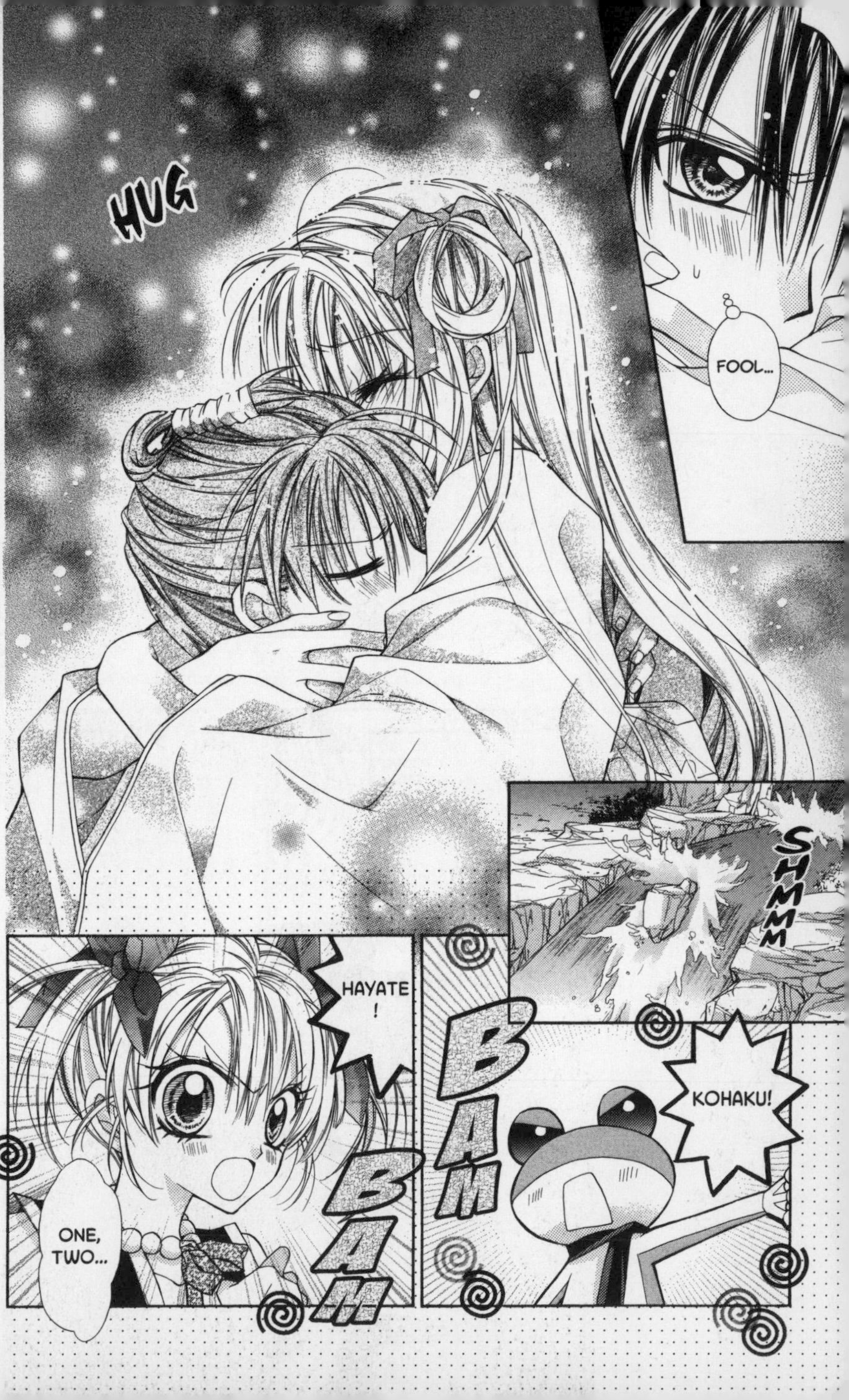
FOOL...
SHMMM
HUG
KOHAKU!
BAM
HAYATE!
BAM
ONE, TWO...

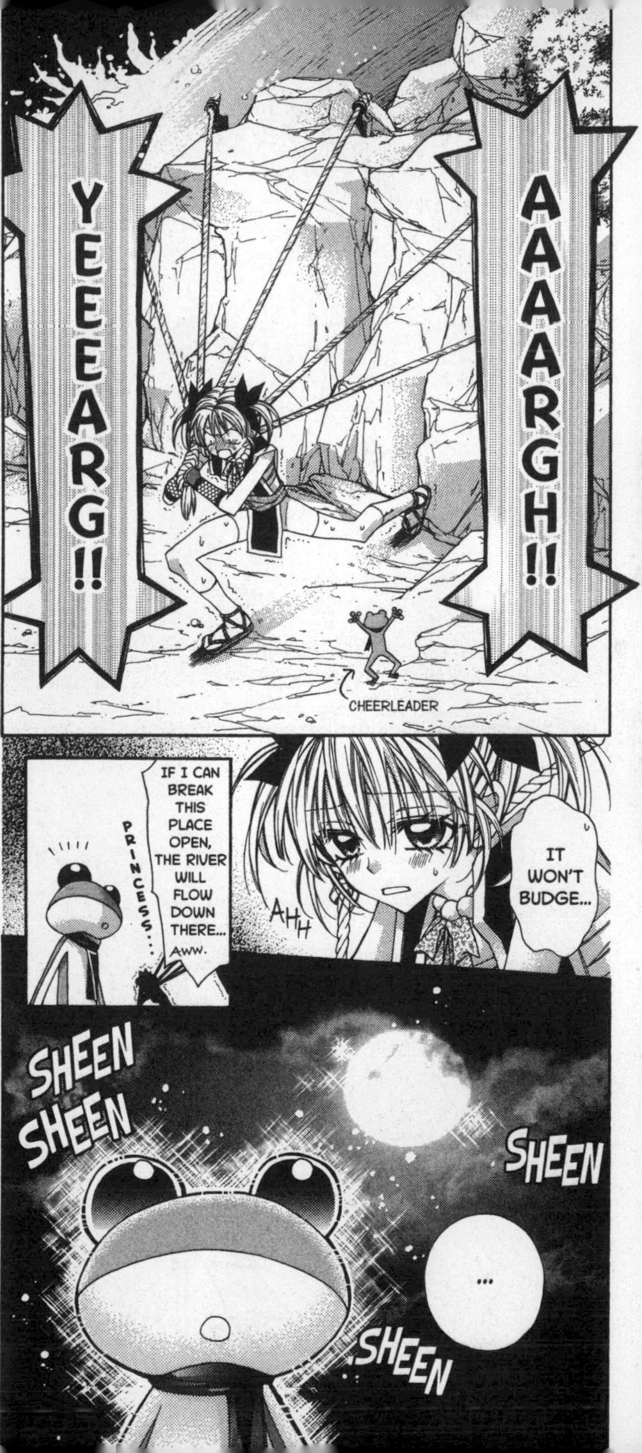
AAAARGH!!
YEEEARG!!
CHEERLEADER
IT WON'T BUDGE...
AHH
IF I CAN BREAK THIS PLACE OPEN, THE RIVER WILL FLOW DOWN THERE... AWW.
PRINCESS...
SHEEN
SHEEN SHEEN
...
SHEEN

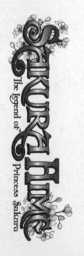

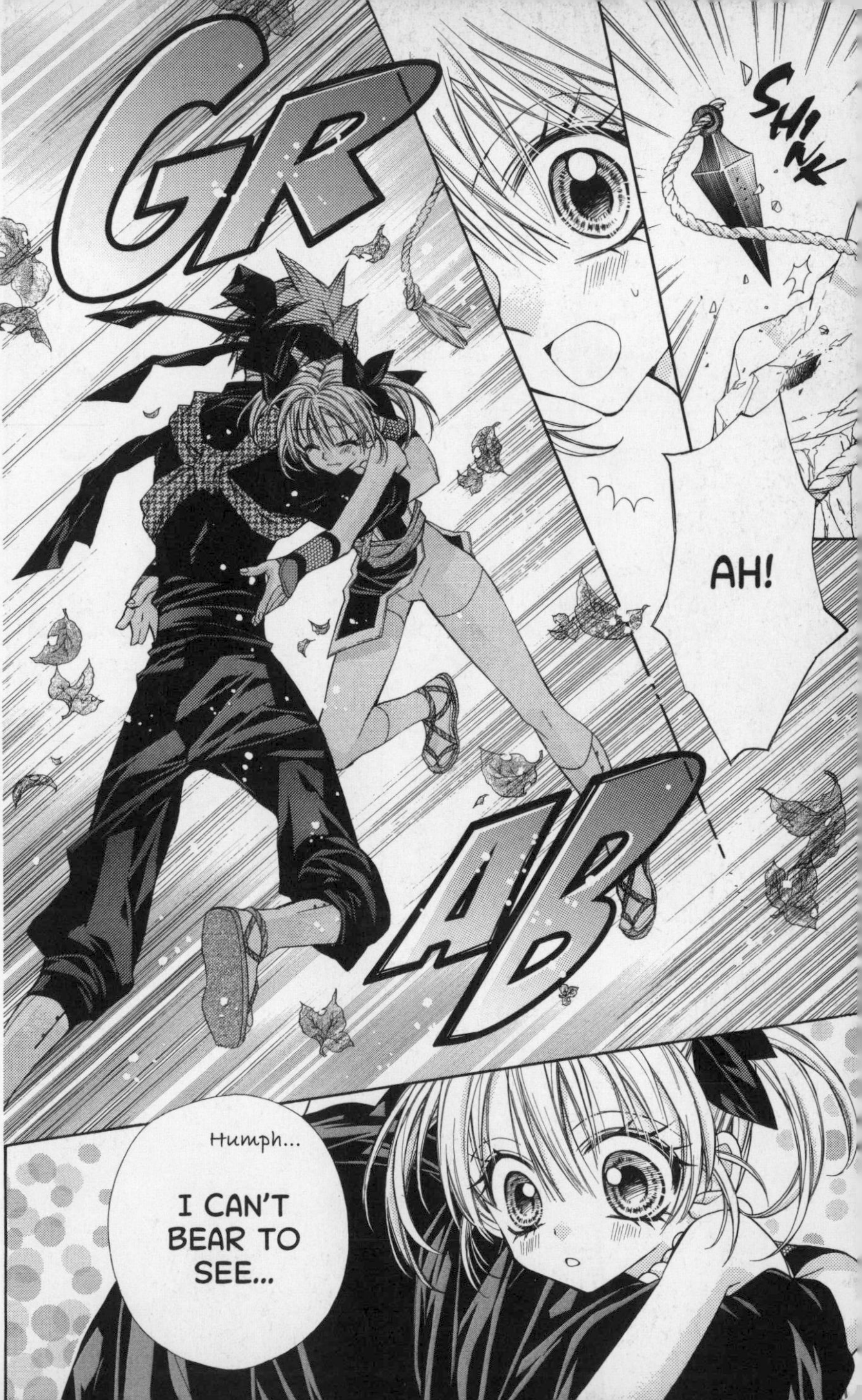
SHINK
AH!
GRAB
Humph...
I CAN'T BEAR TO SEE...

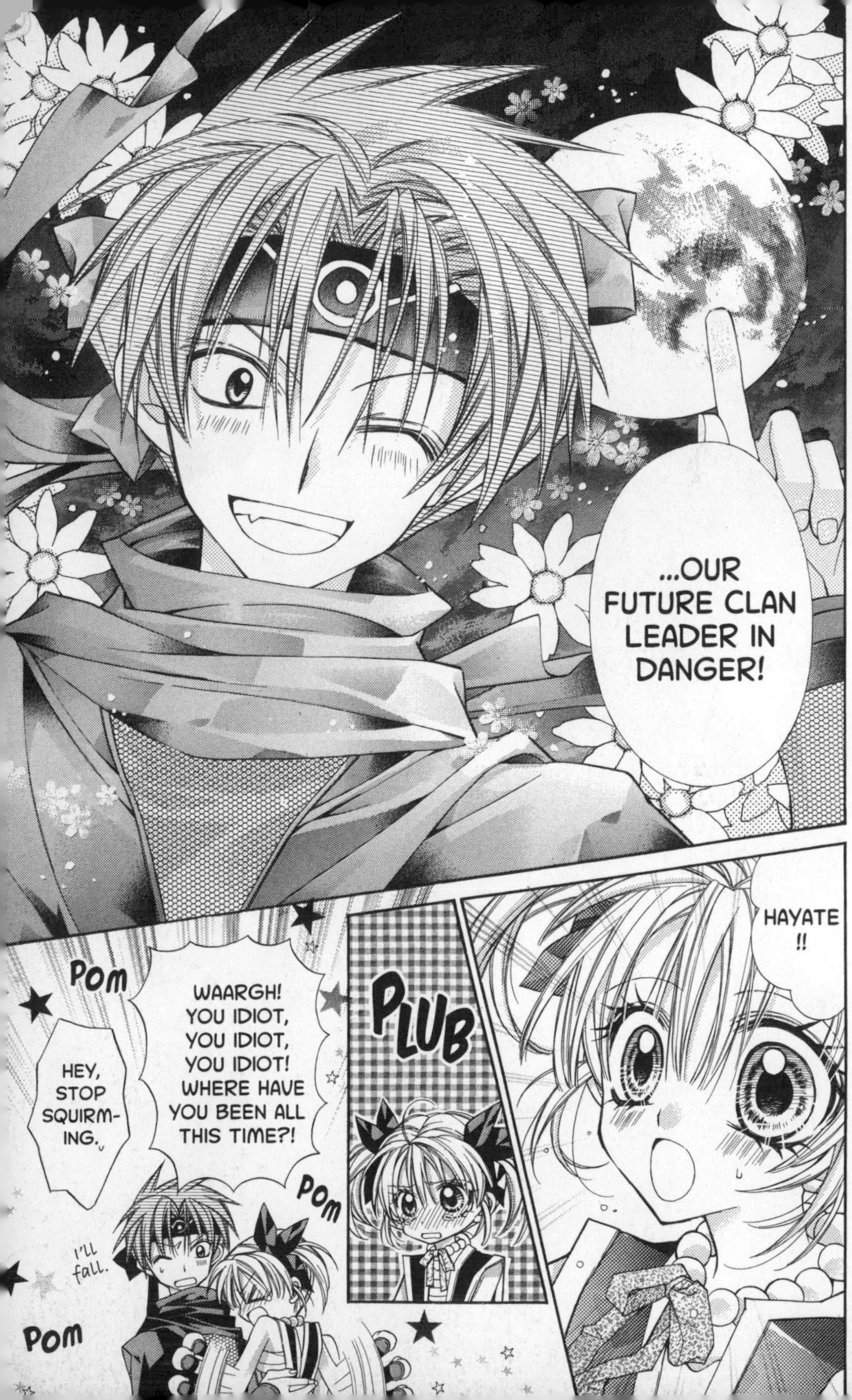
...OUR FUTURE CLAN LEADER IN DANGER!
HAYATE !!
PLUB
WAARGH! YOU IDIOT, YOU IDIOT, YOU IDIOT! WHERE HAVE YOU BEEN ALL THIS TIME?!
POM
HEY, STOP SQUIRM-ING.
POM
I'll fall.
POM

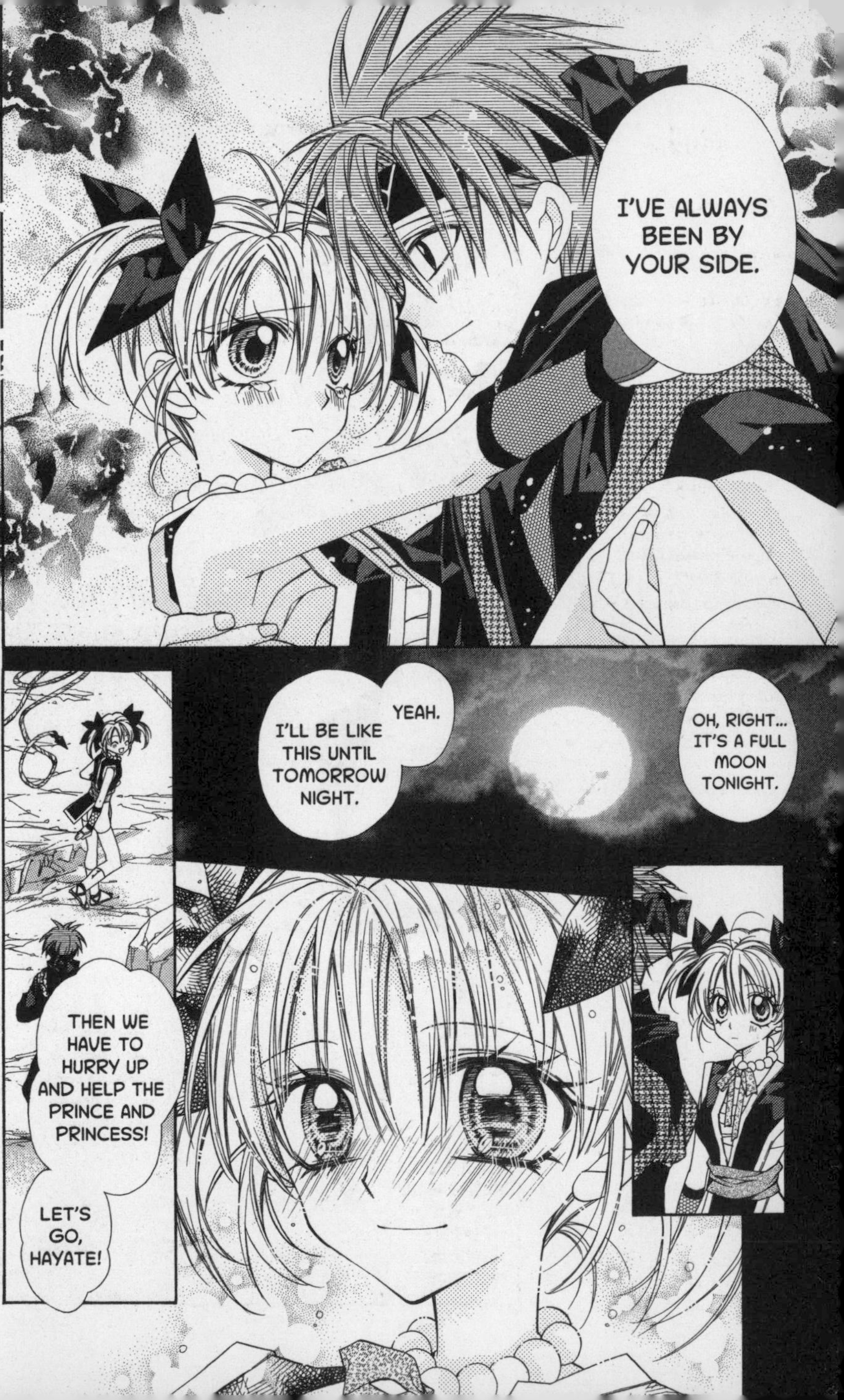
I'VE ALWAYS BEEN BY YOUR SIDE.
OH, RIGHT... IT'S A FULL MOON TONIGHT.
YEAH. I'LL BE LIKE THIS UNTIL TOMORROW NIGHT.
THEN WE HAVE TO HURRY UP AND HELP THE PRINCE AND PRINCESS!
LET'S GO, HAYATE!

Hello.

Tanemura here.
I bring you volume 3 of *Sakura Hime*.

I've only been working these days, so I don't really have much to talk about... (emoticon)

I had an autograph session in Germany, so I'll focus on that. The reason I'm writing about it is because a female fan of mine in Germany asked, "Will you write about the autograph session in Germany somewhere?" I answered, "I'll write about it in volume 3 of *Sakura Hime*!" I'm going to write about it so I can keep my promise. (emoticon) =3

I've uploaded a report of the autograph session with photos on my blog, so please enjoy these if you want to see the photos. ♥

rikukai.arina.lolipop.jp/

I'm going to write about the things I couldn't write on my blog. ♥

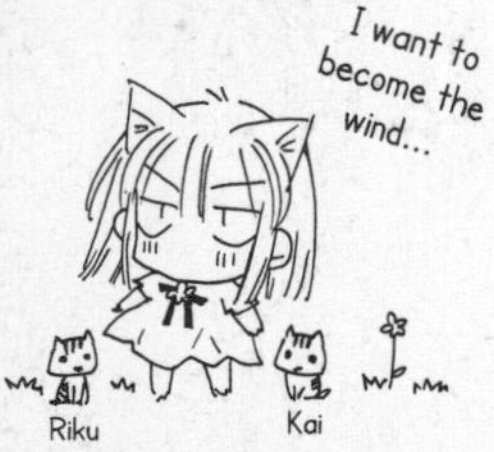
I want to become the wind...
Riku
Kai

The essay "Arina's Seed" is currently serialized in *Cobalt* magazine! ✧
We're also doing a popularity vote in the January 2010 issue of *Ribon*.

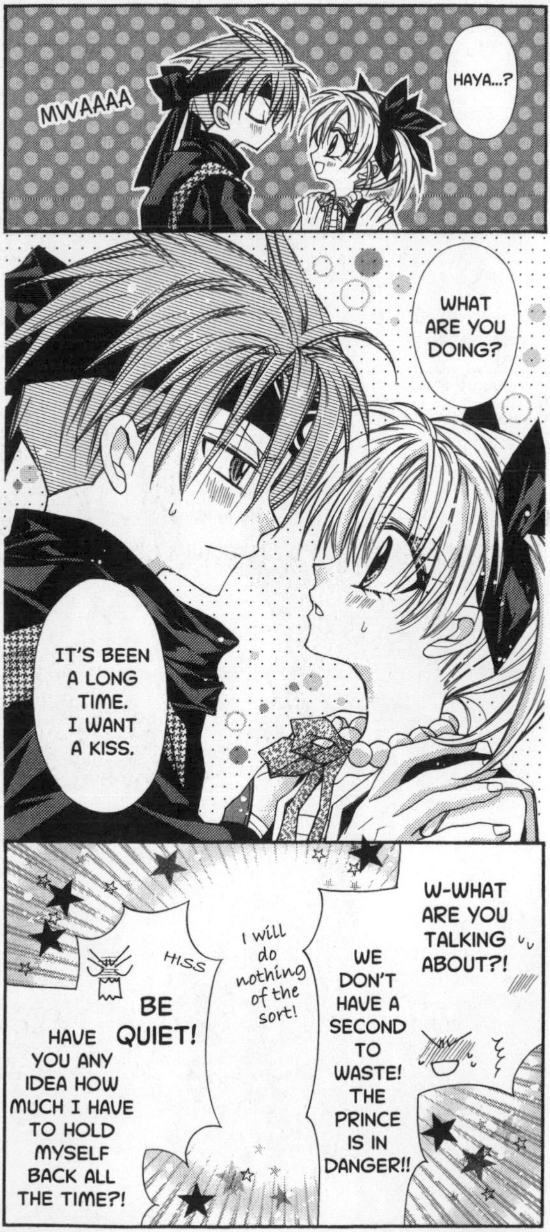
HAYA...?
MWAAAA
WHAT ARE YOU DOING?
IT'S BEEN A LONG TIME. I WANT A KISS.
W-WHAT ARE YOU TALKING ABOUT?!
WE DON'T HAVE A SECOND TO WASTE! THE PRINCE IS IN DANGER!!
I will do nothing of the sort!
HISS
BE QUIET!
HAVE YOU ANY IDEA HOW MUCH I HAVE TO HOLD MYSELF BACK ALL THE TIME?!

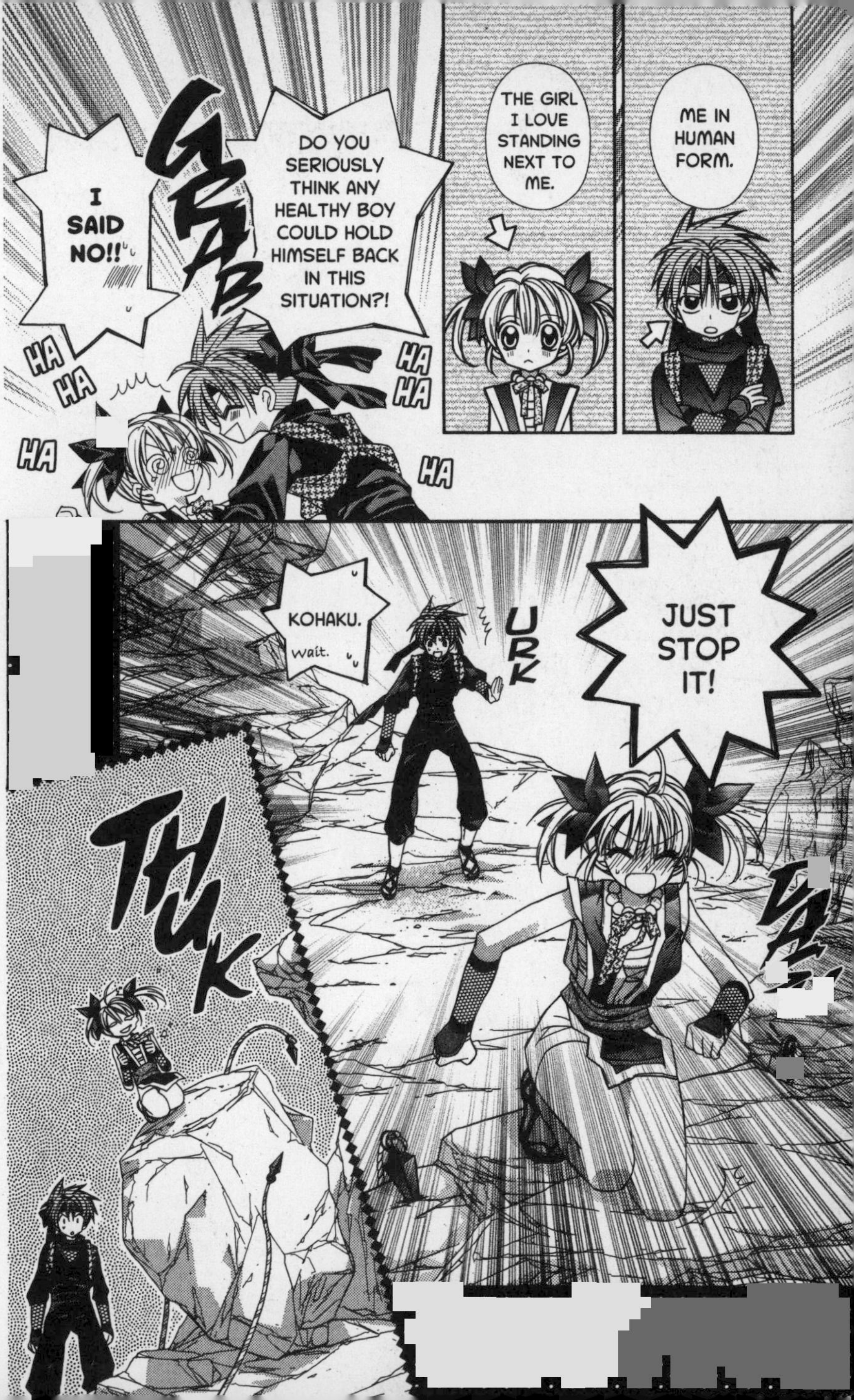
ME IN HUMAN FORM.
THE GIRL I LOVE STANDING NEXT TO ME.
DO YOU SERIOUSLY THINK ANY HEALTHY BOY COULD HOLD HIMSELF BACK IN THIS SITUATION?!
GRAB
I SAID NO!!
HA HA
HA HA
HA
HA
JUST STOP IT!
URK
KOHAKU.
wait.
THUK

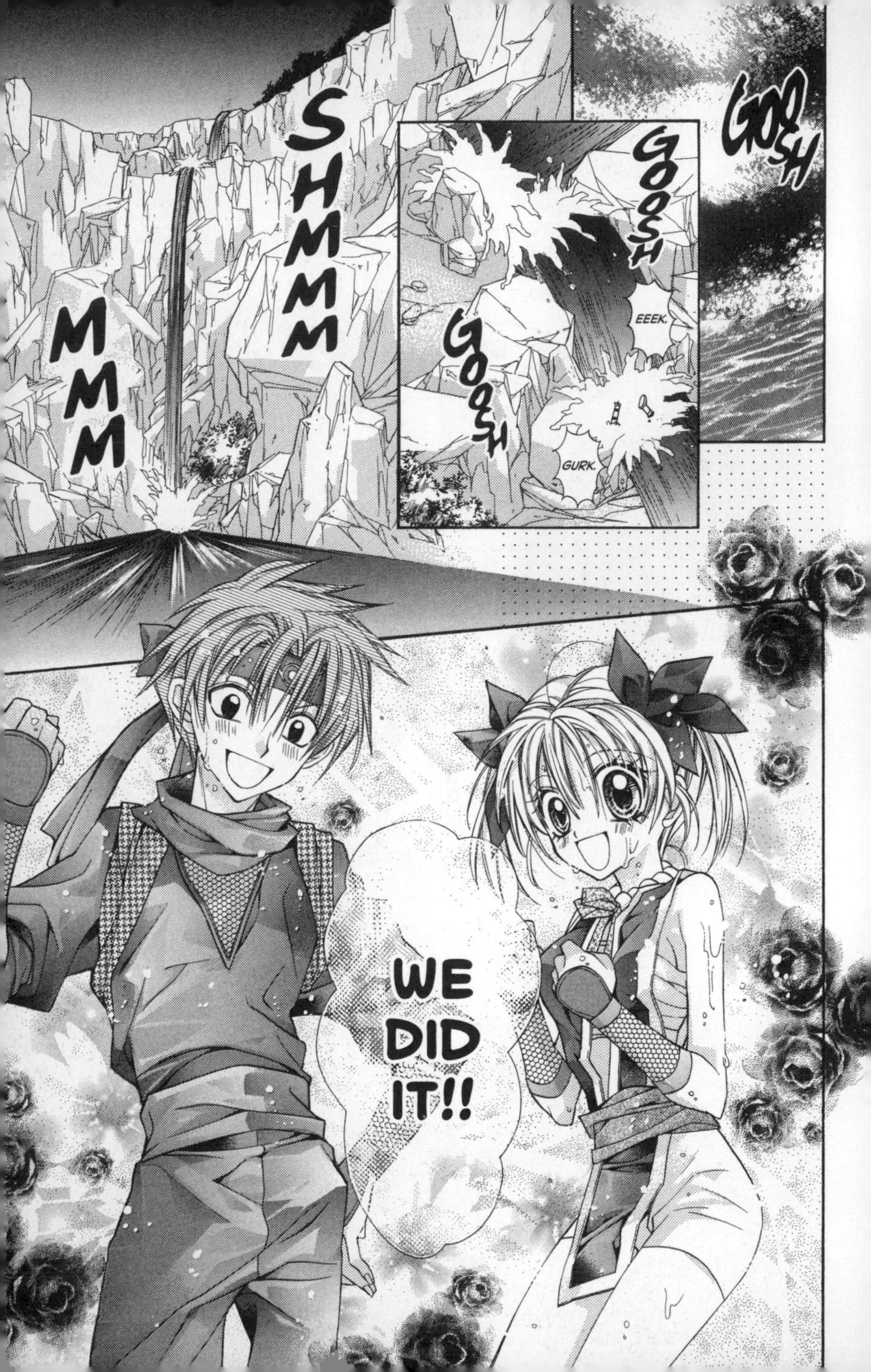
GOOSH
GOOSH
EEEK.
GOOSH
GURK.
SHMMMM
MMM
WE DID IT!!

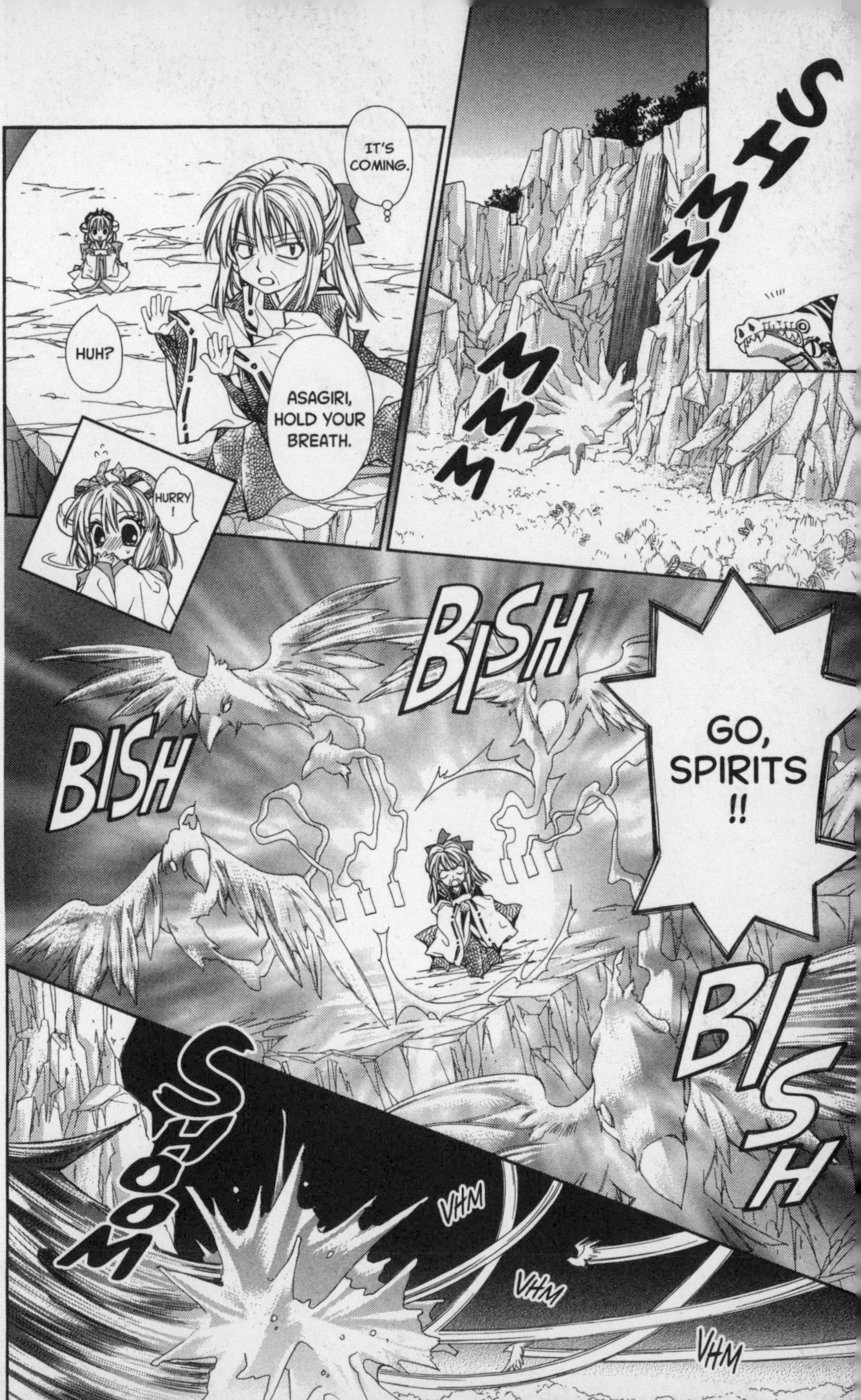
SHHMMM
MMMM
IT'S COMING.
HUH?
ASAGIRI, HOLD YOUR BREATH.
HURRY!
GO, SPIRITS!!
BISH
BISH
BISH
SHOOM
VHM
VHM
VHM

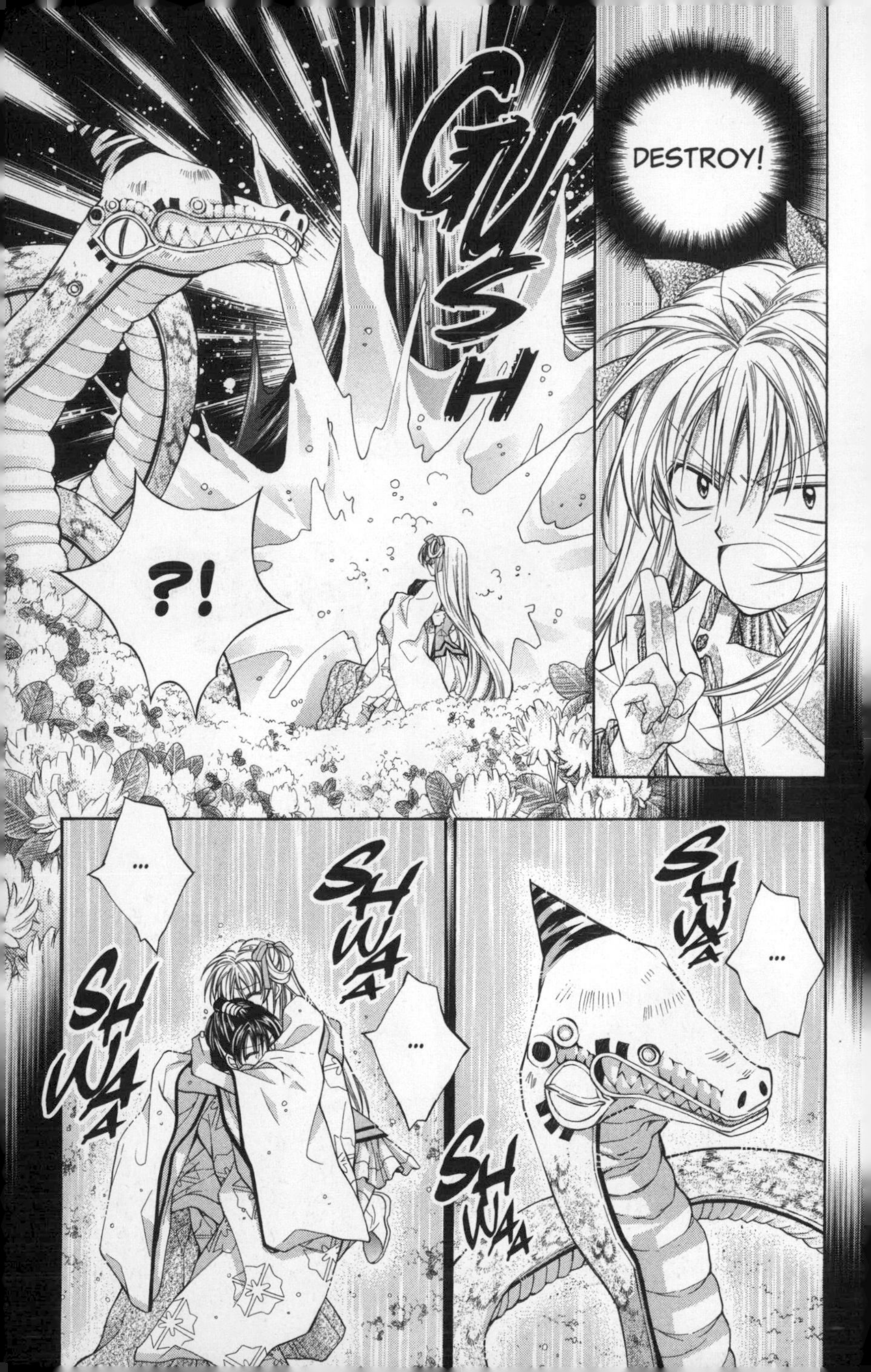
DESTROY!
GUSH
?!
SHWAA
...
SHWAA
...
SHWAA
...
SHWAA

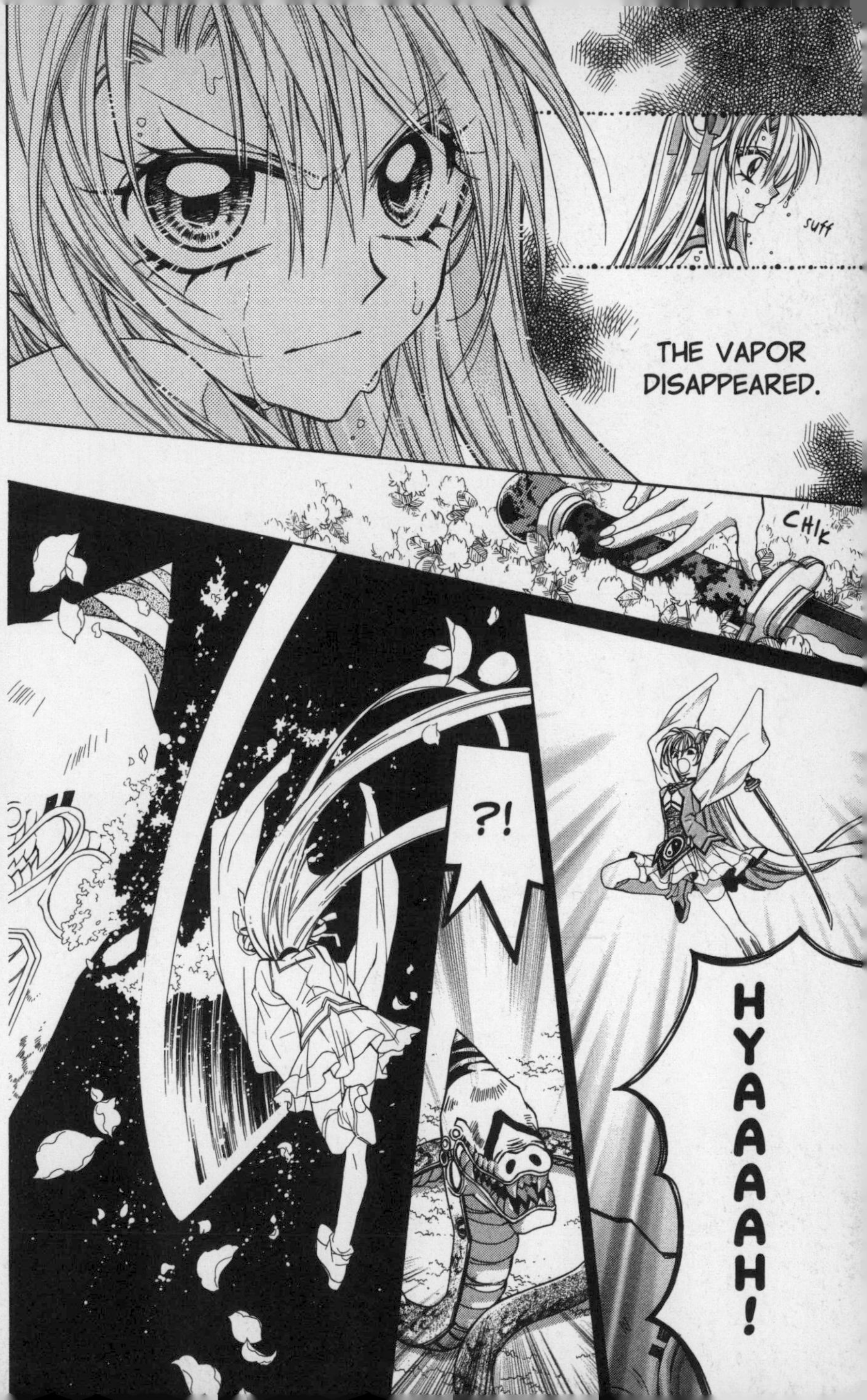
suff
THE VAPOR DISAPPEARED.
CHIK
HYAAAAAH!
?!

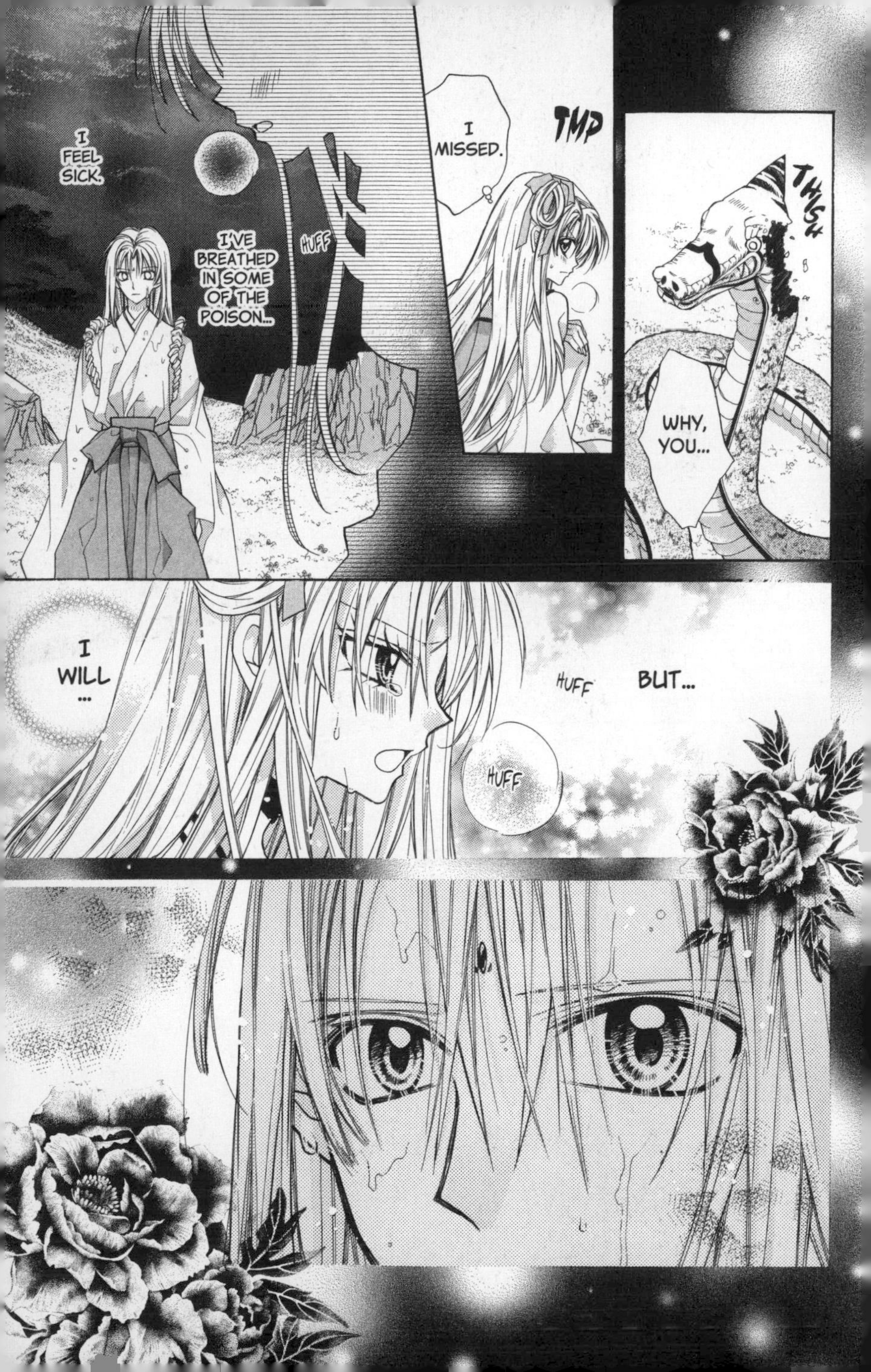
THISH
WHY, YOU...
TMP
I MISSED.
HUFF
I FEEL SICK.
I'VE BREATHED IN SOME OF THE POISON...
BUT...
HUFF
HUFF
I WILL ...

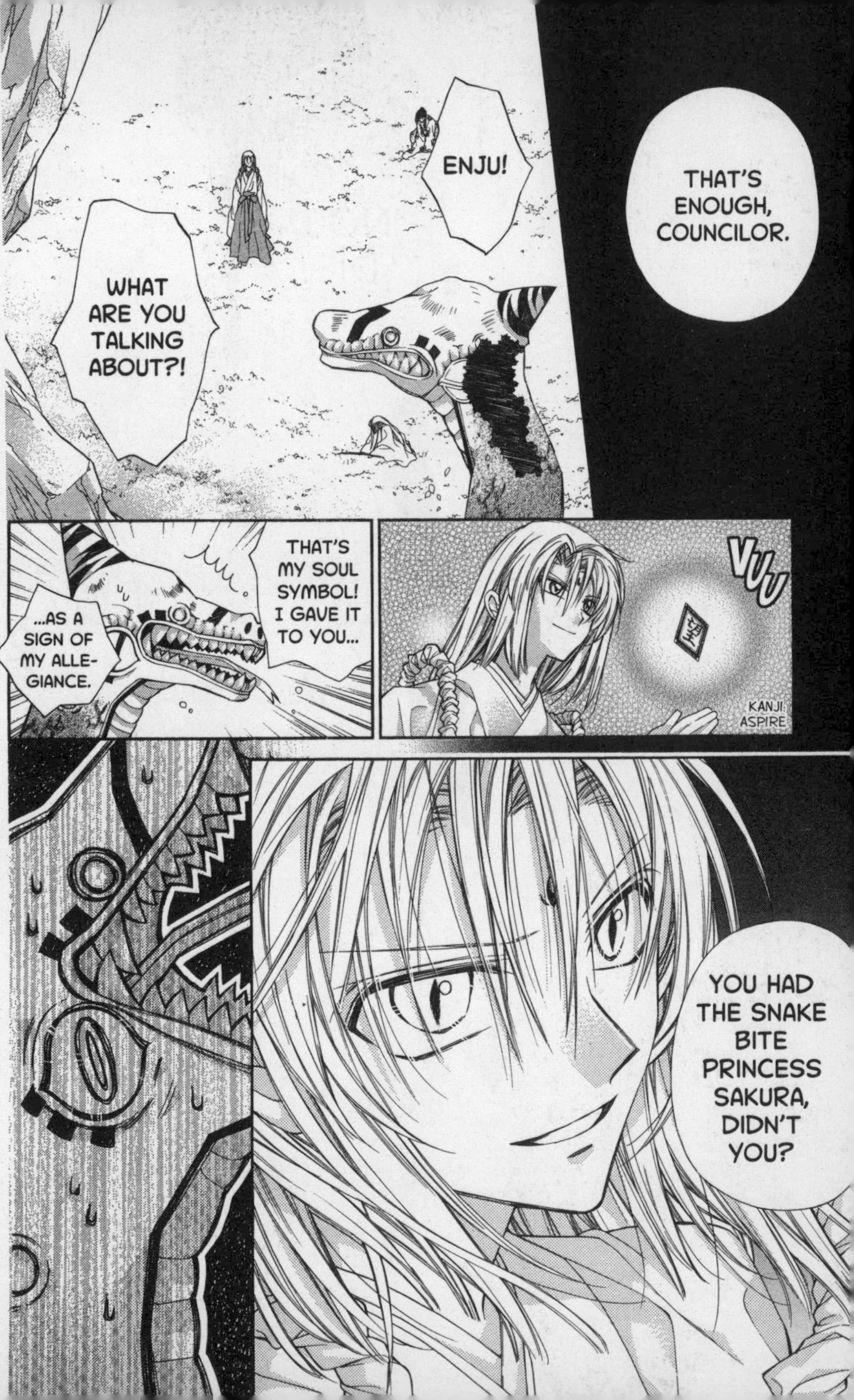
THAT'S ENOUGH, COUNCILOR.
ENJU!
WHAT ARE YOU TALKING ABOUT?!
VUU
KANJI: ASPIRE
THAT'S MY SOUL SYMBOL! I GAVE IT TO YOU...
...AS A SIGN OF MY ALLEGIANCE.
YOU HAD THE SNAKE BITE PRINCESS SAKURA, DIDN'T YOU?

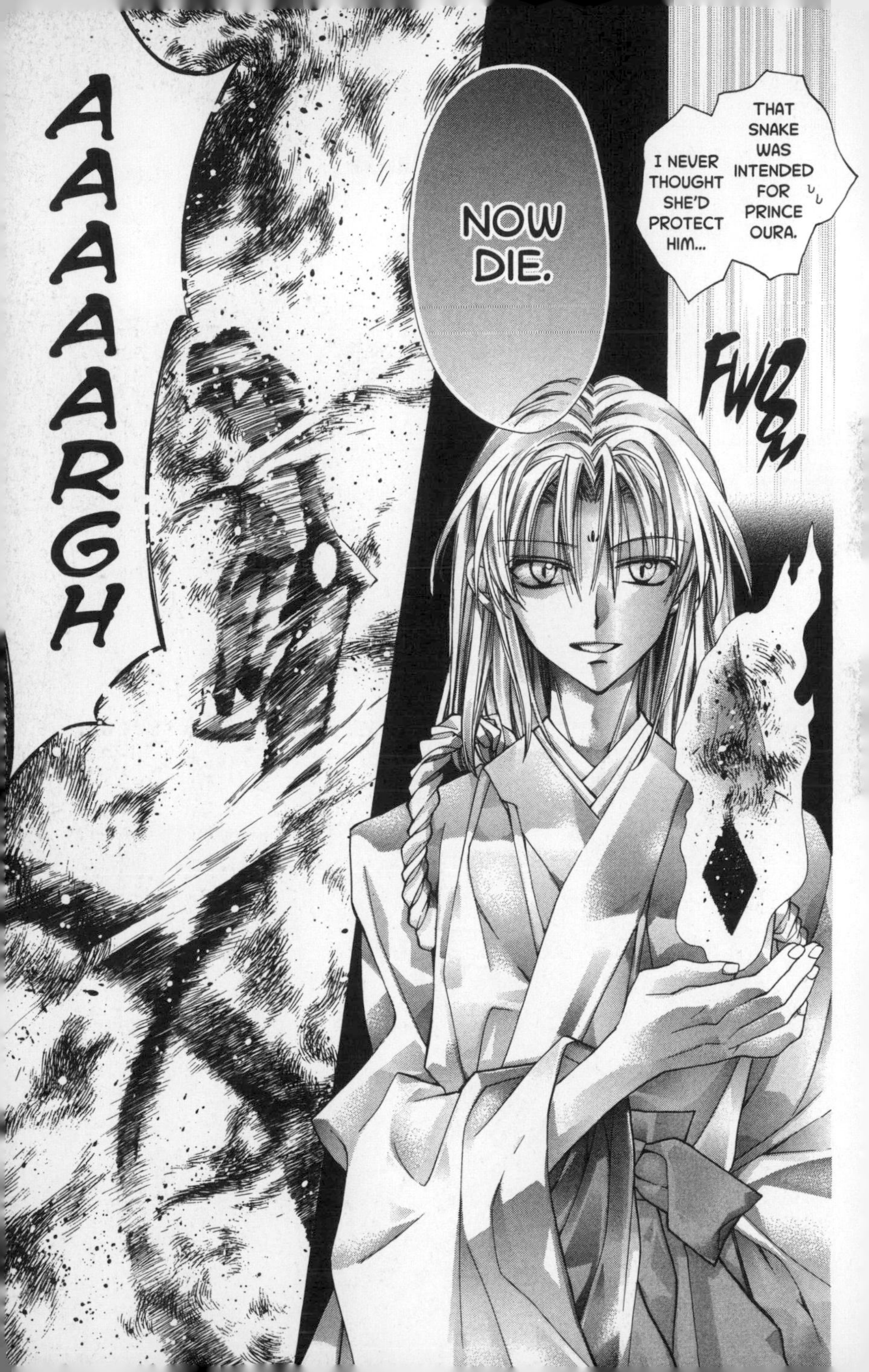
THAT SNAKE WAS INTENDED FOR PRINCE OURA.
I NEVER THOUGHT SHE'D PROTECT HIM...
FWOOM
NOW DIE.
AAAAARGH

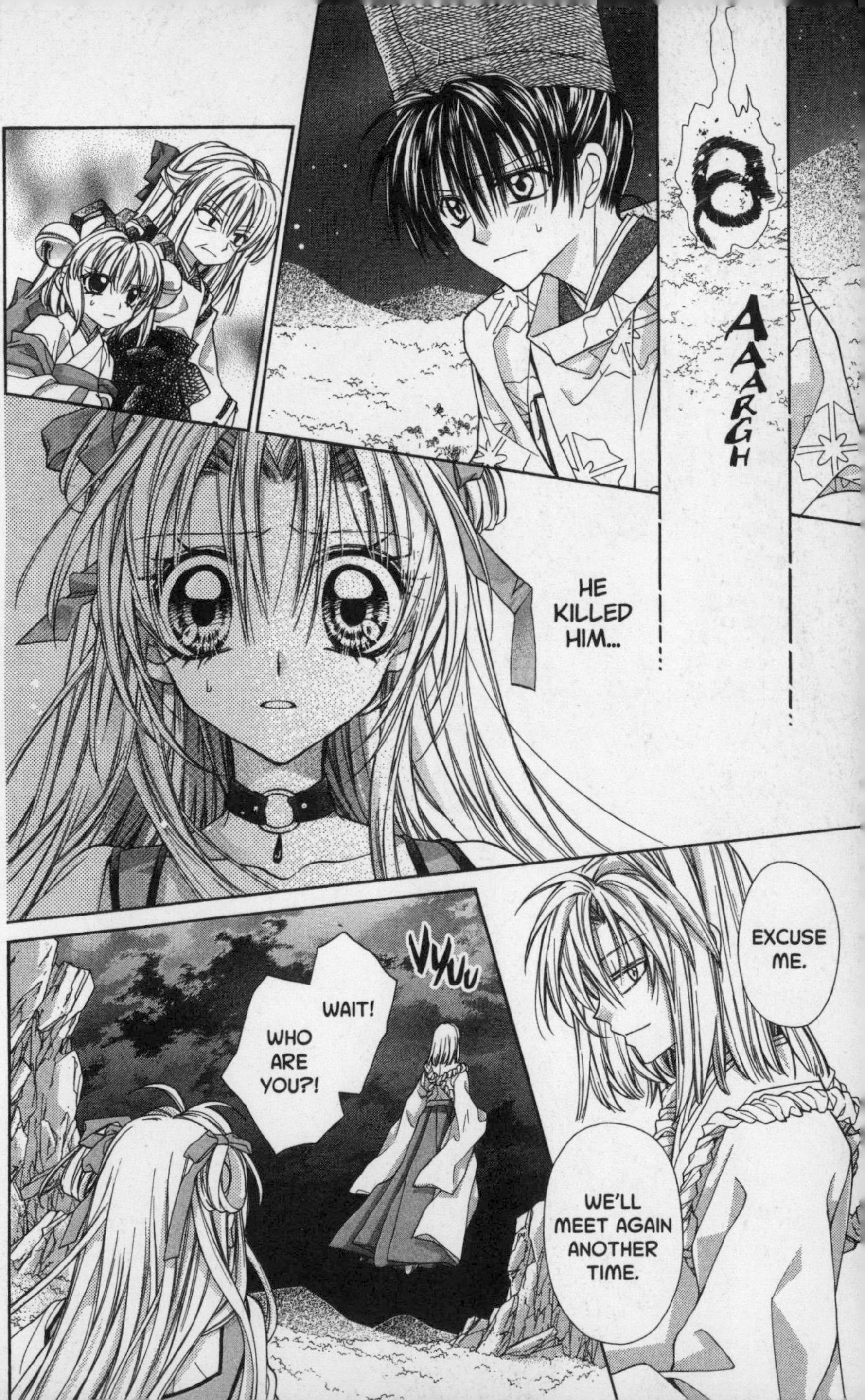
AAARGH
HE KILLED HIM...
EXCUSE ME.
WE'LL MEET AGAIN ANOTHER TIME.
VYUU
WAIT!
WHO ARE YOU?!

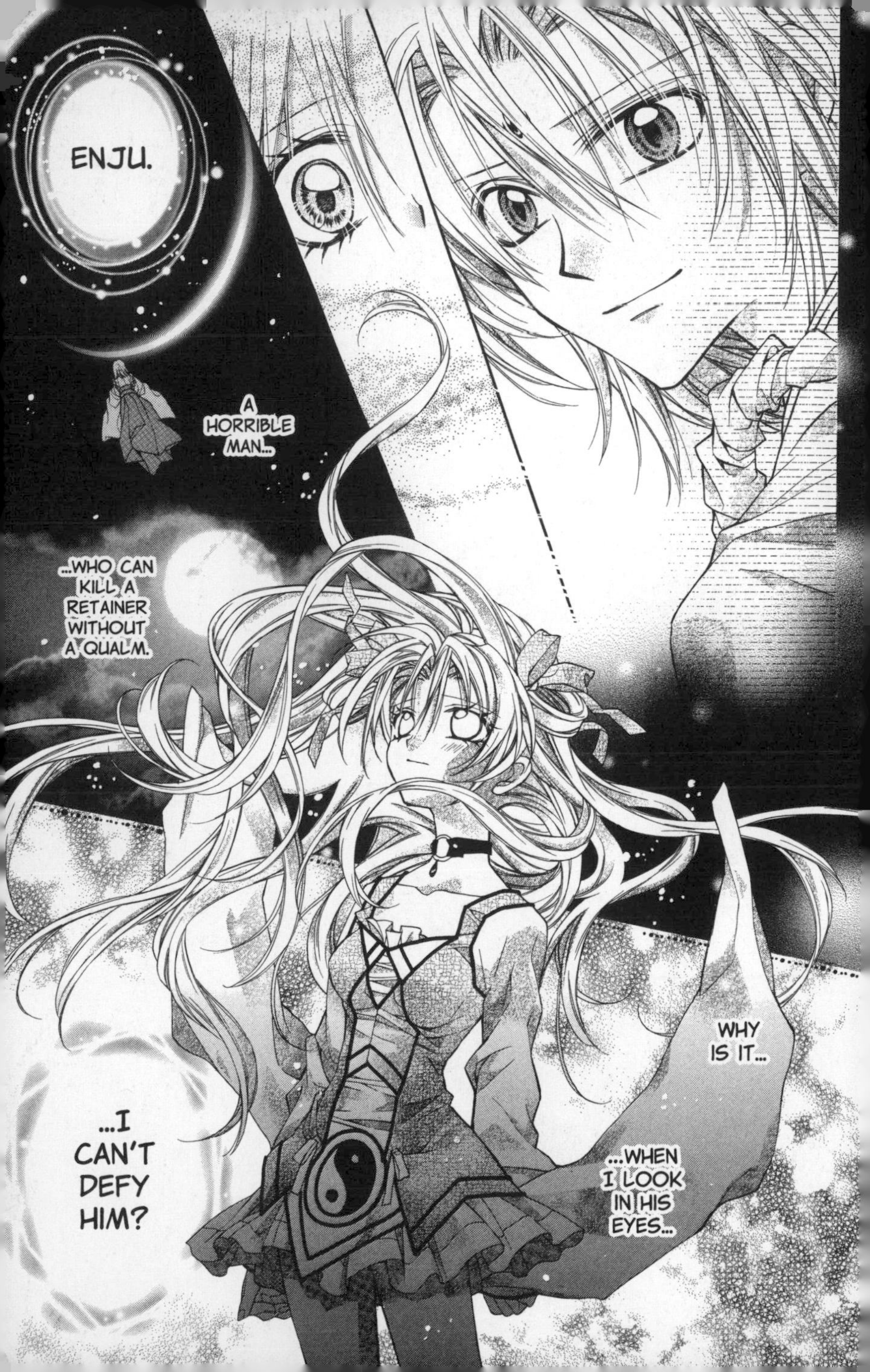
ENJU.
A HORRIBLE MAN...
...WHO CAN KILL A RETAINER WITHOUT A QUALM.
WHY IS IT...
...WHEN I LOOK IN HIS EYES...
...I CAN'T DEFY HIM?

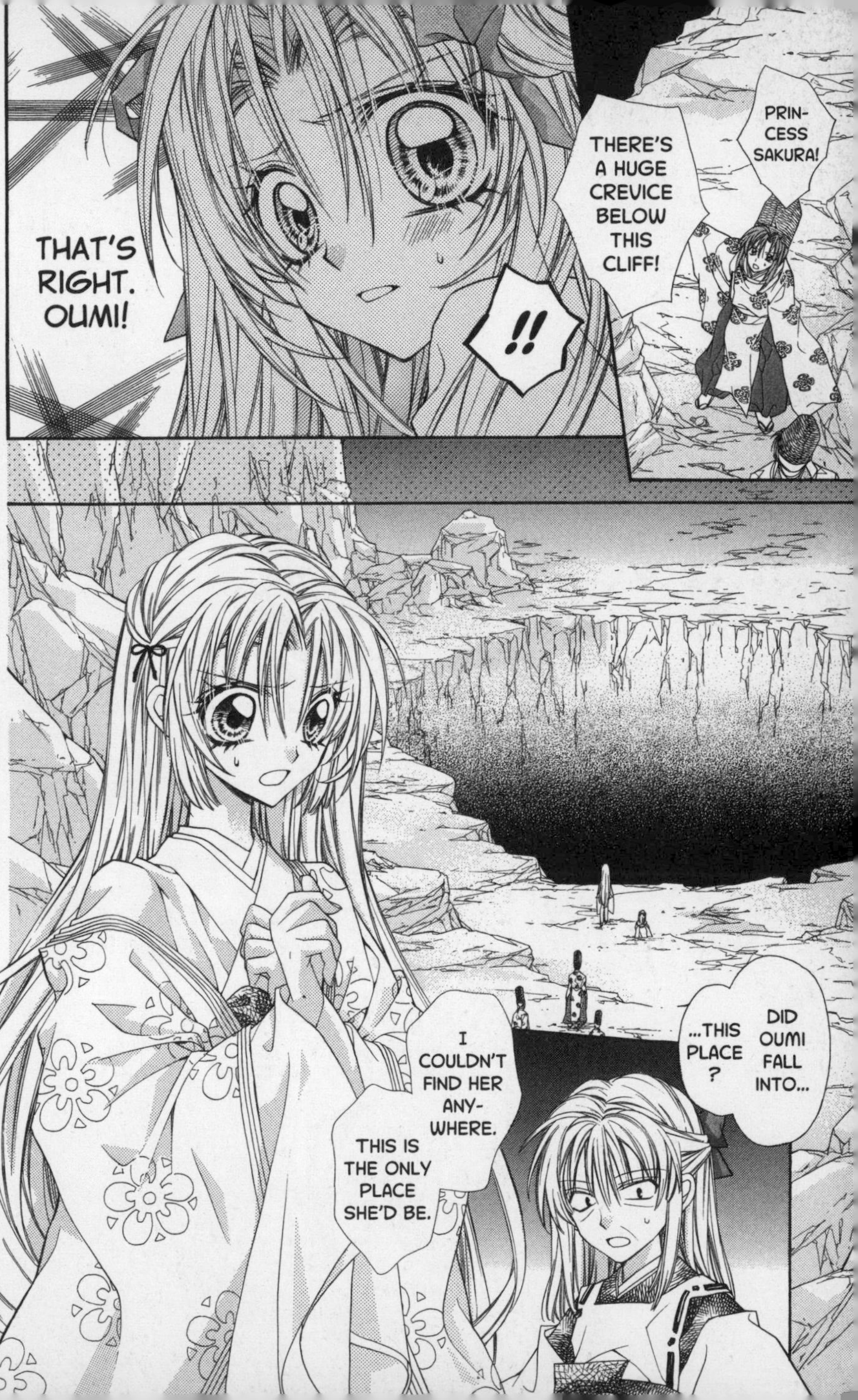
PRIN-CESS SAKURA!
THERE'S A HUGE CREVICE BELOW THIS CLIFF!
!!
THAT'S RIGHT. OUMI!
DID OUMI FALL INTO...
...THIS PLACE?
I COULDN'T FIND HER ANY-WHERE.
THIS IS THE ONLY PLACE SHE'D BE.

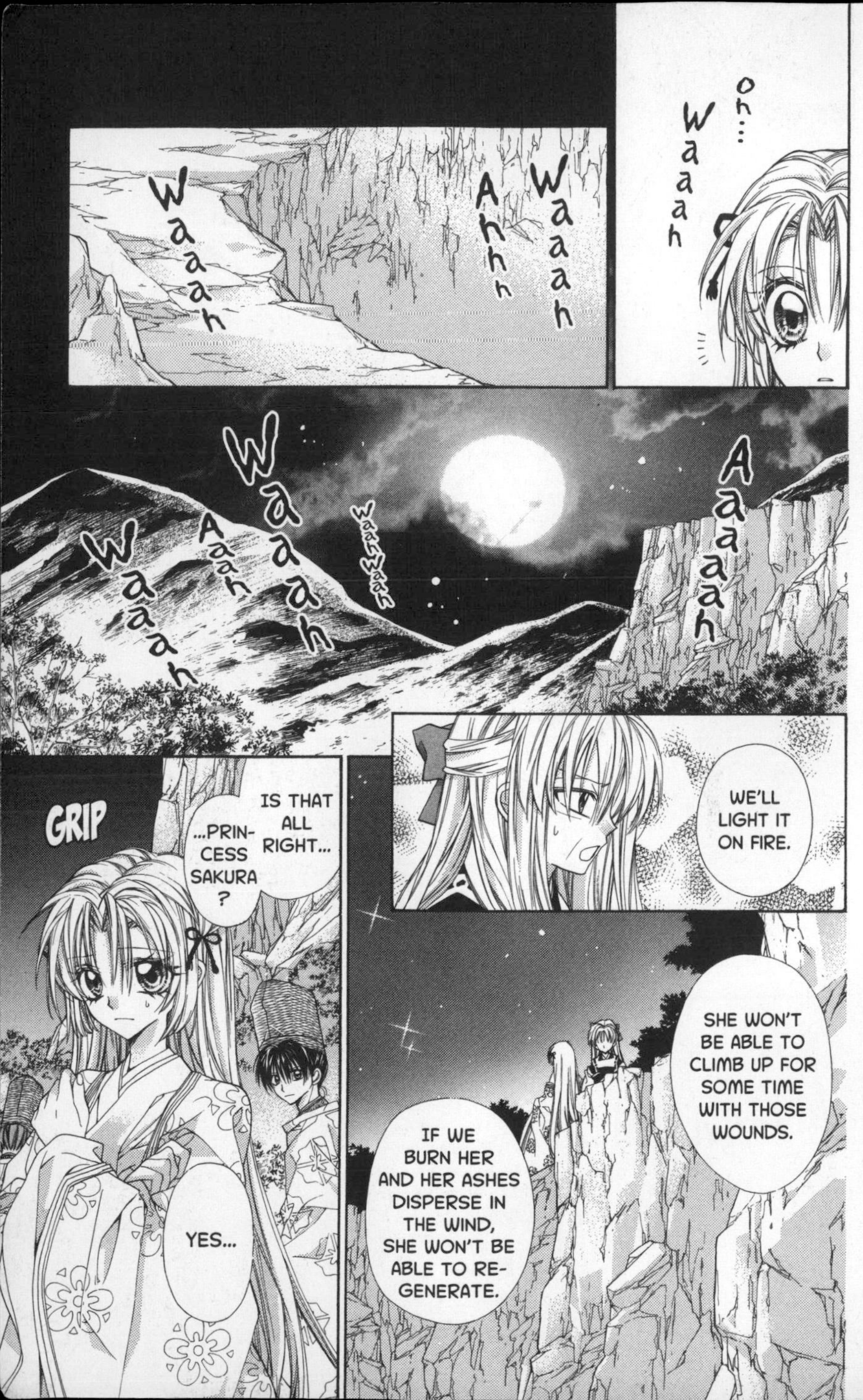

Oh...
Waaaah
Waaaah
Ahhhh
Waaaah
Aaaaaah
WaahWaah
Waaaah
Aaaah
Waaaah
WE'LL LIGHT IT ON FIRE.
SHE WON'T BE ABLE TO CLIMB UP FOR SOME TIME WITH THOSE WOUNDS.
IF WE BURN HER AND HER ASHES DISPERSE IN THE WIND, SHE WON'T BE ABLE TO RE-GENERATE.
GRIP
IS THAT ALL RIGHT...
...PRIN-CESS SAKURA?
YES...

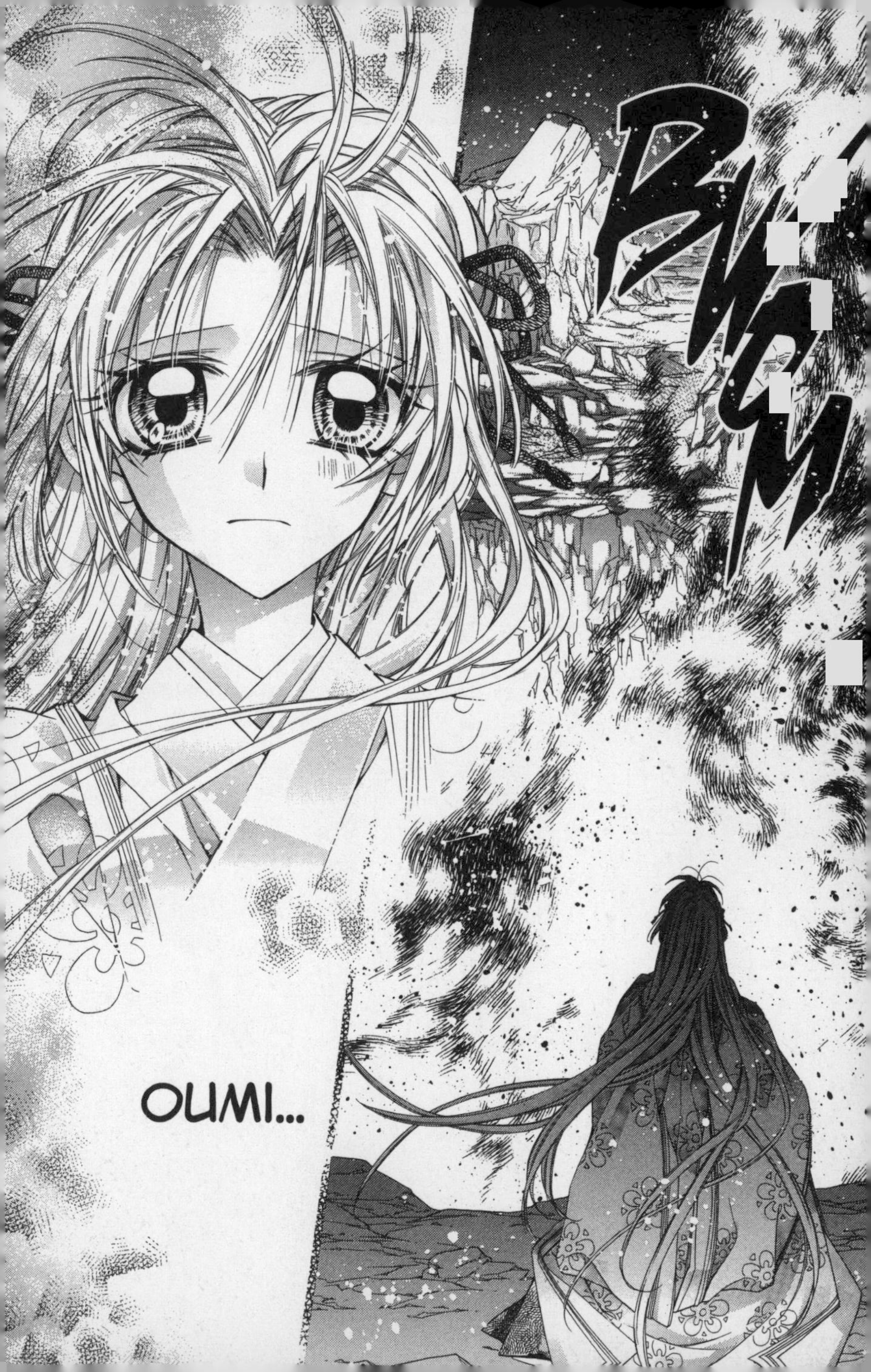
OUMI...

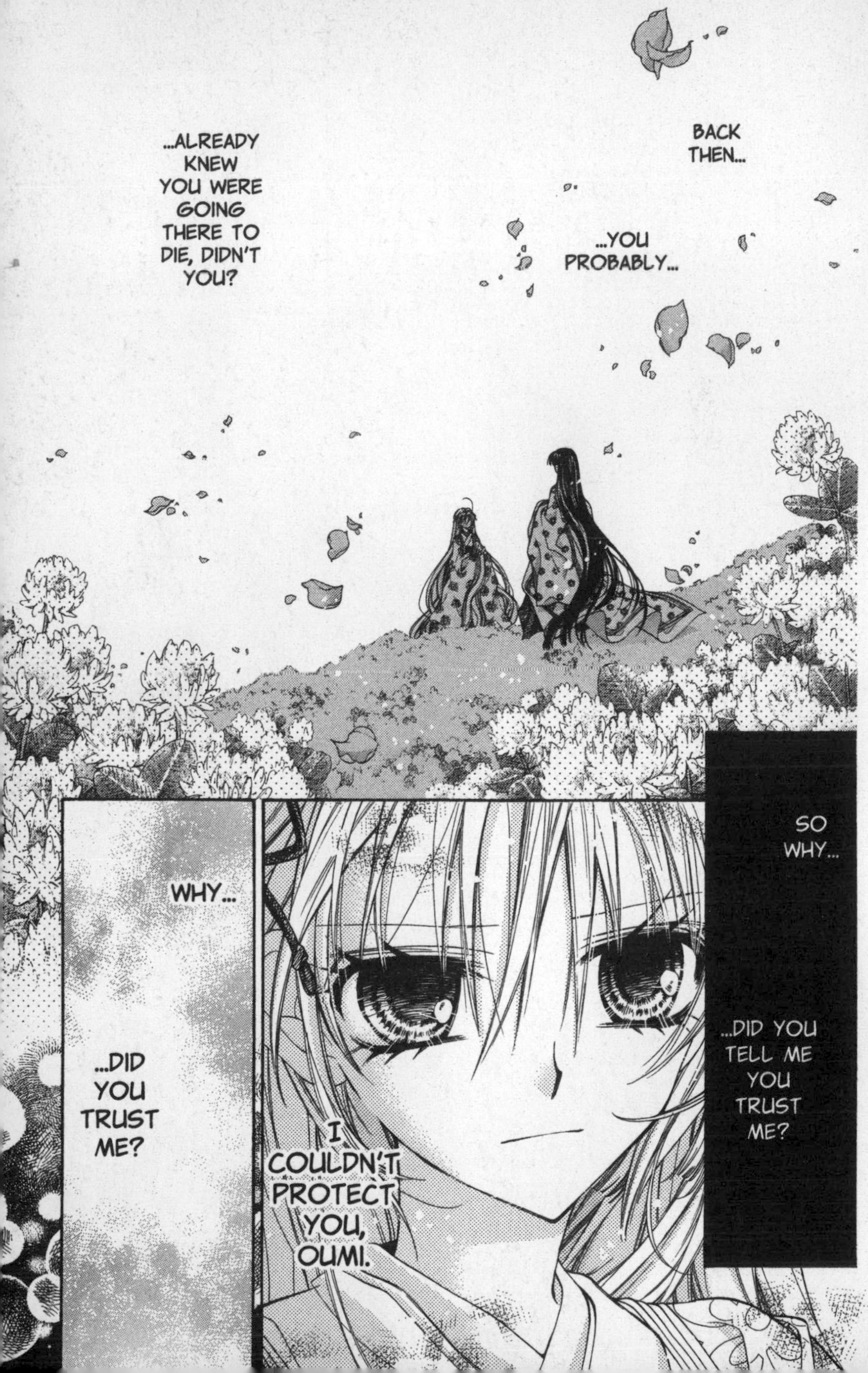
BACK THEN...
...YOU PROBABLY...
...ALREADY KNEW YOU WERE GOING THERE TO DIE, DIDN'T YOU?
SO WHY...
...DID YOU TELL ME YOU TRUST ME?
I COULDN'T PROTECT YOU, OUMI.
WHY...
...DID YOU TRUST ME?

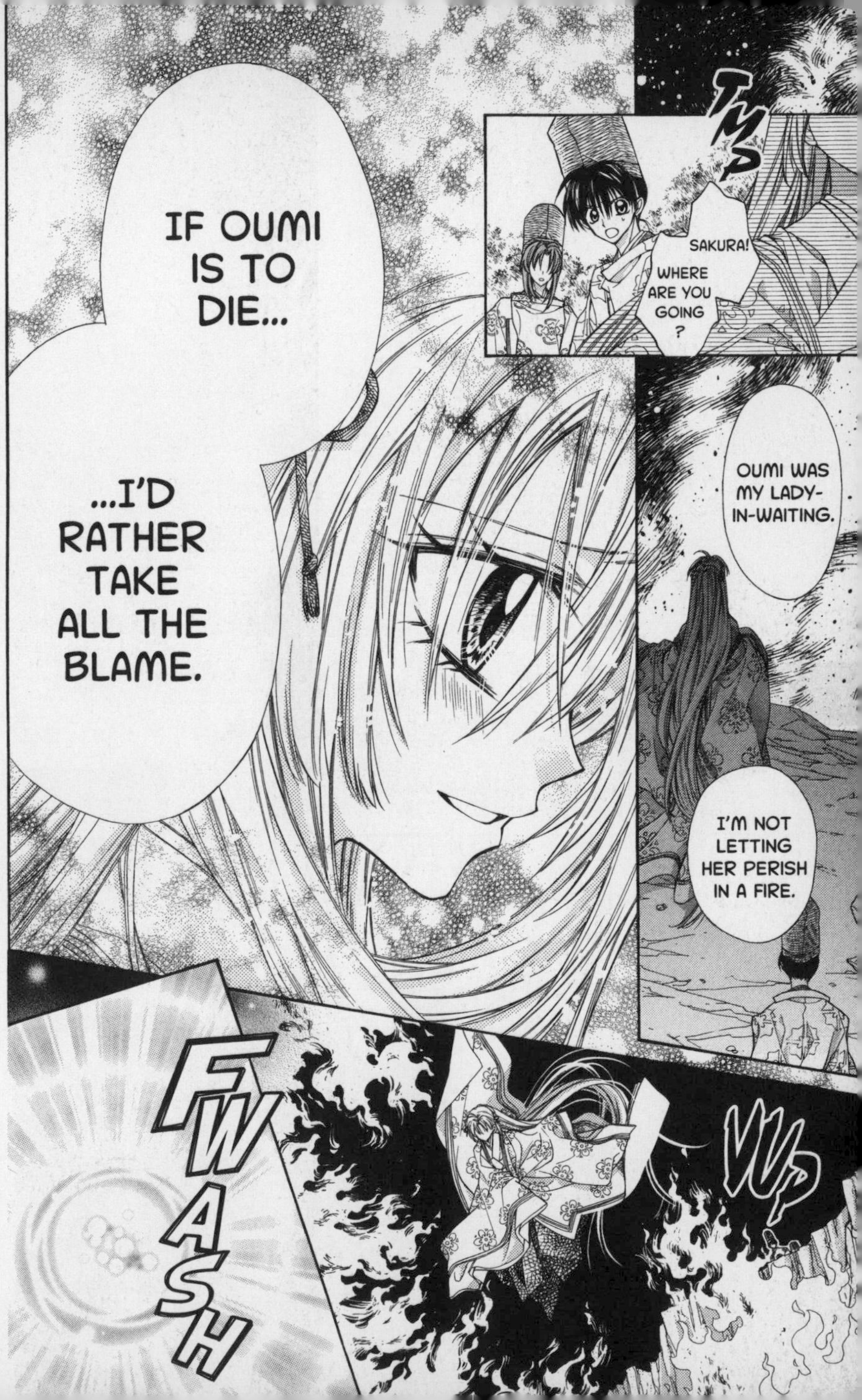
TMP
SAKURA!
WHERE ARE YOU GOING?
OUMI WAS MY LADY-IN-WAITING.
I'M NOT LETTING HER PERISH IN A FIRE.
IF OUMI IS TO DIE...
...I'D RATHER TAKE ALL THE BLAME.
VVP
FWASH

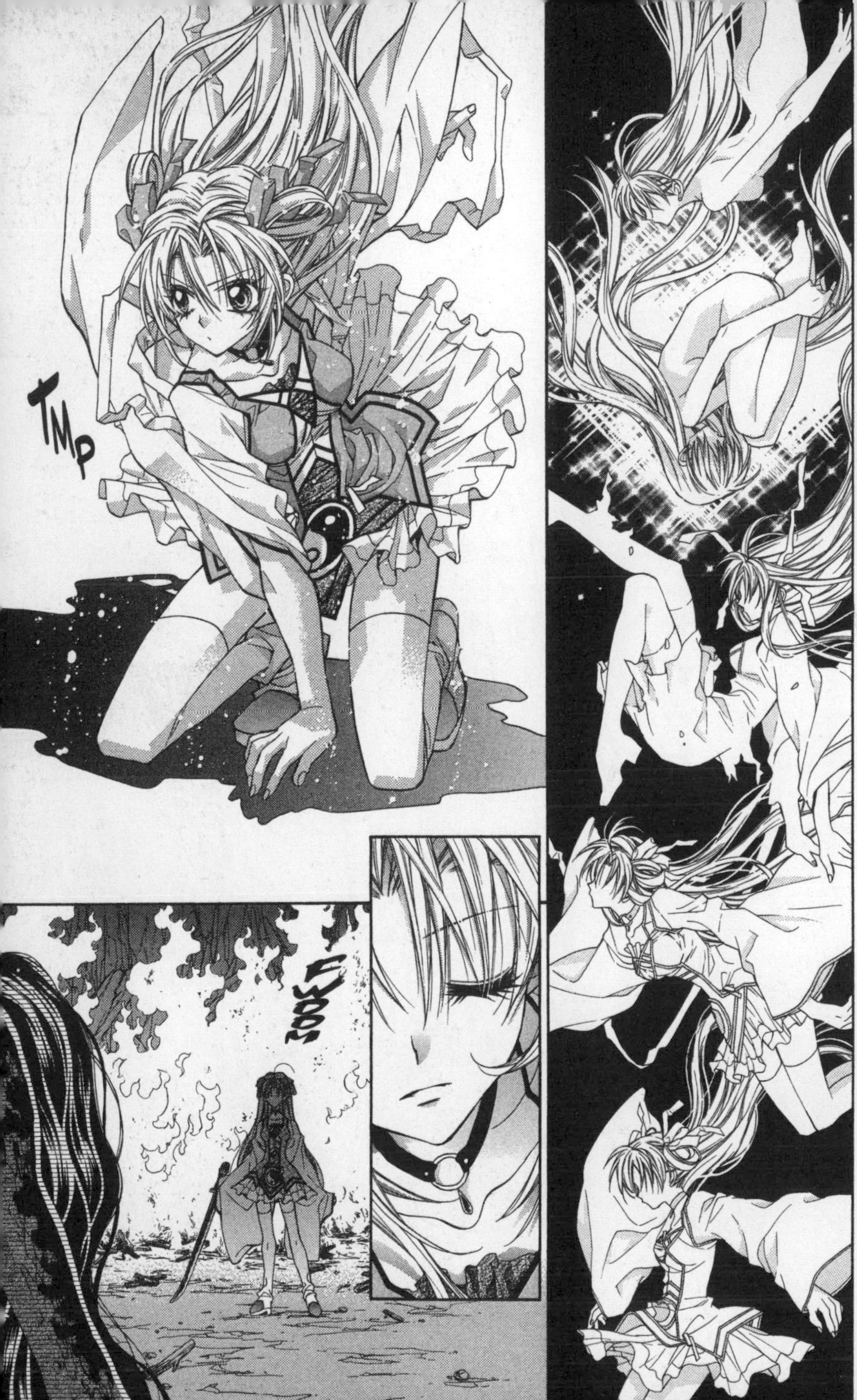
TMP
FWOOM

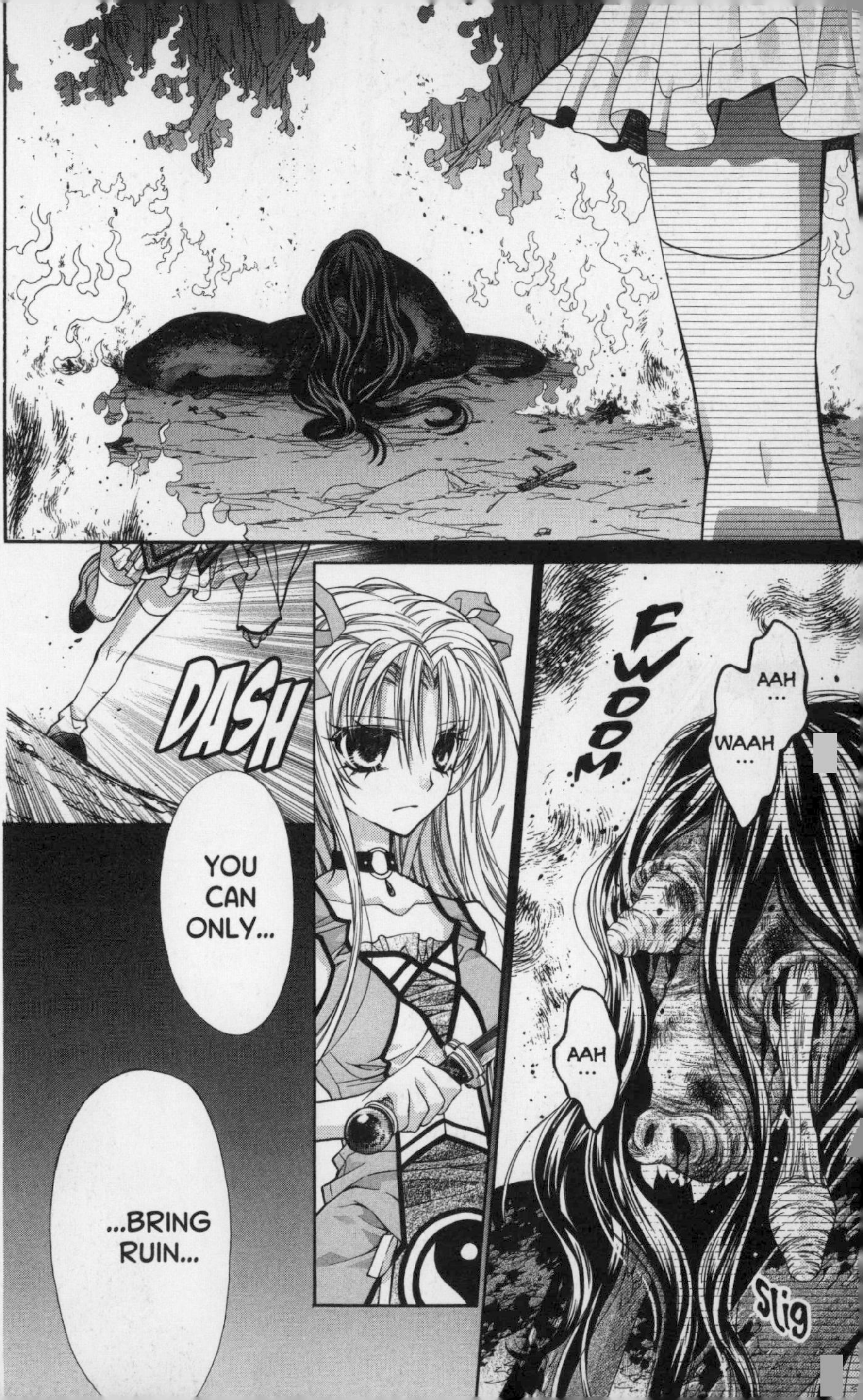
AAH... WAAH...
FWOOM
AAH...
Slig
DASH
YOU CAN ONLY...
...BRING RUIN...

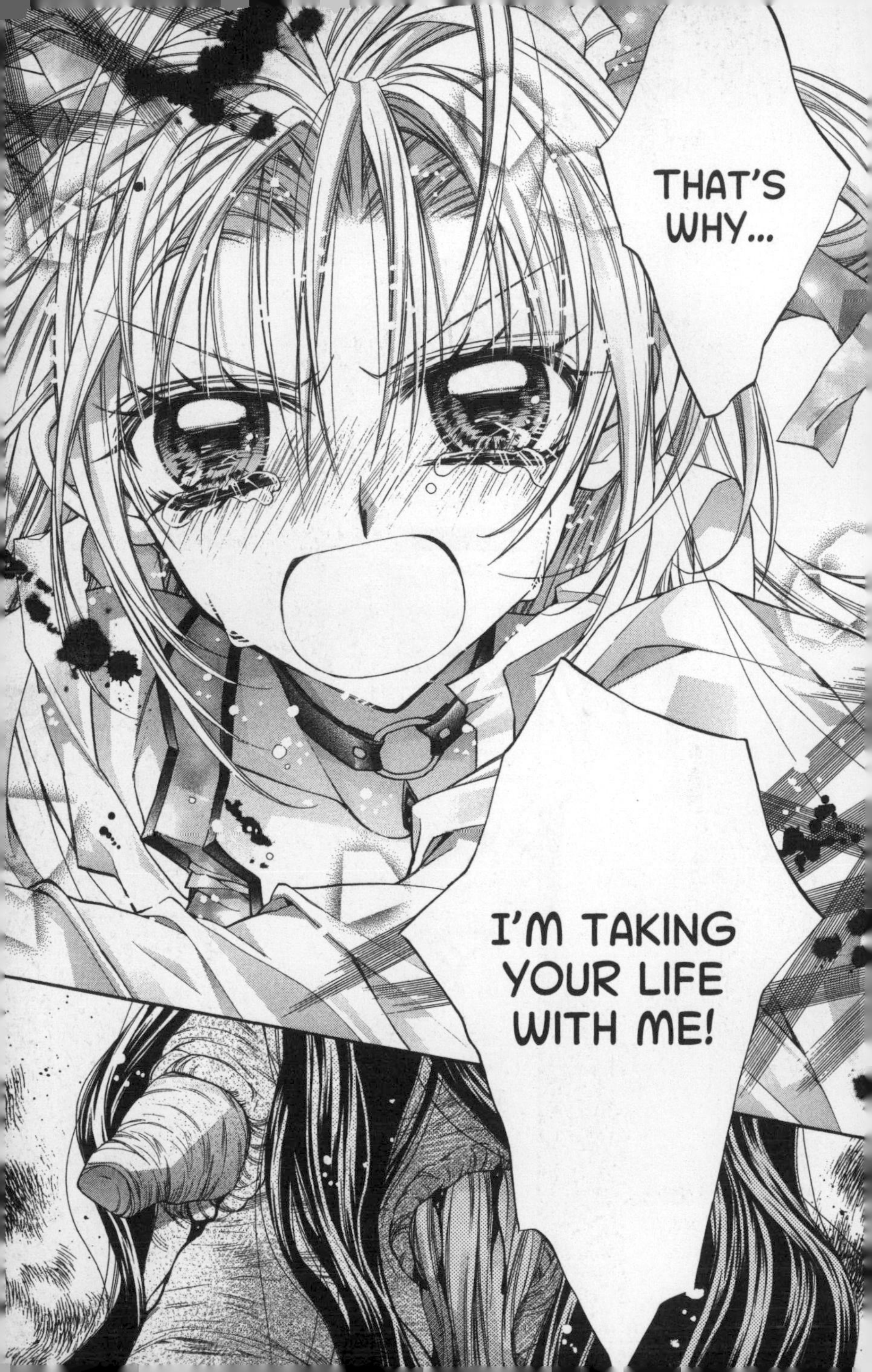
THAT'S WHY...
I'M TAKING YOUR LIFE WITH ME!

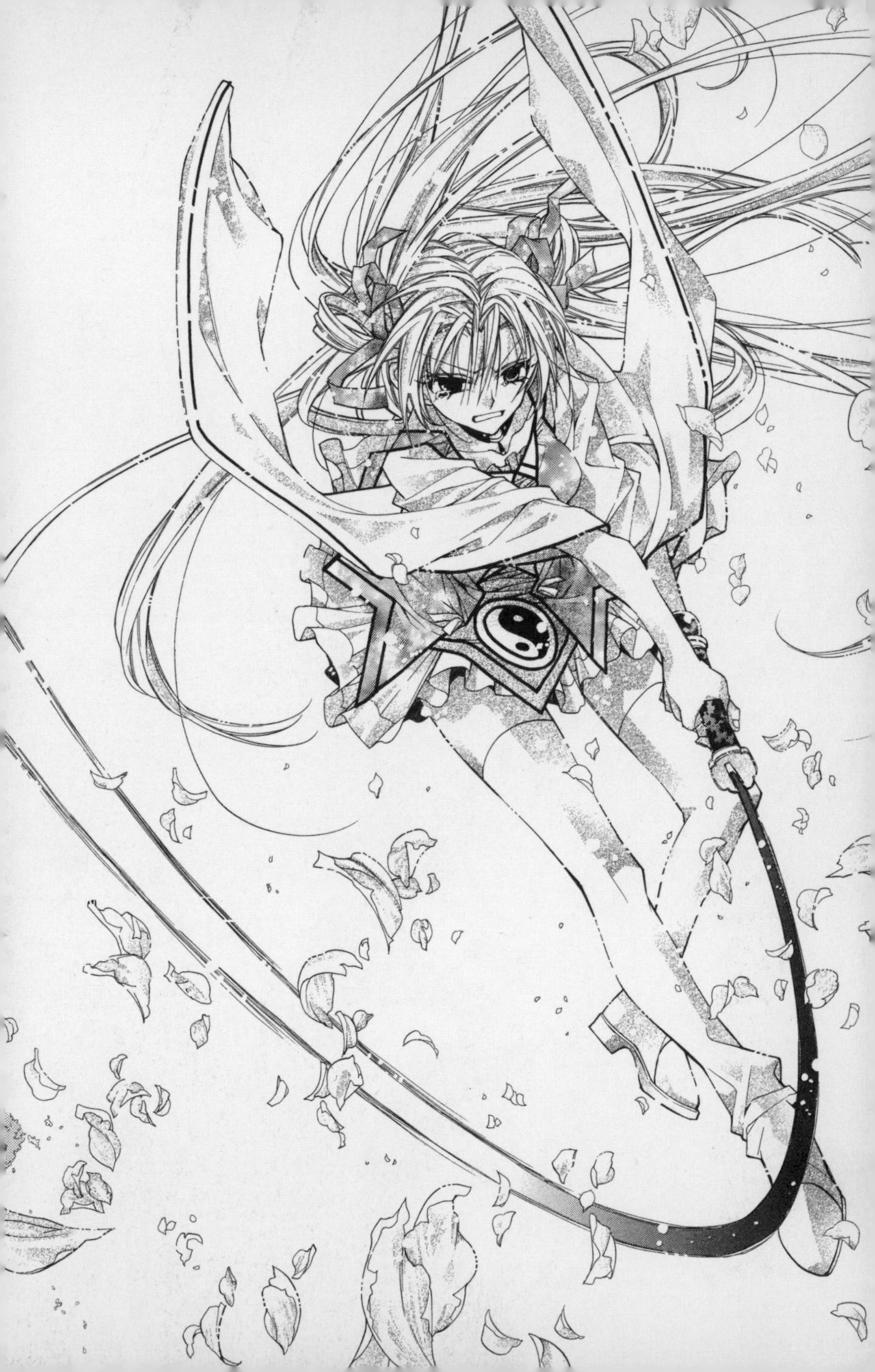

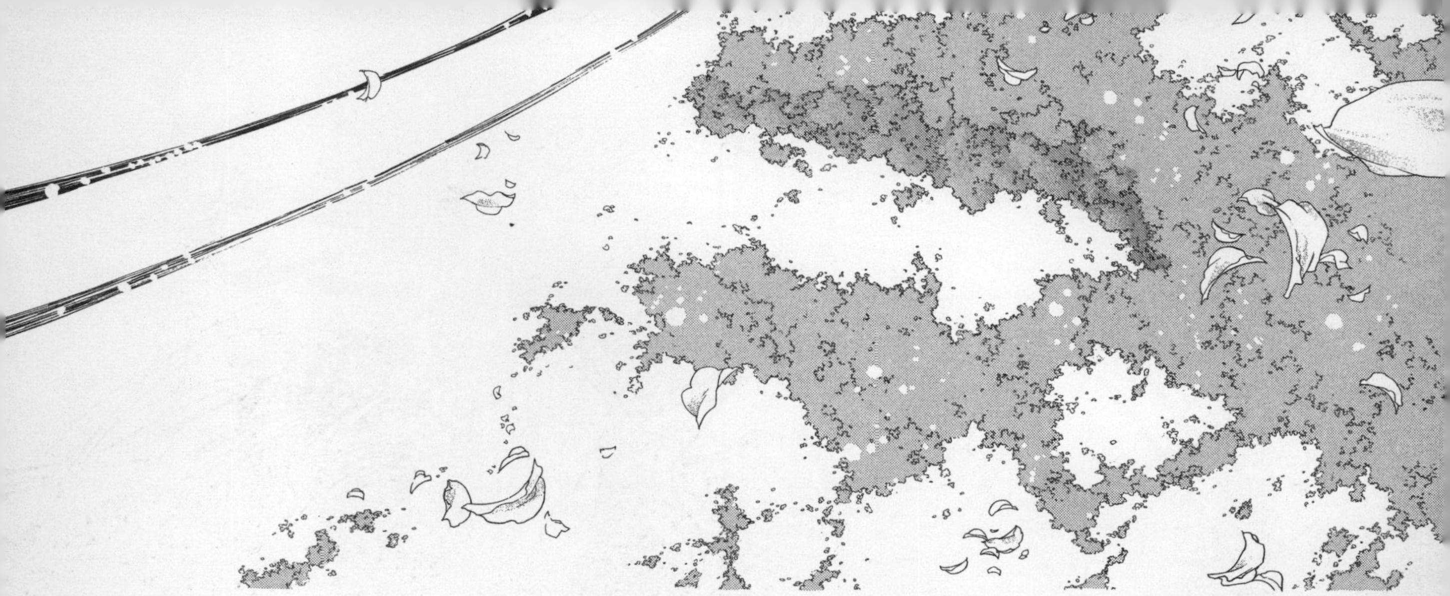

Sakura Hime
The Legend of Princess Sakura

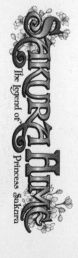

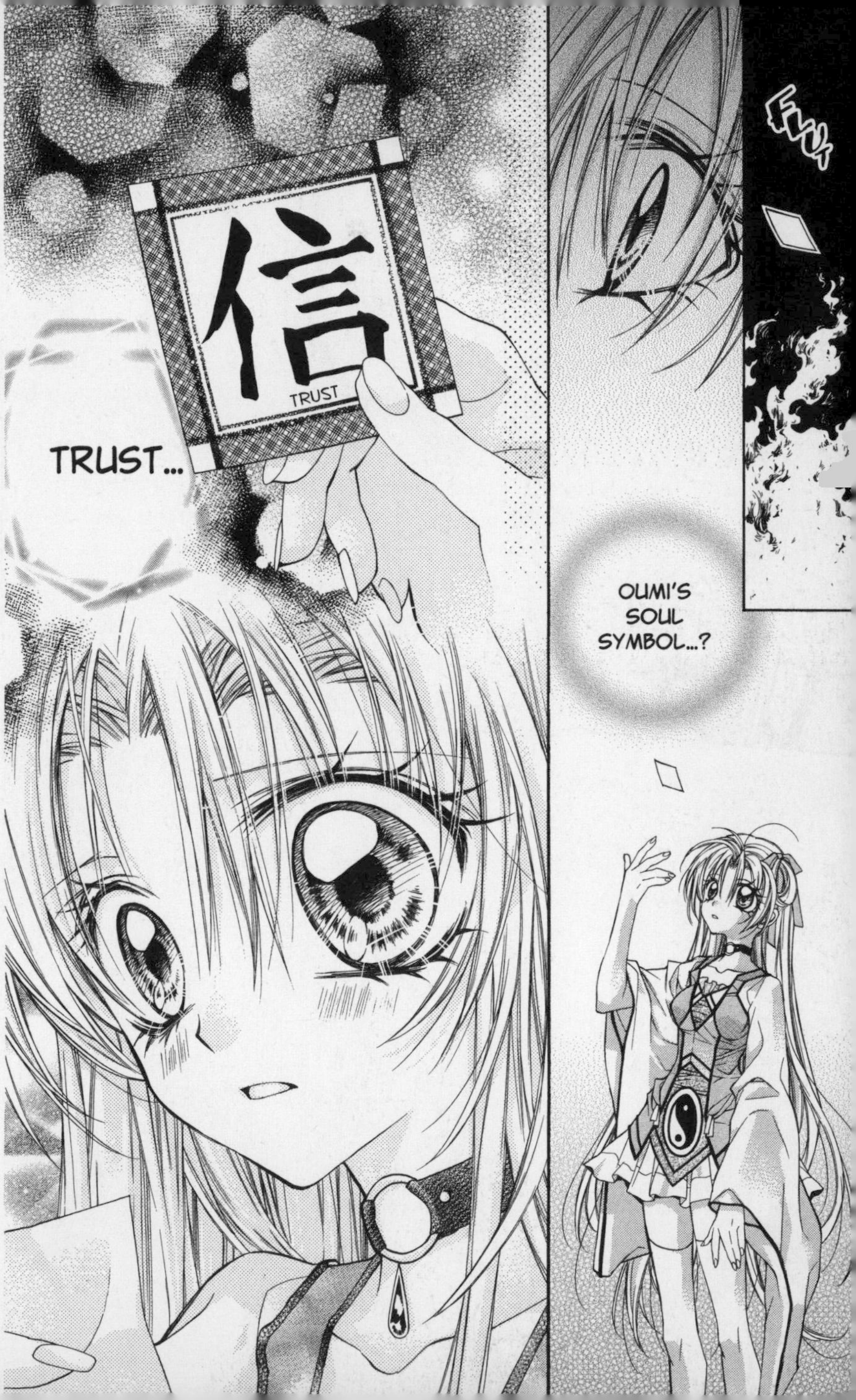
FLUX
OUMI'S SOUL SYMBOL...?
信
TRUST
TRUST...

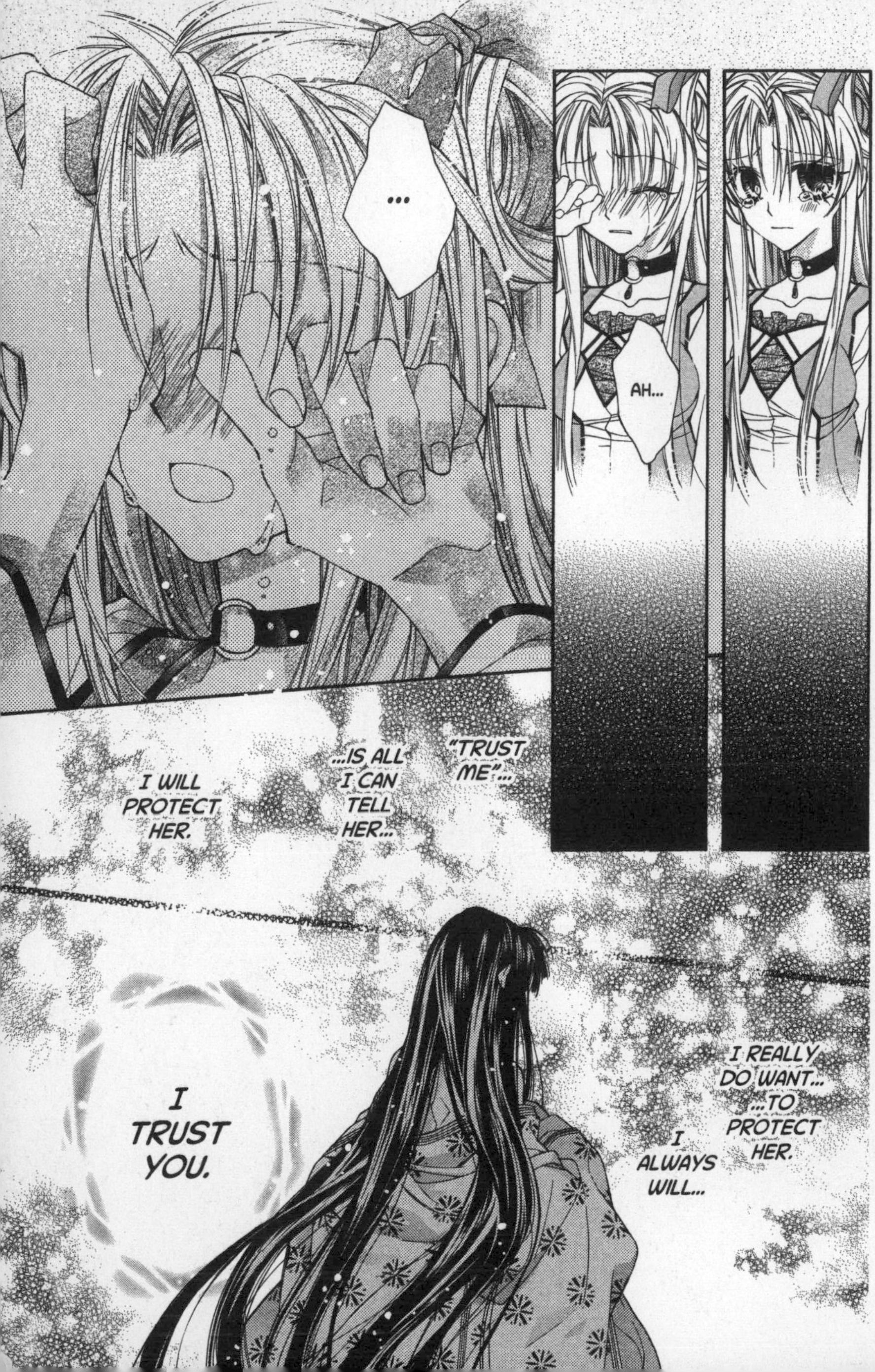
AH...
...
"TRUST ME"...
...IS ALL I CAN TELL HER...
I WILL PROTECT HER.
I REALLY DO WANT... ...TO PROTECT HER.
I ALWAYS WILL...
I TRUST YOU.

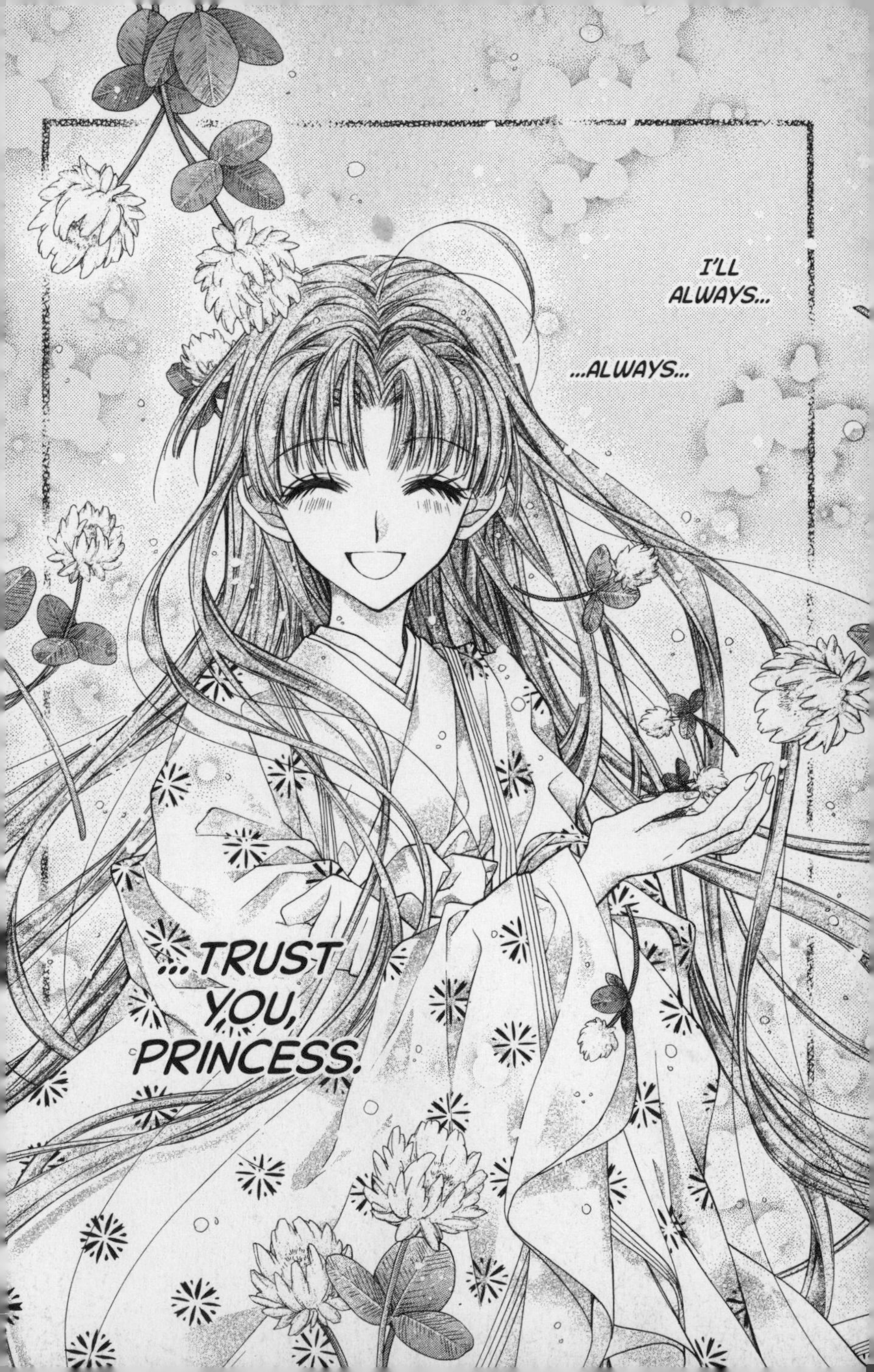
I'LL ALWAYS...
...ALWAYS...
...TRUST YOU, PRINCESS.

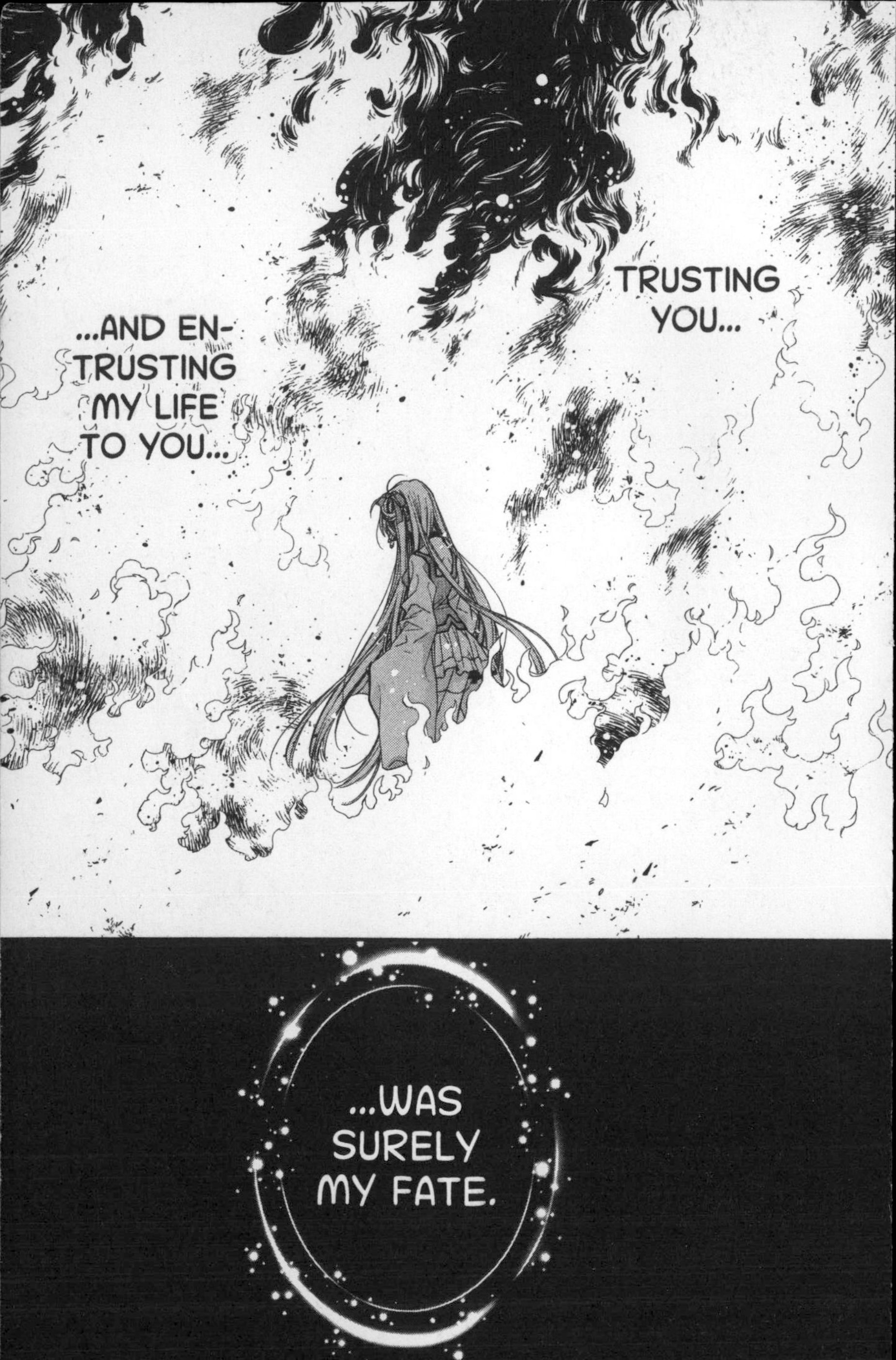
TRUSTING YOU...
...AND EN-TRUSTING MY LIFE TO YOU...
...WAS SURELY MY FATE.

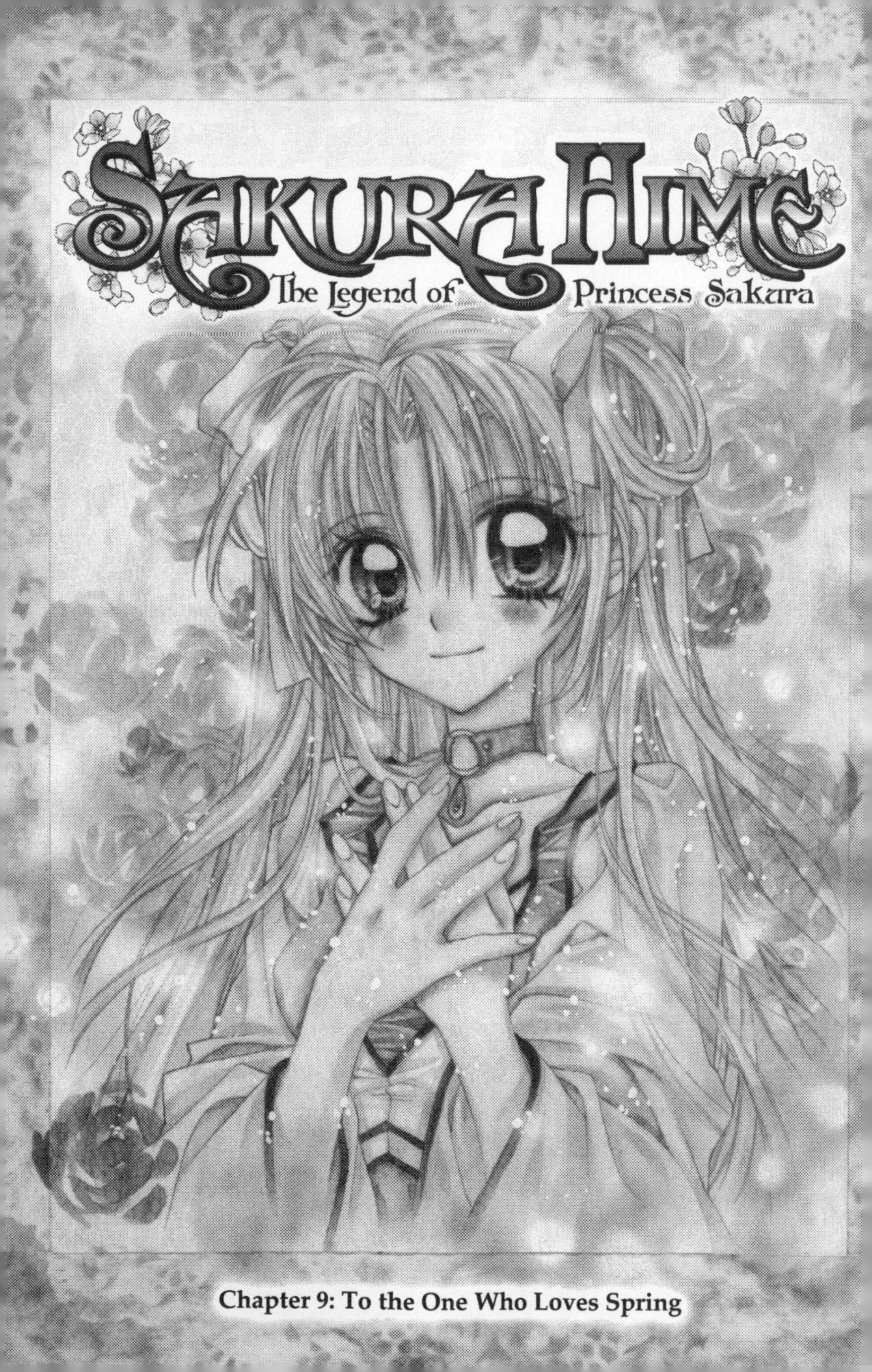
SAKURA HIME
The Legend of Princess Sakura

Chapter 9: To the One Who Loves Spring

flut

flut

Chapter 9: To the One Who Loves Spring [Lead-in]

The kanji for "people" and "dream" make up the kanji for "ephemeral." The kanji for "me" and "dream" must make up the kanji for "love"...

※ I'm giving away the story. Please read this after you read the chapter.

Ah, this brings back memories...
I put in the first two pages just because I wanted to, but when I was deep in thought while working on my final draft, I started to think, "Maybe this is the underlying theme of this manga..." I never thought I'd learn that from Oumi. Now that I've figured that out, I'll make an effort to express it.

Hayate is a character I created to challenge Aoba's cool façade. Aoba doesn't have to act proud in front of a friend who is his same age. I'm glad Hayate turned out to be that kind of character.

"Immortality" is a term you often see and read about in manga, but I (personally) had never read anything that really went into depth about the subject, so I enjoy writing about it.
The elixir of immortality appears at the end of "The Tale of the Bamboo Cutter," so I came to the conclusion that the people on the moon were immortal, but I didn't want their wounds to heal miraculously. Well, it's got its positives and negatives... In other words, there are risks involved.

It would get too depressing if the story continued to dwell on Oumi, so I've drawn it rather blandly. I feel somewhat sorry for traumatizing Princess Sakura... Well, there are still more things to write about this subject, so please keep your eyes on Sakura.

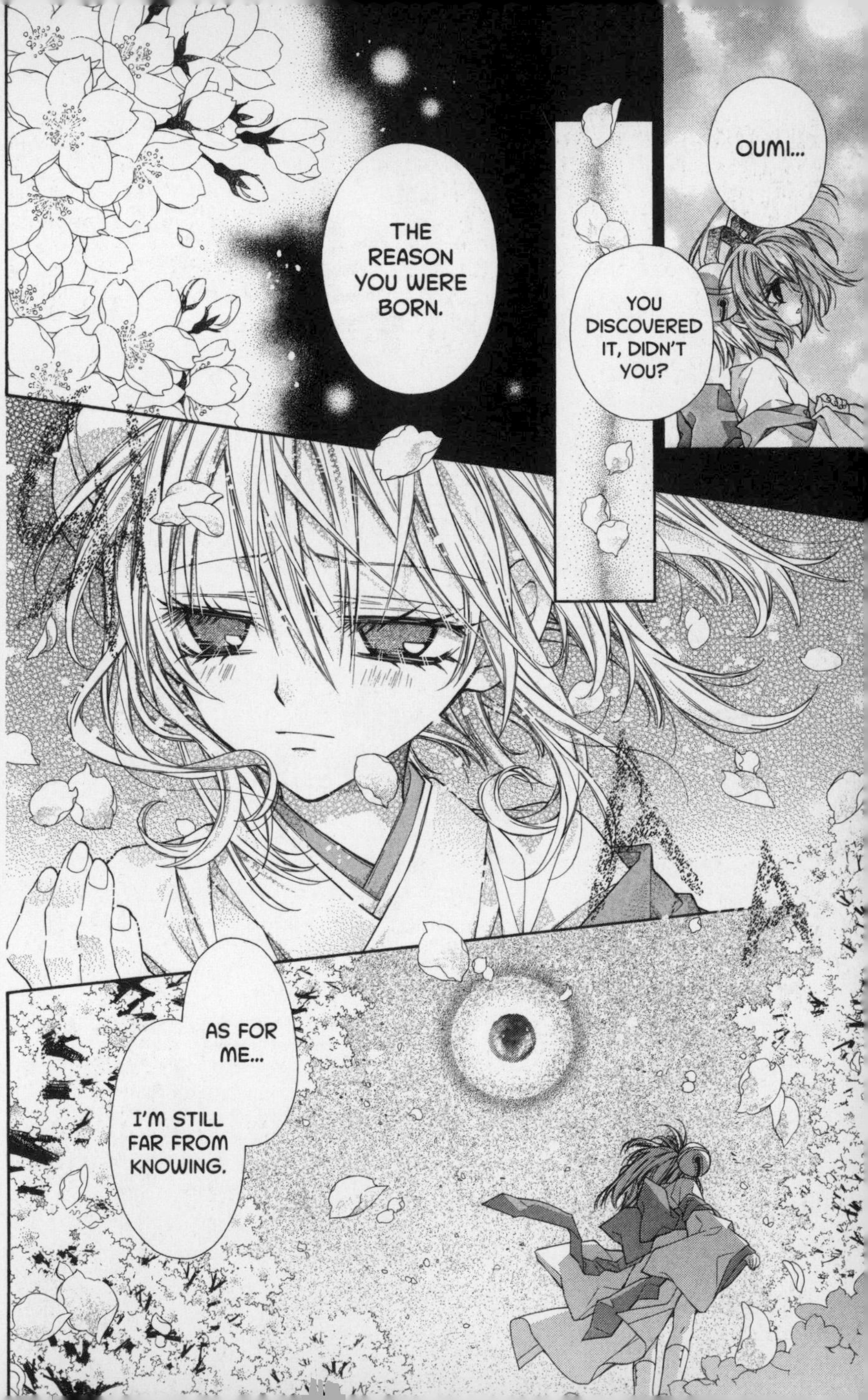
OUMI...
YOU DISCOVERED IT, DIDN'T YOU?
THE REASON YOU WERE BORN.
AS FOR ME...
I'M STILL FAR FROM KNOWING.

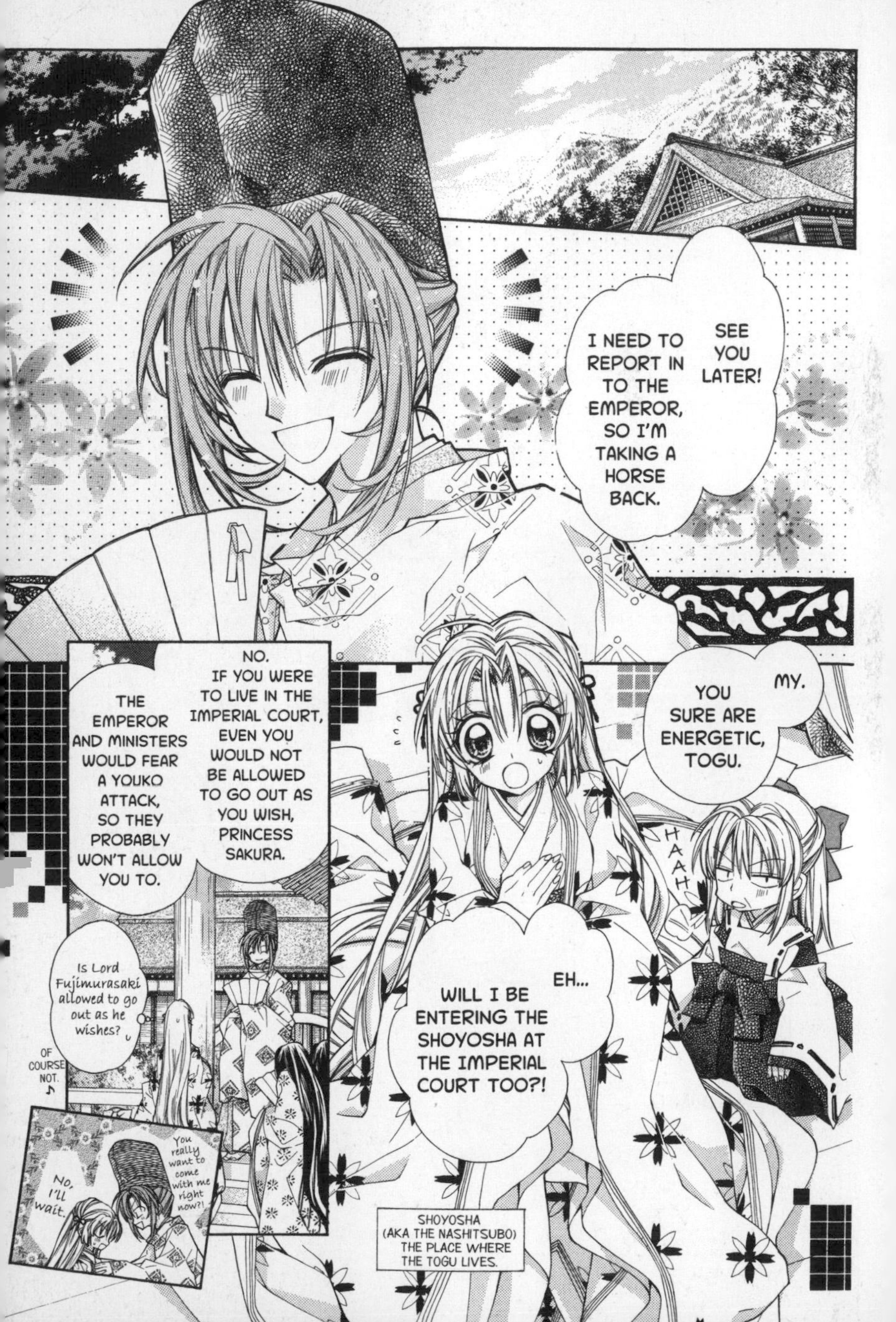
I NEED TO REPORT IN TO THE EMPEROR, SO I'M TAKING A HORSE BACK.
SEE YOU LATER!
MY.
YOU SURE ARE ENERGETIC, TOGU.
HAAH
EH...
WILL I BE ENTERING THE SHOYOSHA AT THE IMPERIAL COURT TOO?!
SHOYOSHA (AKA THE NASHITSUBO) THE PLACE WHERE THE TOGU LIVES.
NO. IF YOU WERE TO LIVE IN THE IMPERIAL COURT, EVEN YOU WOULD NOT BE ALLOWED TO GO OUT AS YOU WISH, PRINCESS SAKURA.
THE EMPEROR AND MINISTERS WOULD FEAR A YOUKO ATTACK, SO THEY PROBABLY WON'T ALLOW YOU TO.
Is Lord Fujimurasaki allowed to go out as he wishes?
OF COURSE NOT. ♪
You really want to come with me right now?!
No, I'll wait.

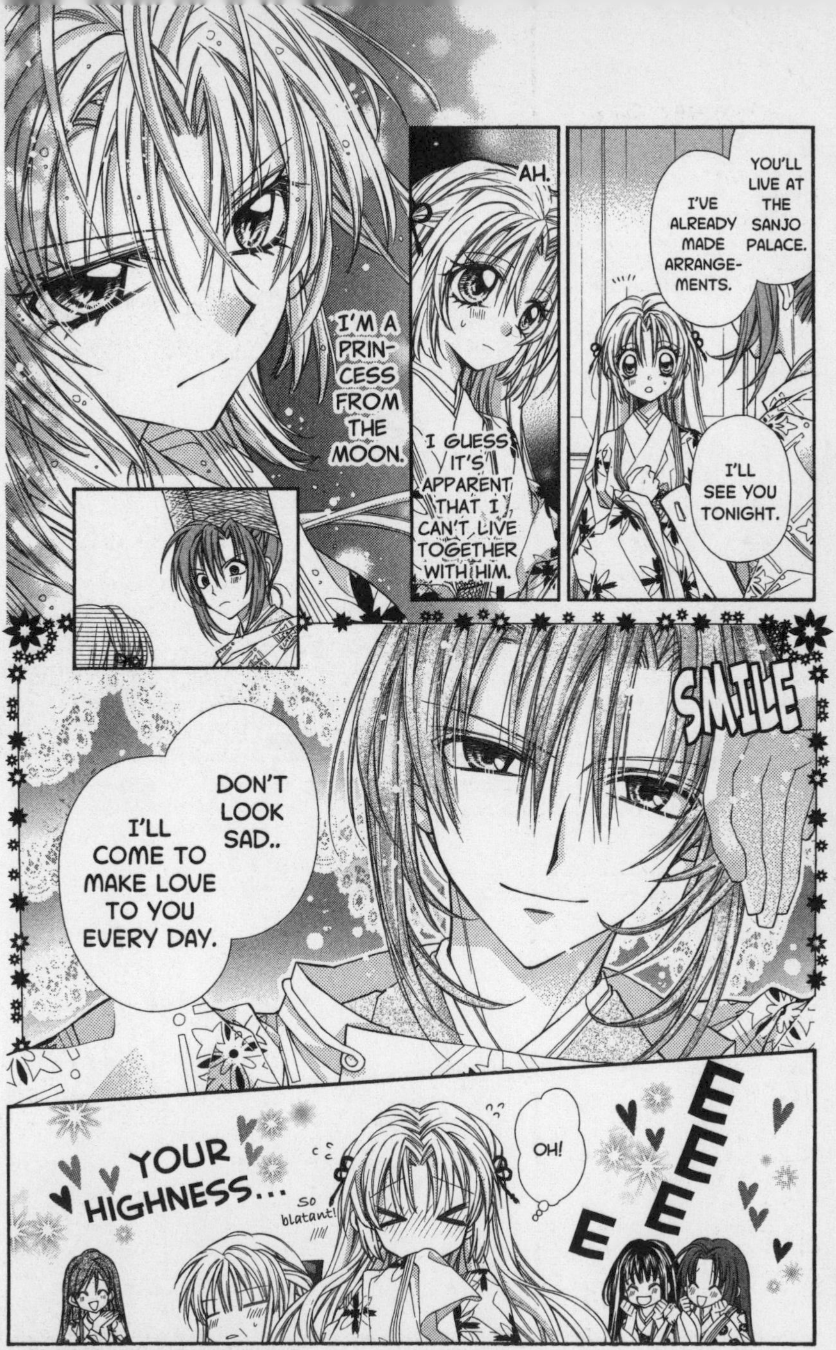
YOU'LL LIVE AT THE SANJO PALACE.
I'VE ALREADY MADE ARRANGEMENTS.
I'LL SEE YOU TONIGHT.
AH.
I GUESS IT'S APPARENT THAT I CAN'T LIVE TOGETHER WITH HIM.
I'M A PRINCESS FROM THE MOON.
SMILE
DON'T LOOK SAD..
I'LL COME TO MAKE LOVE TO YOU EVERY DAY.
EEEEE
OH!
YOUR HIGHNESS...
So blatant!

TOGU IS VERY POPULAR WITH THE LADIES.

✽ Germany Diary

I traveled from Narita Airport→ the Netherlands→Germany and finally got there!
It's so great that I get to travel on business class when I'm traveling for work. ♥ (Sorry... My sense of money is like that of a high school student's.)

I love planes (especially the business class). ♪I really like that strange feeling of having a meal somewhere very high up in the air.

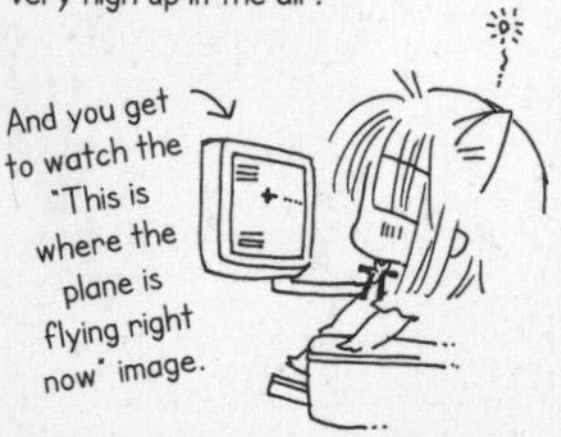
And you get to watch the "This is where the plane is flying right now" image.

I stayed at Dorint Hotel in the mountains. ♪
And my room faced the inner court-yard too! I don't have to do anything like making reservations for a wonder-ful hotel like this when I go somewhere for work. ♥♥ (I'm being persistent.)

I got to go sightseeing the first day, and my autograph session was scheduled for the next day.
I attended the opening ceremony. The hall, which was large enough for two thousand people or so, was standing room only!
From what I heard, they don't have these kinds of otaku events that often... And the government decides how many people may attend the event depending on the size of the location, so they are only allowed to sell so many tickets.

The tickets sold out very fast, and the people who couldn't enter the event hall were all in cosplay in the large open space outside.

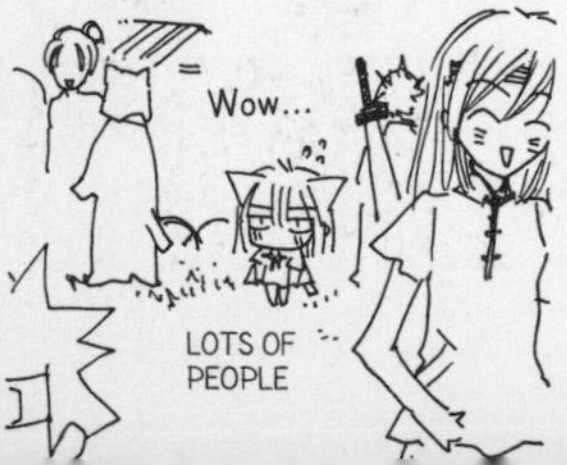
Wow...
LOTS OF PEOPLE

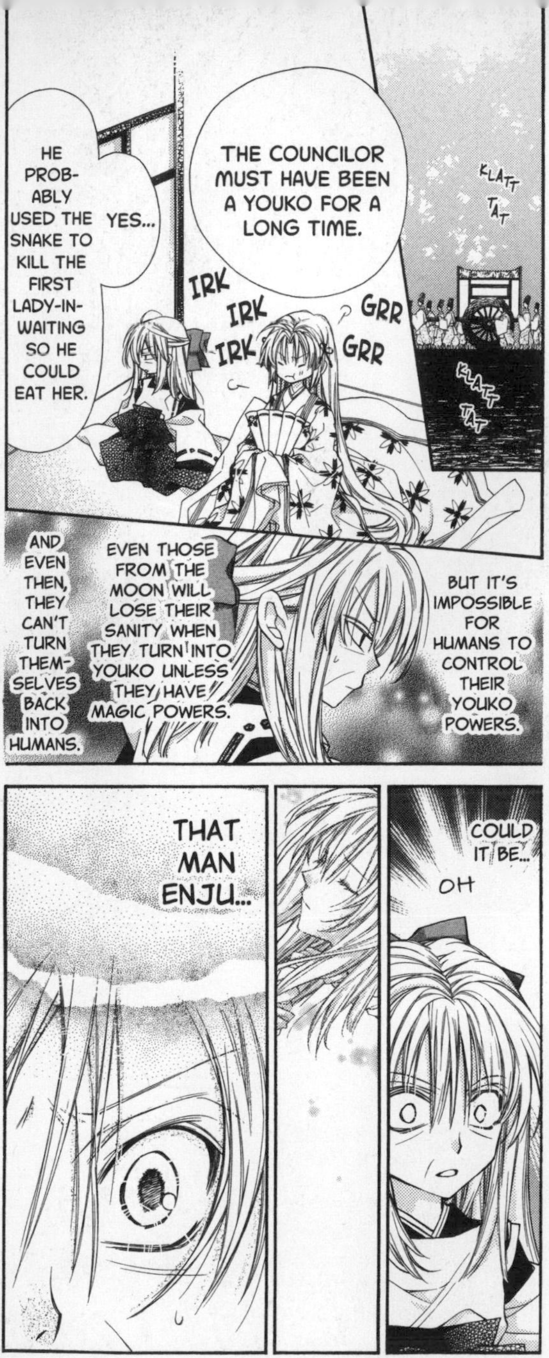
KLATT TAT
KLATT TAT
THE COUNCILOR MUST HAVE BEEN A YOUKO FOR A LONG TIME.
YES...
HE PROBABLY USED THE SNAKE TO KILL THE FIRST LADY-IN-WAITING SO HE COULD EAT HER.
GRR GRR
IRK IRK IRK
BUT IT'S IMPOSSIBLE FOR HUMANS TO CONTROL THEIR YOUKO POWERS.
EVEN THOSE FROM THE MOON WILL LOSE THEIR SANITY WHEN THEY TURN INTO YOUKO UNLESS THEY HAVE MAGIC POWERS.
AND EVEN THEN, THEY CAN'T TURN THEMSELVES BACK INTO HUMANS.
COULD IT BE...
OH
THAT MAN ENJU...

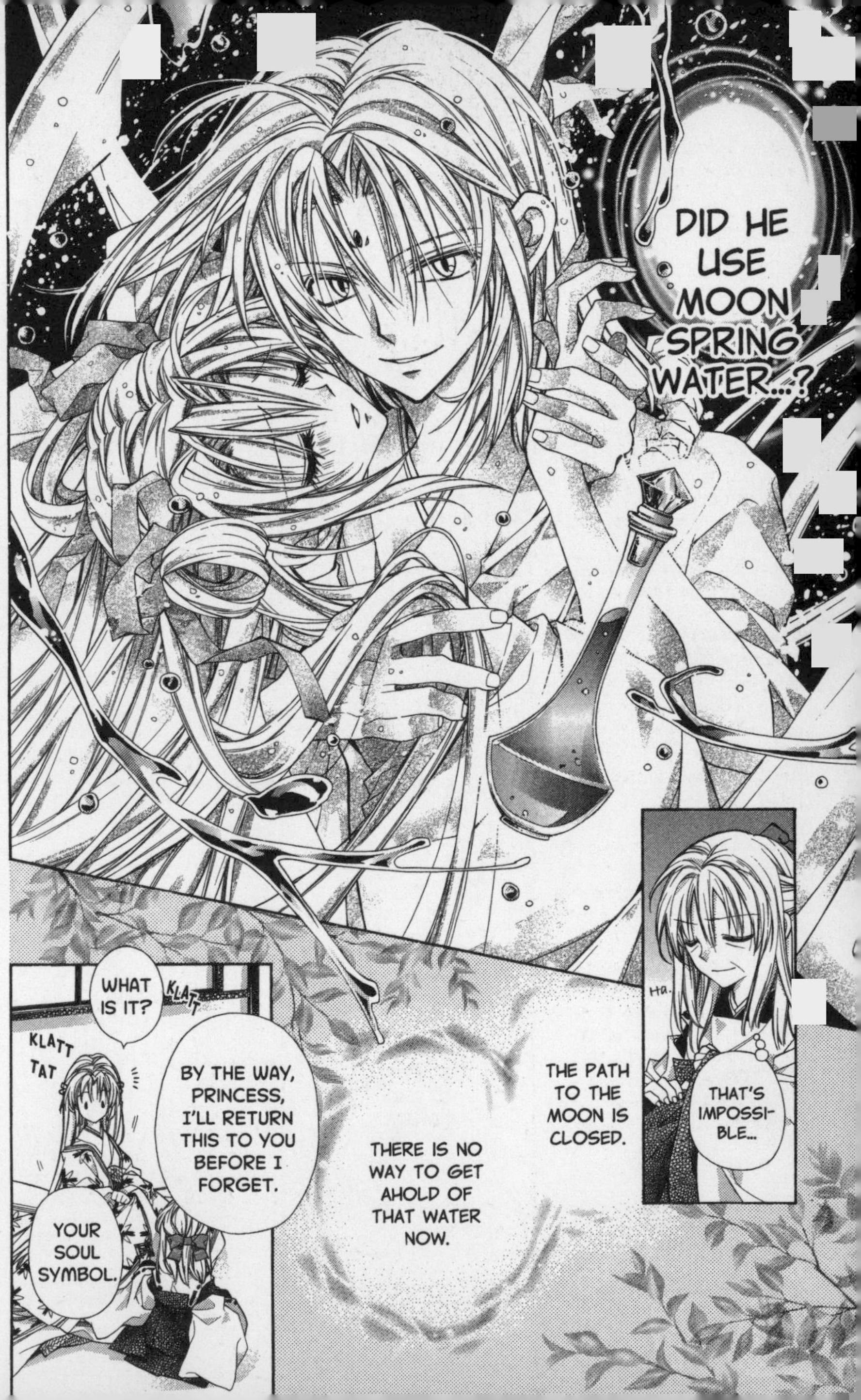
DID HE USE MOON SPRING WATER...?
Ha.
THAT'S IMPOSSI-BLE...
THE PATH TO THE MOON IS CLOSED.
THERE IS NO WAY TO GET AHOLD OF THAT WATER NOW.
KLATT
WHAT IS IT?
KLATT TAT
BY THE WAY, PRINCESS, I'LL RETURN THIS TO YOU BEFORE I FORGET.
YOUR SOUL SYMBOL.

Germany Diary 2

I was screaming joyfully at all the cosplayers around me when I heard an "Excuse me..." in Japanese!

There were two Japanese girls! For some reason, things like onigiri and takoyaki were being sold in the open space outside. (I thought it looked more like a "We Like Japan Festival" rather than an "Anime Festival.")

They were Japanese girls who were born in Germany, and they were working a stall. They also had *Ribon* sent to them from Japan and had read my work before. We shook hands.
Hmm... But I wonder how they figured out I was Tanemura...

There was an hour for audience questions and an hour for autographs.
I came to Germany three years ago, and a girl who was at that autograph session came again this time. She cosplayed Haine. It was great.
I want to go back to Germany just to see her again.

A staff member at Tokyopop (the company which publishes my work in Germany) interpreted for me, but everybody would laugh for questions like "What is your favorite color?" "Pink." I would answer using an English word. (They were happy they understood something I said.)
↳ Of course they speak German in Germany, but they understand English too.

(Continues)

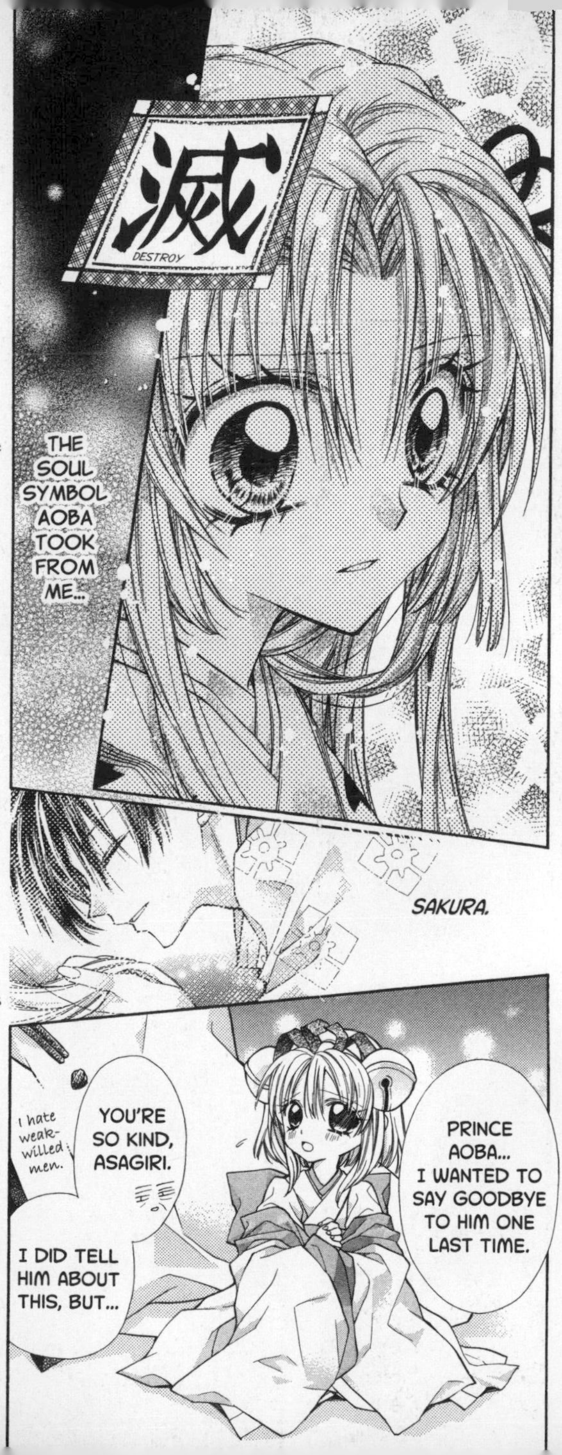
滅
DESTROY
THE SOUL SYMBOL AOBA TOOK FROM ME...
SAKURA.
PRINCE AOBA... I WANTED TO SAY GOODBYE TO HIM ONE LAST TIME.
YOU'RE SO KIND, ASAGIRI.
I hate weak-willed men.
I DID TELL HIM ABOUT THIS, BUT...

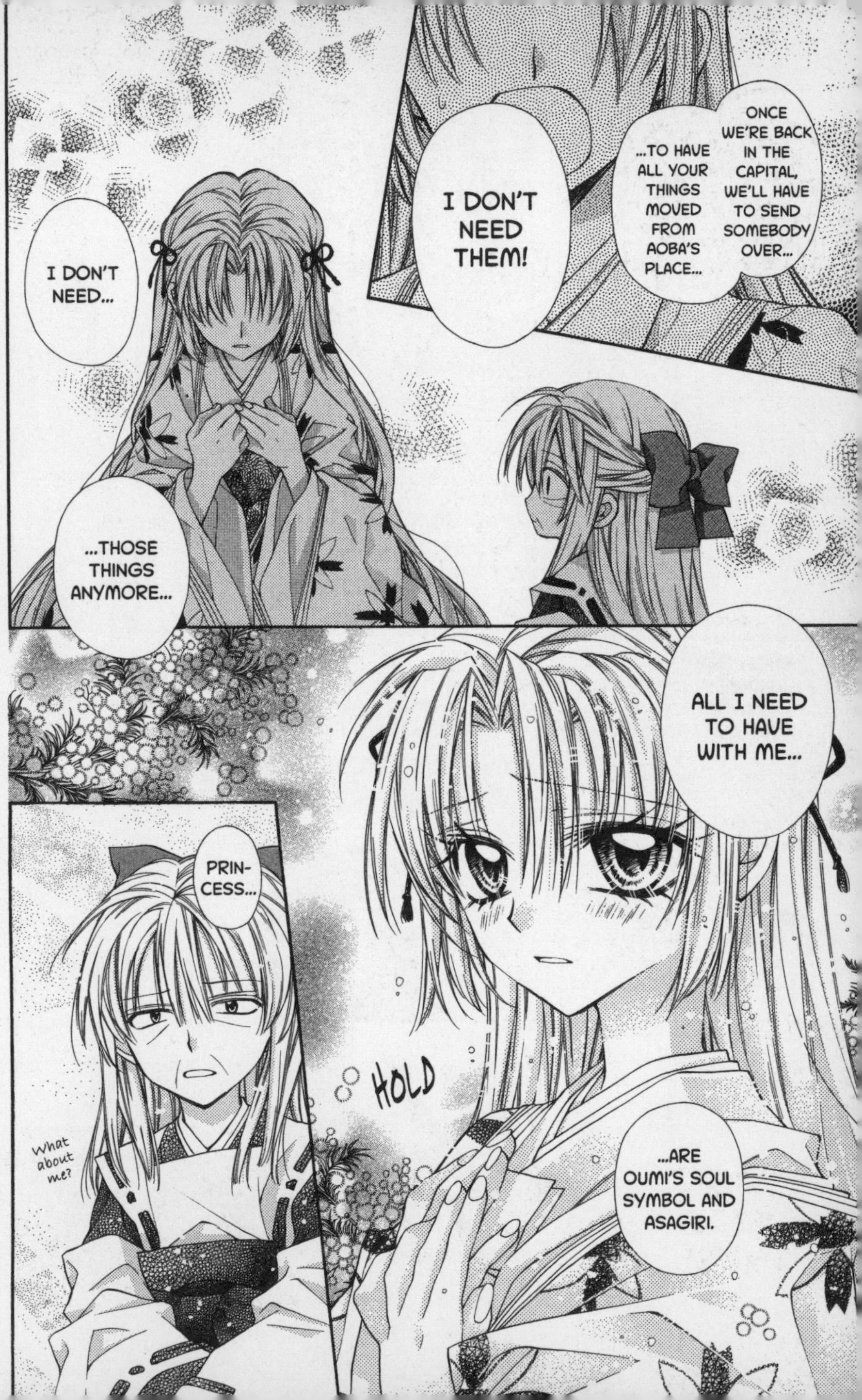
ONCE WE'RE BACK IN THE CAPITAL, WE'LL HAVE TO SEND SOMEBODY OVER...
...TO HAVE ALL YOUR THINGS MOVED FROM AOBA'S PLACE...
I DON'T NEED THEM!
I DON'T NEED...
...THOSE THINGS ANYMORE...
ALL I NEED TO HAVE WITH ME...
HOLD
...ARE OUMI'S SOUL SYMBOL AND ASAGIRI.
PRIN-CESS...
What about me?

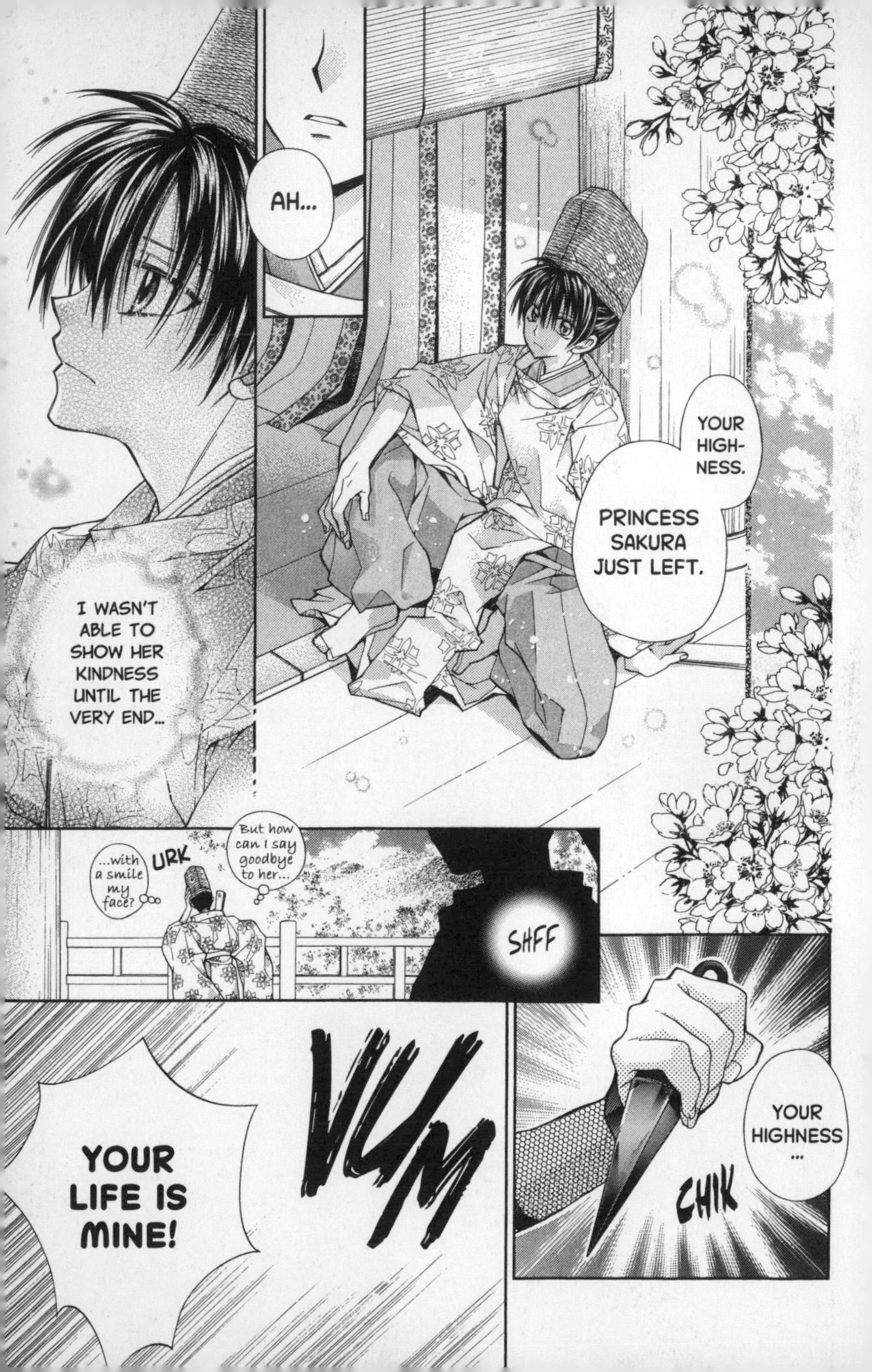

YOUR HIGHNESS.
PRINCESS SAKURA JUST LEFT.
AH...
I WASN'T ABLE TO SHOW HER KINDNESS UNTIL THE VERY END...
SHFF
But how can I say goodbye to her...
...with a smile my face?
URK
YOUR HIGHNESS ...
CHIK
VUM
YOUR LIFE IS MINE!

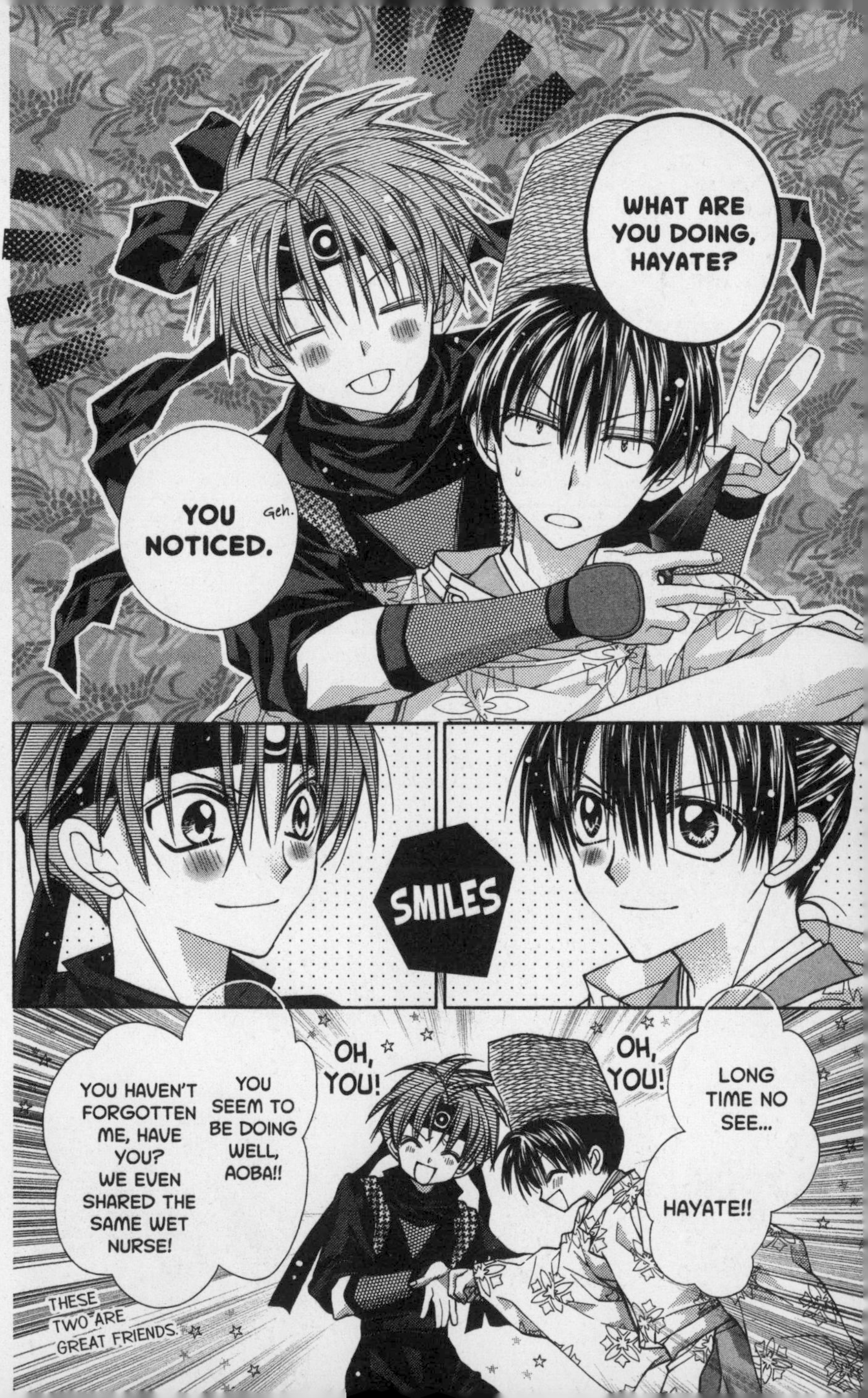
WHAT ARE YOU DOING, HAYATE?
YOU NOTICED.
Geh.
SMILES
LONG TIME NO SEE...
HAYATE!!
OH, YOU!
OH, YOU!
YOU SEEM TO BE DOING WELL, AOBA!!
YOU HAVEN'T FORGOTTEN ME, HAVE YOU? WE EVEN SHARED THE SAME WET NURSE!
THESE TWO ARE GREAT FRIENDS.

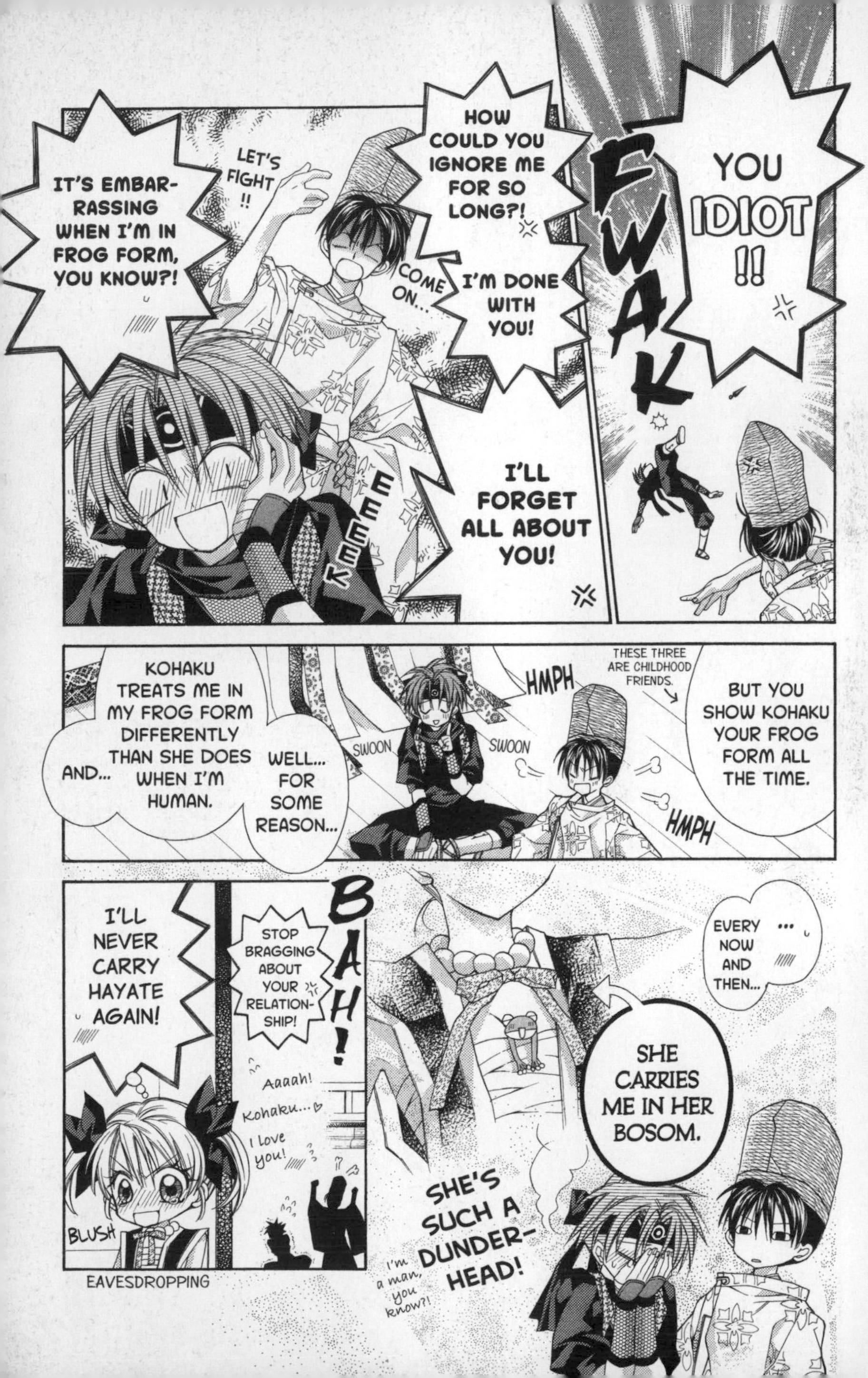
YOU IDIOT!!
FWAK
HOW COULD YOU IGNORE ME FOR SO LONG?!
I'M DONE WITH YOU!
COME ON...
LET'S FIGHT!!
IT'S EMBARRASSING WHEN I'M IN FROG FORM, YOU KNOW?!
I'LL FORGET ALL ABOUT YOU!
EEEEEK
BUT YOU SHOW KOHAKU YOUR FROG FORM ALL THE TIME.
THESE THREE ARE CHILDHOOD FRIENDS.
HMPH
HMPH
SWOON
SWOON
WELL... FOR SOME REASON...
KOHAKU TREATS ME IN MY FROG FORM DIFFERENTLY THAN SHE DOES WHEN I'M HUMAN.
AND...
...
EVERY NOW AND THEN...
SHE CARRIES ME IN HER BOSOM.
SHE'S SUCH A DUNDER-HEAD!
I'm a man, you know?!
BAH!
STOP BRAGGING ABOUT YOUR RELATION-SHIP!
I'LL NEVER CARRY HAYATE AGAIN!
Aaaah!
Kohaku...
I love you!
BLUSH
EAVESDROPPING

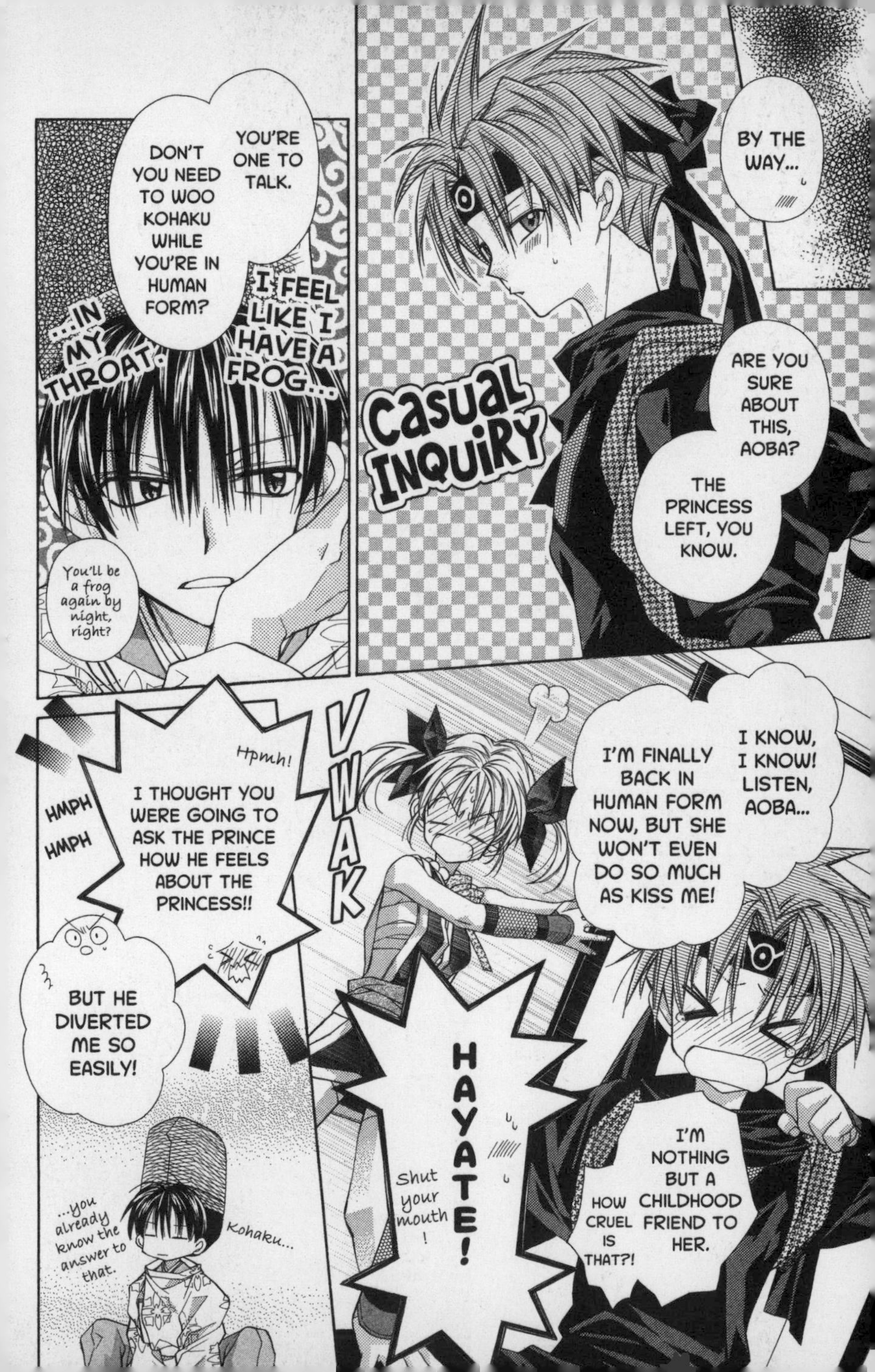
BY THE WAY...
ARE YOU SURE ABOUT THIS, AOBA?
THE PRINCESS LEFT, YOU KNOW.
CASUAL INQUIRY
YOU'RE ONE TO TALK.
DON'T YOU NEED TO WOO KOHAKU WHILE YOU'RE IN HUMAN FORM?
I FEEL LIKE I HAVE A FROG...
...IN MY THROAT.
You'll be a frog again by night, right?
I KNOW, I KNOW! LISTEN, AOBA...
I'M FINALLY BACK IN HUMAN FORM NOW, BUT SHE WON'T EVEN DO SO MUCH AS KISS ME!
VWAK
I'M NOTHING BUT A CHILDHOOD FRIEND TO HER.
HOW CRUEL IS THAT?!
HAYATE!
Shut your mouth!
Hpmh!
I THOUGHT YOU WERE GOING TO ASK THE PRINCE HOW HE FEELS ABOUT THE PRINCESS!!
HMPH HMPH
BUT HE DIVERTED ME SO EASILY!
Kohaku...
...you already know the answer to that.

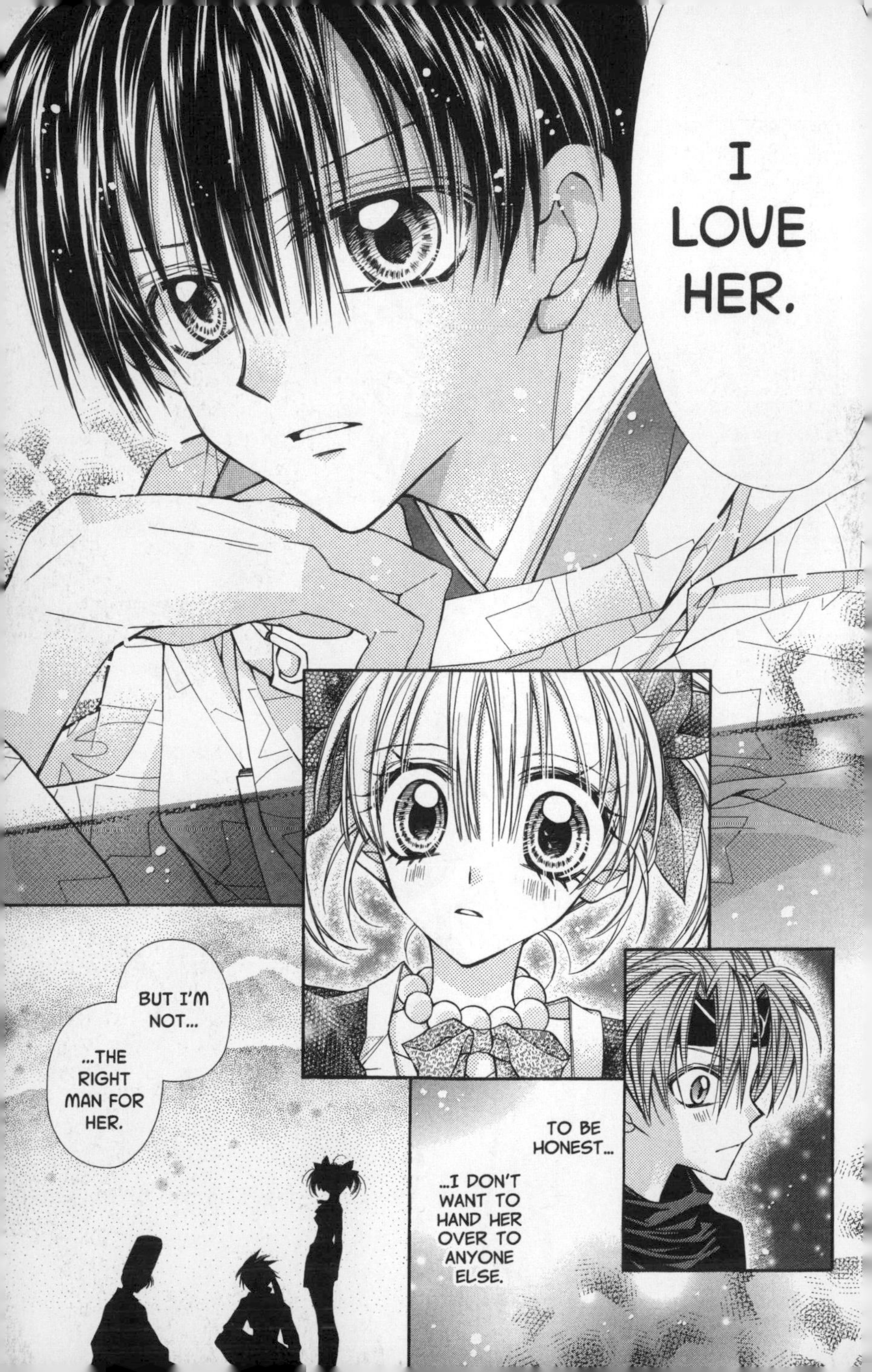
I LOVE HER.
TO BE HONEST...
...I DON'T WANT TO HAND HER OVER TO ANYONE ELSE.
BUT I'M NOT...
...THE RIGHT MAN FOR HER.

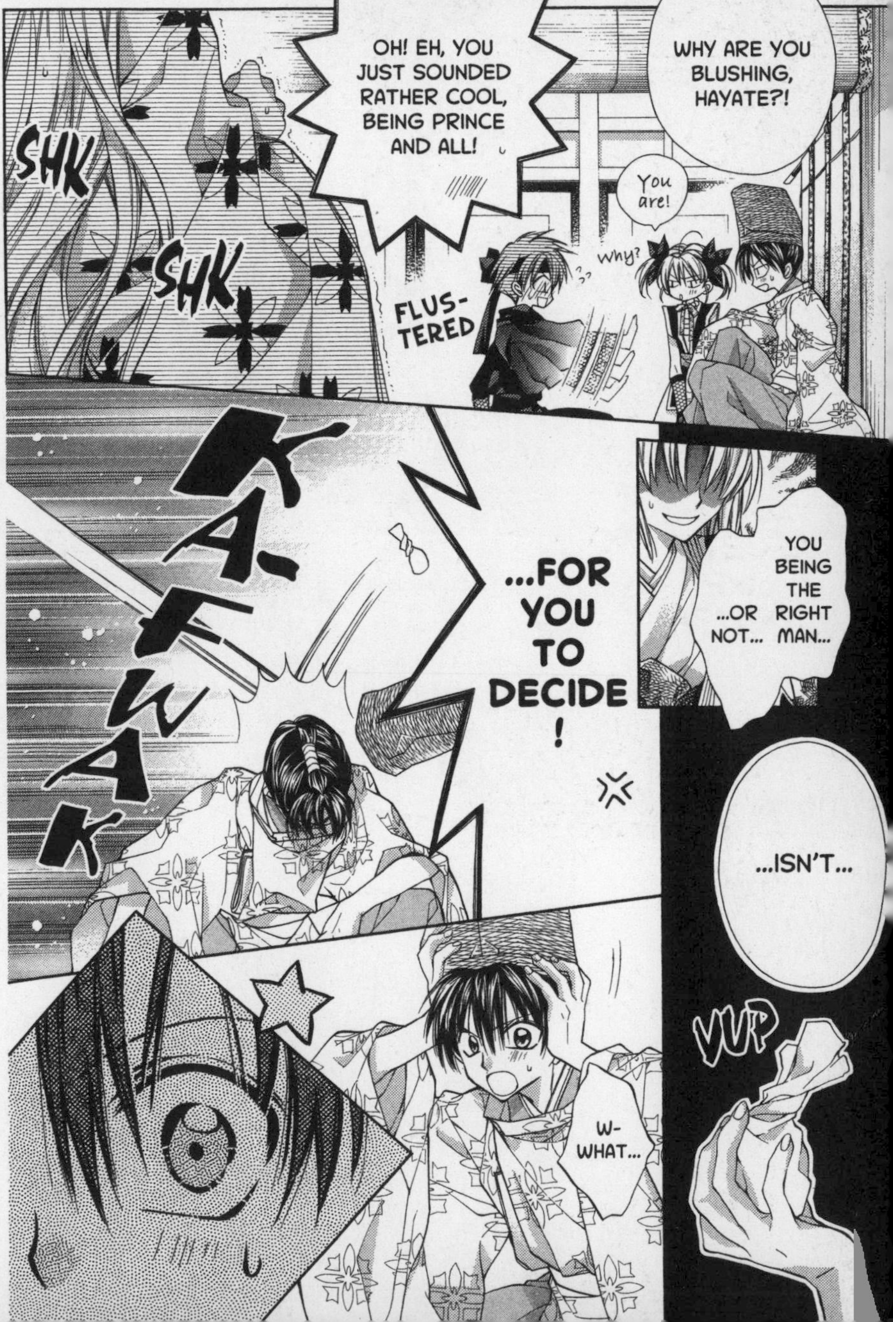
WHY ARE YOU BLUSHING, HAYATE?!
You are!
Why?
OH! EH, YOU JUST SOUNDED RATHER COOL, BEING PRINCE AND ALL!
FLUS-TERED
SHK
SHK
YOU BEING THE RIGHT MAN...
...OR NOT...
...ISN'T...
VUP
...FOR YOU TO DECIDE!
KA-FWAK
W-WHAT...

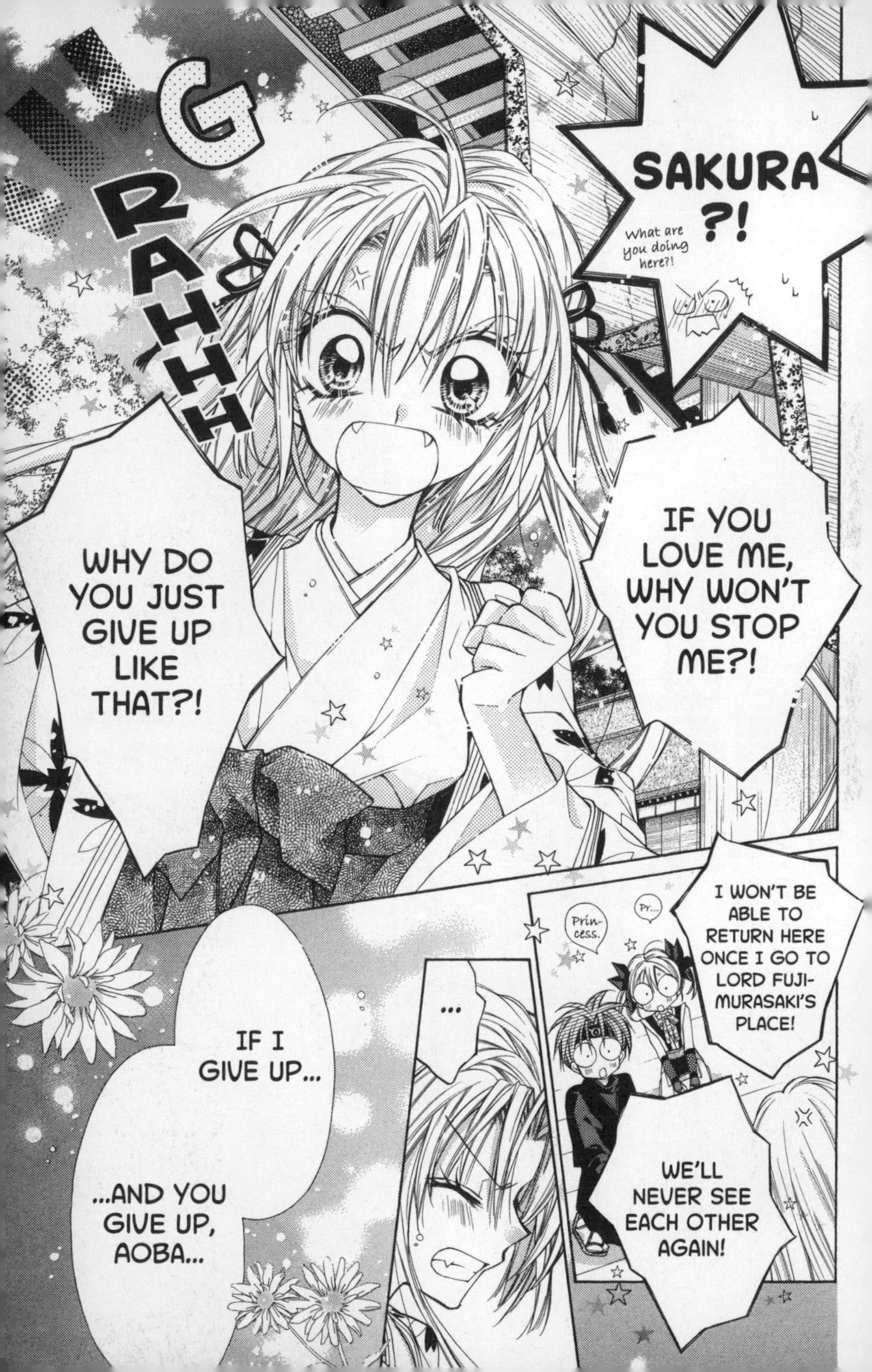
SAKURA ?!
What are you doing here?!
GRAHHH
WHY DO YOU JUST GIVE UP LIKE THAT?!
IF YOU LOVE ME, WHY WON'T YOU STOP ME?!
I WON'T BE ABLE TO RETURN HERE ONCE I GO TO LORD FUJI-MURASAKI'S PLACE!
Pr...
Prin-cess.
WE'LL NEVER SEE EACH OTHER AGAIN!
...
IF I GIVE UP...
...AND YOU GIVE UP, AOBA...

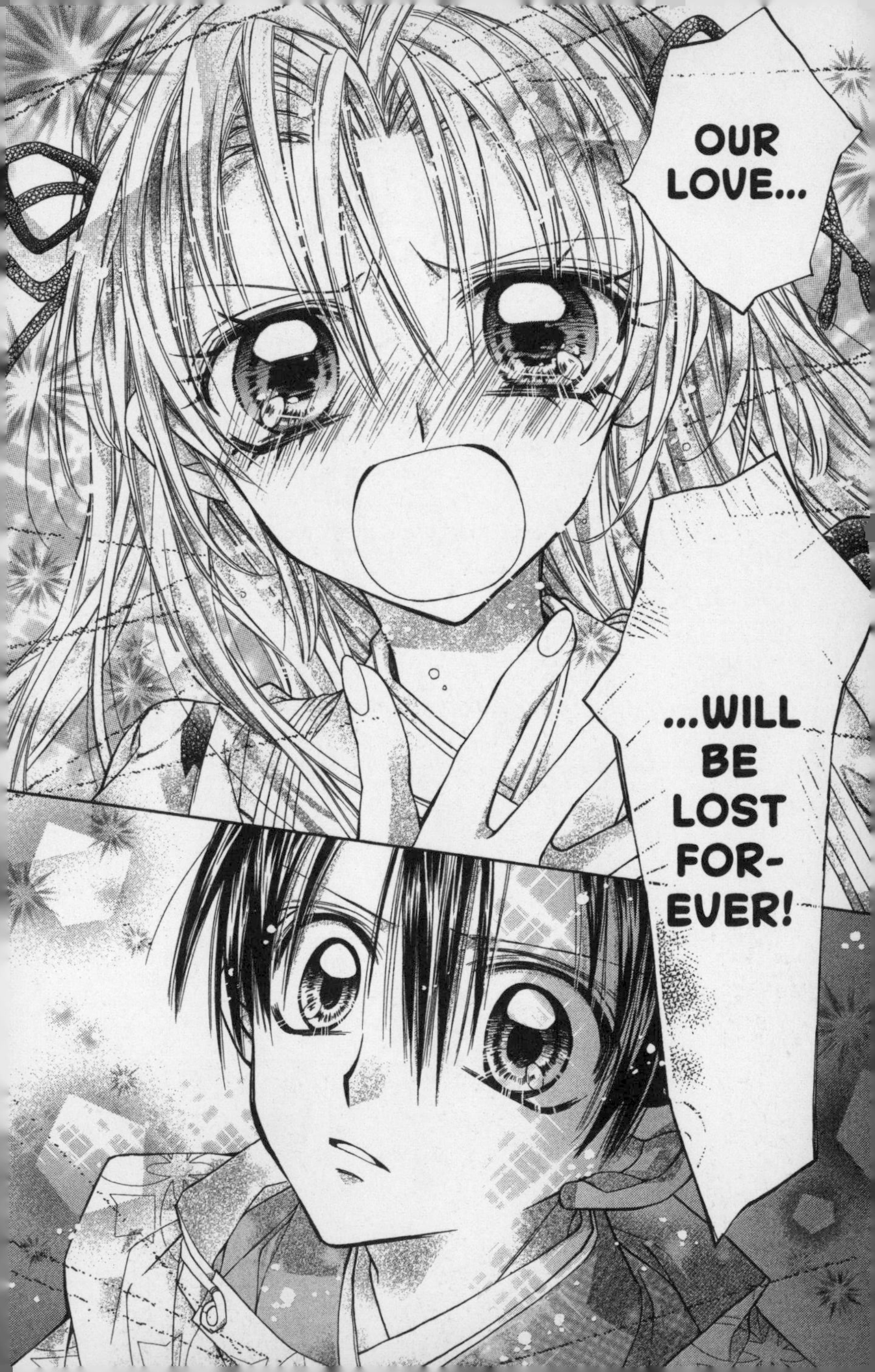
OUR LOVE...
...WILL BE LOST FOR-EVER!

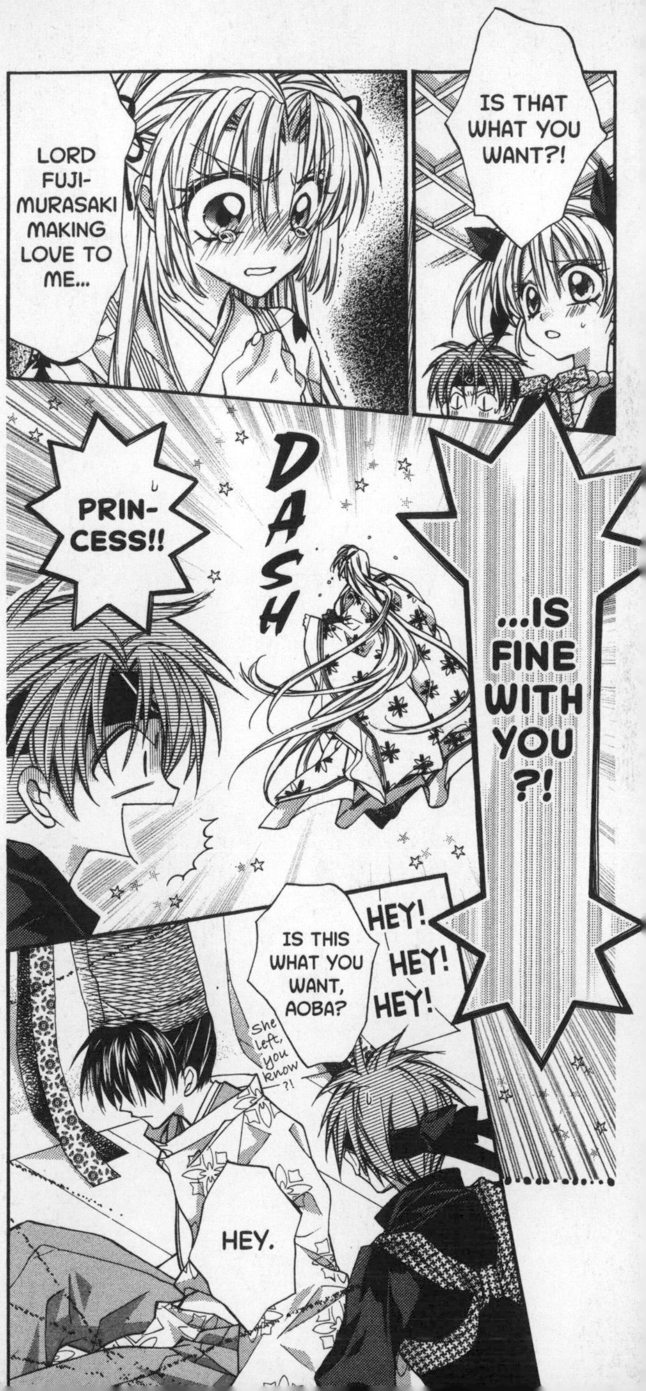
IS THAT WHAT YOU WANT?!
LORD FUJI-MURASAKI MAKING LOVE TO ME...
...IS FINE WITH YOU?!
....
PRIN-CESS!!
DASH
HEY! HEY! HEY!
IS THIS WHAT YOU WANT, AOBA?
She left, you know?!
HEY.

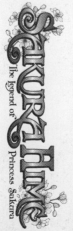

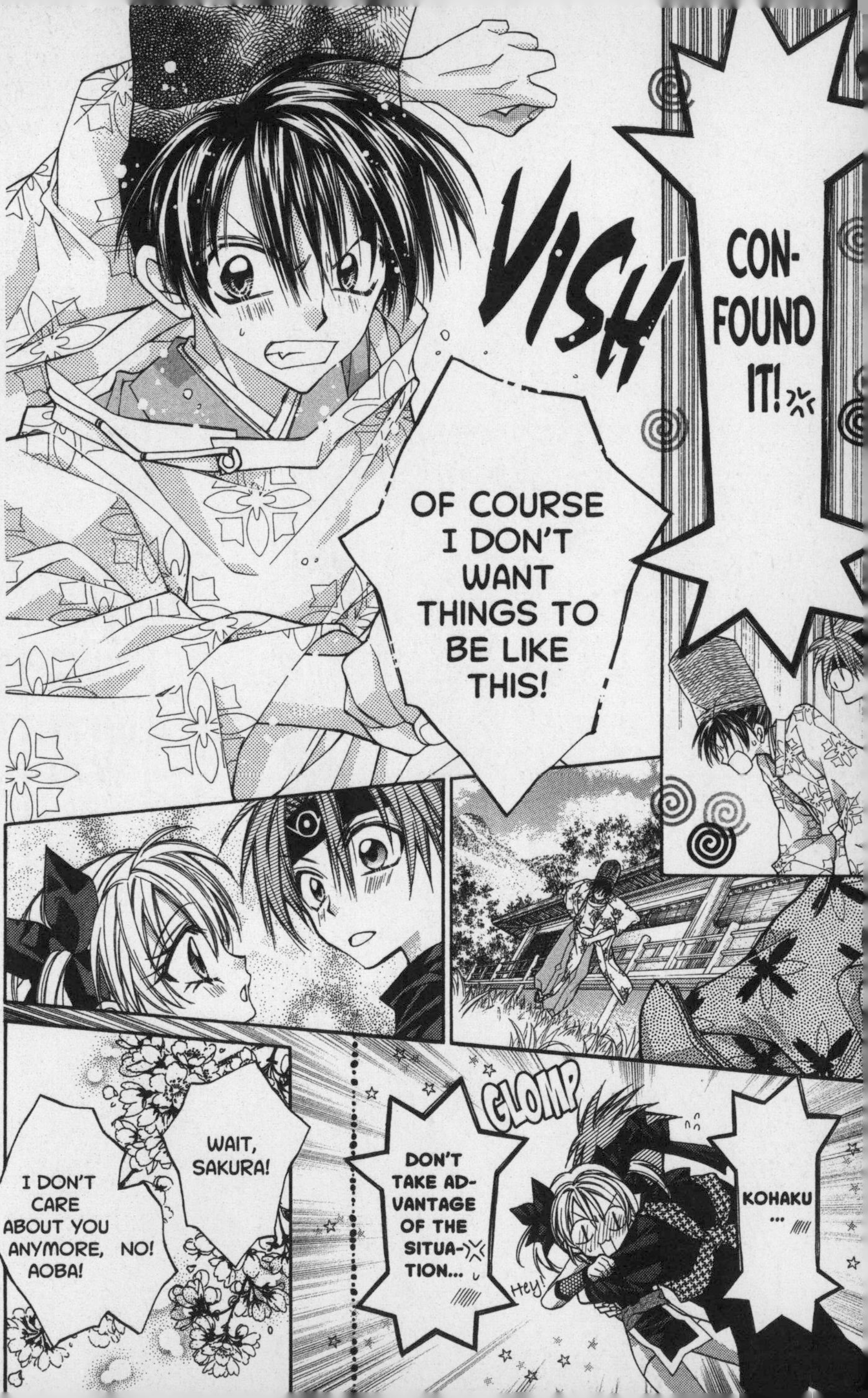
CON-FOUND IT!
VISH
OF COURSE I DON'T WANT THINGS TO BE LIKE THIS!
KOHAKU...
GLOMP
Hey!
DON'T TAKE AD-VANTAGE OF THE SITUA-TION...
WAIT, SAKURA!
NO!
I DON'T CARE ABOUT YOU ANYMORE, AOBA!

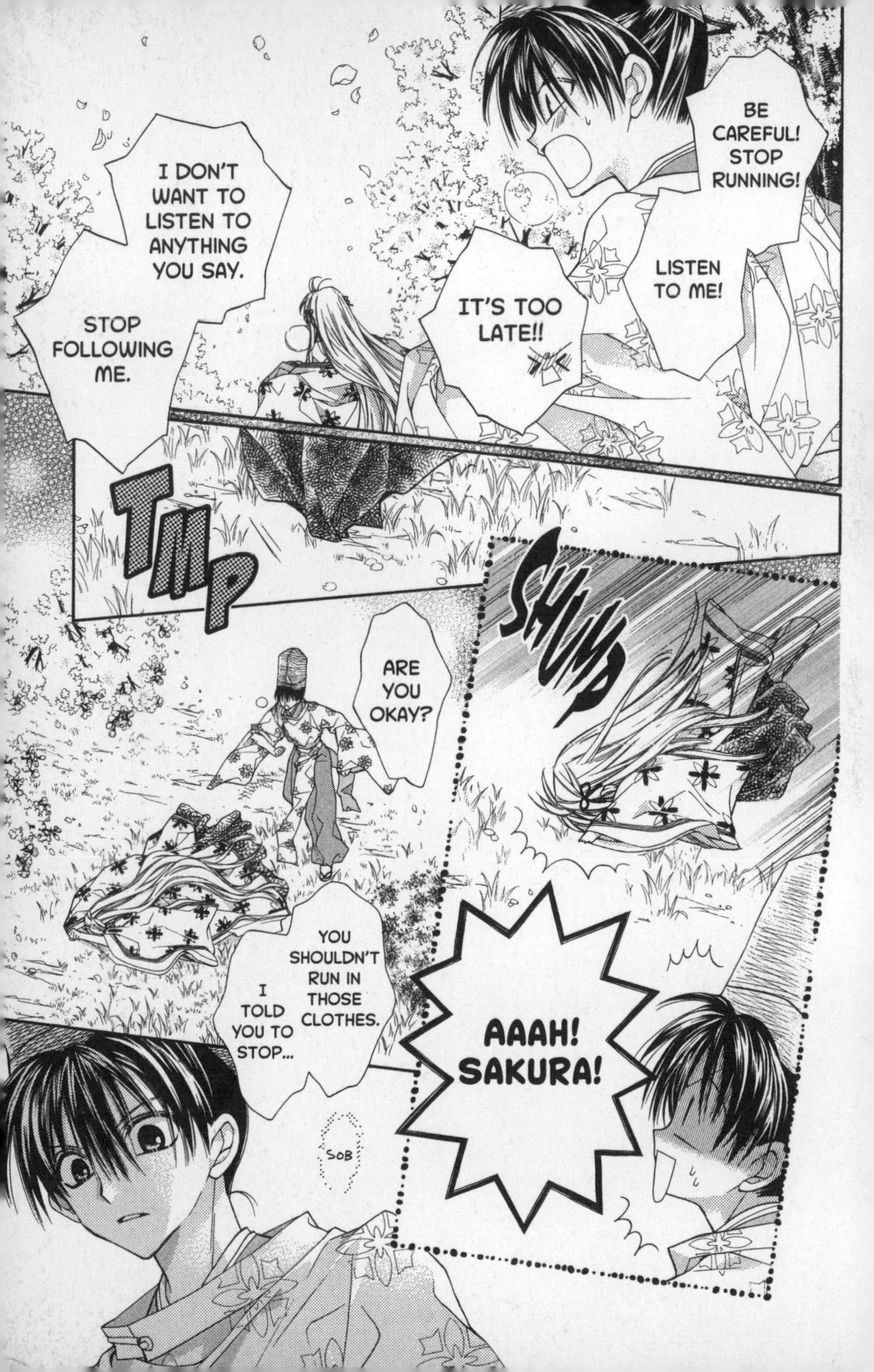
BE CAREFUL! STOP RUNNING!
LISTEN TO ME!
IT'S TOO LATE!!
I DON'T WANT TO LISTEN TO ANYTHING YOU SAY.
STOP FOLLOWING ME.
TMP
SHUMP
AAAH! SAKURA!
ARE YOU OKAY?
YOU SHOULDN'T RUN IN THOSE CLOTHES.
I TOLD YOU TO STOP...
SOB

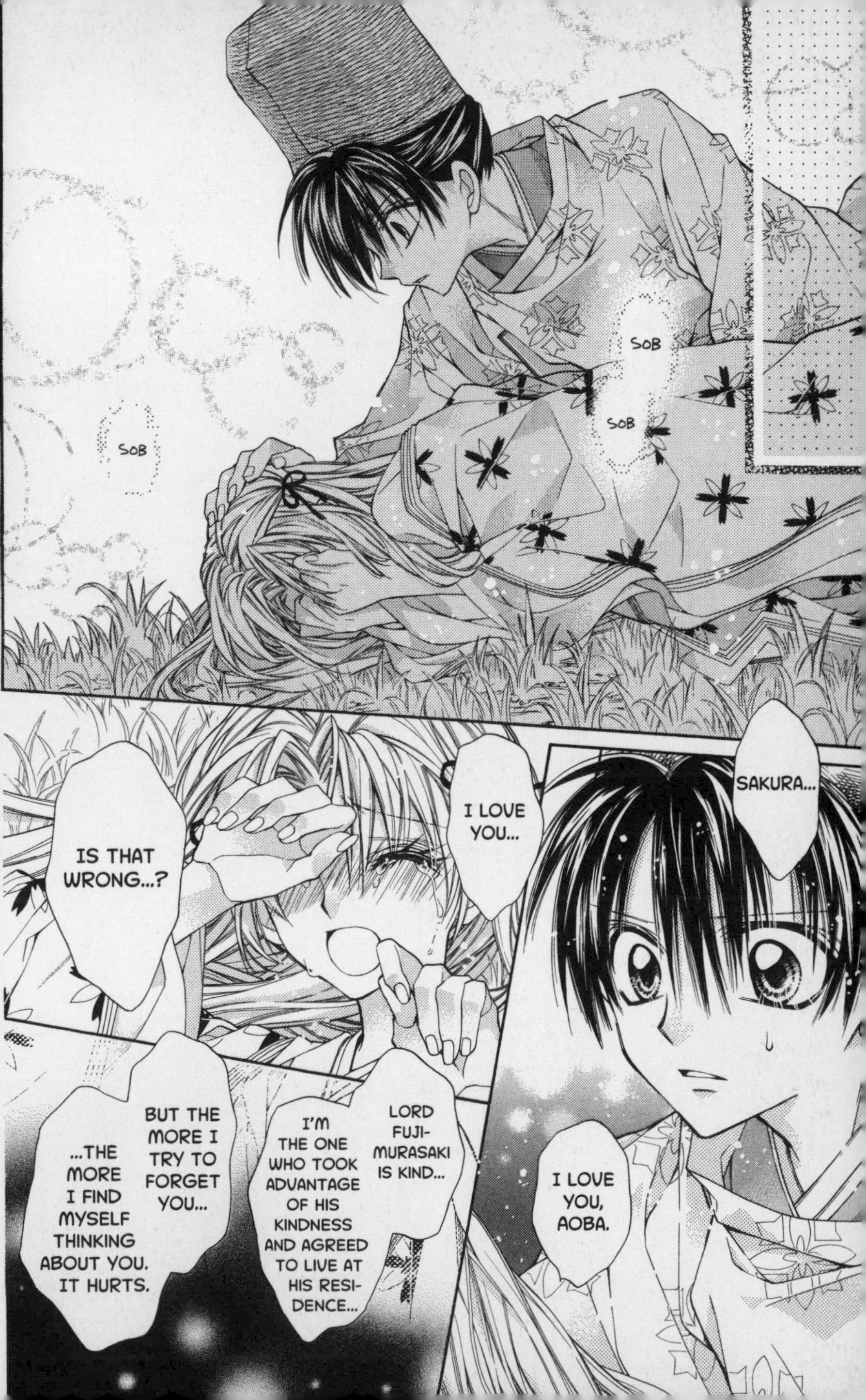
SOB
SOB
SOB
SAKURA...
I LOVE YOU...
IS THAT WRONG...?
LORD FUJI-MURASAKI IS KIND...
I'M THE ONE WHO TOOK ADVANTAGE OF HIS KINDNESS AND AGREED TO LIVE AT HIS RESI-DENCE...
BUT THE MORE I TRY TO FORGET YOU...
...THE MORE I FIND MYSELF THINKING ABOUT YOU. IT HURTS.
I LOVE YOU, AOBA.

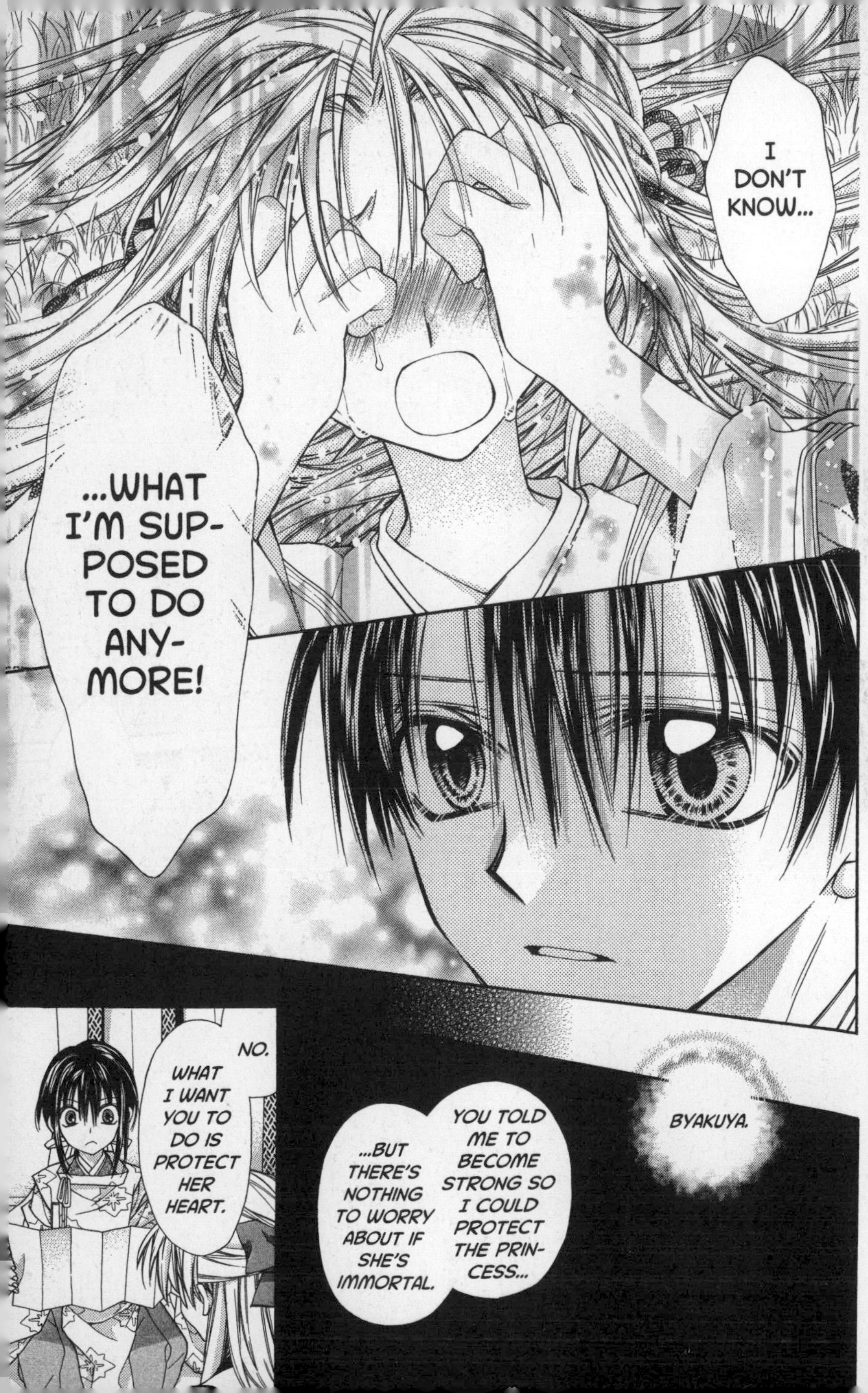
I DON'T KNOW...
...WHAT I'M SUPPOSED TO DO ANYMORE!
BYAKUYA.
YOU TOLD ME TO BECOME STRONG SO I COULD PROTECT THE PRINCESS...
...BUT THERE'S NOTHING TO WORRY ABOUT IF SHE'S IMMORTAL.
NO.
WHAT I WANT YOU TO DO IS PROTECT HER HEART.

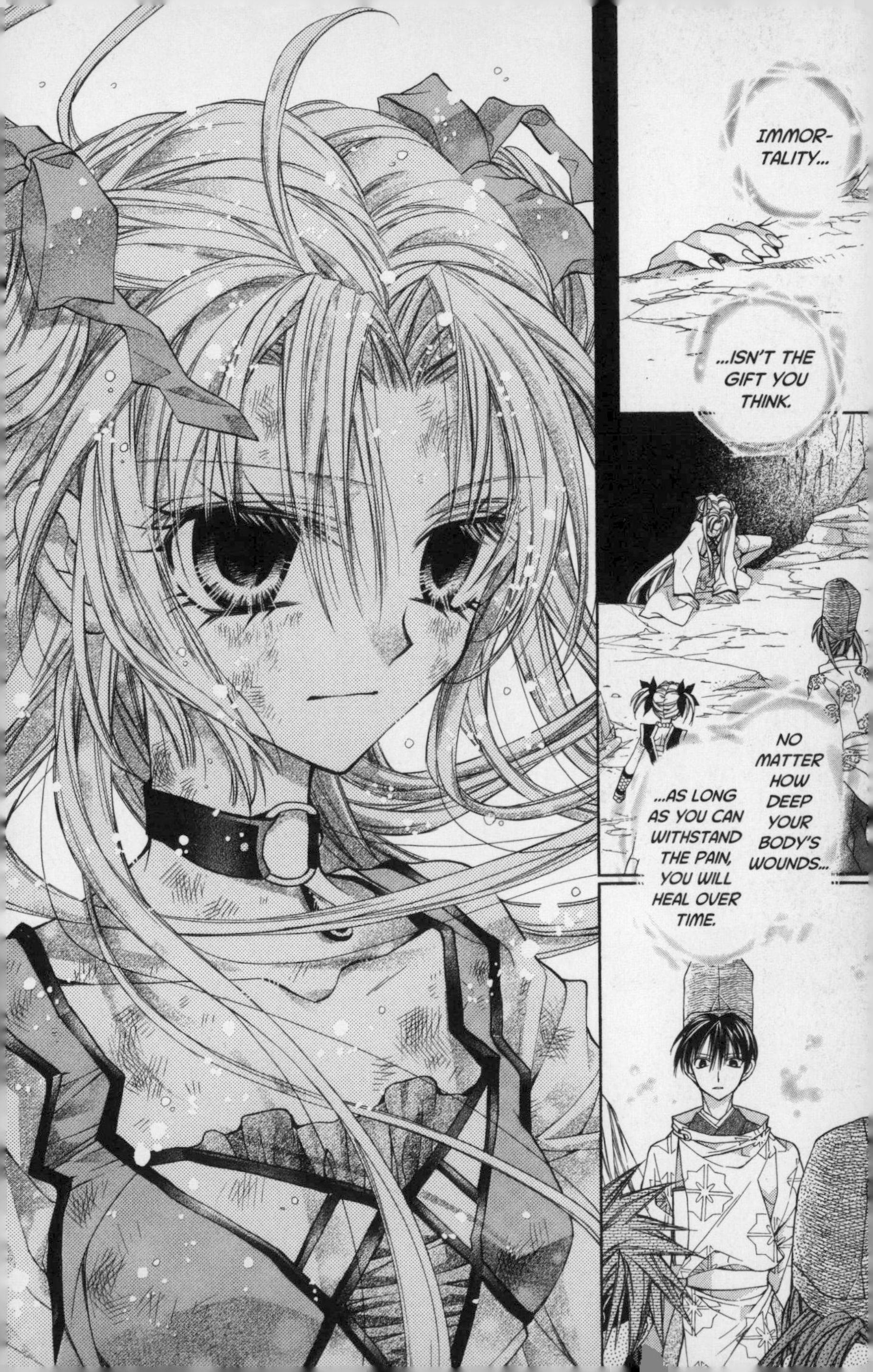
IMMOR-TALITY...
...ISN'T THE GIFT YOU THINK.
NO MATTER HOW DEEP YOUR BODY'S WOUNDS...
...AS LONG AS YOU CAN WITHSTAND THE PAIN, YOU WILL HEAL OVER TIME.

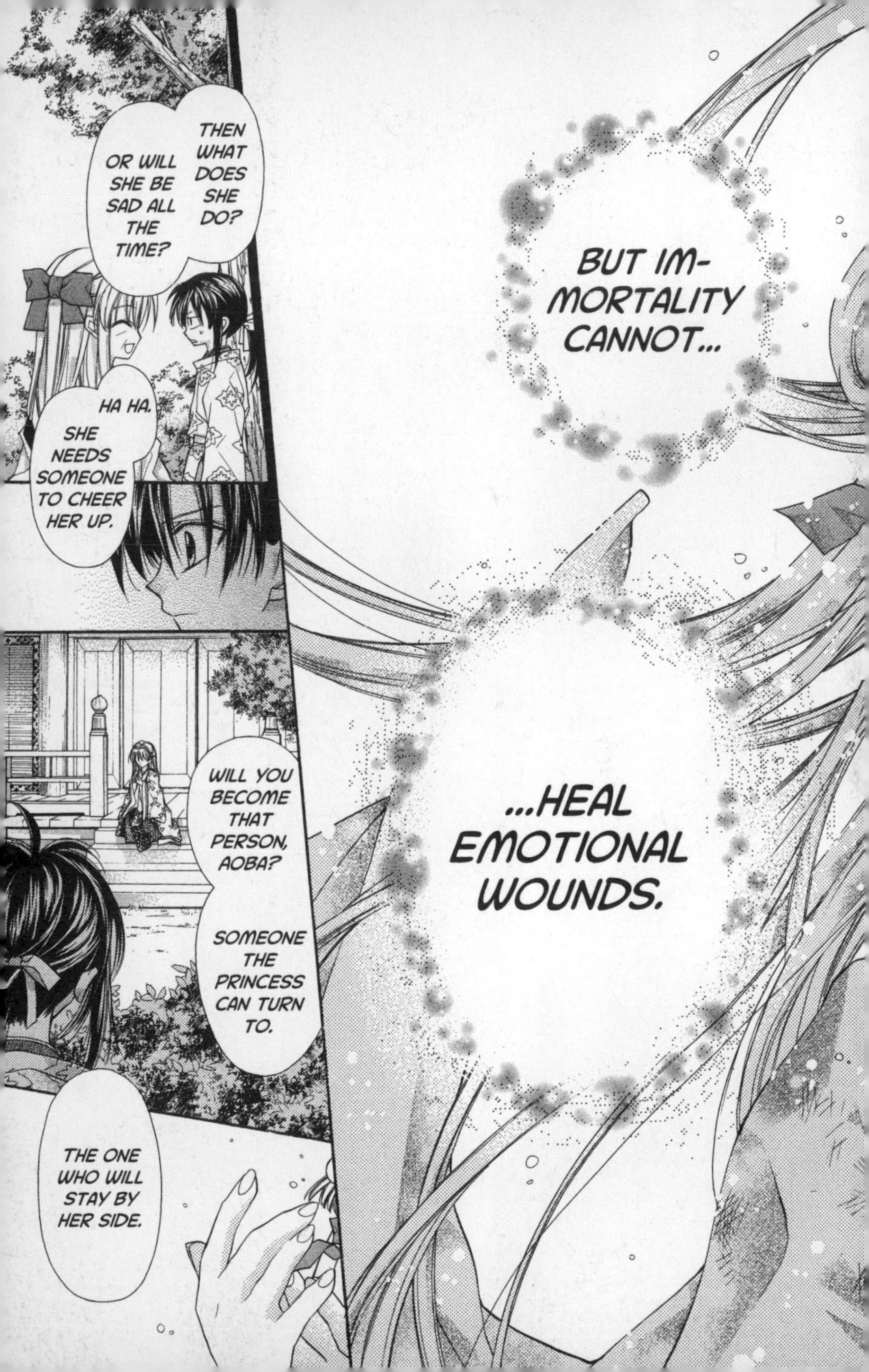
BUT IM-MORTALITY CANNOT...
...HEAL EMOTIONAL WOUNDS.
THEN WHAT DOES SHE DO?
OR WILL SHE BE SAD ALL THE TIME?
HA HA. SHE NEEDS SOMEONE TO CHEER HER UP.
WILL YOU BECOME THAT PERSON, AOBA?
SOMEONE THE PRINCESS CAN TURN TO.
THE ONE WHO WILL STAY BY HER SIDE.

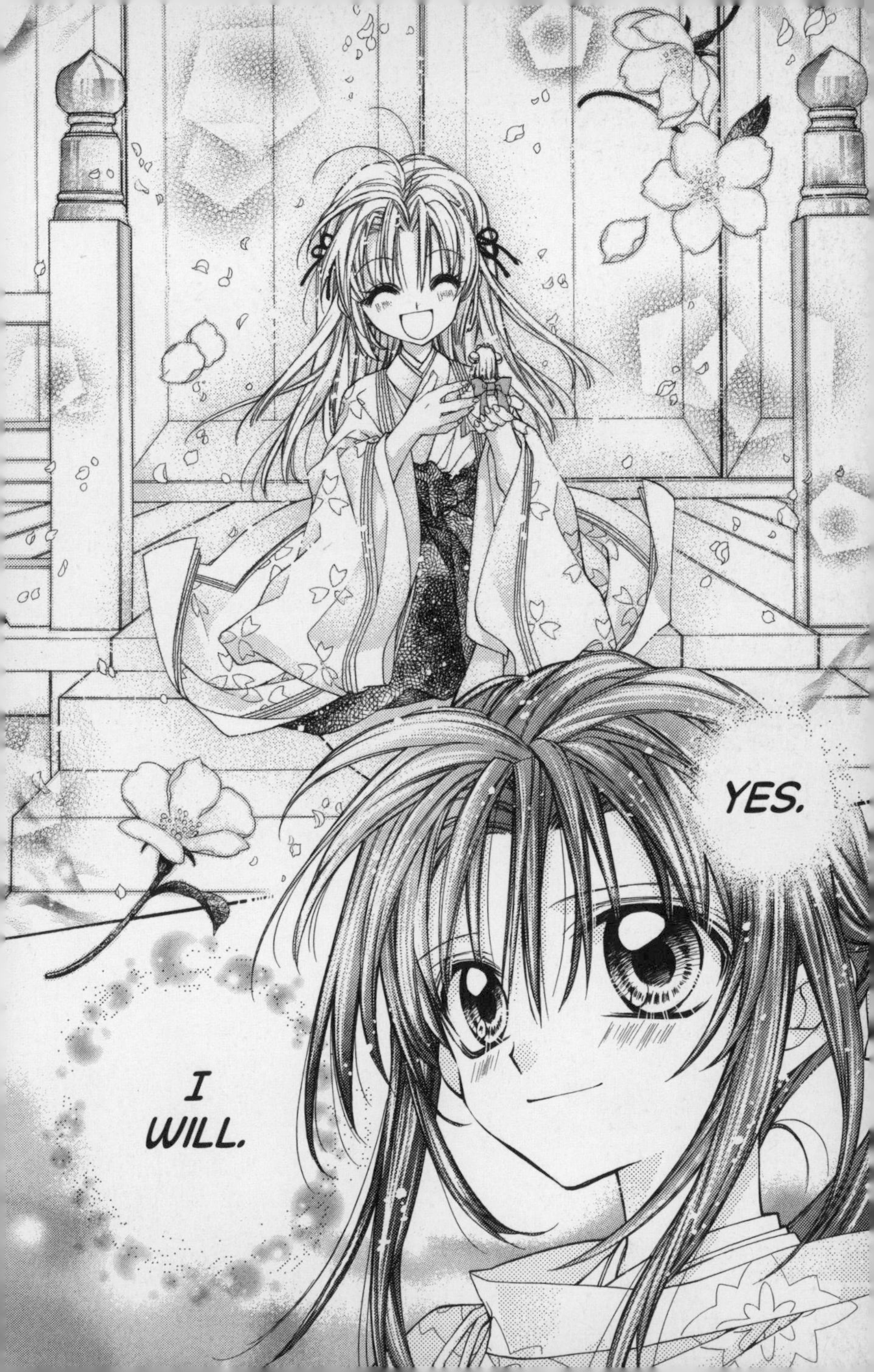
YES.
I WILL.

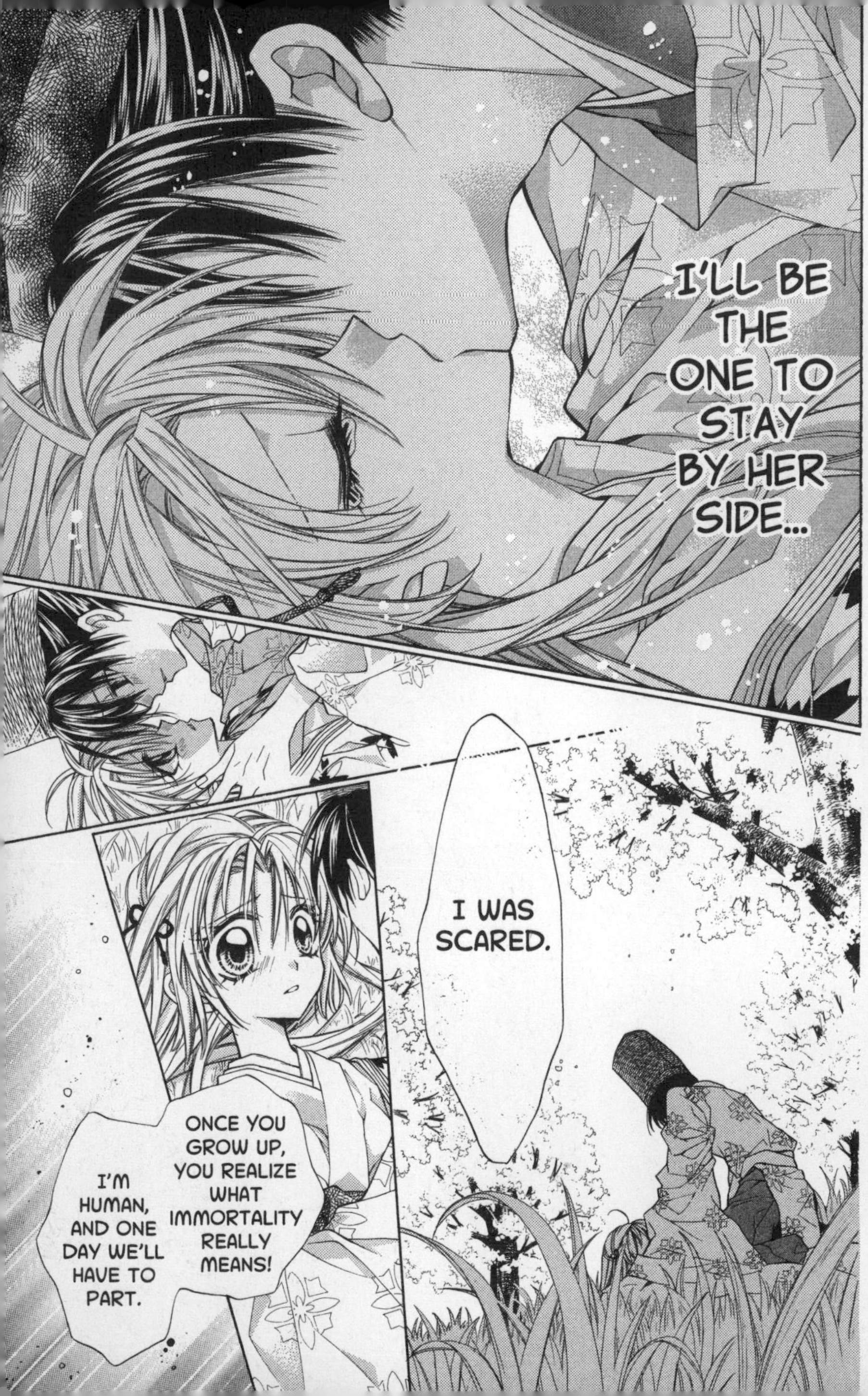
I'LL BE THE ONE TO STAY BY HER SIDE...
I WAS SCARED.
ONCE YOU GROW UP, YOU REALIZE WHAT IMMORTALITY REALLY MEANS!
I'M HUMAN, AND ONE DAY WE'LL HAVE TO PART.

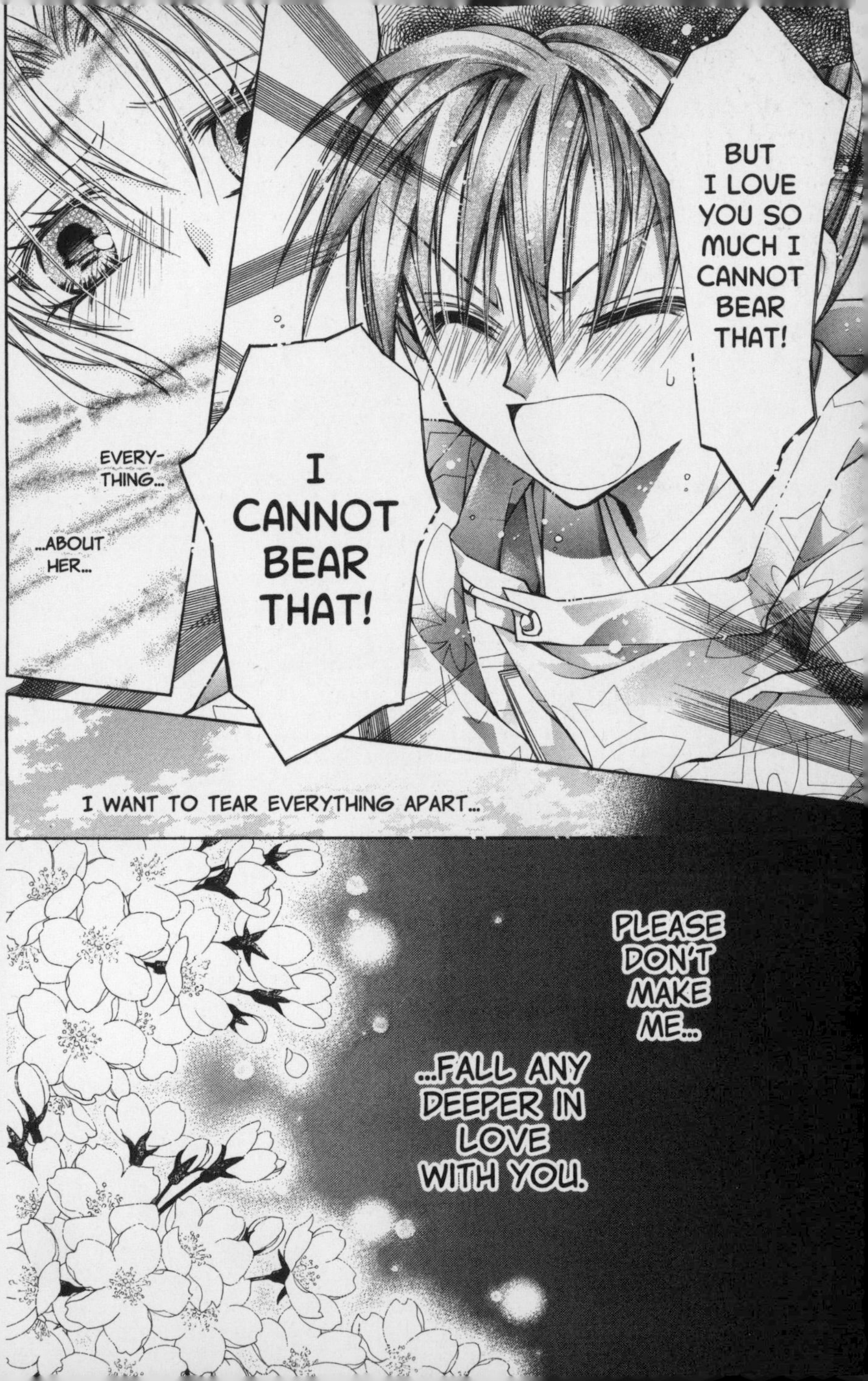
BUT I LOVE YOU SO MUCH I CANNOT BEAR THAT!
I CANNOT BEAR THAT!
EVERY-THING...
...ABOUT HER...
I WANT TO TEAR EVERYTHING APART...
PLEASE DON'T MAKE ME...
...FALL ANY DEEPER IN LOVE WITH YOU.

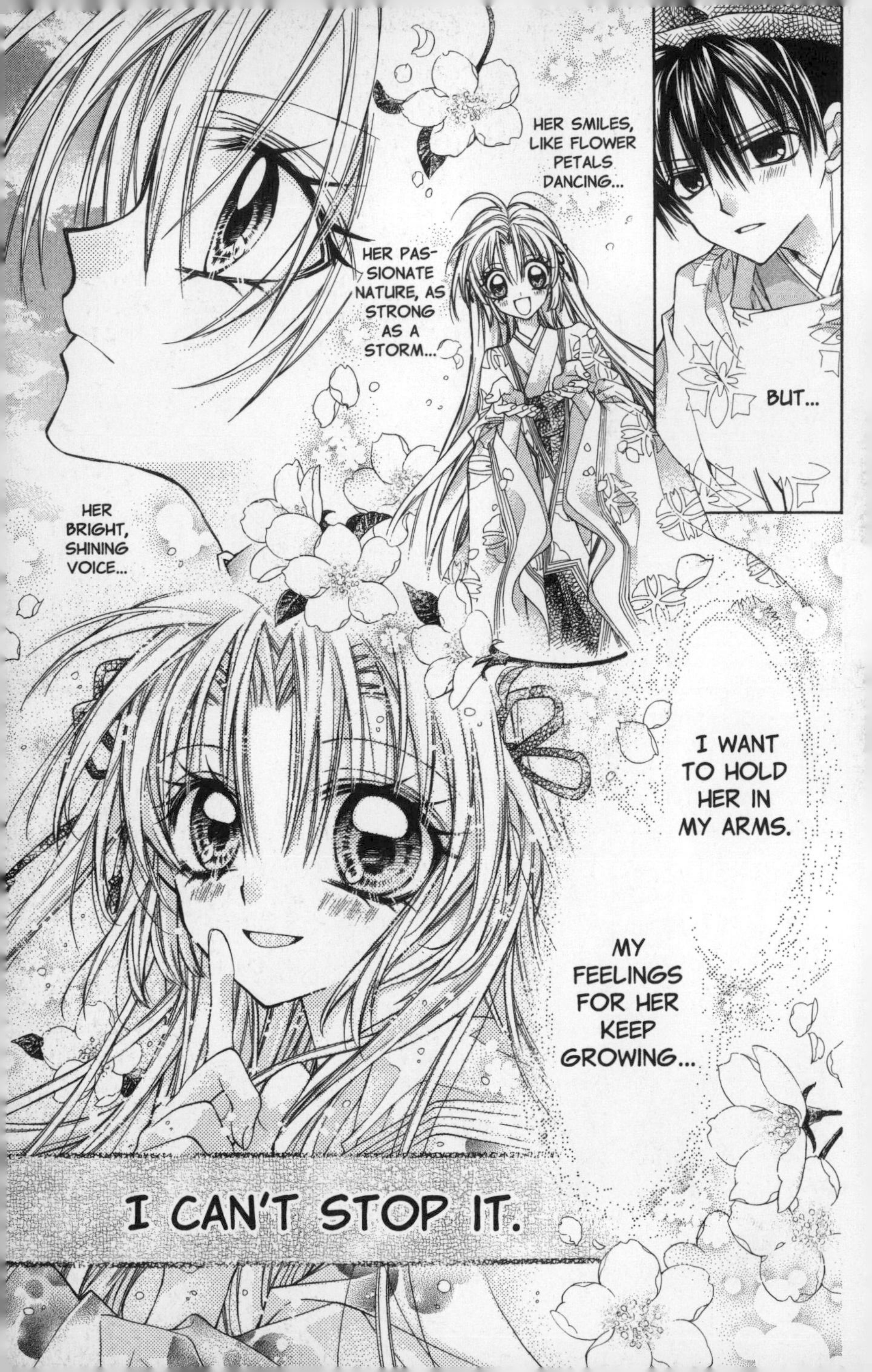
HER SMILES, LIKE FLOWER PETALS DANCING...
HER PASSIONATE NATURE, AS STRONG AS A STORM...
HER BRIGHT, SHINING VOICE...
BUT...
I WANT TO HOLD HER IN MY ARMS.
MY FEELINGS FOR HER KEEP GROWING...
I CAN'T STOP IT.

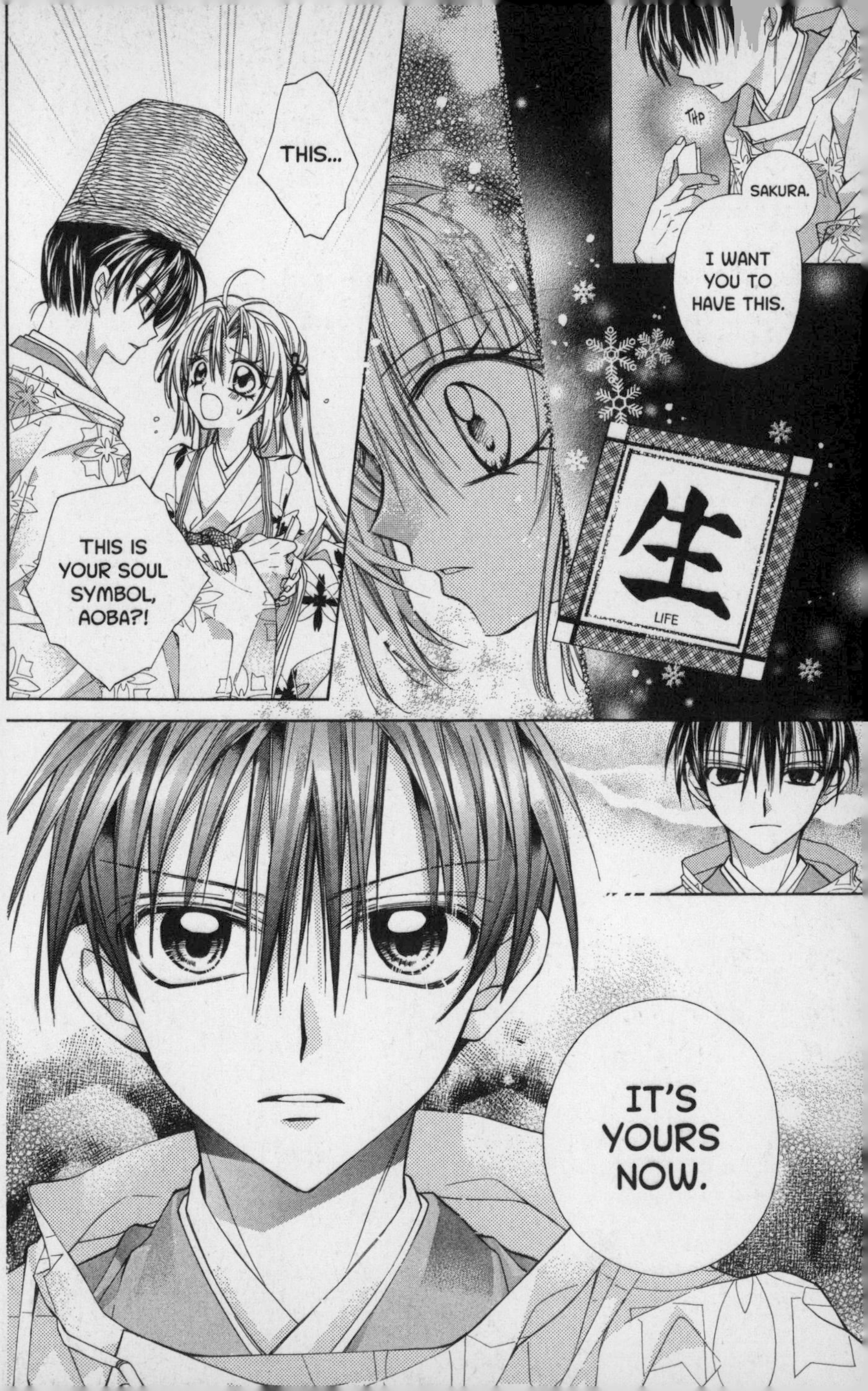
THP
SAKURA.
I WANT YOU TO HAVE THIS.
生
LIFE
THIS...
THIS IS YOUR SOUL SYMBOL, AOBA?!
IT'S YOURS NOW.

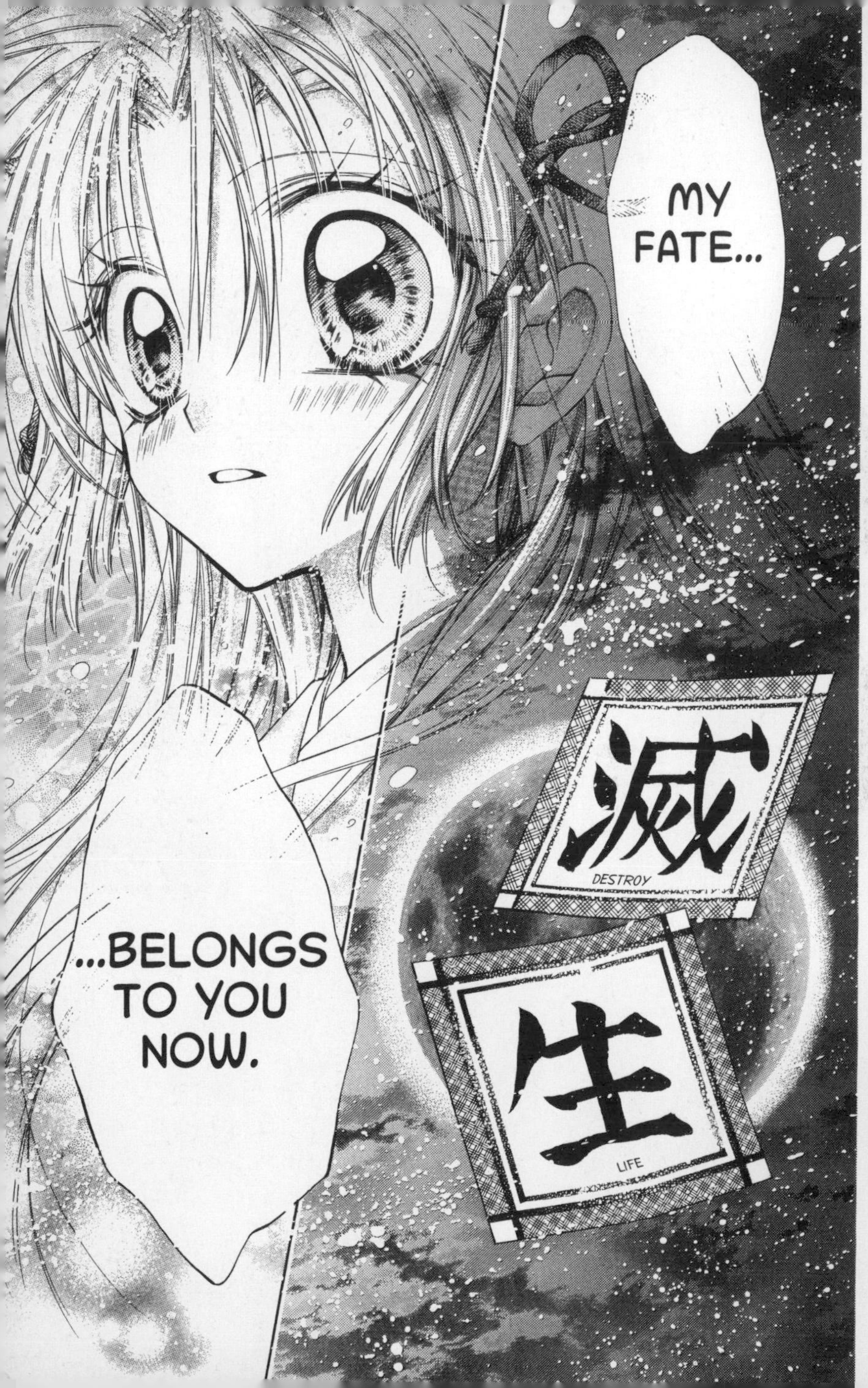
MY FATE...
滅
DESTROY
生
LIFE
...BELONGS TO YOU NOW.

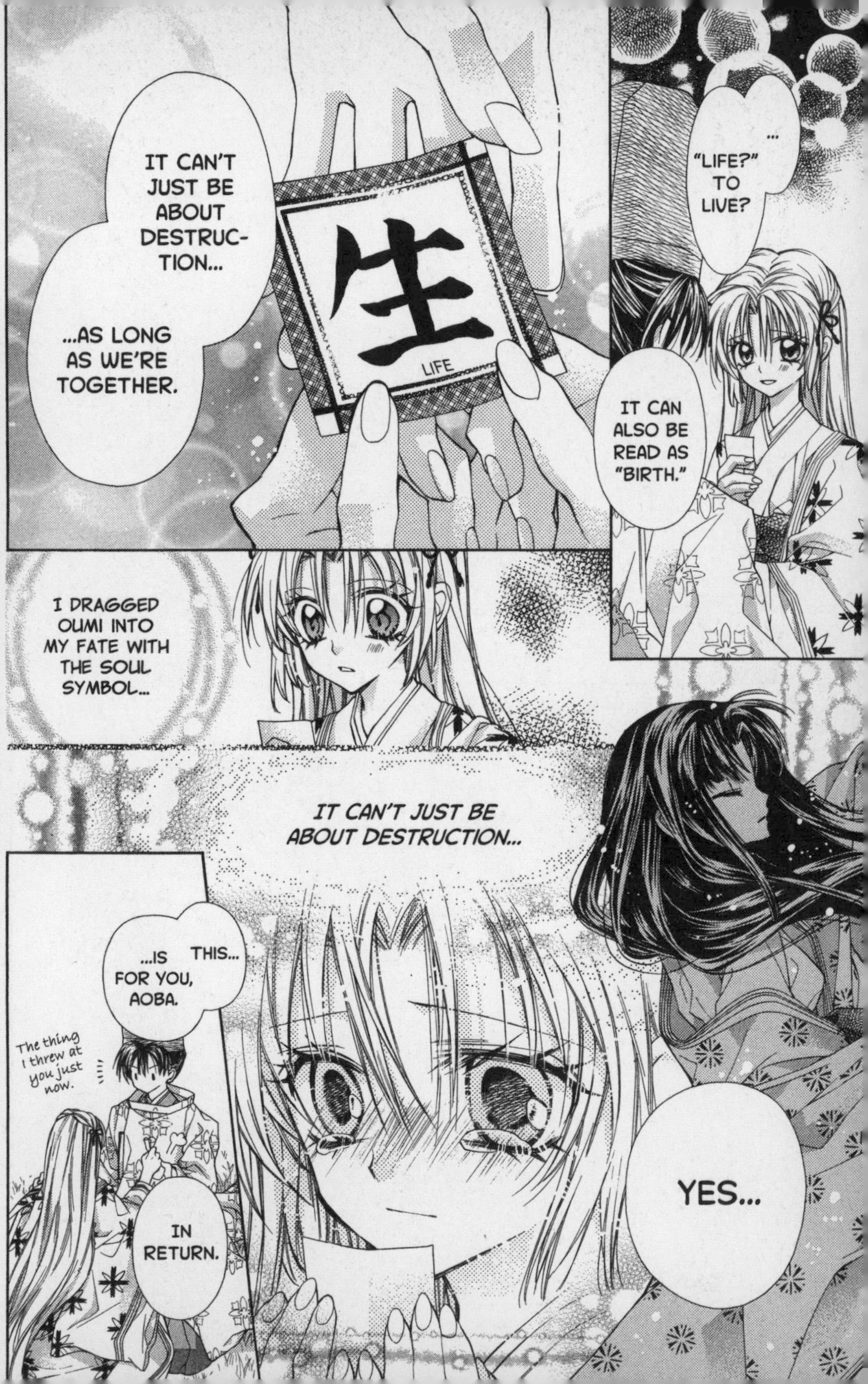

... "LIFE?" TO LIVE?
IT CAN ALSO BE READ AS "BIRTH."
IT CAN'T JUST BE ABOUT DESTRUCTION...
...AS LONG AS WE'RE TOGETHER.
LIFE
I DRAGGED OUMI INTO MY FATE WITH THE SOUL SYMBOL...
IT CAN'T JUST BE ABOUT DESTRUCTION...
THIS... ...IS FOR YOU, AOBA.
The thing I threw at you just now.
IN RETURN.
YES...

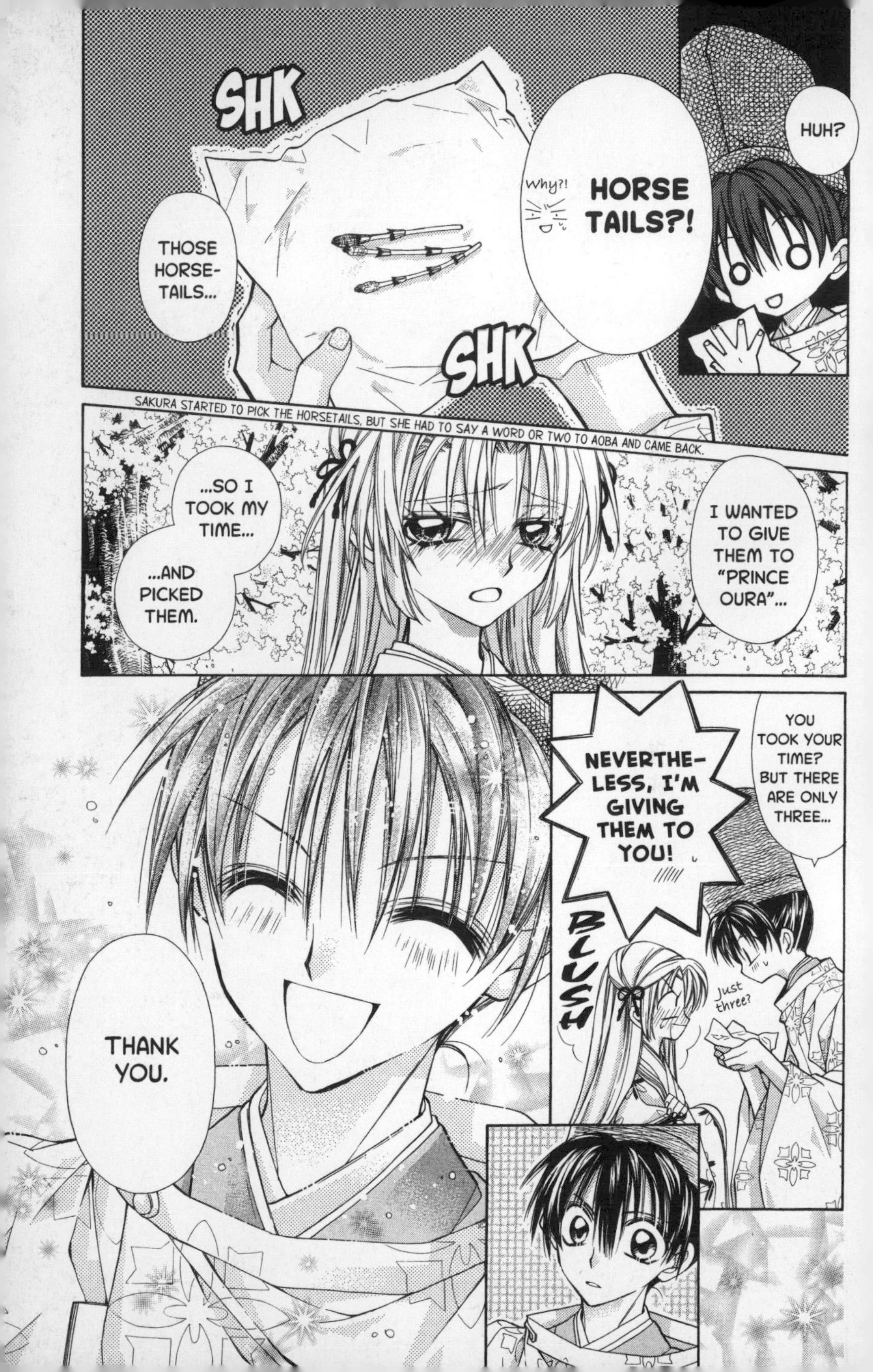
HUH?
Why?!
HORSE TAILS?!
SHK
THOSE HORSE-TAILS...
SHK
SAKURA STARTED TO PICK THE HORSETAILS, BUT SHE HAD TO SAY A WORD OR TWO TO AOBA AND CAME BACK.
I WANTED TO GIVE THEM TO "PRINCE OURA"...
...SO I TOOK MY TIME...
...AND PICKED THEM.
YOU TOOK YOUR TIME? BUT THERE ARE ONLY THREE...
NEVERTHE-LESS, I'M GIVING THEM TO YOU!
BLUSH
Just three?
THANK YOU.

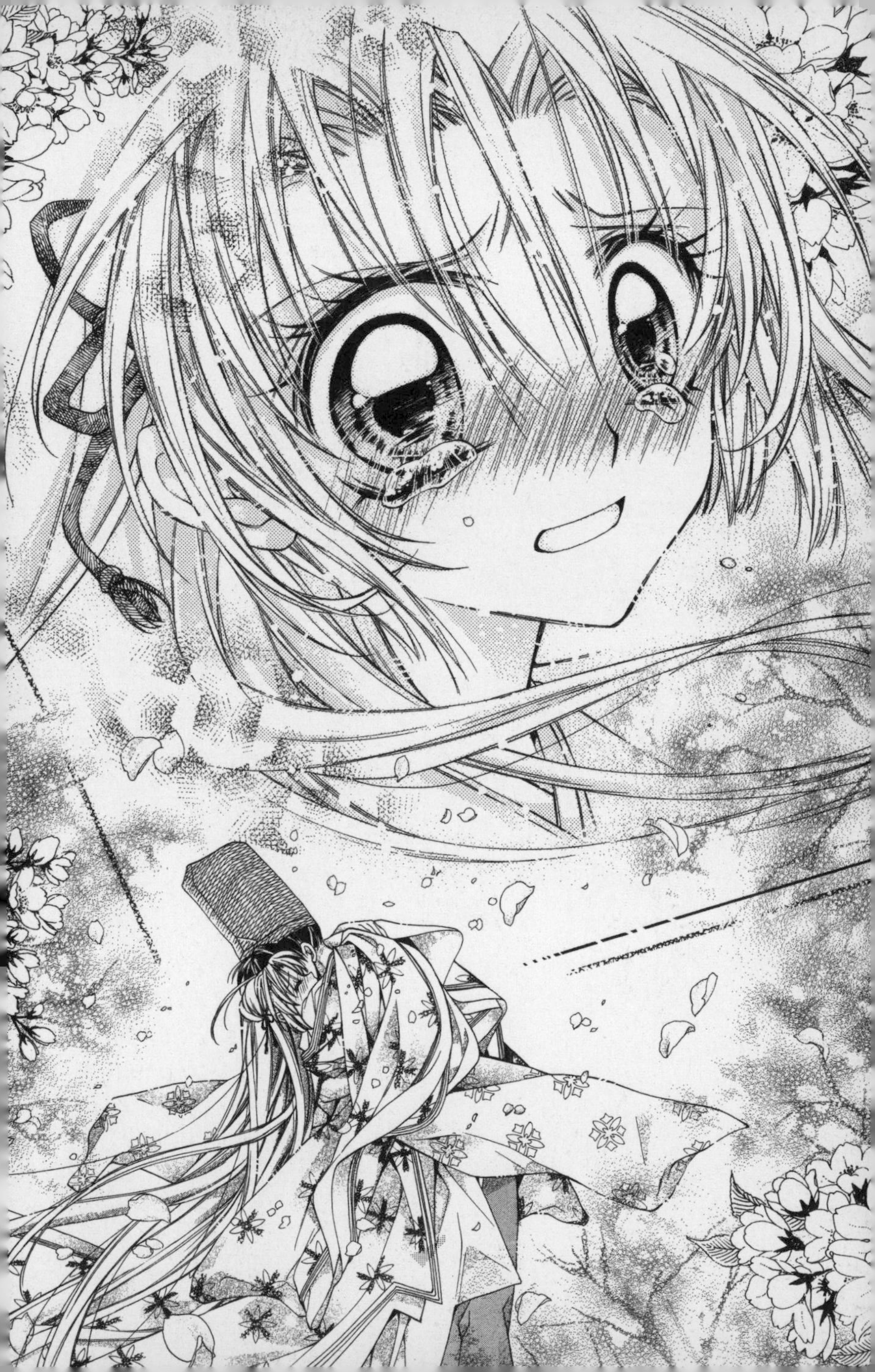

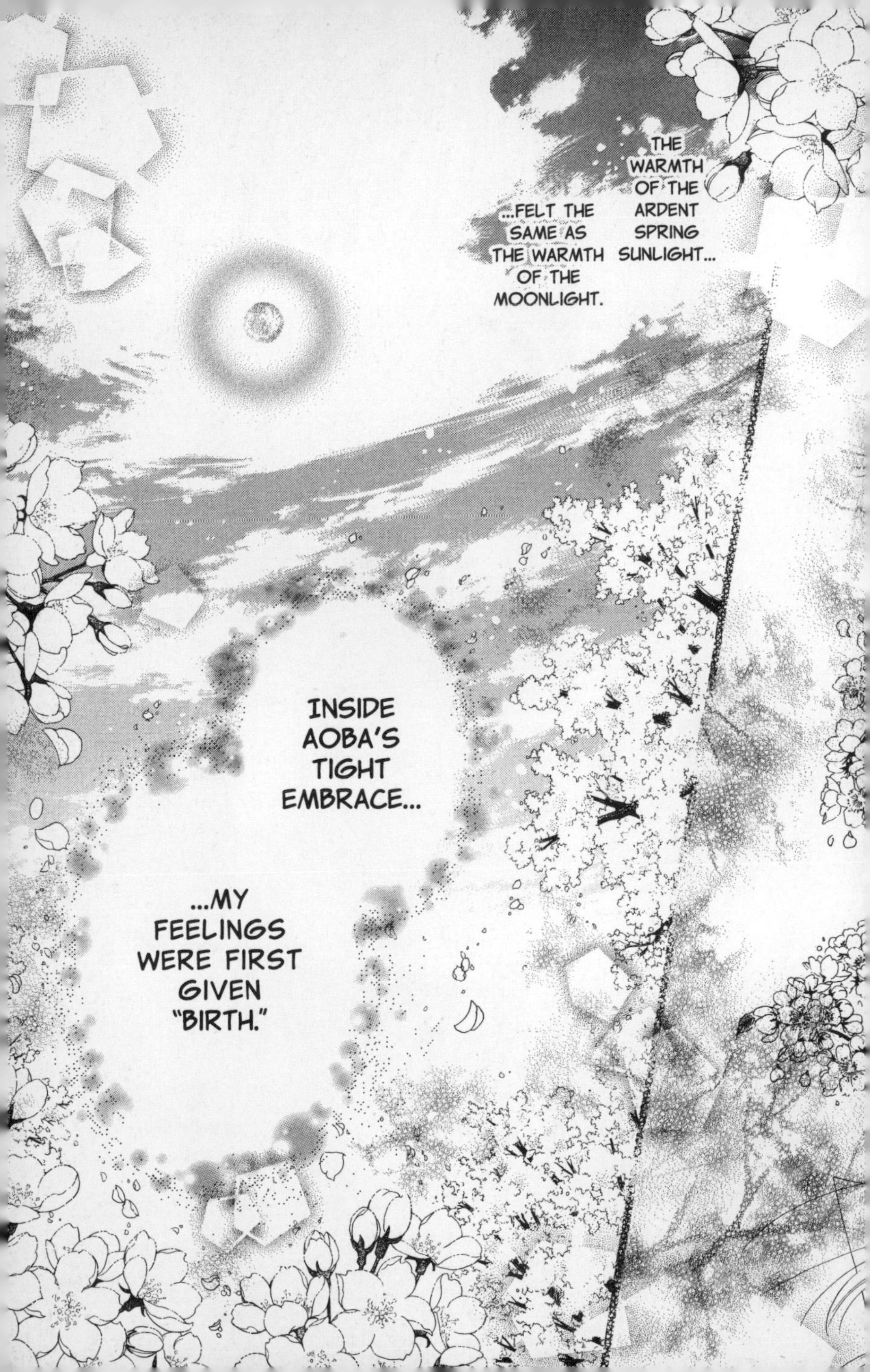
THE WARMTH OF THE ARDENT SPRING SUNLIGHT...
...FELT THE SAME AS THE WARMTH OF THE MOONLIGHT.
INSIDE AOBA'S TIGHT EMBRACE...
...MY FEELINGS WERE FIRST GIVEN "BIRTH."

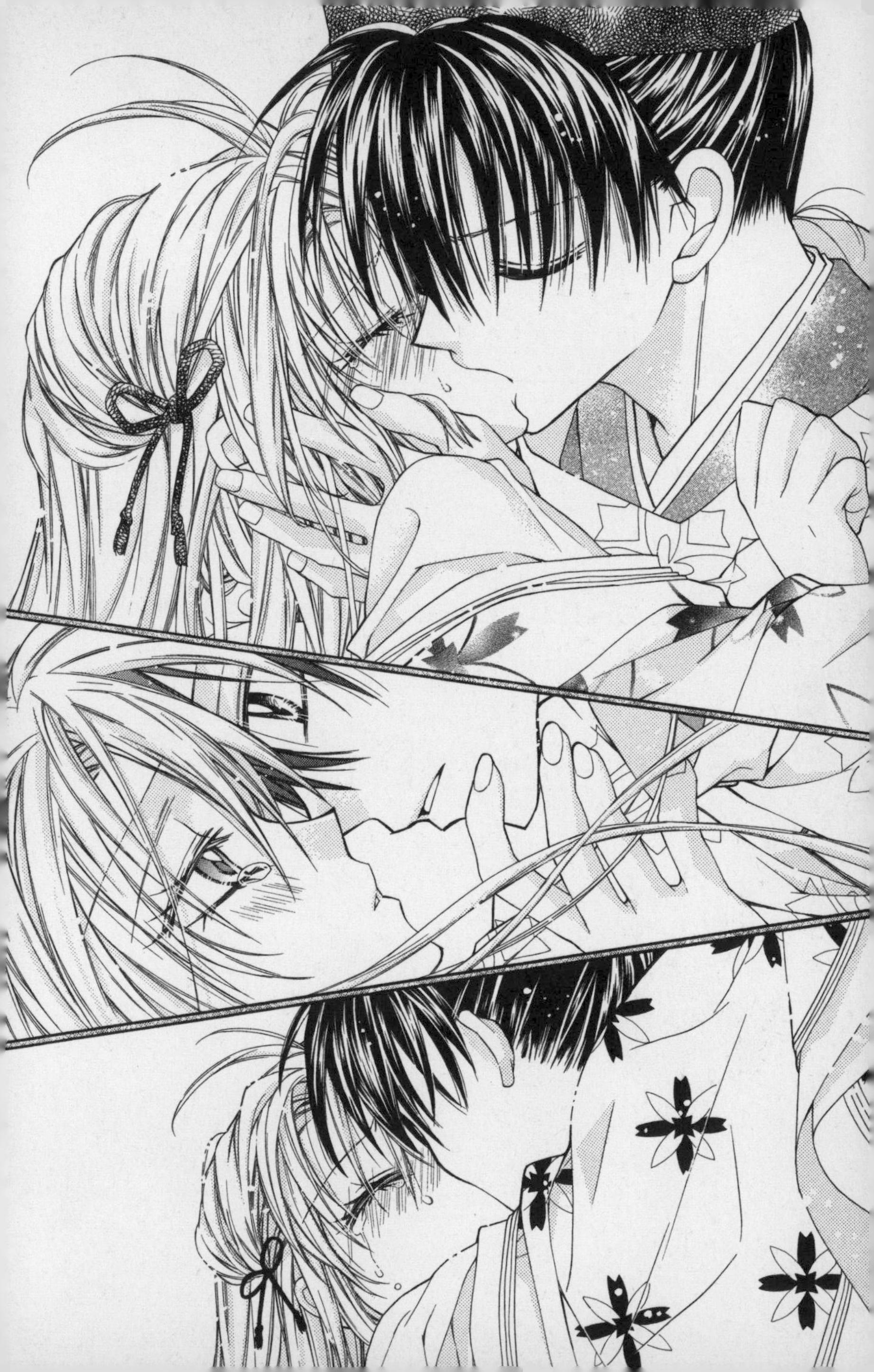

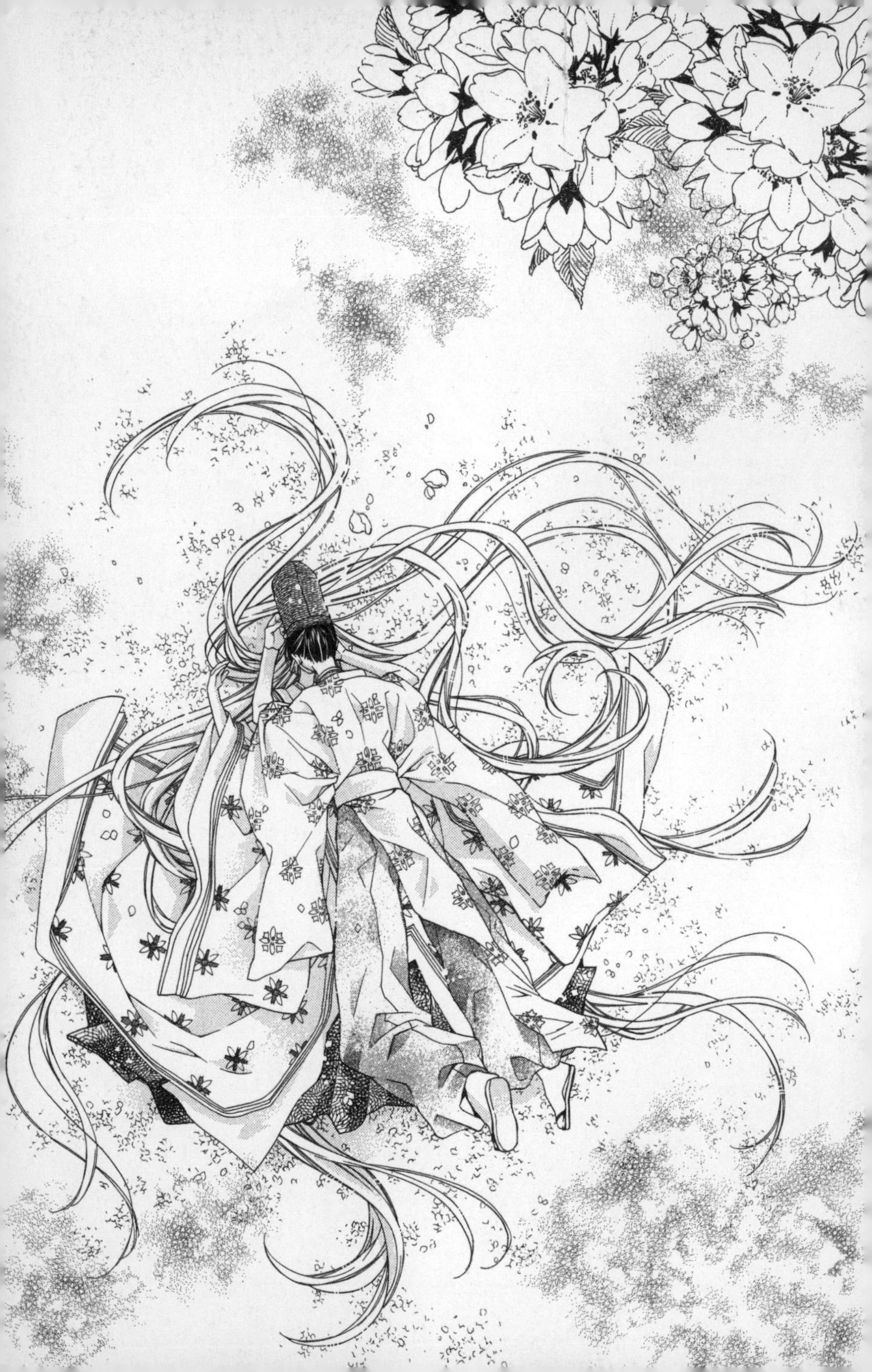

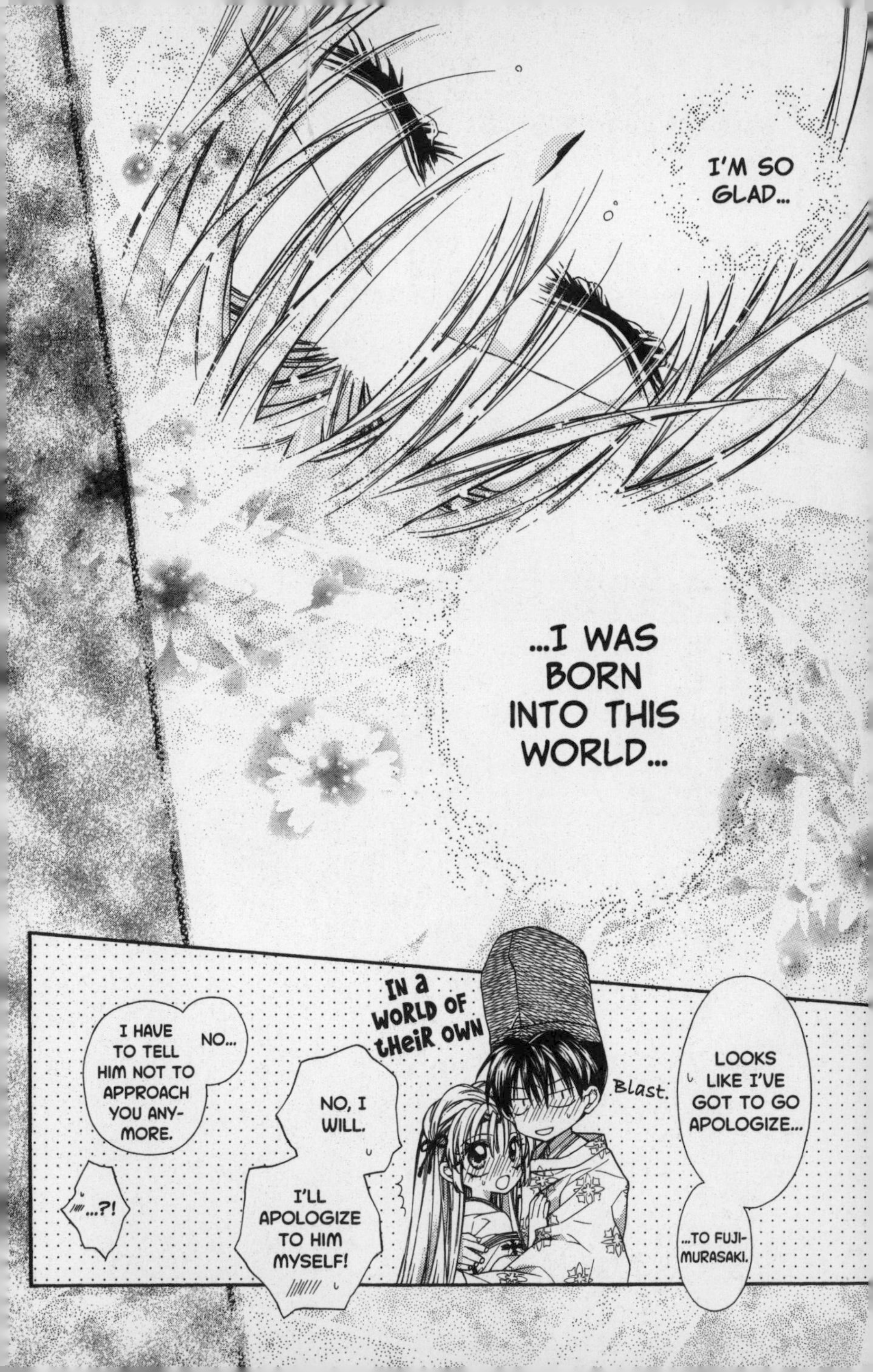
I'M SO GLAD...
...I WAS BORN INTO THIS WORLD...
LOOKS LIKE I'VE GOT TO GO APOLOGIZE...
...TO FUJI-MURASAKI.
Blast.
IN a WORLD OF theiR OWN
NO, I WILL.
I'LL APOLOGIZE TO HIM MYSELF!
NO...
I HAVE TO TELL HIM NOT TO APPROACH YOU ANY-MORE.
...?!

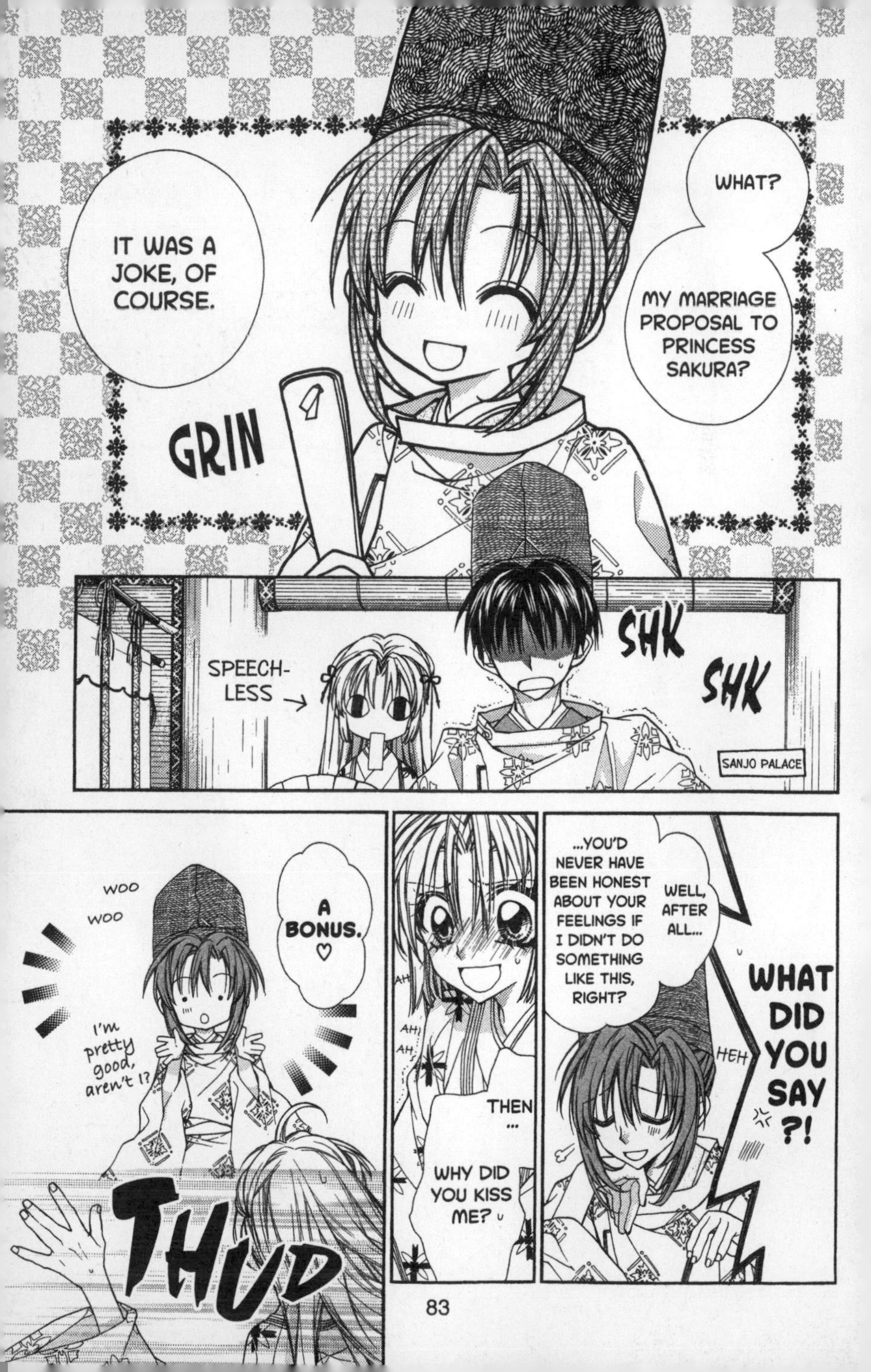
WHAT?
MY MARRIAGE PROPOSAL TO PRINCESS SAKURA?
IT WAS A JOKE, OF COURSE.
GRIN
SHK
SHK
SANJO PALACE
SPEECH-LESS
WHAT DID YOU SAY ?!
WELL, AFTER ALL...
...YOU'D NEVER HAVE BEEN HONEST ABOUT YOUR FEELINGS IF I DIDN'T DO SOMETHING LIKE THIS, RIGHT?
HEH
AH AH AH
THEN ...
WHY DID YOU KISS ME?
A BONUS. ♡
WOO WOO
I'm pretty good, aren't I?
THUD

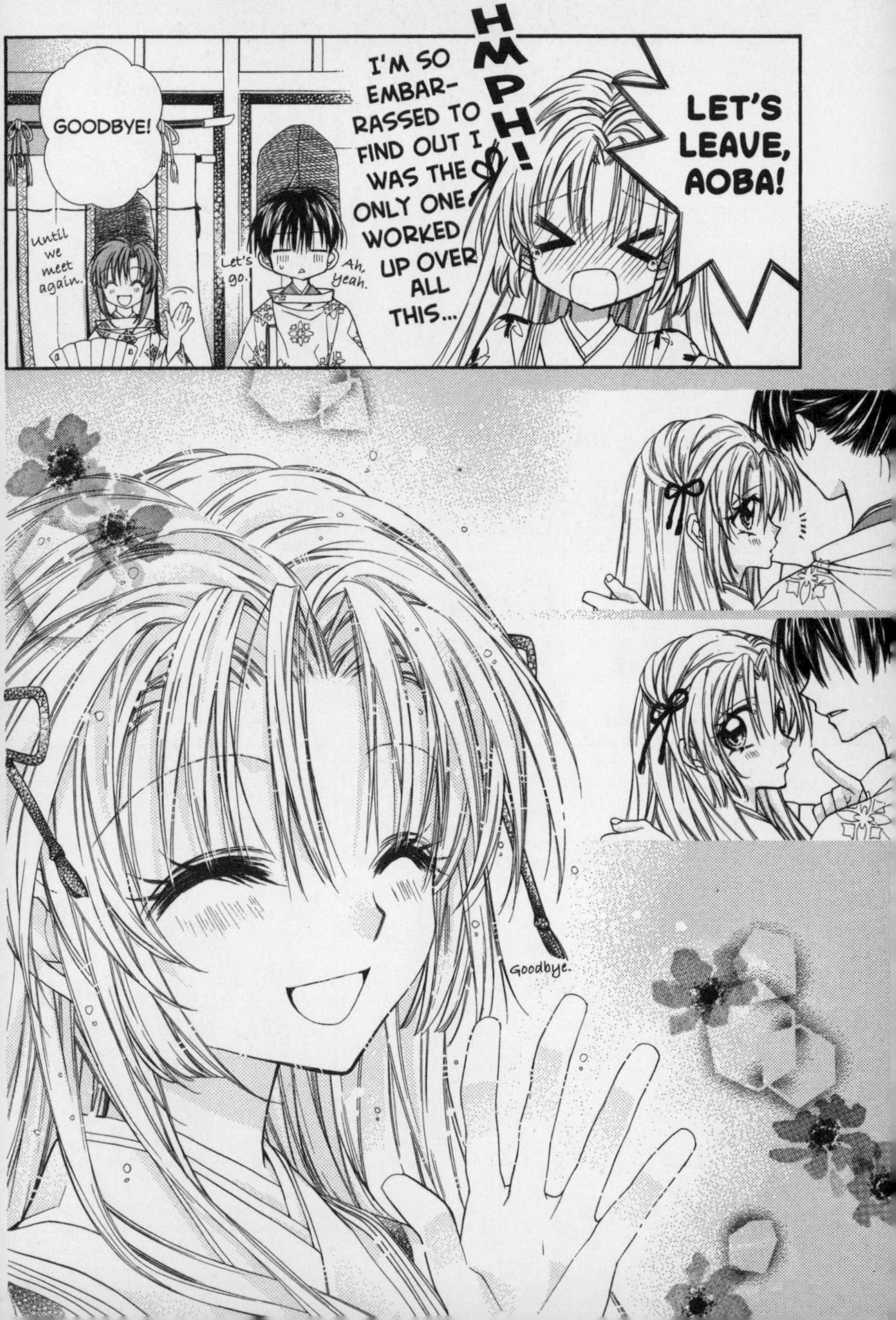
LET'S LEAVE, AOBA!
HMPH!
I'M SO EMBAR-RASSED TO FIND OUT I WAS THE ONLY ONE WORKED UP OVER ALL THIS...
Ah, yeah.
Let's go.
GOODBYE!
Until we meet again.
Goodbye.

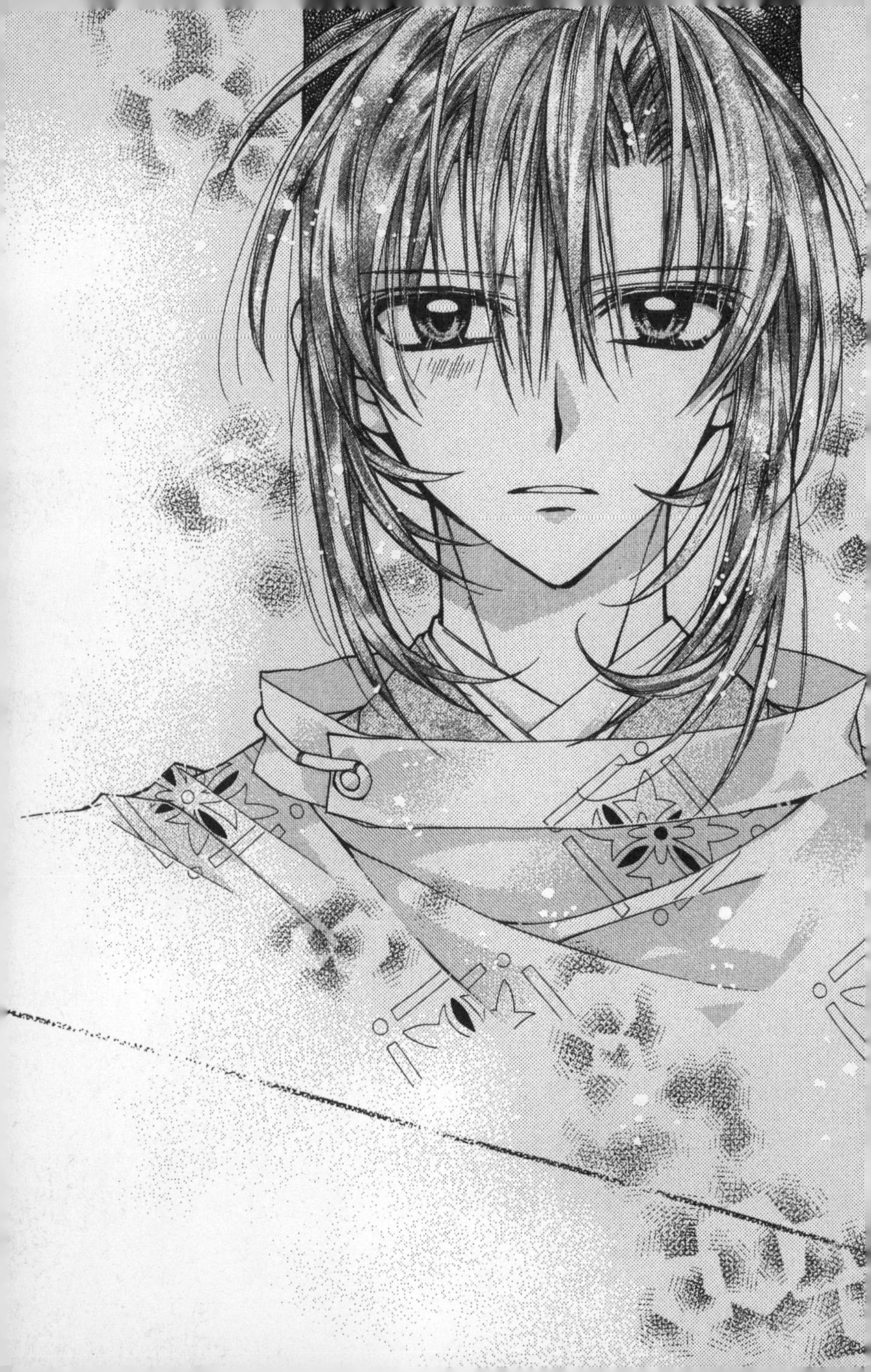

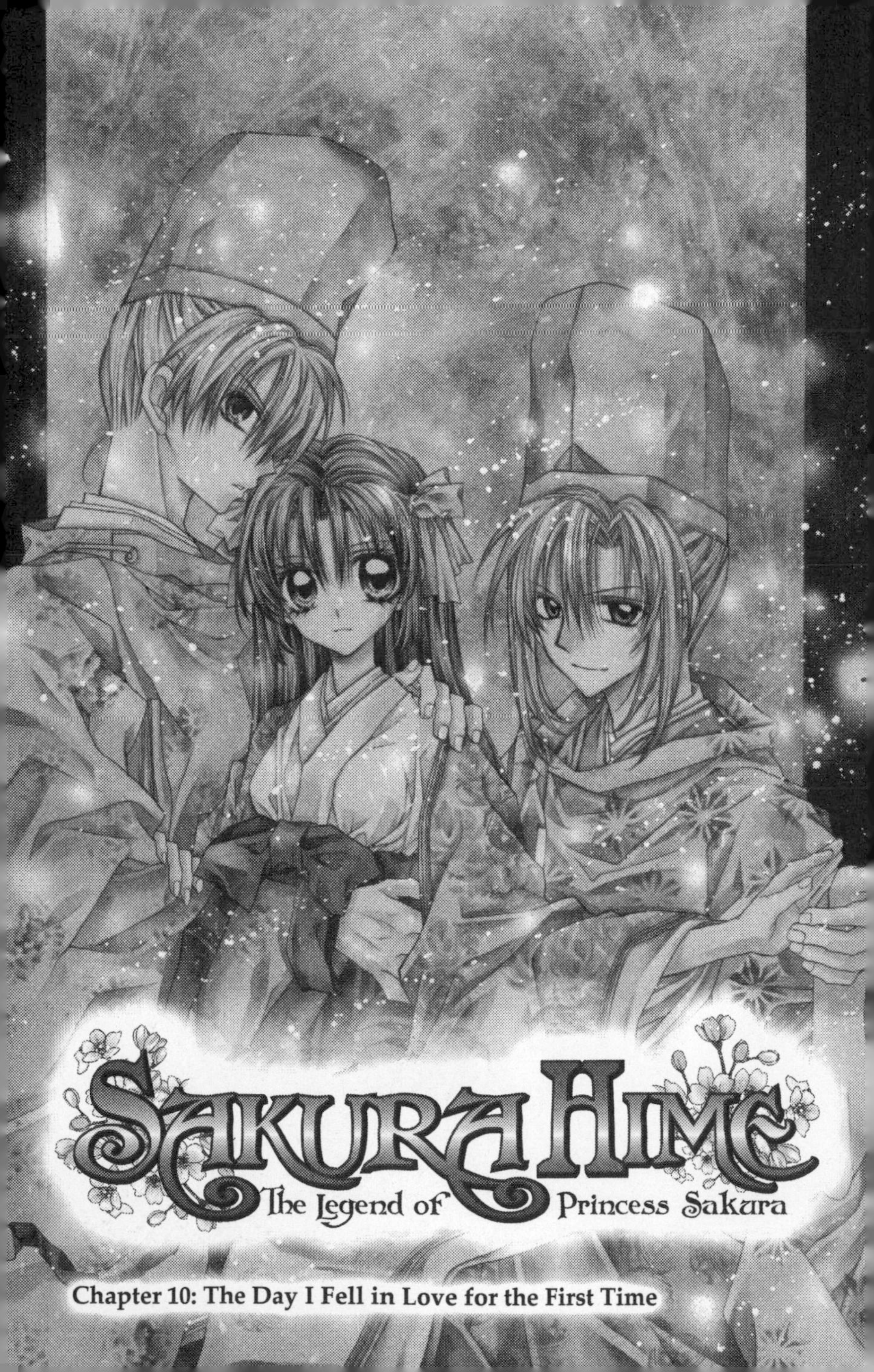
SAKURA HIME
The Legend of Princess Sakura
Chapter 10: The Day I Fell in Love for the First Time

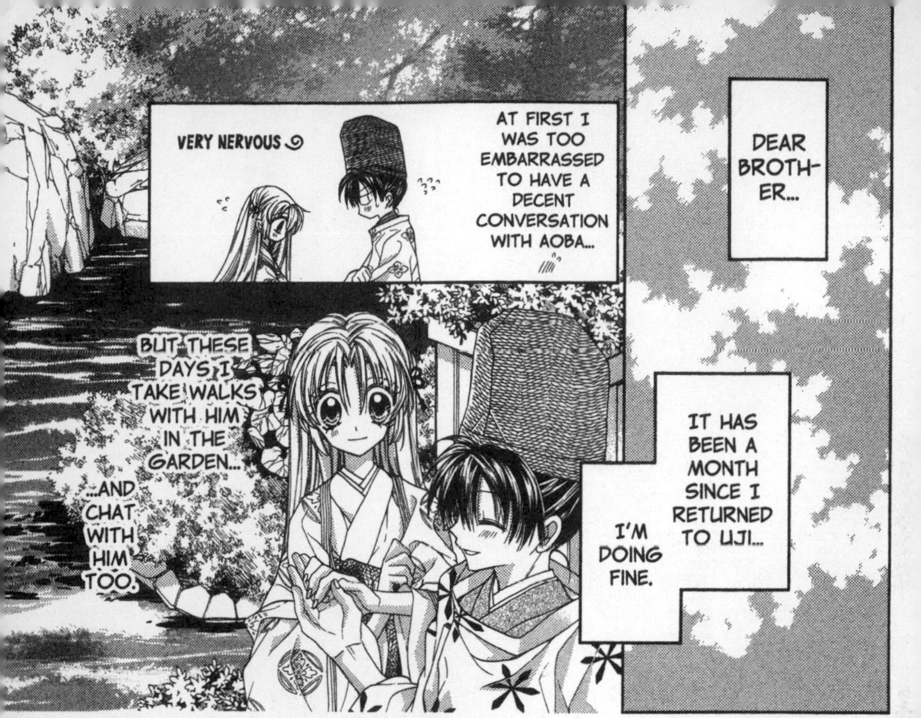

Chapter 10: The Day I Fell in Love for the First Time

Lead-in My Princess of the Moon, I will never let anyone have you; my Cherry Blossom Princess, I shall never let you go.

※ I'm giving away the story. Please read this after you read the chapter.

A new turn. I still have lots to write about, so it's like I've finally reached the starting point. Please take your time in following the story.

I was aiming for Aoba and Sakura to become a "cute couple." What do you think? They happen to be the first pair in all my manga who have become a couple prior to the end of the series. (A senior mangaka once advised me, "You shouldn't have the hero and heroine become a couple until the very last chapter." I agreed with that idea, so I have been doing that up till now, but I had them get together because I don't think this story centers around love?)

As for Fujimurasaki... Hmm... The last three pages turned out to be like this after I thought it over many, many times. You'll find out what his soul symbol is in the bonus funnies at the end. It is deeply connected to all this. One thing I can say is that he is the most pure-hearted character in the series. I really recommend him! ← What for...?
What? You think the most pure-hearted character is Kai? Well... I guess... "Kai" is. But then again, Enju is... Well, you know. (What do I mean by "you know"?)

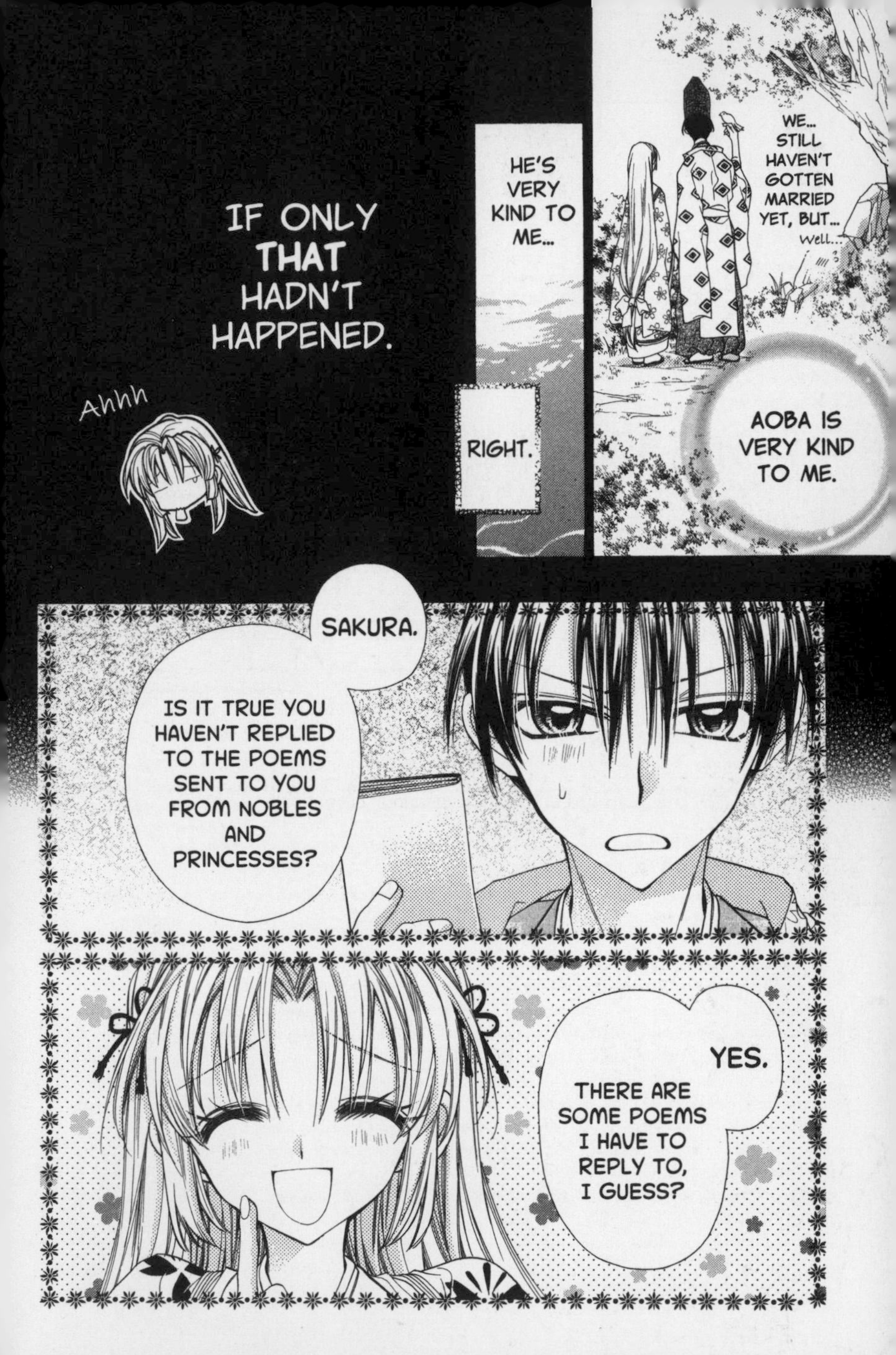
WE... STILL HAVEN'T GOTTEN MARRIED YET, BUT...
Well...
AOBA IS VERY KIND TO ME.
HE'S VERY KIND TO ME...
RIGHT.
IF ONLY THAT HADN'T HAPPENED.
Ahhh
SAKURA.
IS IT TRUE YOU HAVEN'T REPLIED TO THE POEMS SENT TO YOU FROM NOBLES AND PRINCESSES?
YES.
THERE ARE SOME POEMS I HAVE TO REPLY TO, I GUESS?

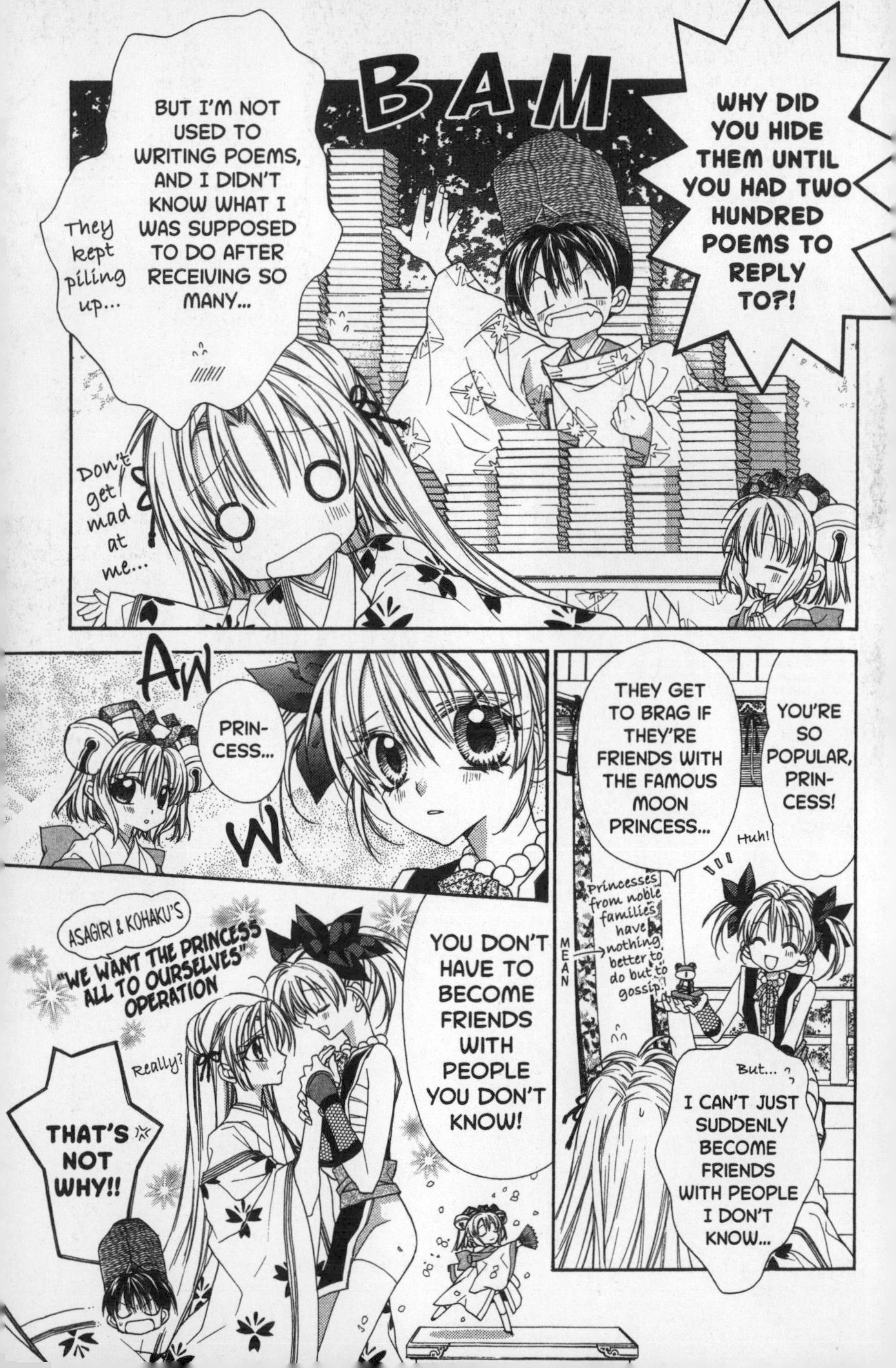
WHY DID YOU HIDE THEM UNTIL YOU HAD TWO HUNDRED POEMS TO REPLY TO?!
BAM
BUT I'M NOT USED TO WRITING POEMS, AND I DIDN'T KNOW WHAT I WAS SUPPOSED TO DO AFTER RECEIVING SO MANY...
They kept piling up...
Don't get mad at me...
YOU'RE SO POPULAR, PRIN-CESS!
THEY GET TO BRAG IF THEY'RE FRIENDS WITH THE FAMOUS MOON PRINCESS...
Huh!
MEAN
Princesses from noble families have nothing better to do but to gossip.
But...
I CAN'T JUST SUDDENLY BECOME FRIENDS WITH PEOPLE I DON'T KNOW...
AW
W
PRIN-CESS...
ASAGIRI & KOHAKU'S
"WE WANT THE PRINCESS ALL TO OURSELVES" OPERATION
YOU DON'T HAVE TO BECOME FRIENDS WITH PEOPLE YOU DON'T KNOW!
Really?
THAT'S NOT WHY!!

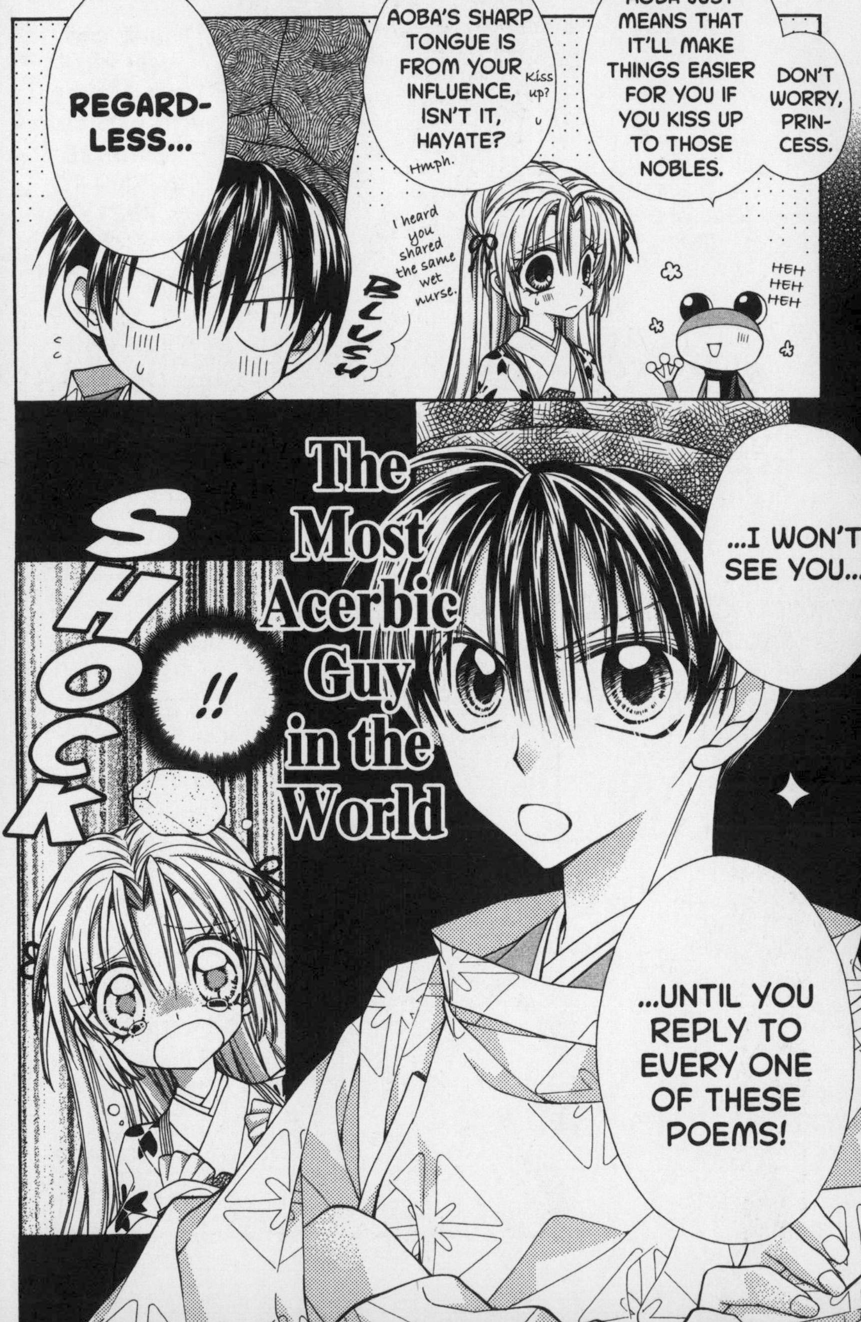
DON'T WORRY, PRINCESS.
AOBA JUST MEANS THAT IT'LL MAKE THINGS EASIER FOR YOU IF YOU KISS UP TO THOSE NOBLES.
HEH HEH HEH
AOBA'S SHARP TONGUE IS FROM YOUR INFLUENCE, ISN'T IT, HAYATE?
Kiss up?
Hmph.
I heard you shared the same wet nurse.
BLUSH
REGARD-LESS...
...I WON'T SEE YOU...
...UNTIL YOU REPLY TO EVERY ONE OF THESE POEMS!
The Most Acerbic Guy in the World
!!
SHOCK

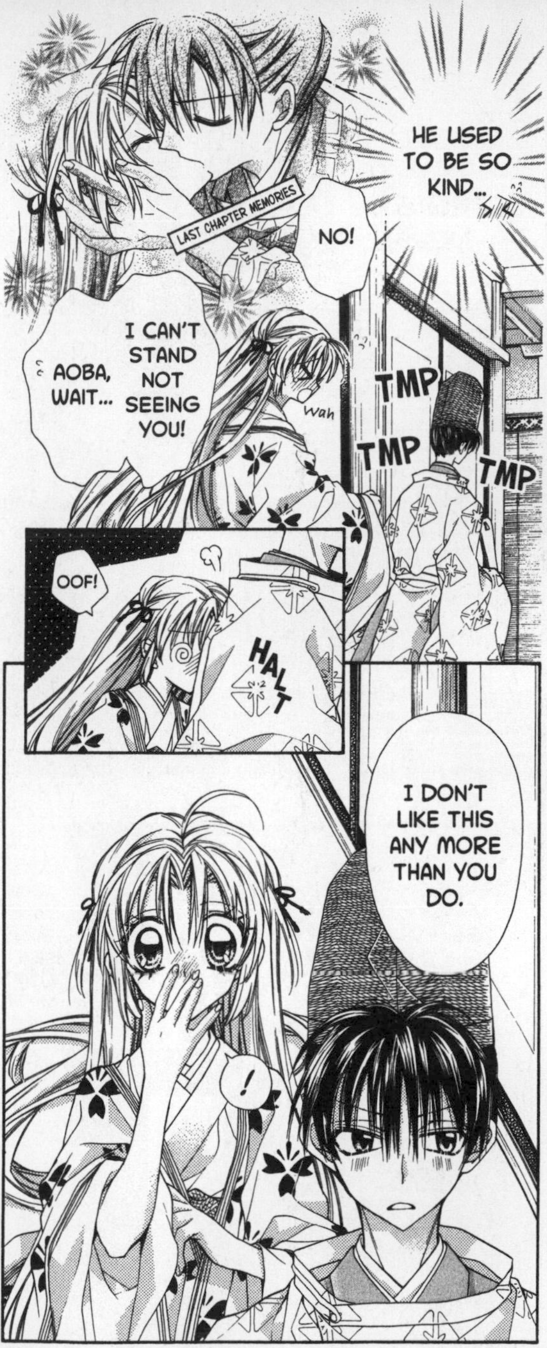
HE USED TO BE SO KIND...
LAST CHAPTER MEMORIES
NO!
I CAN'T STAND NOT SEEING YOU!
AOBA, WAIT...
Wah
TMP
TMP
TMP
OOF!
HALT
I DON'T LIKE THIS ANY MORE THAN YOU DO.
!

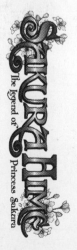

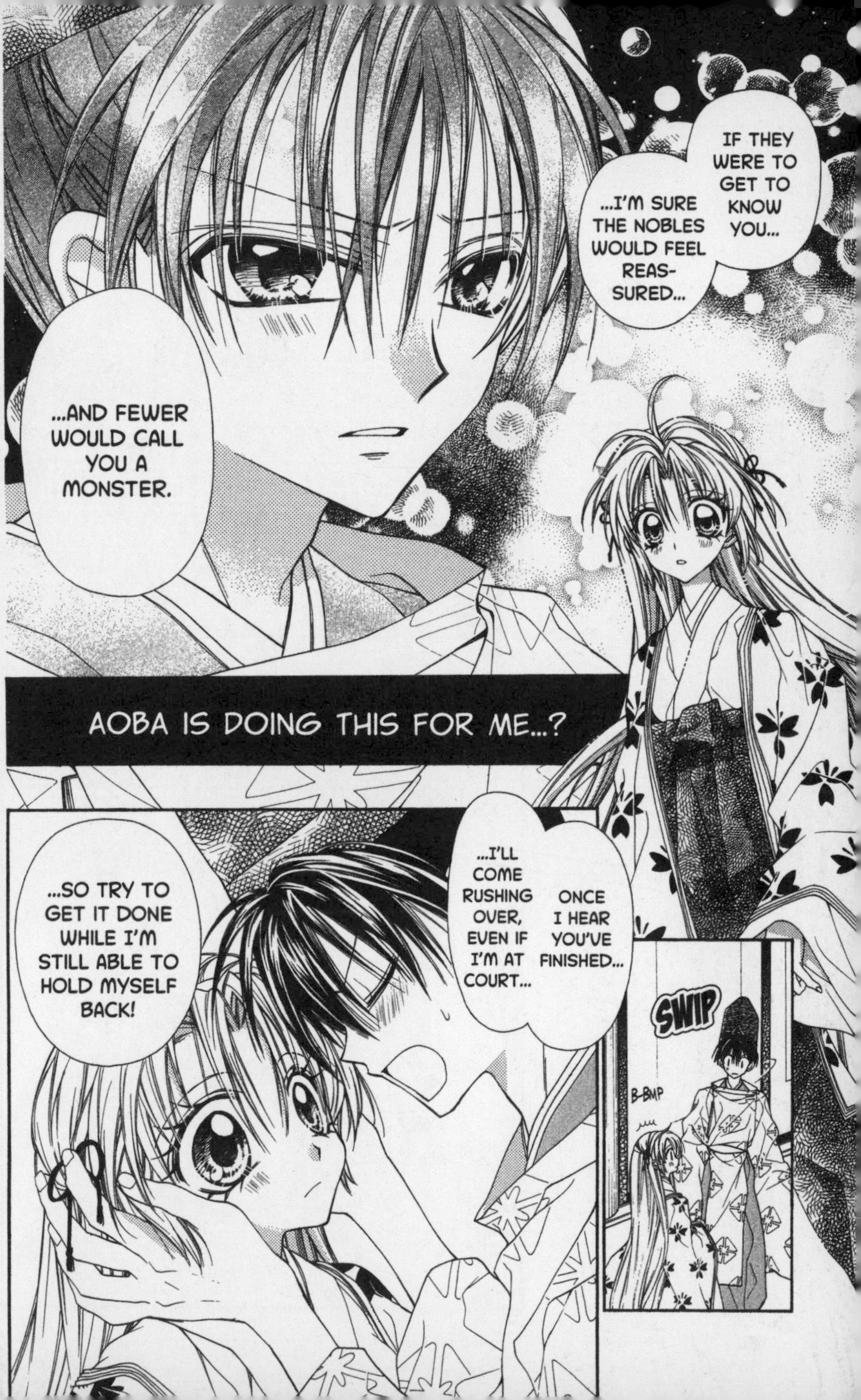
IF THEY WERE TO GET TO KNOW YOU...
...I'M SURE THE NOBLES WOULD FEEL REAS-SURED...
...AND FEWER WOULD CALL YOU A MONSTER.
AOBA IS DOING THIS FOR ME...?
SWIP
B-BMP
ONCE I HEAR YOU'VE FINISHED...
...I'LL COME RUSHING OVER, EVEN IF I'M AT COURT...
...SO TRY TO GET IT DONE WHILE I'M STILL ABLE TO HOLD MYSELF BACK!

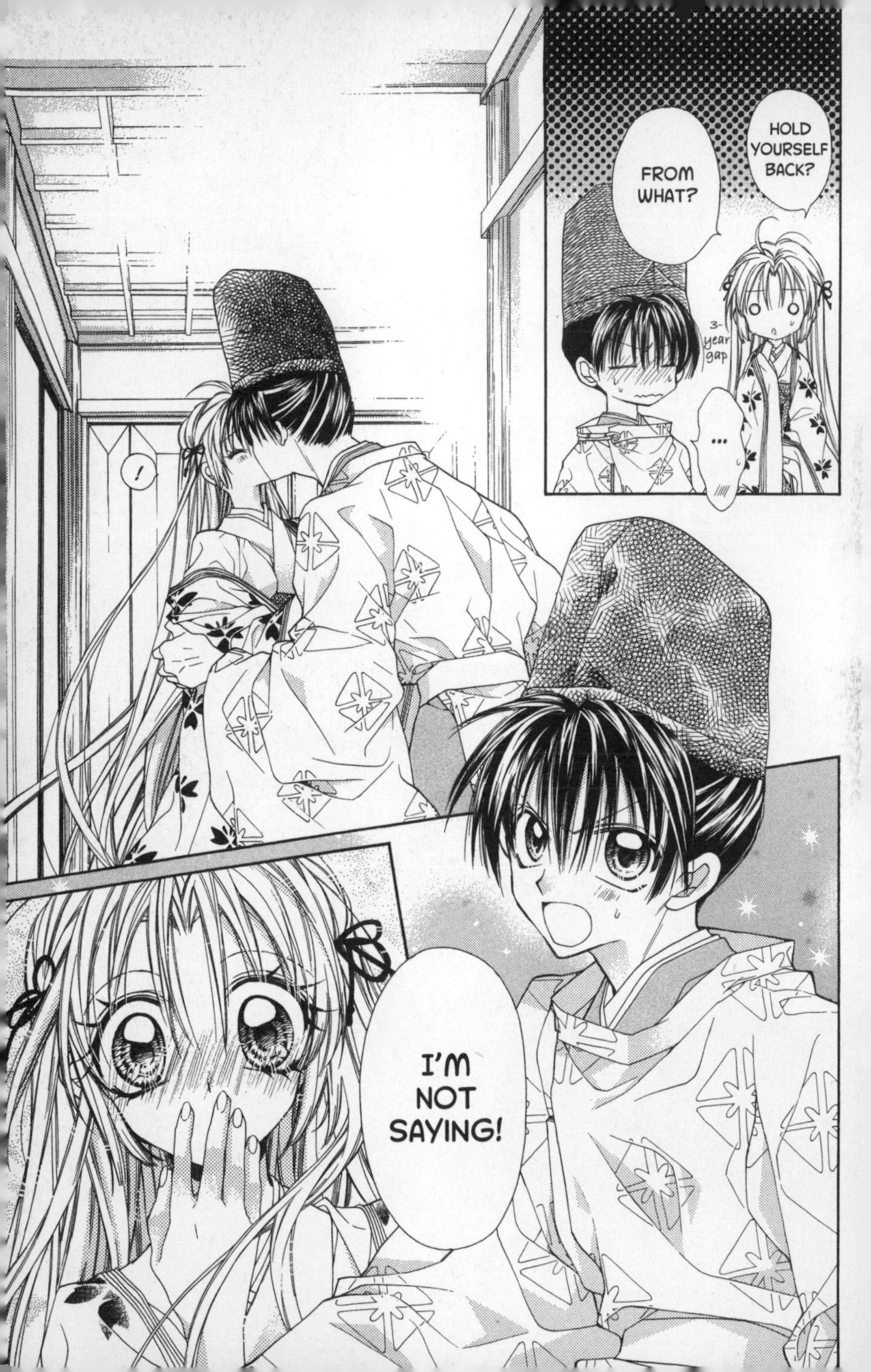
HOLD YOURSELF BACK?
FROM WHAT?
3-year gap
...
!
I'M NOT SAYING!

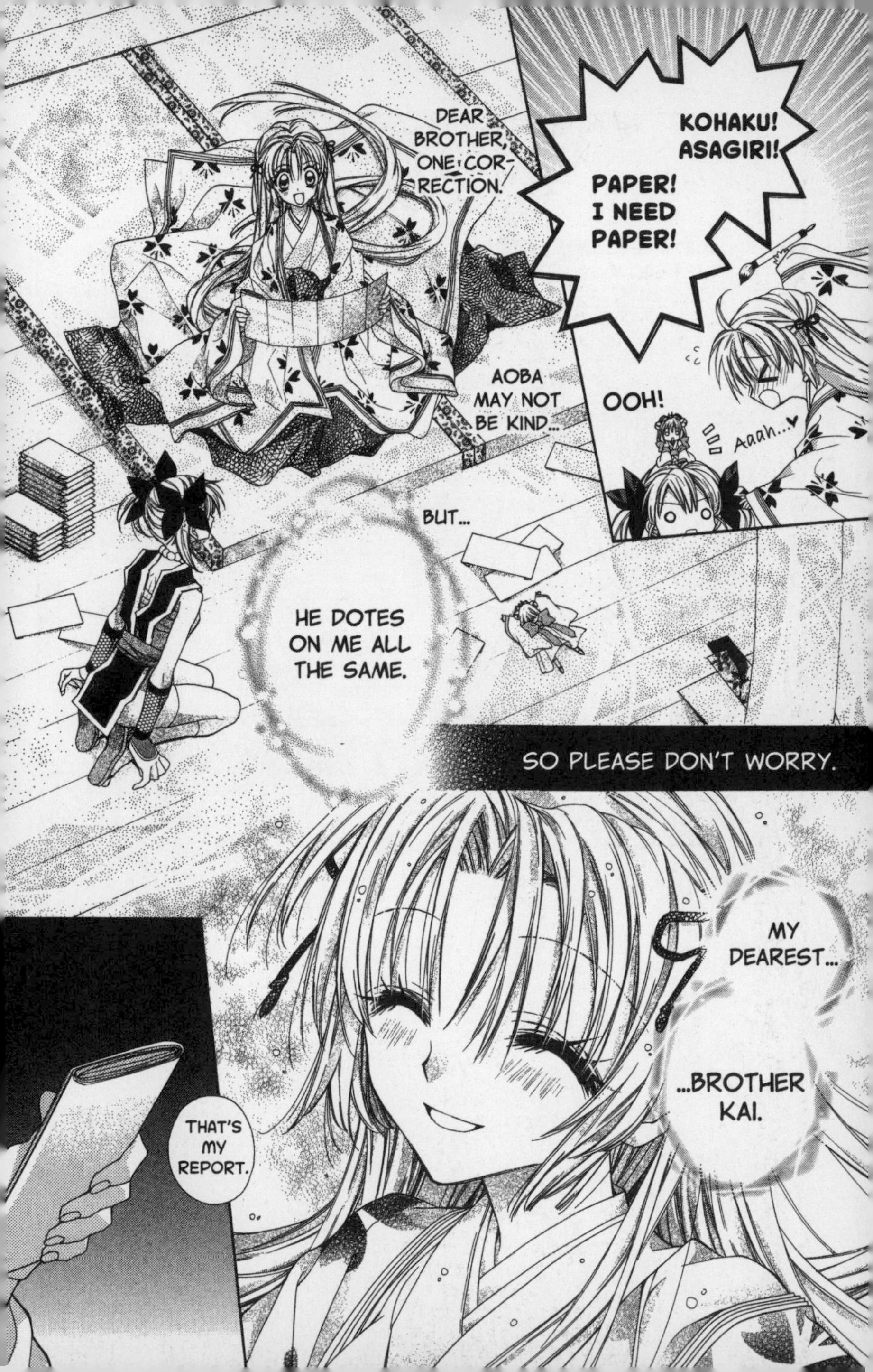
KOHAKU! ASAGIRI!
PAPER! I NEED PAPER!
OOH!
Aaah...♥
DEAR BROTHER, ONE CORRECTION.
AOBA MAY NOT BE KIND...
BUT...
HE DOTES ON ME ALL THE SAME.
SO PLEASE DON'T WORRY.
MY DEAREST...
...BROTHER KAI.
THAT'S MY REPORT.

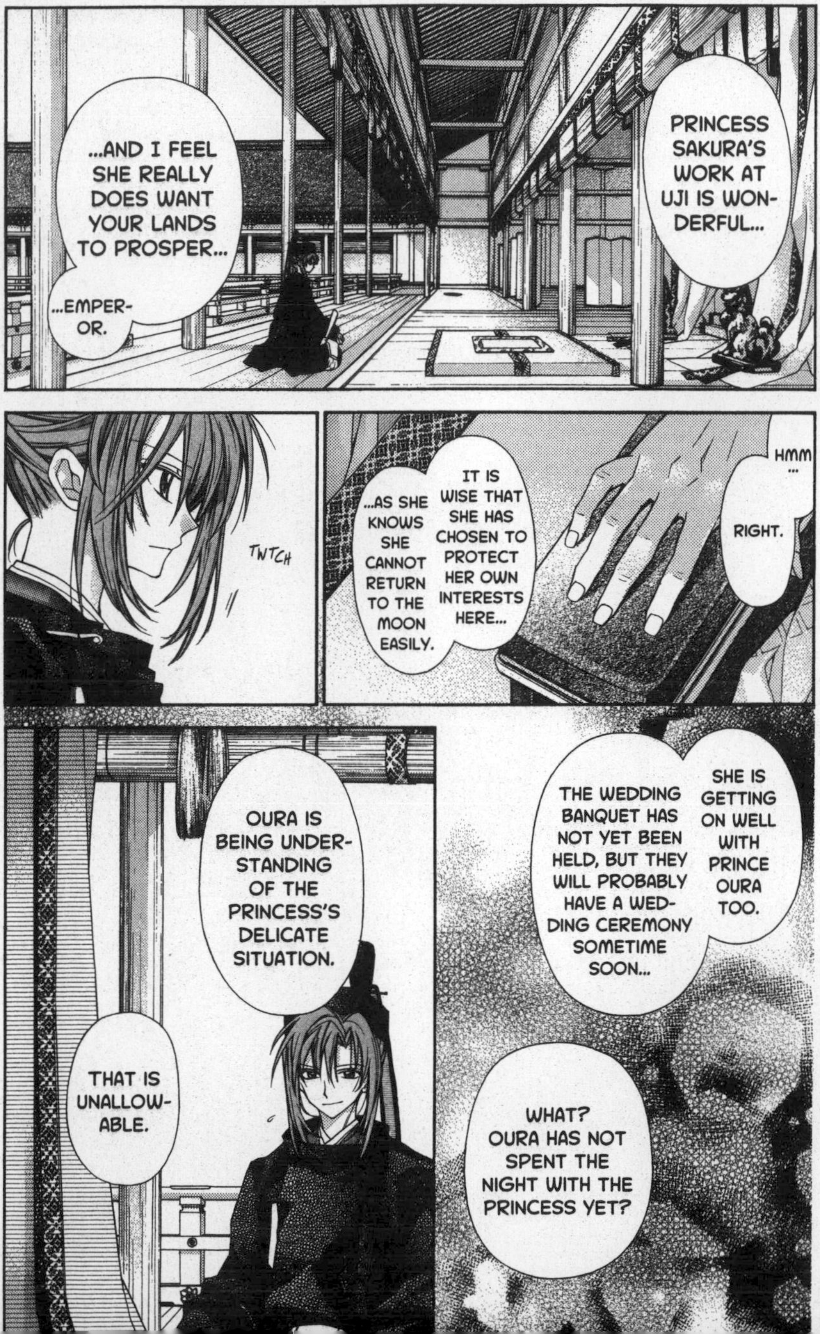
PRINCESS SAKURA'S WORK AT UJI IS WONDERFUL...
...AND I FEEL SHE REALLY DOES WANT YOUR LANDS TO PROSPER...
...EMPEROR.
HMM...
RIGHT.
IT IS WISE THAT SHE HAS CHOSEN TO PROTECT HER OWN INTERESTS HERE...
...AS SHE KNOWS SHE CANNOT RETURN TO THE MOON EASILY.
TWTCH
SHE IS GETTING ON WELL WITH PRINCE OURA TOO.
THE WEDDING BANQUET HAS NOT YET BEEN HELD, BUT THEY WILL PROBABLY HAVE A WEDDING CEREMONY SOMETIME SOON...
WHAT? OURA HAS NOT SPENT THE NIGHT WITH THE PRINCESS YET?
OURA IS BEING UNDERSTANDING OF THE PRINCESS'S DELICATE SITUATION.
THAT IS UNALLOWABLE.

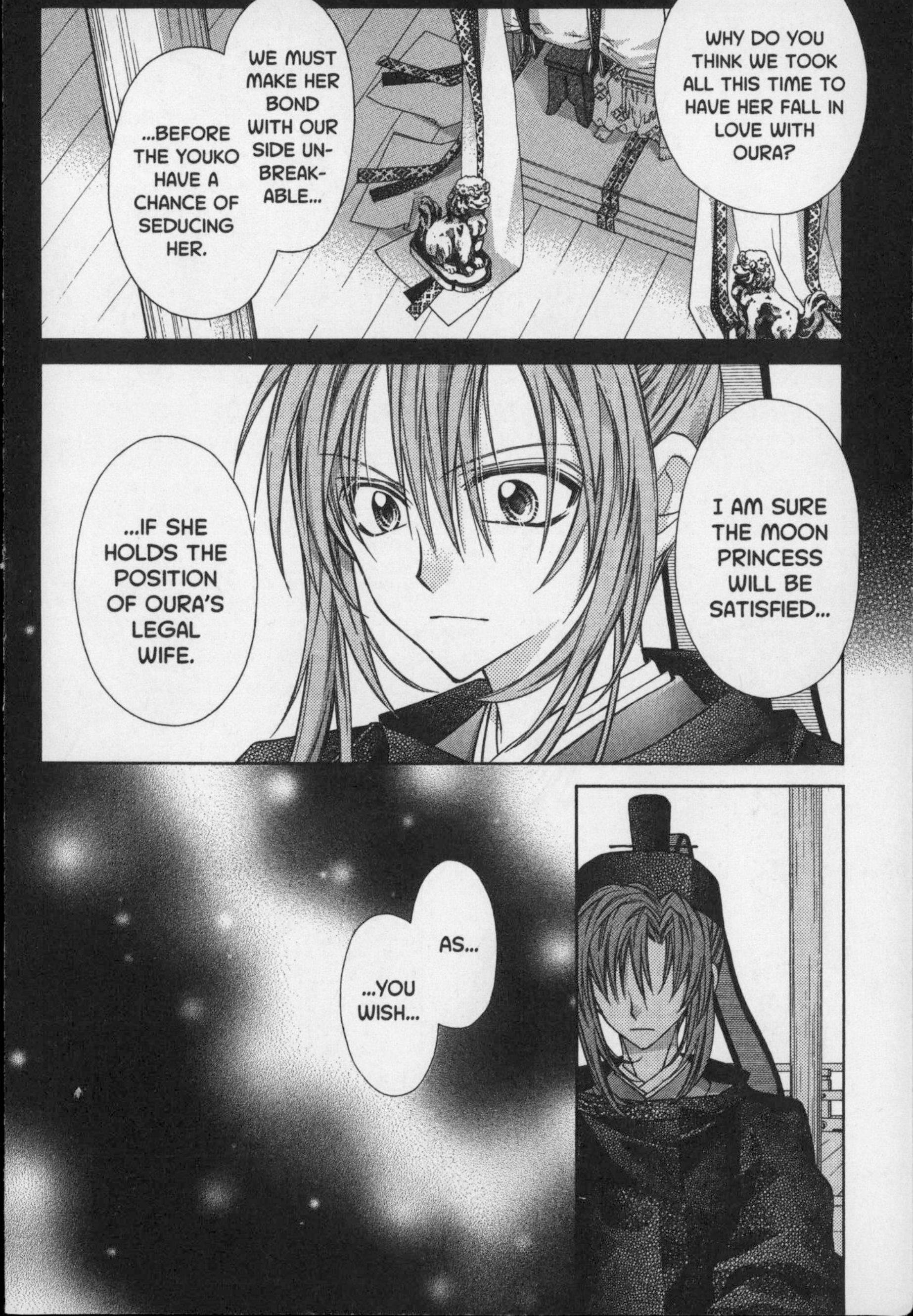
WHY DO YOU THINK WE TOOK ALL THIS TIME TO HAVE HER FALL IN LOVE WITH OURA?
WE MUST MAKE HER BOND WITH OUR SIDE UN-BREAK-ABLE...
...BEFORE THE YOUKO HAVE A CHANCE OF SEDUCING HER.
I AM SURE THE MOON PRINCESS WILL BE SATISFIED...
...IF SHE HOLDS THE POSITION OF OURA'S LEGAL WIFE.
AS...
...YOU WISH...

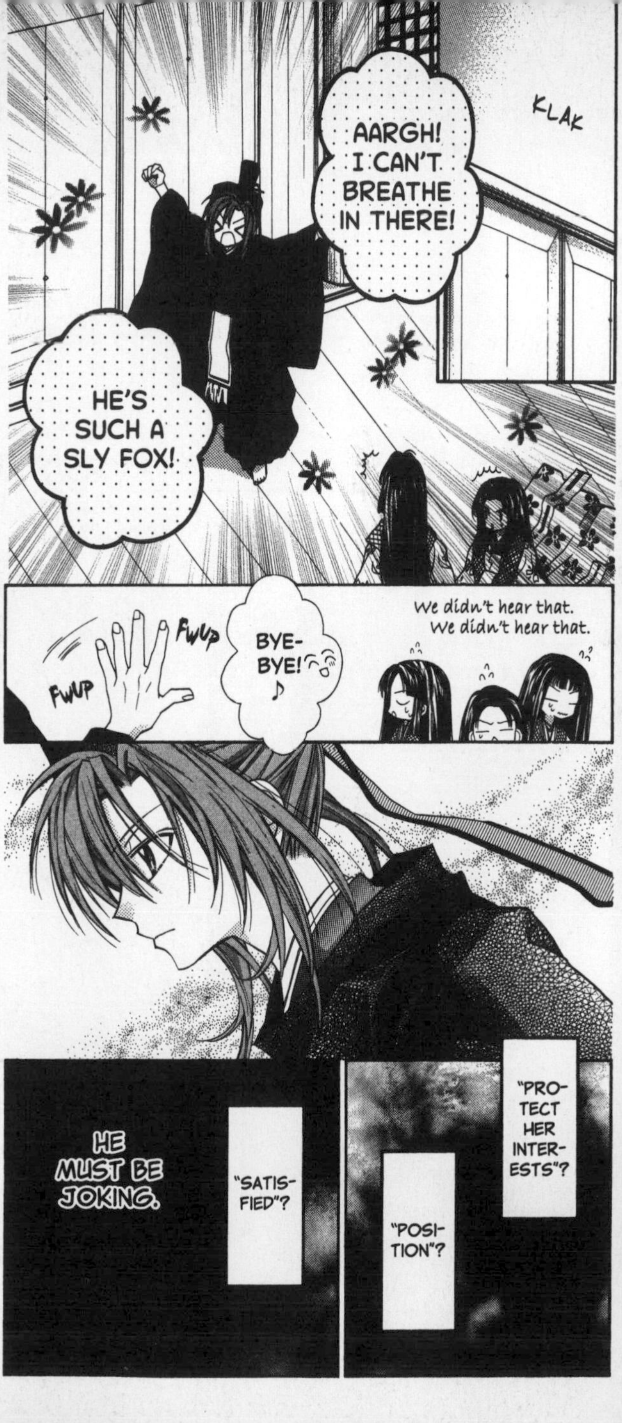
KLAK
AARGH! I CAN'T BREATHE IN THERE!
HE'S SUCH A SLY FOX!
We didn't hear that. We didn't hear that.
BYE-BYE! ♪
FWUP
FWUP
"PROTECT HER INTERESTS"?
"POSITION"?
"SATISFIED"?
HE MUST BE JOKING.

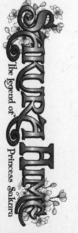

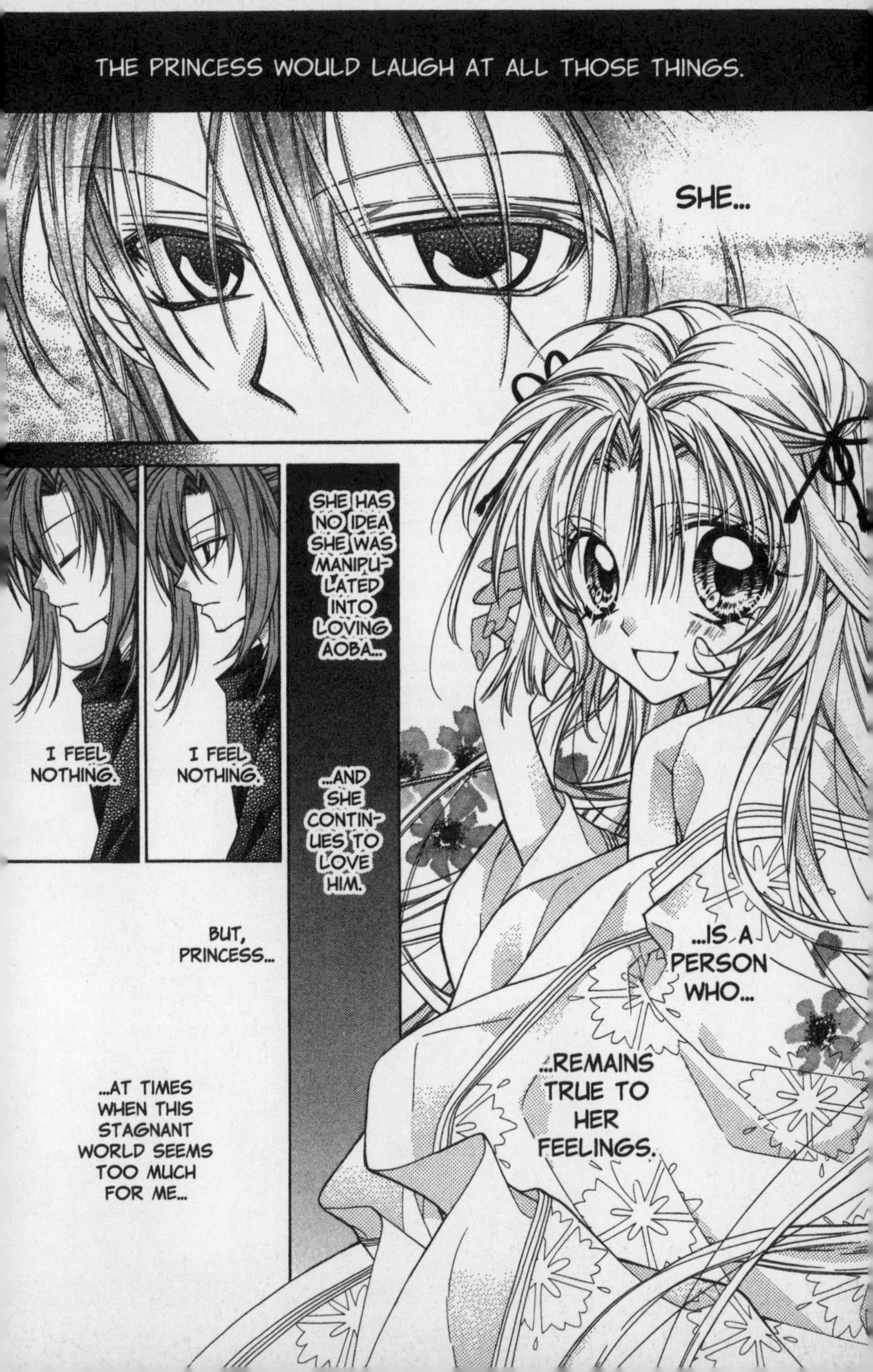
THE PRINCESS WOULD LAUGH AT ALL THOSE THINGS.
SHE...
...IS A PERSON WHO...
...REMAINS TRUE TO HER FEELINGS.
SHE HAS NO IDEA SHE WAS MANIPU-LATED INTO LOVING AOBA...
...AND SHE CONTIN-UES TO LOVE HIM.
I FEEL NOTHING.
I FEEL NOTHING.
BUT, PRINCESS...
...AT TIMES WHEN THIS STAGNANT WORLD SEEMS TOO MUCH FOR ME...

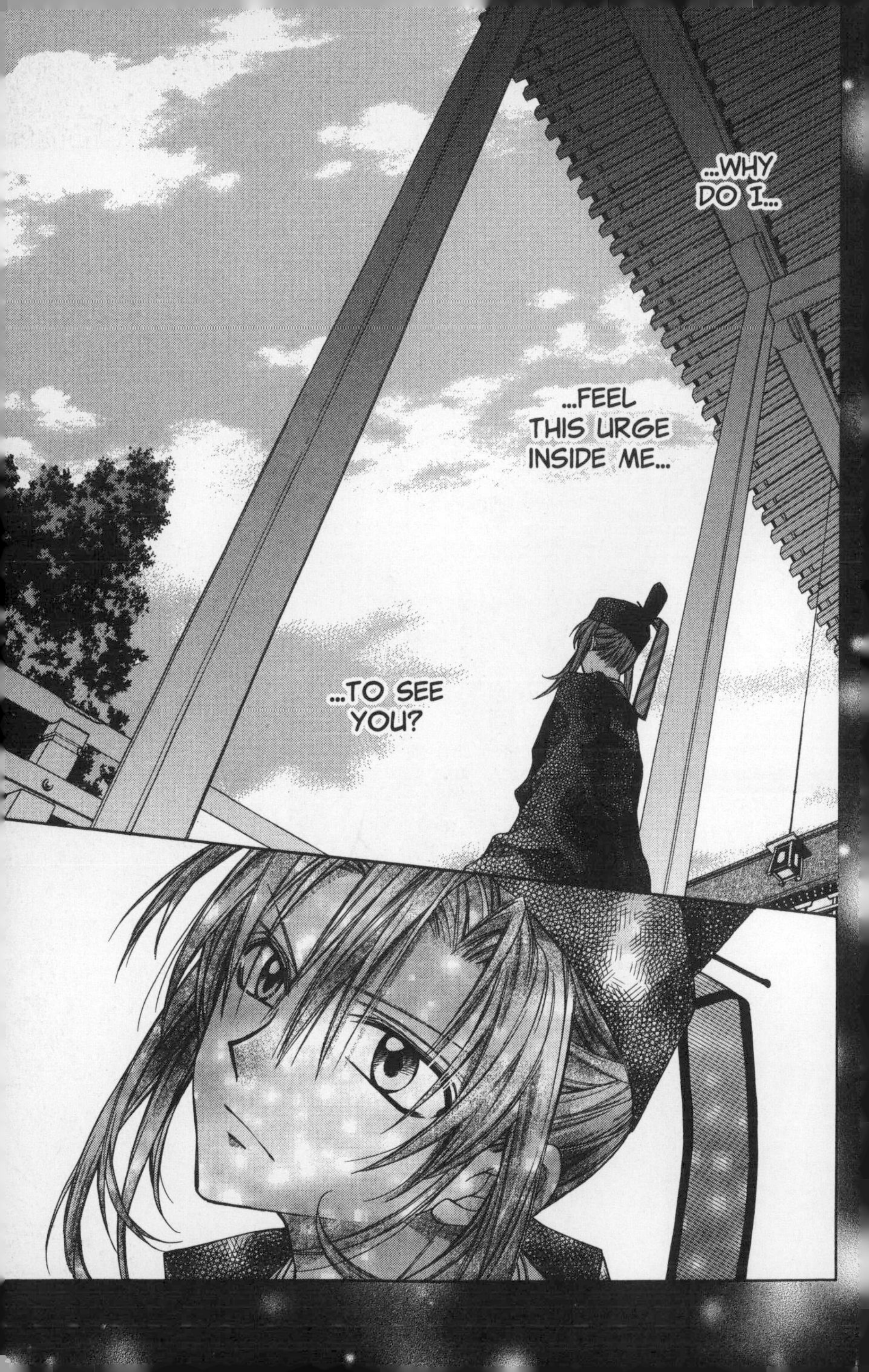
...WHY DO I...
...FEEL THIS URGE INSIDE ME...
...TO SEE YOU?

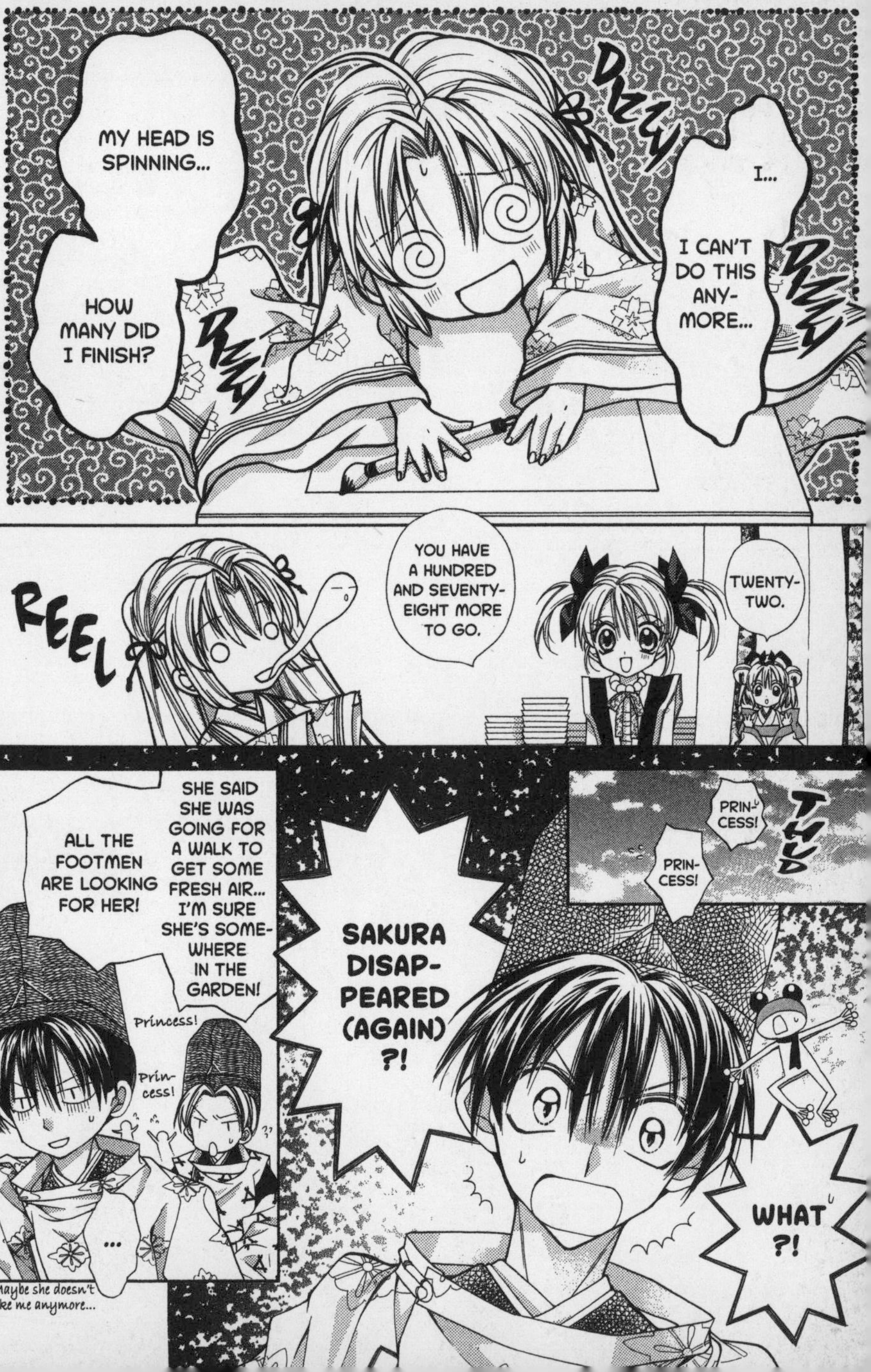
DIZZY
I...
I CAN'T DO THIS ANY-MORE...
DIZZY
MY HEAD IS SPINNING...
HOW MANY DID I FINISH?
DIZZY
TWENTY-TWO.
YOU HAVE A HUNDRED AND SEVENTY-EIGHT MORE TO GO.
REEL
PRIN-CESS!
THUD
PRIN-CESS!
WHAT?!
SAKURA DISAP-PEARED (AGAIN)?!
SHE SAID SHE WAS GOING FOR A WALK TO GET SOME FRESH AIR... I'M SURE SHE'S SOME-WHERE IN THE GARDEN!
ALL THE FOOTMEN ARE LOOKING FOR HER!
Princess!
Prin-cess!
...
Maybe she doesn't like me anymore...

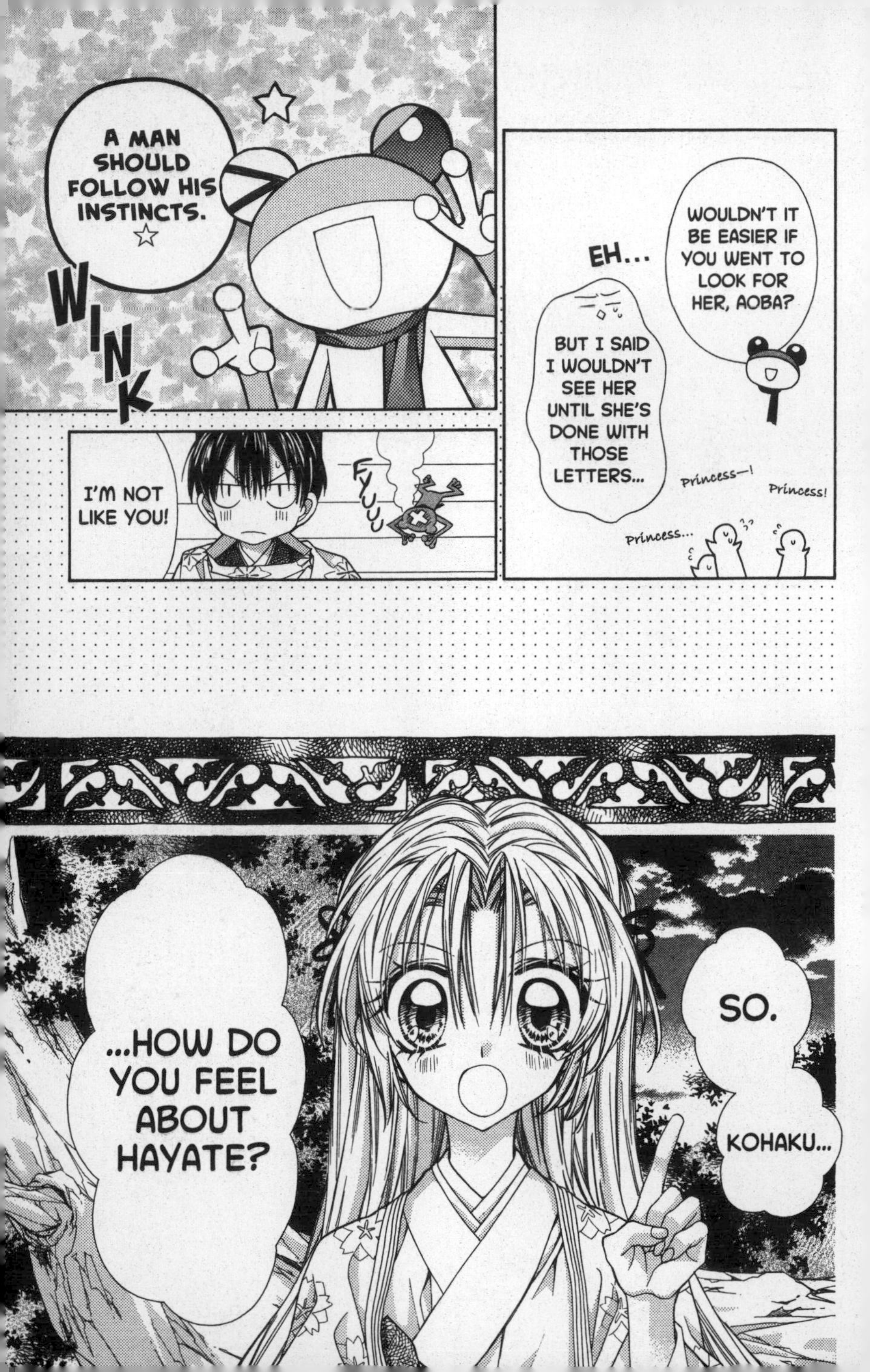
WOULDN'T IT BE EASIER IF YOU WENT TO LOOK FOR HER, AOBA?
EH...
BUT I SAID I WOULDN'T SEE HER UNTIL SHE'S DONE WITH THOSE LETTERS...
Princess—!
Princess!
Princess...
A MAN SHOULD FOLLOW HIS INSTINCTS. ☆
WINK
I'M NOT LIKE YOU!
FYUUU
SO.
KOHAKU...
...HOW DO YOU FEEL ABOUT HAYATE?

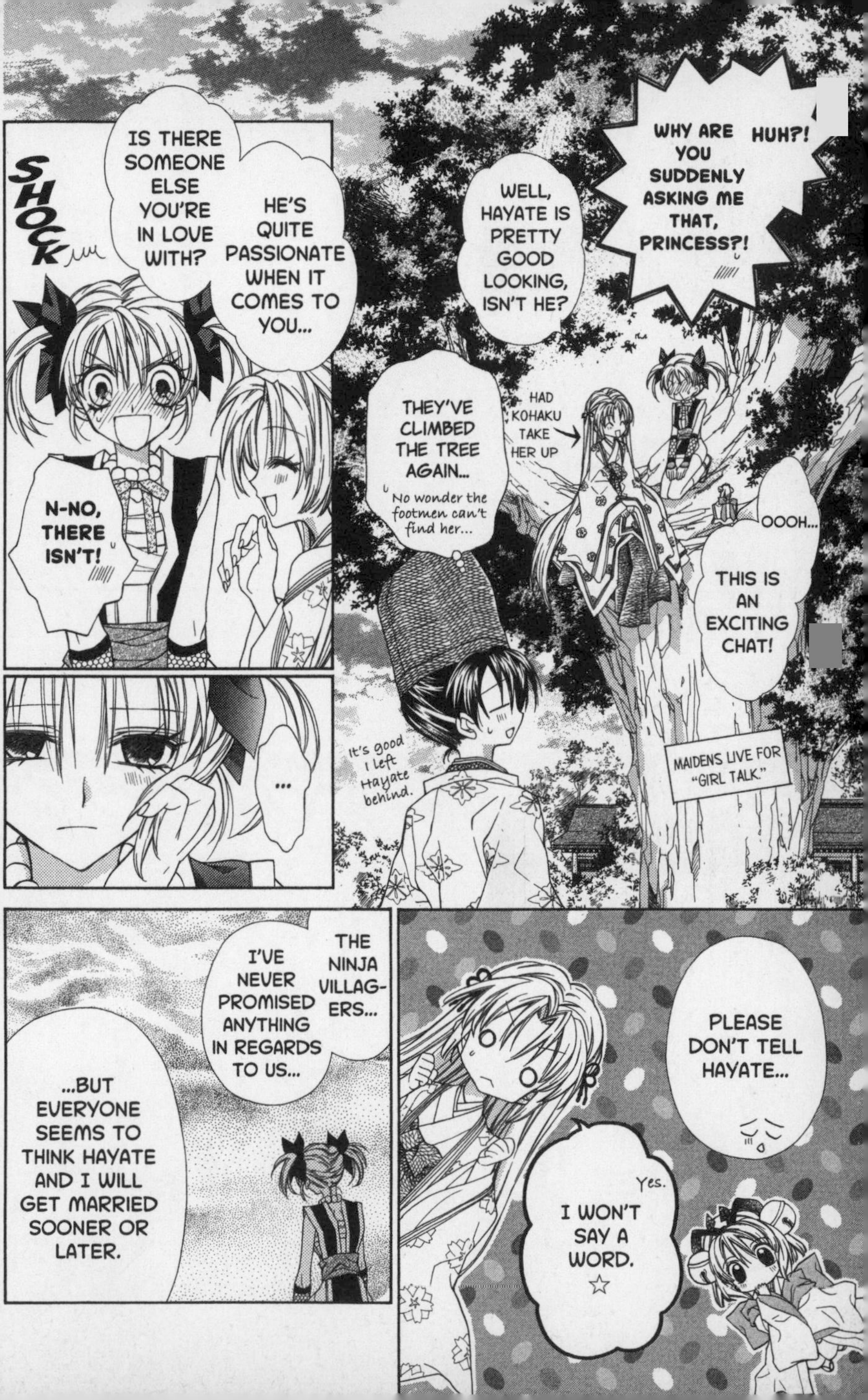
HUH?!
WHY ARE YOU SUDDENLY ASKING ME THAT, PRINCESS?!
WELL, HAYATE IS PRETTY GOOD LOOKING, ISN'T HE?
HAD KOHAKU TAKE HER UP
OOOH...
THIS IS AN EXCITING CHAT!
THEY'VE CLIMBED THE TREE AGAIN...
No wonder the footmen can't find her...
MAIDENS LIVE FOR "GIRL TALK."
It's good I left Hayate behind.
HE'S QUITE PASSIONATE WHEN IT COMES TO YOU...
IS THERE SOMEONE ELSE YOU'RE IN LOVE WITH?
SHOCK
N-NO, THERE ISN'T!
...
PLEASE DON'T TELL HAYATE...
Yes.
I WON'T SAY A WORD. ☆
THE NINJA VILLAGERS...
I'VE NEVER PROMISED ANYTHING IN REGARDS TO US...
...BUT EVERYONE SEEMS TO THINK HAYATE AND I WILL GET MARRIED SOONER OR LATER.

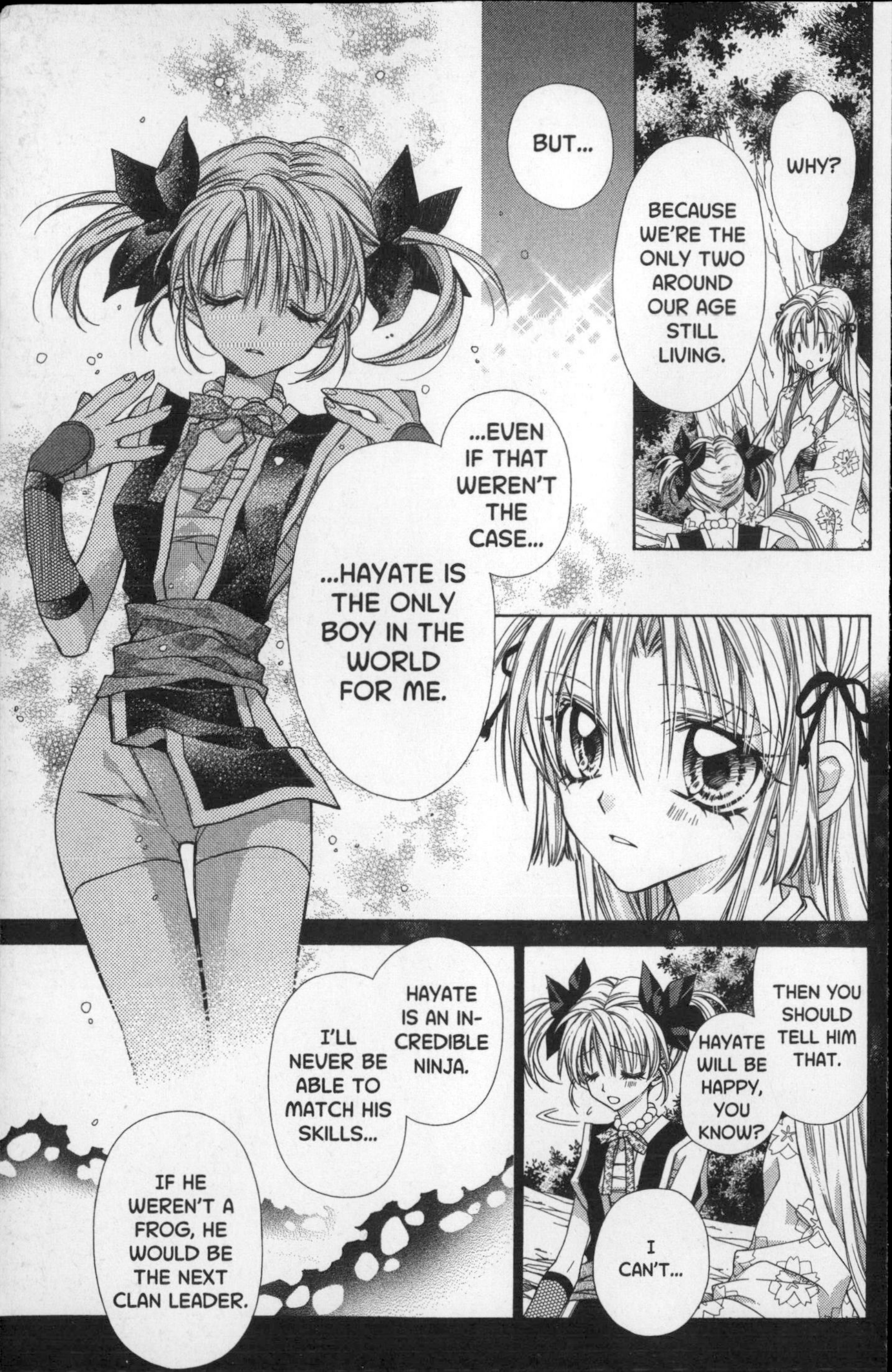
WHY?
BECAUSE WE'RE THE ONLY TWO AROUND OUR AGE STILL LIVING.
BUT...
...EVEN IF THAT WEREN'T THE CASE...
...HAYATE IS THE ONLY BOY IN THE WORLD FOR ME.
THEN YOU SHOULD TELL HIM THAT.
HAYATE WILL BE HAPPY, YOU KNOW?
I CAN'T...
HAYATE IS AN IN-CREDIBLE NINJA.
I'LL NEVER BE ABLE TO MATCH HIS SKILLS...
IF HE WEREN'T A FROG, HE WOULD BE THE NEXT CLAN LEADER.

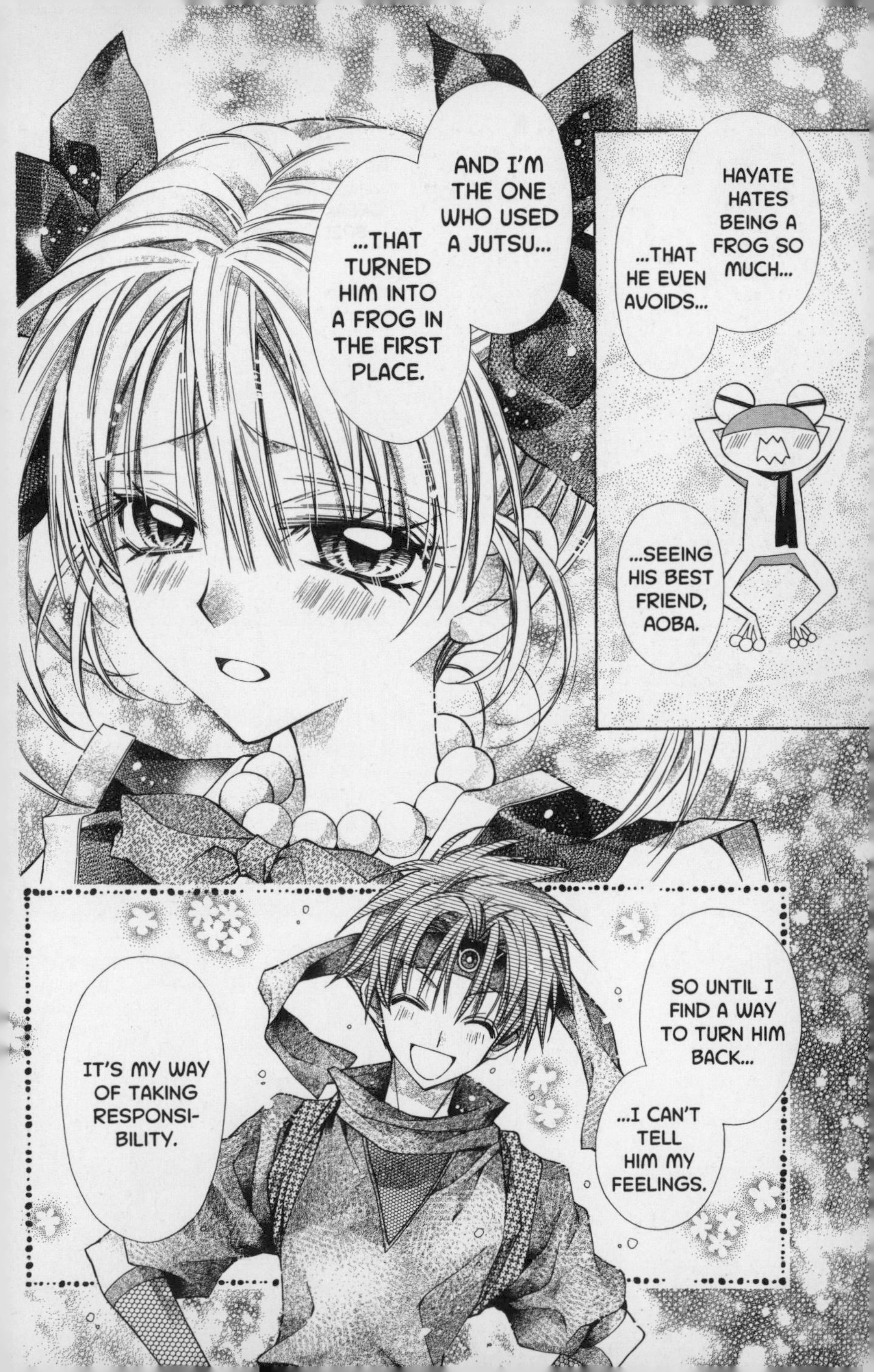
HAYATE HATES BEING A FROG SO MUCH...
...THAT HE EVEN AVOIDS...
...SEEING HIS BEST FRIEND, AOBA.
AND I'M THE ONE WHO USED A JUTSU...
...THAT TURNED HIM INTO A FROG IN THE FIRST PLACE.
SO UNTIL I FIND A WAY TO TURN HIM BACK...
...I CAN'T TELL HIM MY FEELINGS.
IT'S MY WAY OF TAKING RESPONSI-BILITY.

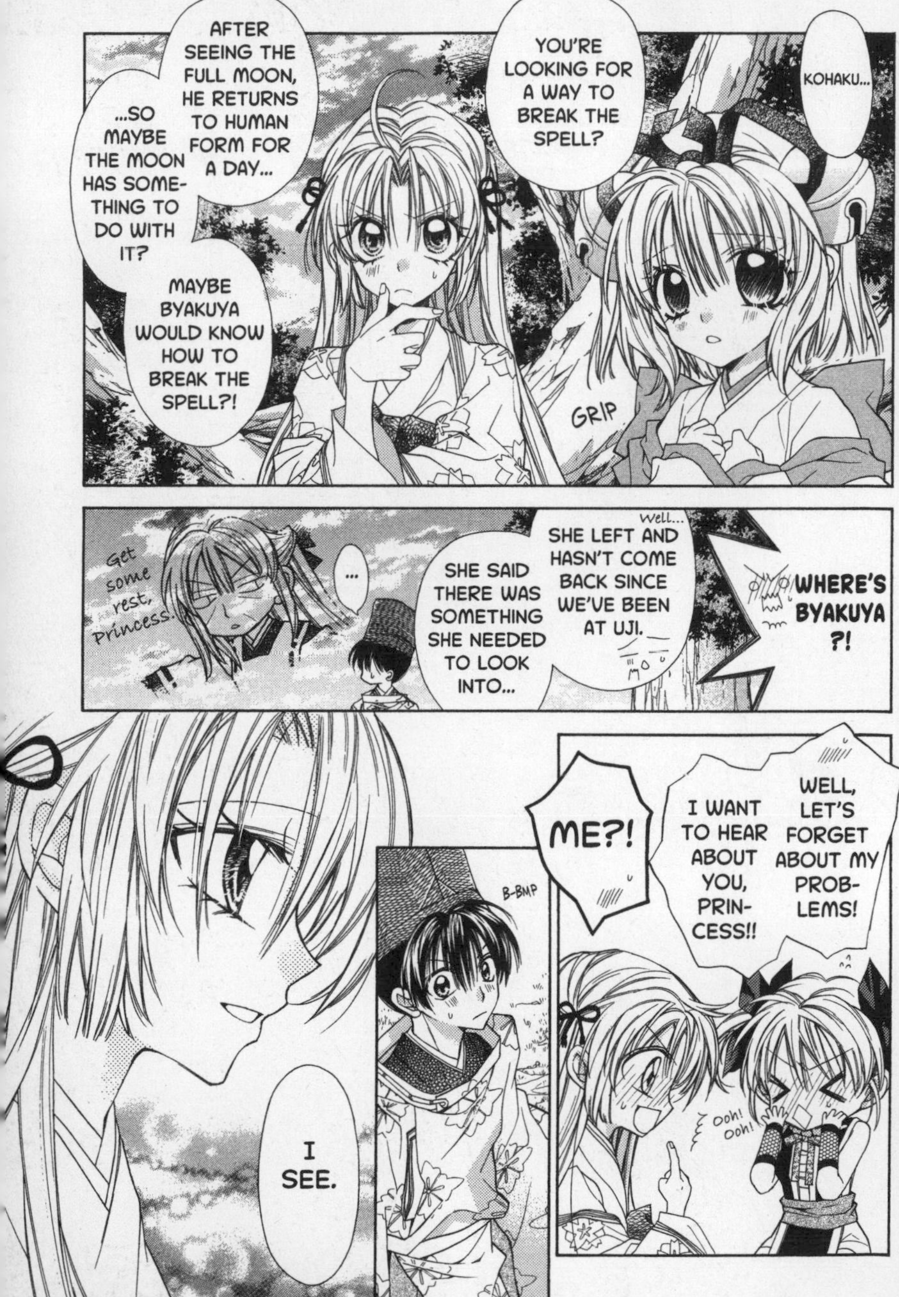
KOHAKU...
YOU'RE LOOKING FOR A WAY TO BREAK THE SPELL?
AFTER SEEING THE FULL MOON, HE RETURNS TO HUMAN FORM FOR A DAY...
...SO MAYBE THE MOON HAS SOME-THING TO DO WITH IT?
MAYBE BYAKUYA WOULD KNOW HOW TO BREAK THE SPELL?!
GRIP
WHERE'S BYAKUYA?!
Well...
SHE LEFT AND HASN'T COME BACK SINCE WE'VE BEEN AT UJI.
SHE SAID THERE WAS SOMETHING SHE NEEDED TO LOOK INTO...
...
Get some rest, Princess.
WELL, LET'S FORGET ABOUT MY PROB-LEMS!
I WANT TO HEAR ABOUT YOU, PRIN-CESS!!
ME?!
Ooh! Ooh!
B-BMP
I SEE.

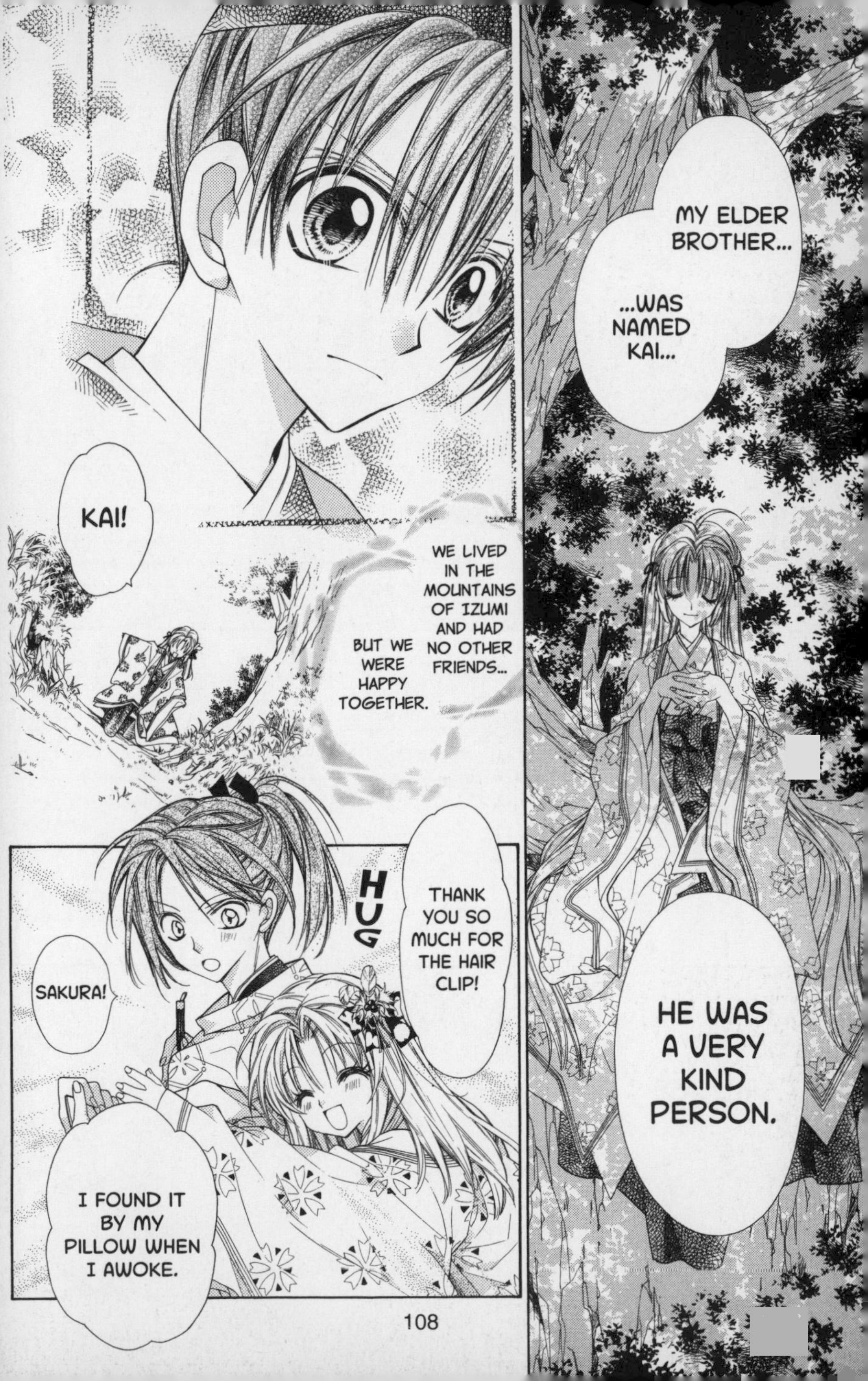
MY ELDER BROTHER...
...WAS NAMED KAI...
HE WAS A VERY KIND PERSON.
WE LIVED IN THE MOUNTAINS OF IZUMI AND HAD NO OTHER FRIENDS...
BUT WE WERE HAPPY TOGETHER.
KAI!
THANK YOU SO MUCH FOR THE HAIR CLIP!
HUG
SAKURA!
I FOUND IT BY MY PILLOW WHEN I AWOKE.

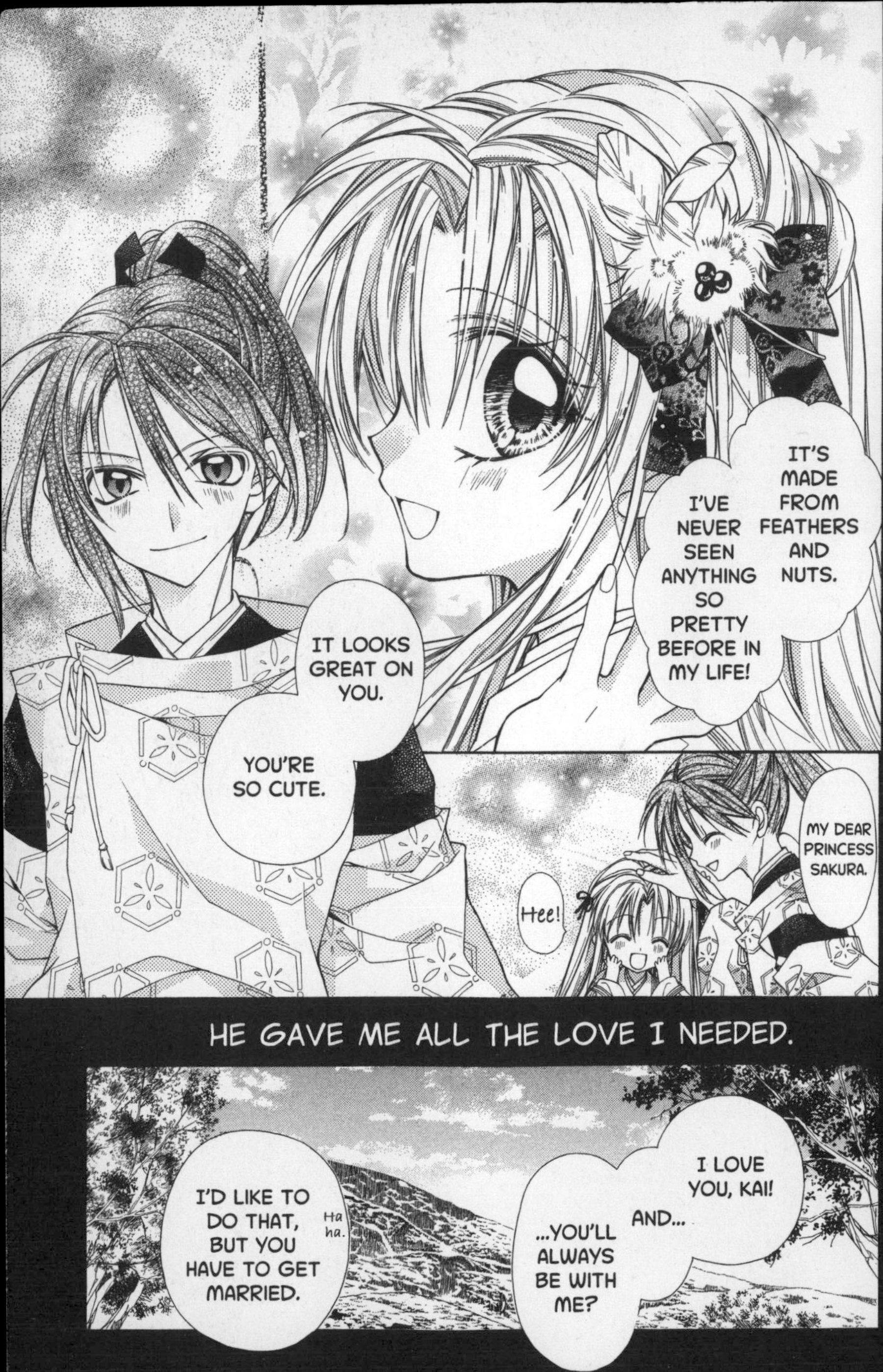
IT'S MADE FROM FEATHERS AND NUTS.
I'VE NEVER SEEN ANYTHING SO PRETTY BEFORE IN MY LIFE!
IT LOOKS GREAT ON YOU.
YOU'RE SO CUTE.
MY DEAR PRINCESS SAKURA.
Hee!
HE GAVE ME ALL THE LOVE I NEEDED.
I LOVE YOU, KAI!
AND...
...YOU'LL ALWAYS BE WITH ME?
Ha ha.
I'D LIKE TO DO THAT, BUT YOU HAVE TO GET MARRIED.

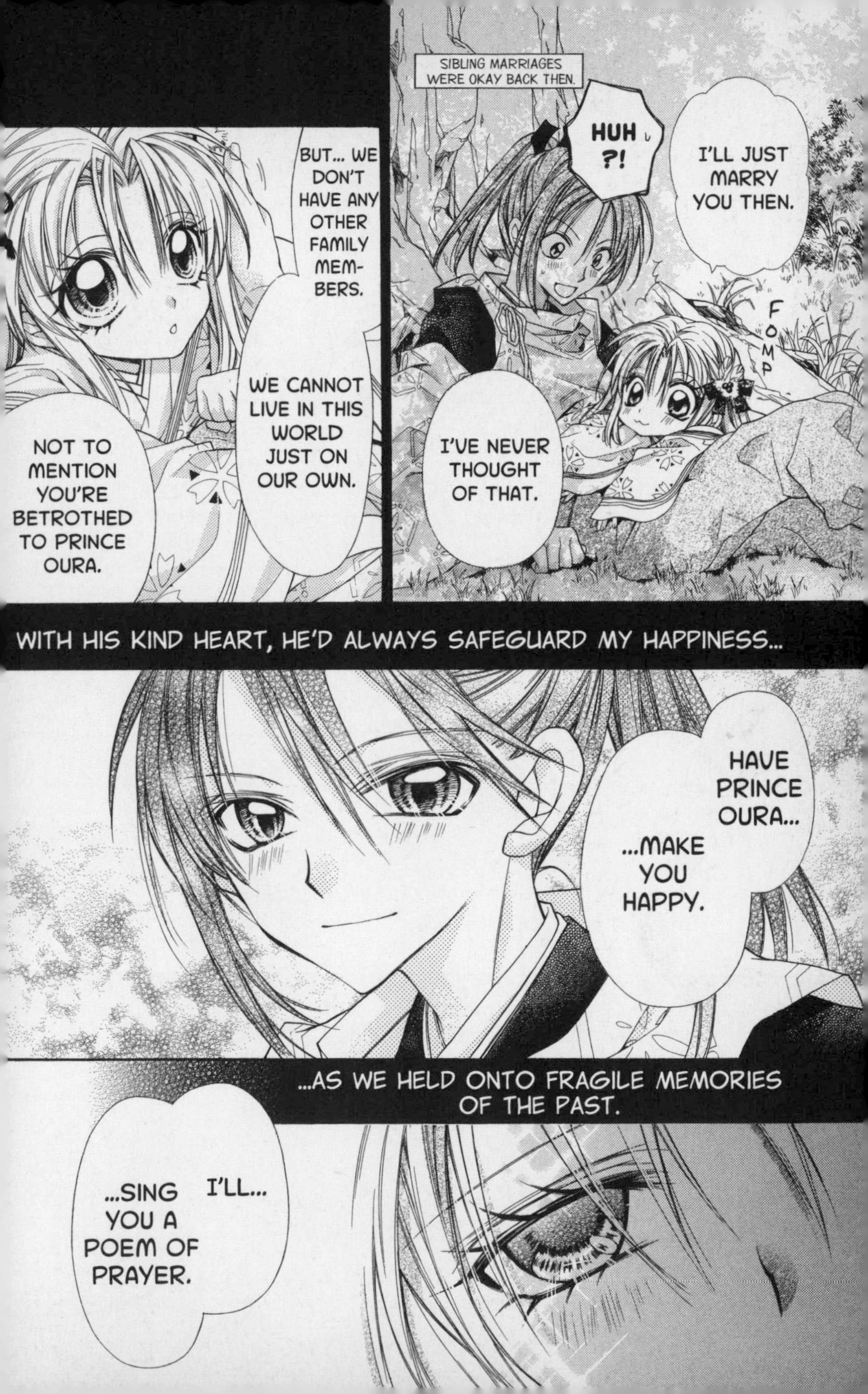
I'LL JUST MARRY YOU THEN.
HUH ?!
SIBLING MARRIAGES WERE OKAY BACK THEN.
FOMP
I'VE NEVER THOUGHT OF THAT.
BUT... WE DON'T HAVE ANY OTHER FAMILY MEM-BERS.
WE CANNOT LIVE IN THIS WORLD JUST ON OUR OWN.
NOT TO MENTION YOU'RE BETROTHED TO PRINCE OURA.
WITH HIS KIND HEART, HE'D ALWAYS SAFEGUARD MY HAPPINESS...
HAVE PRINCE OURA...
...MAKE YOU HAPPY.
...AS WE HELD ONTO FRAGILE MEMORIES OF THE PAST.
I'LL...
...SING YOU A POEM OF PRAYER.

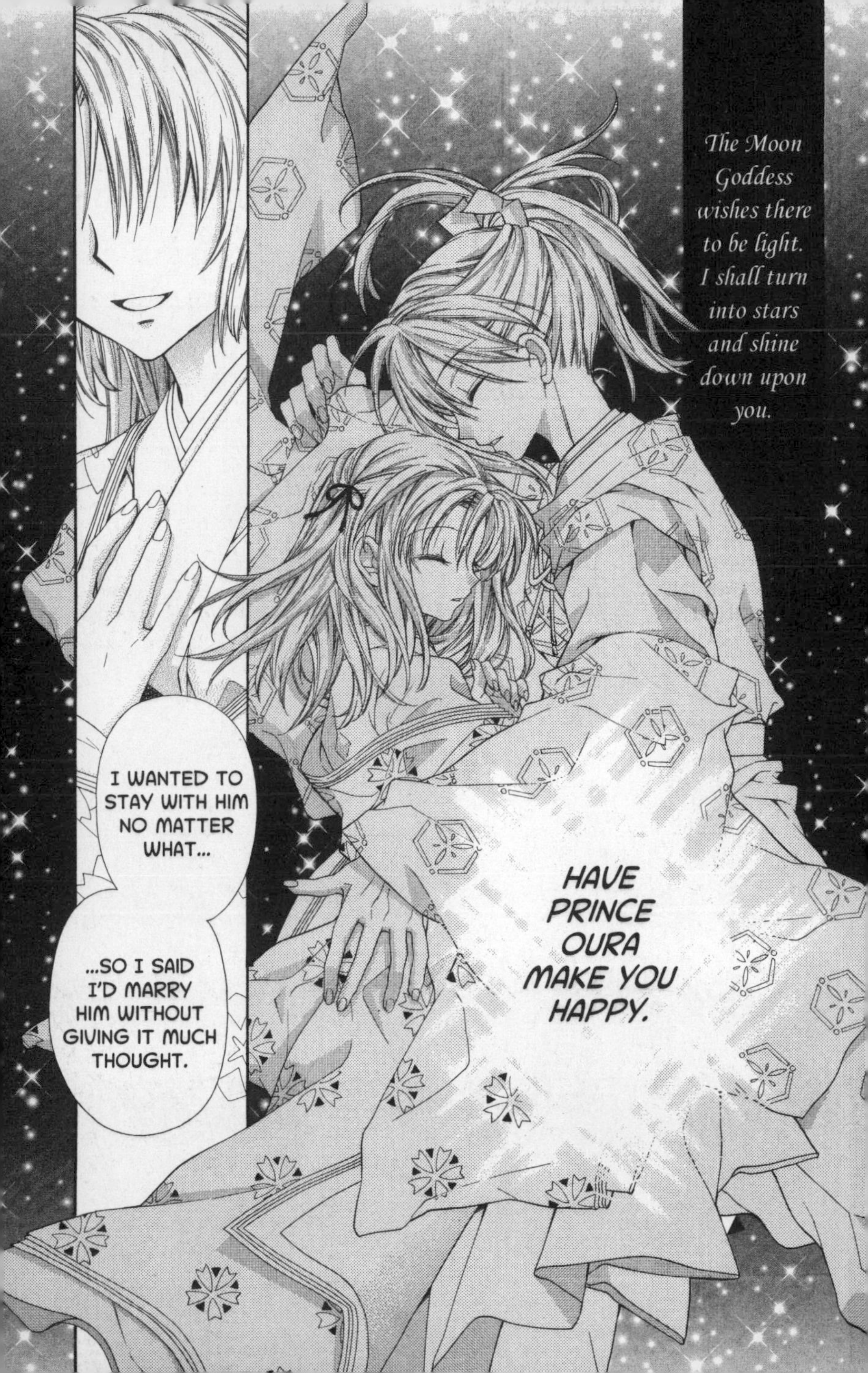
The Moon Goddess wishes there to be light. I shall turn into stars and shine down upon you.
HAVE PRINCE OURA MAKE YOU HAPPY.
I WANTED TO STAY WITH HIM NO MATTER WHAT...
...SO I SAID I'D MARRY HIM WITHOUT GIVING IT MUCH THOUGHT.

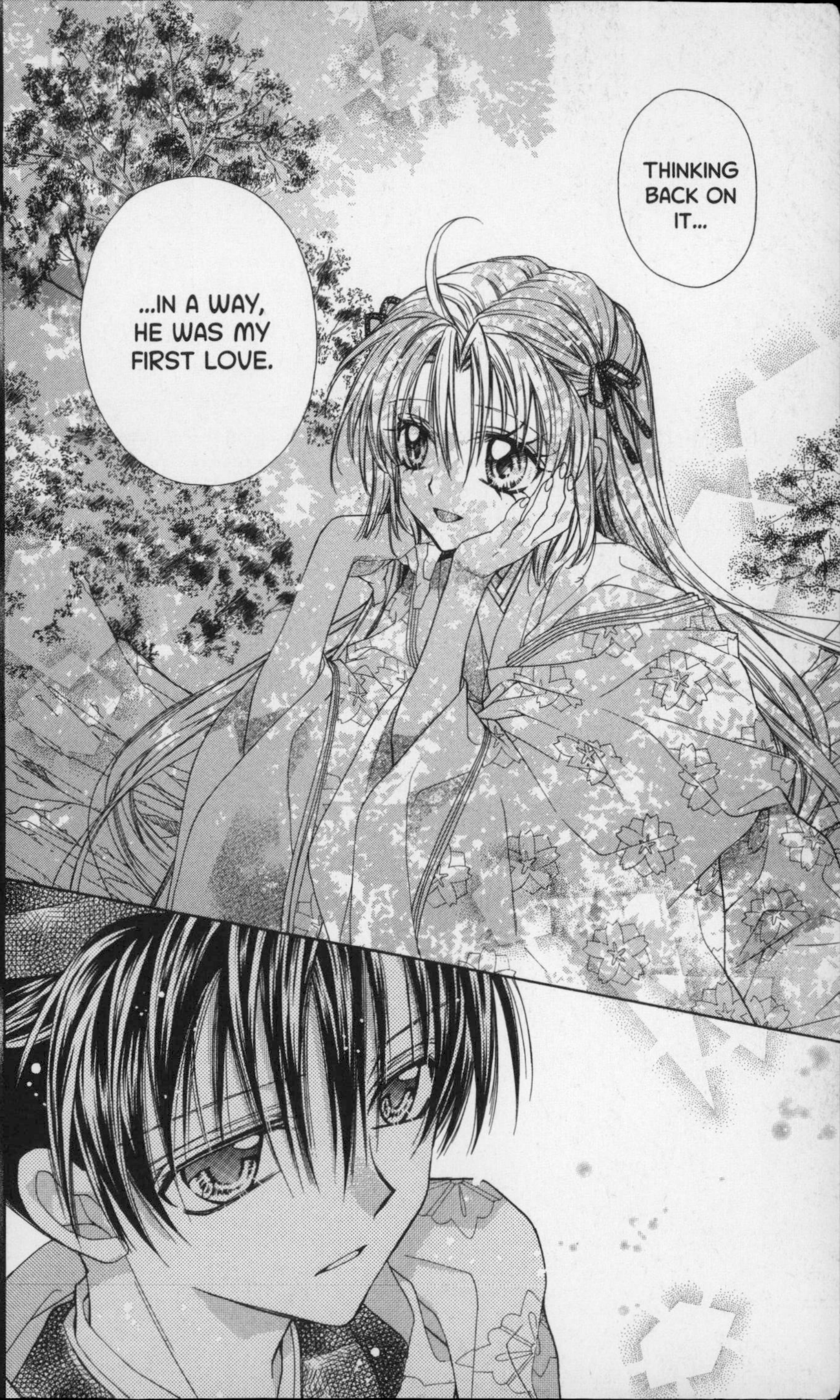
THINKING BACK ON IT...
...IN A WAY, HE WAS MY FIRST LOVE.

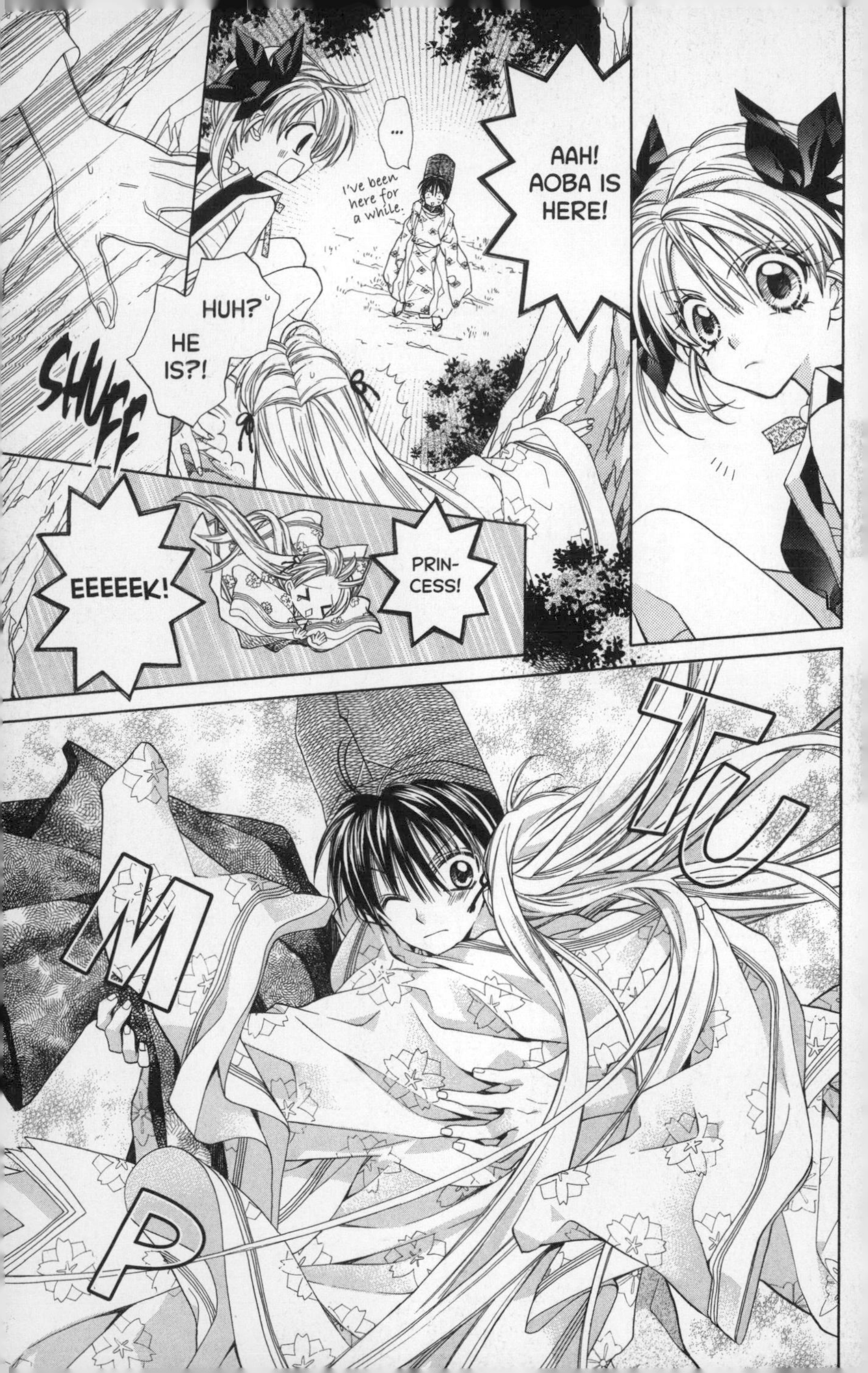
AAH! AOBA IS HERE!
...
I've been here for a while.
HUH?
HE IS?!
SHUFF
PRIN-CESS!
EEEEEK!
T U M P

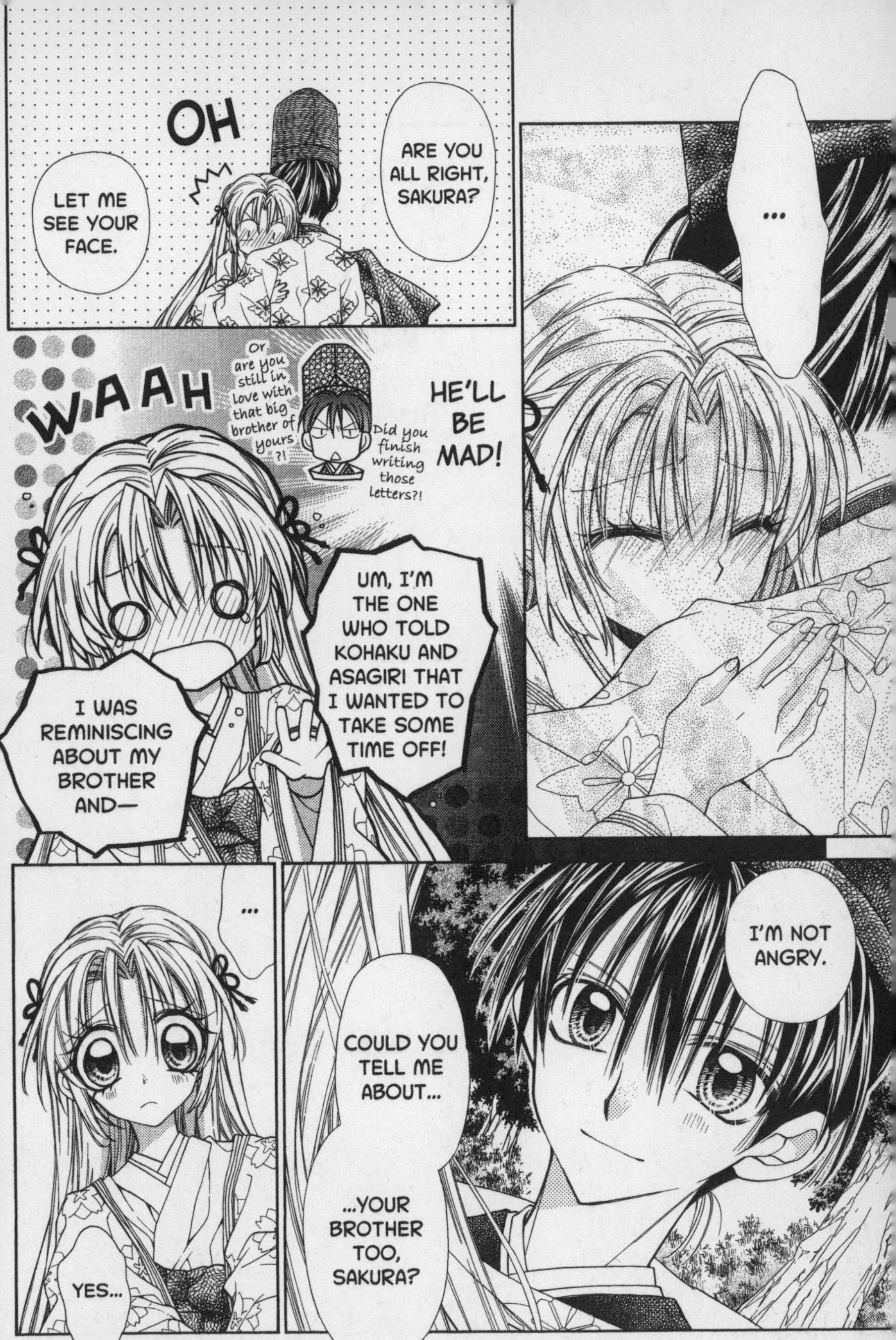
...
ARE YOU ALL RIGHT, SAKURA?
OH
LET ME SEE YOUR FACE.
HE'LL BE MAD!
Did you finish writing those letters?!
Or are you still in love with that big brother of yours ?!
WAAH
UM, I'M THE ONE WHO TOLD KOHAKU AND ASAGIRI THAT I WANTED TO TAKE SOME TIME OFF!
I WAS REMINISCING ABOUT MY BROTHER AND—
I'M NOT ANGRY.
COULD YOU TELL ME ABOUT...
...YOUR BROTHER TOO, SAKURA?
...
YES...

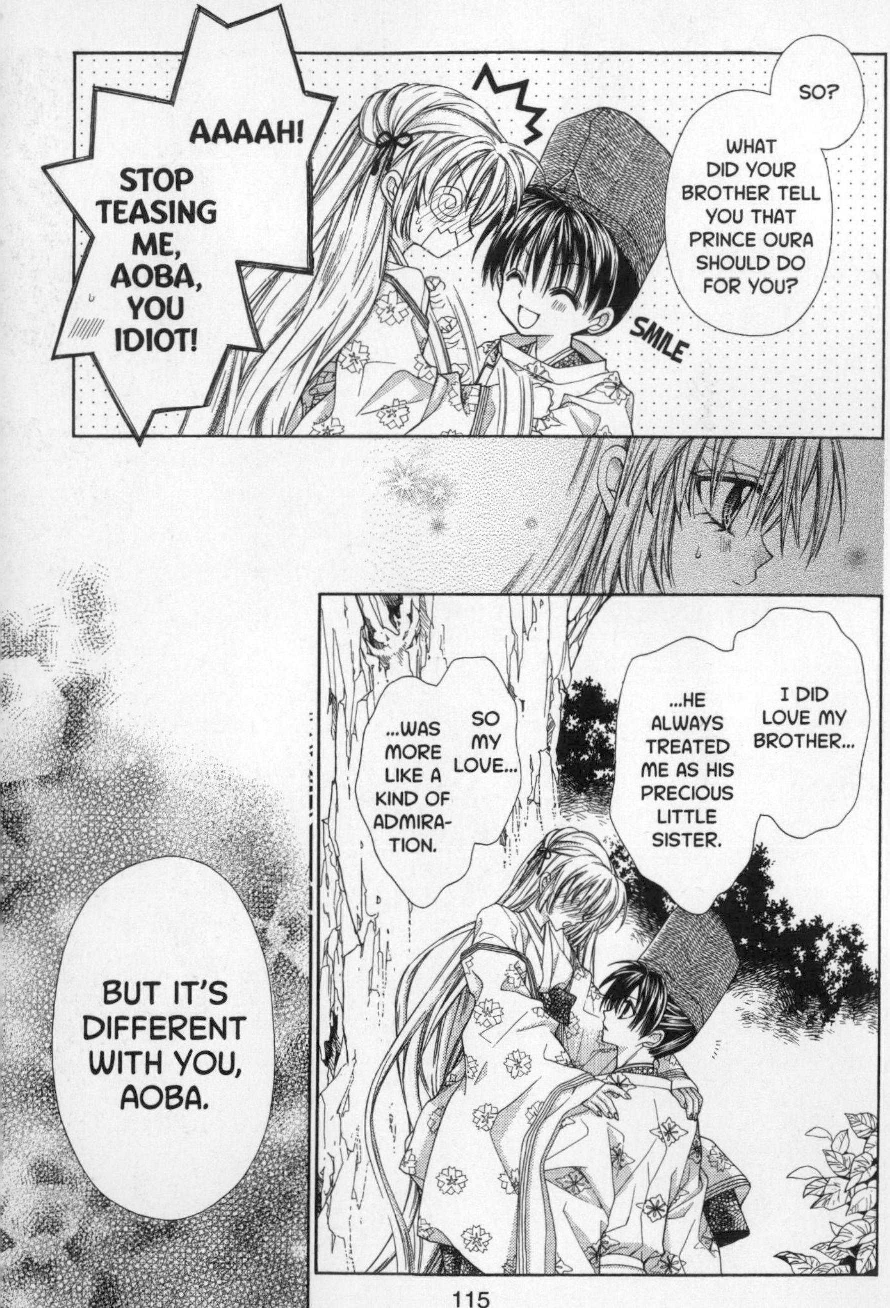
SO?
WHAT DID YOUR BROTHER TELL YOU THAT PRINCE OURA SHOULD DO FOR YOU?
SMILE
AAAAH!
STOP TEASING ME, AOBA, YOU IDIOT!
I DID LOVE MY BROTHER...
...HE ALWAYS TREATED ME AS HIS PRECIOUS LITTLE SISTER.
SO MY LOVE...
...WAS MORE LIKE A KIND OF ADMIRA-TION.
BUT IT'S DIFFERENT WITH YOU, AOBA.

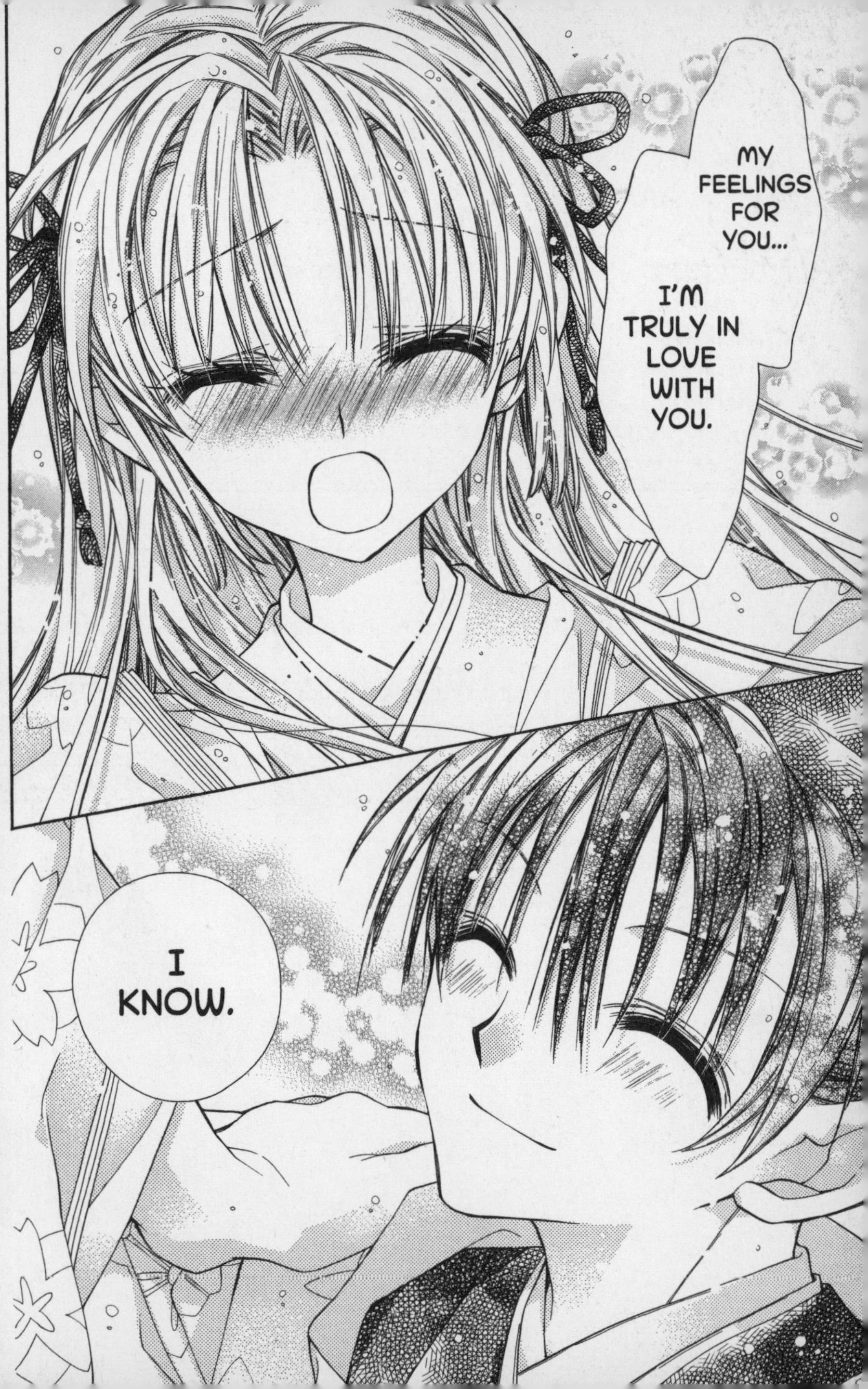
MY FEELINGS FOR YOU...
I'M TRULY IN LOVE WITH YOU.
I KNOW.

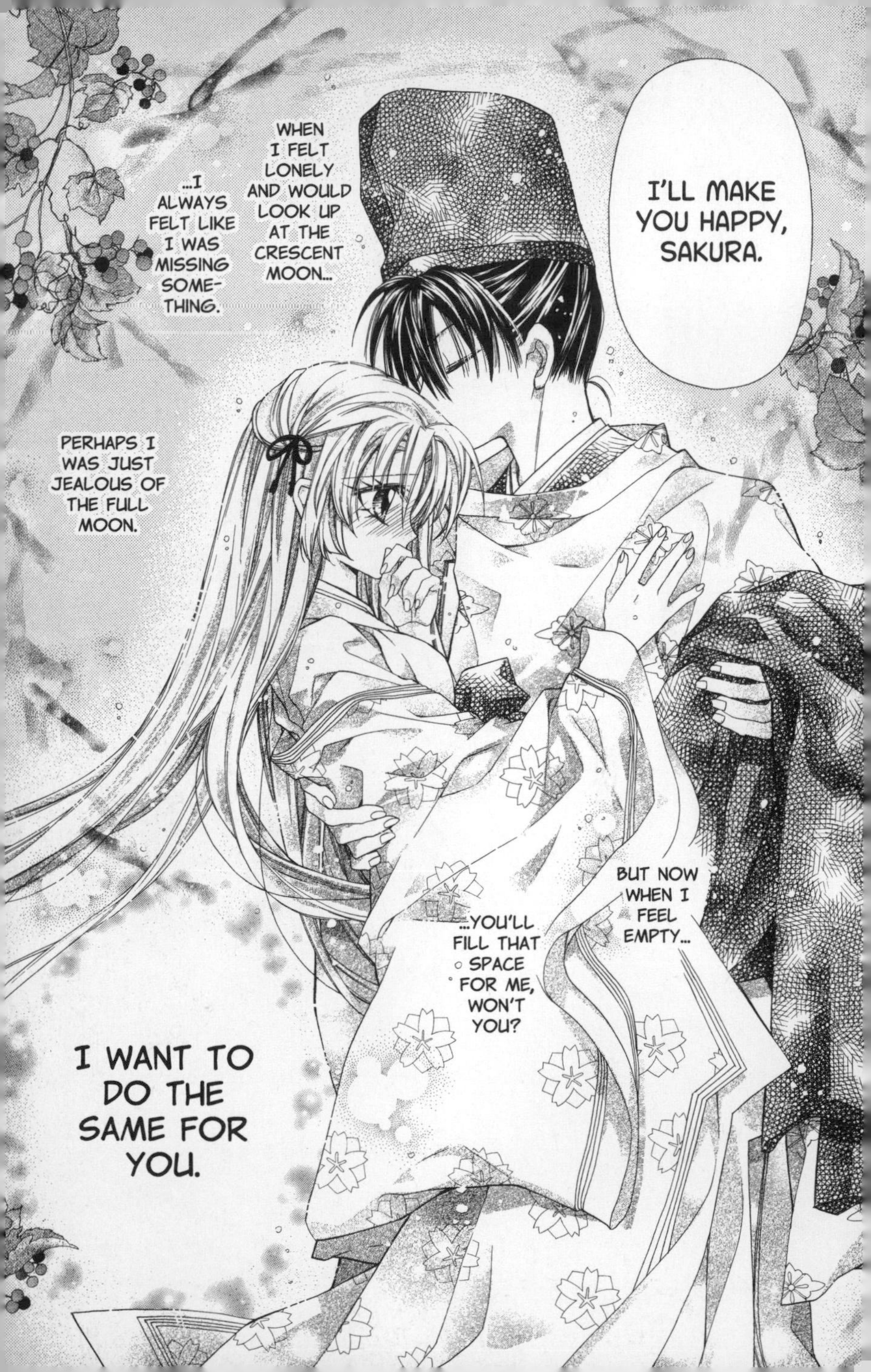
I'LL MAKE YOU HAPPY, SAKURA.
WHEN I FELT LONELY AND WOULD LOOK UP AT THE CRESCENT MOON...
...I ALWAYS FELT LIKE I WAS MISSING SOME-THING.
PERHAPS I WAS JUST JEALOUS OF THE FULL MOON.
BUT NOW WHEN I FEEL EMPTY...
...YOU'LL FILL THAT SPACE FOR ME, WON'T YOU?
I WANT TO DO THE SAME FOR YOU.

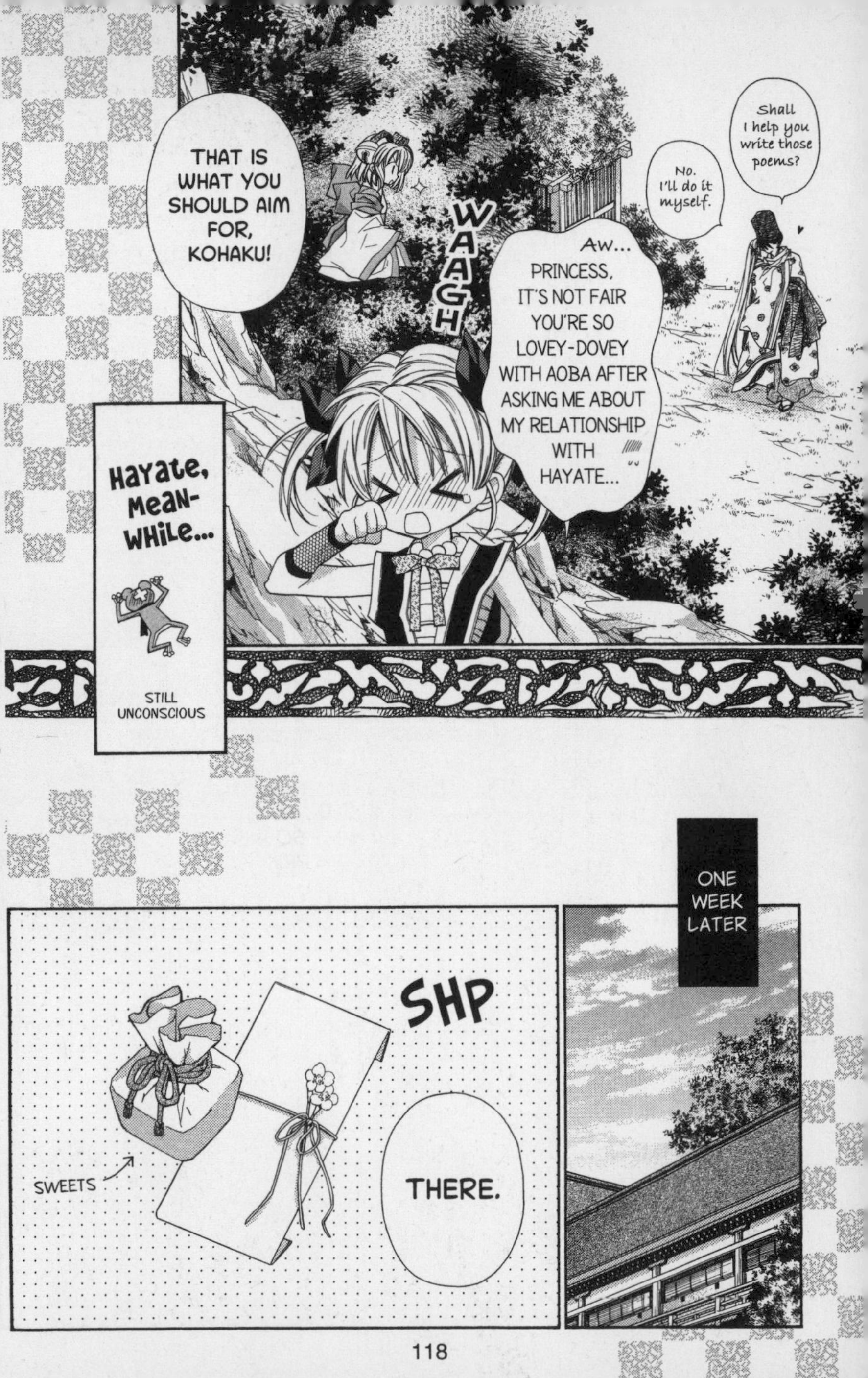
Shall I help you write those poems?
No. I'll do it myself.
Aw... PRINCESS, IT'S NOT FAIR YOU'RE SO LOVEY-DOVEY WITH AOBA AFTER ASKING ME ABOUT MY RELATIONSHIP WITH HAYATE...
WAAAGH
THAT IS WHAT YOU SHOULD AIM FOR, KOHAKU!
Hayate, Mean-while...
STILL UNCONSCIOUS
ONE WEEK LATER
SHP
THERE.
SWEETS

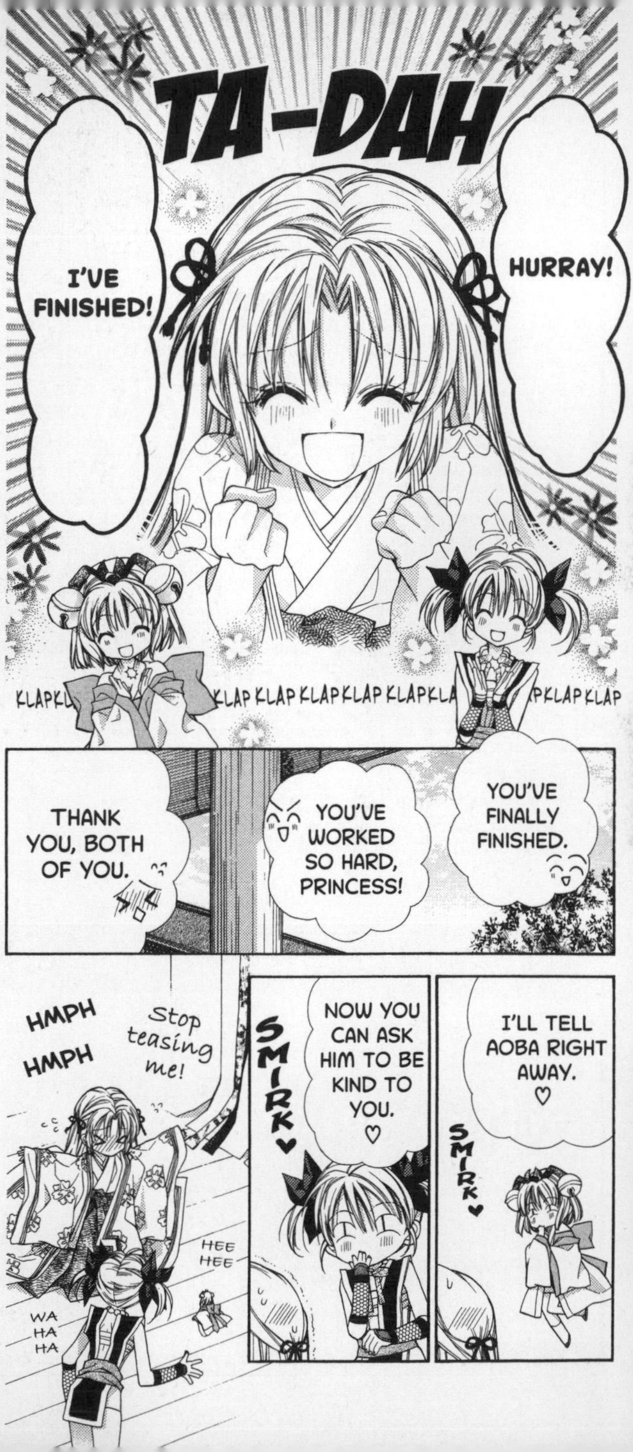
TA-DAH
HURRAY!
I'VE FINISHED!
KLAPKLAP KLAP KLAP KLAPKLAP KLAPKLAP KLAPKLAP KLAP
YOU'VE FINALLY FINISHED.
YOU'VE WORKED SO HARD, PRINCESS!
THANK YOU, BOTH OF YOU.
I'LL TELL AOBA RIGHT AWAY. ♡
SMIRK♥
NOW YOU CAN ASK HIM TO BE KIND TO YOU. ♡
SMIRK♥
Stop teasing me!
HMPH
HMPH
HEE HEE
WA HA HA

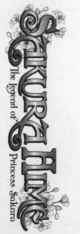

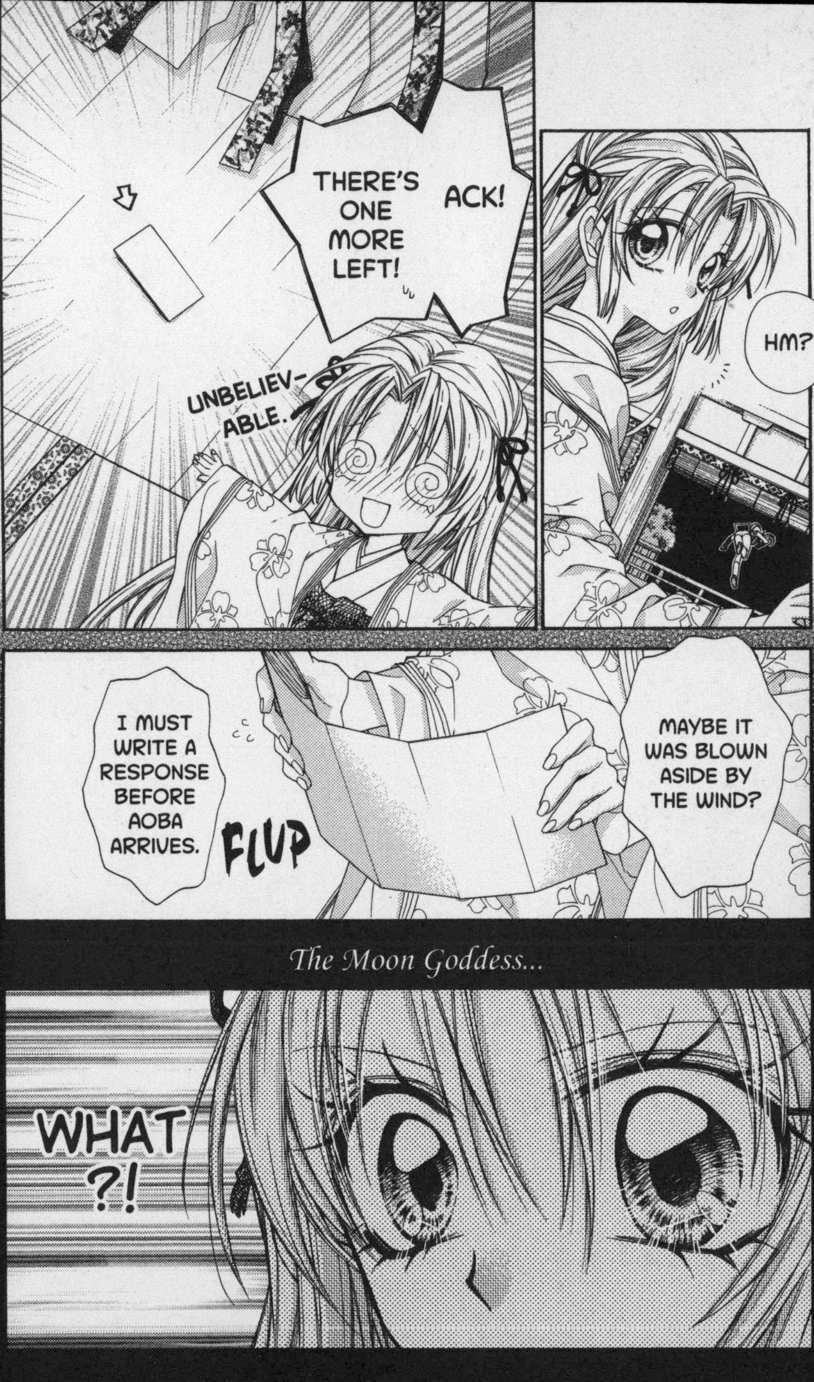
HM?
ACK!
THERE'S ONE MORE LEFT!
UNBELIEV-ABLE.
MAYBE IT WAS BLOWN ASIDE BY THE WIND?
FLUP
I MUST WRITE A RESPONSE BEFORE AOBA ARRIVES.
The Moon Goddess...
WHAT?!

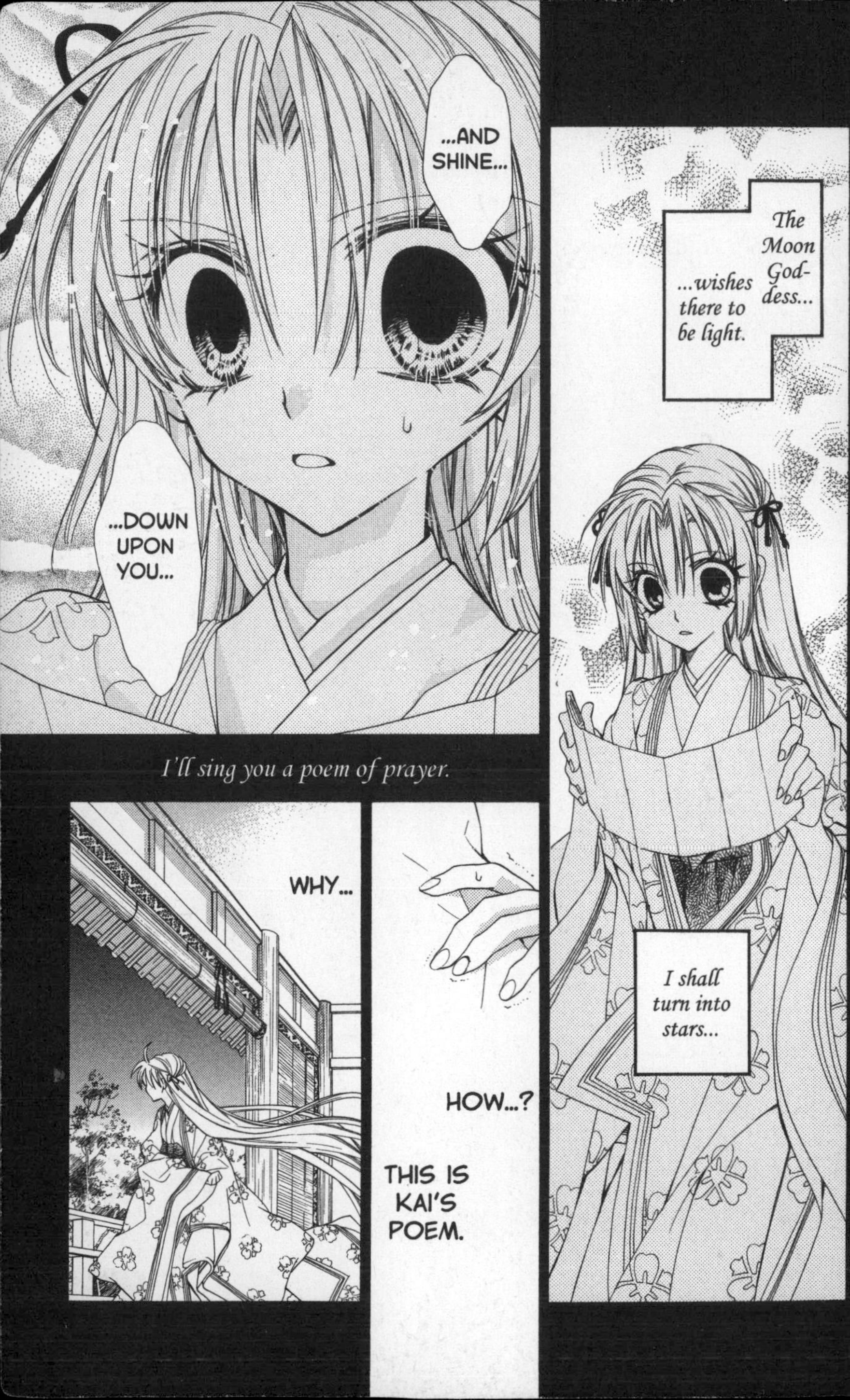
The Moon God-dess...
...wishes there to be light.
I shall turn into stars...
...AND SHINE...
...DOWN UPON YOU...
I'll sing you a poem of prayer.
HOW...?
THIS IS KAI'S POEM.
WHY...

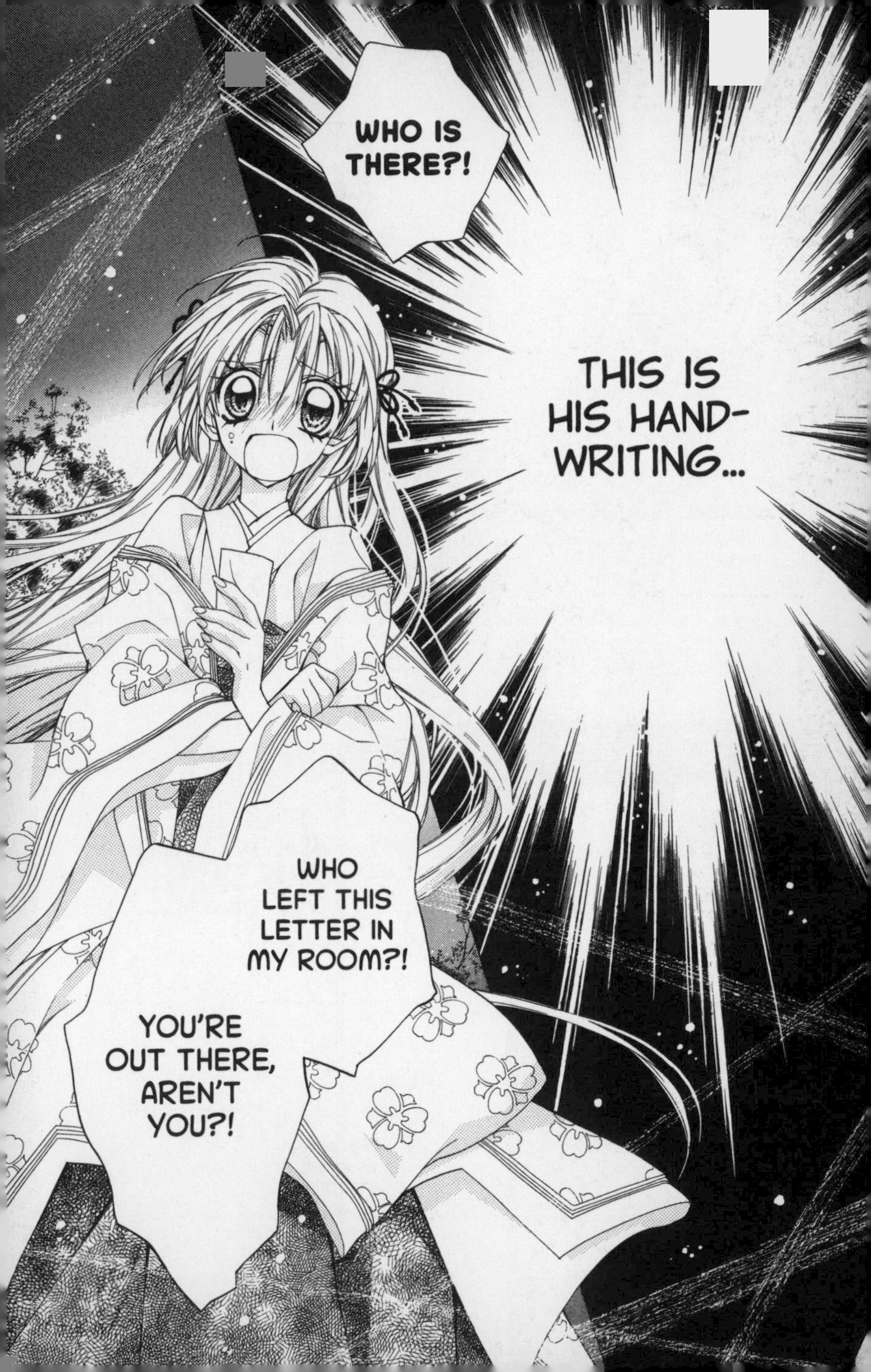
WHO IS THERE?!
THIS IS HIS HAND-WRITING...
WHO LEFT THIS LETTER IN MY ROOM?!
YOU'RE OUT THERE, AREN'T YOU?!

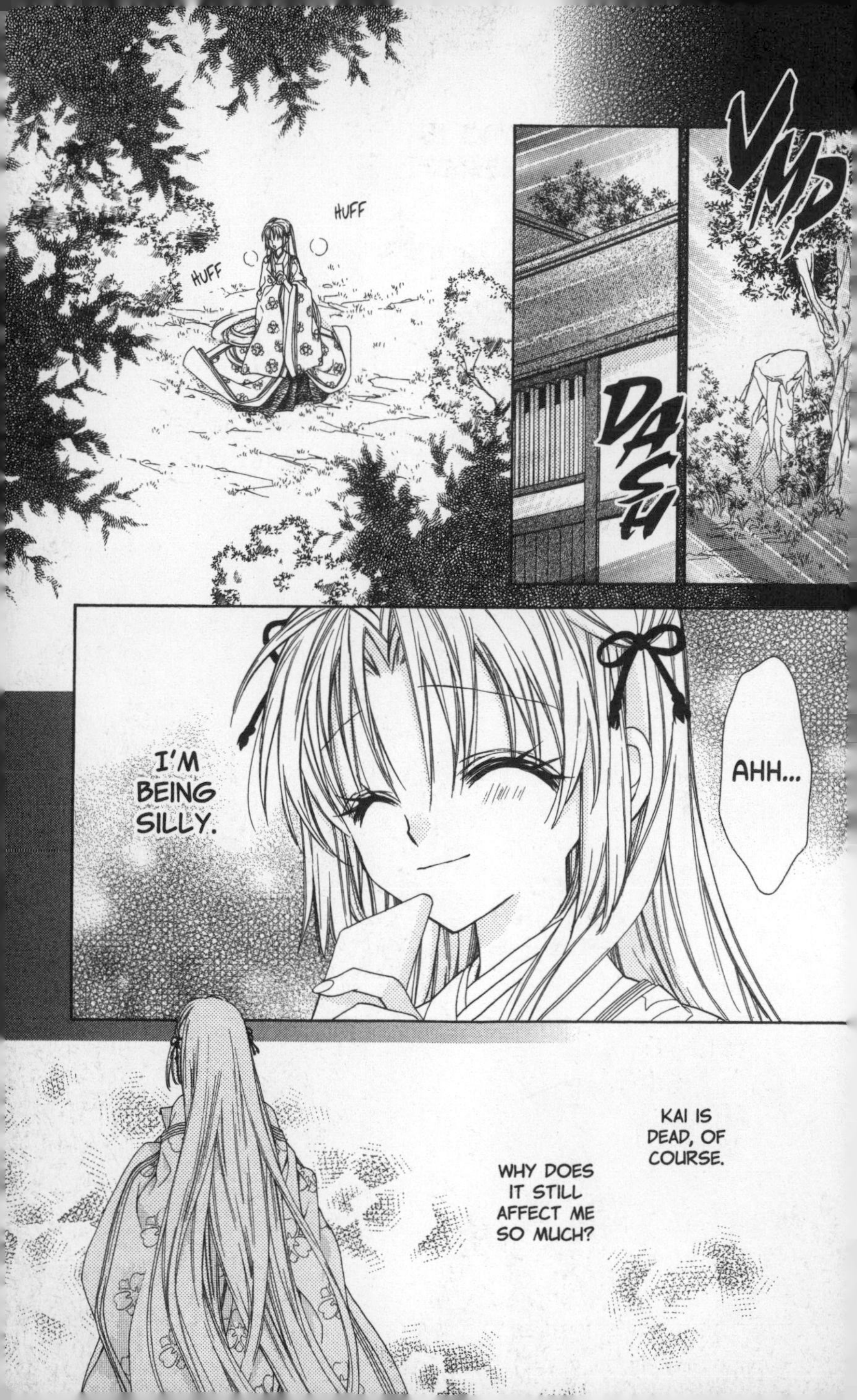
VMP
DASH
HUFF
HUFF
AHH...
I'M BEING SILLY.
KAI IS DEAD, OF COURSE.
WHY DOES IT STILL AFFECT ME SO MUCH?

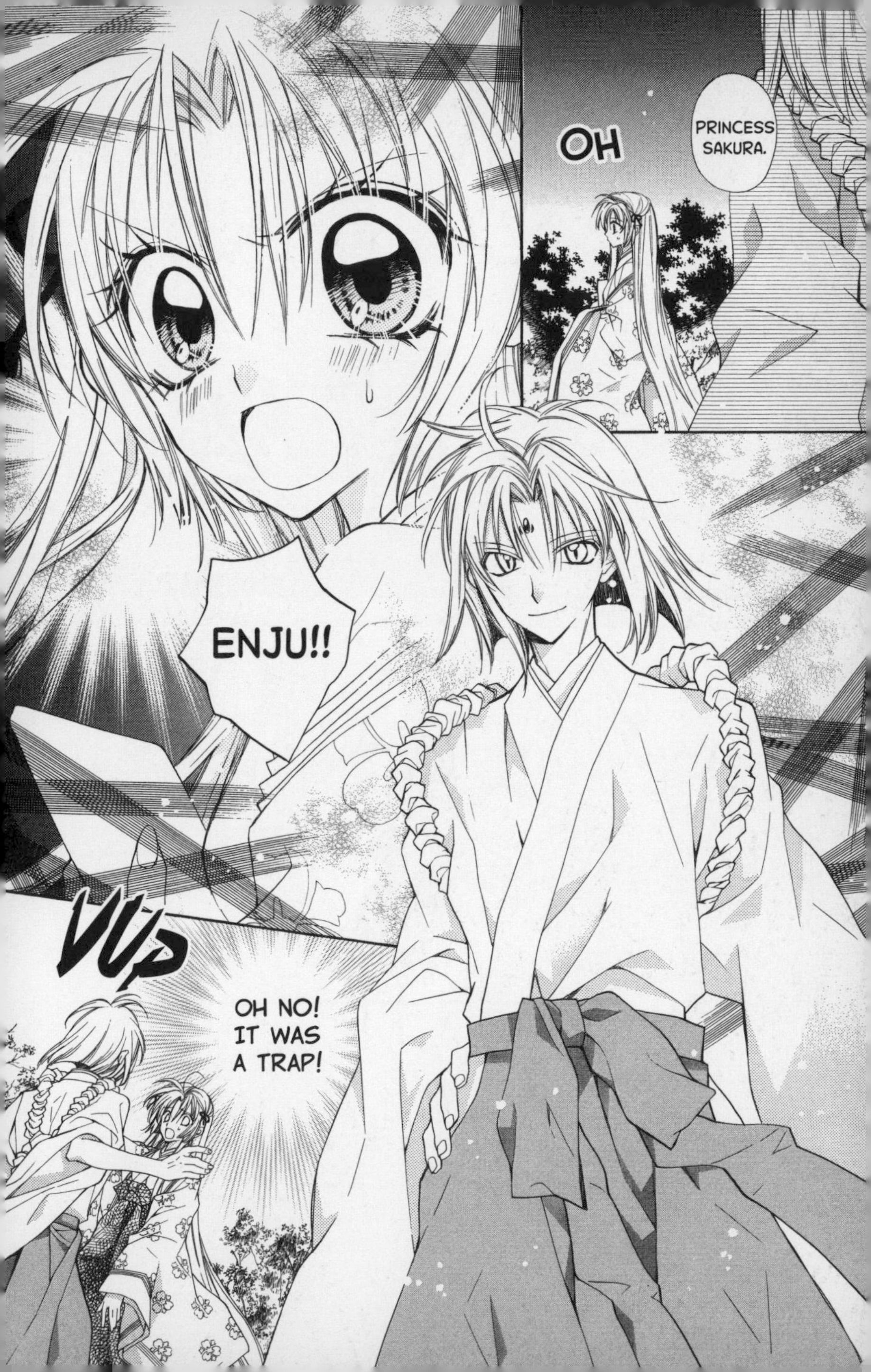
PRINCESS SAKURA.
OH
ENJU!!
VUP
OH NO! IT WAS A TRAP!

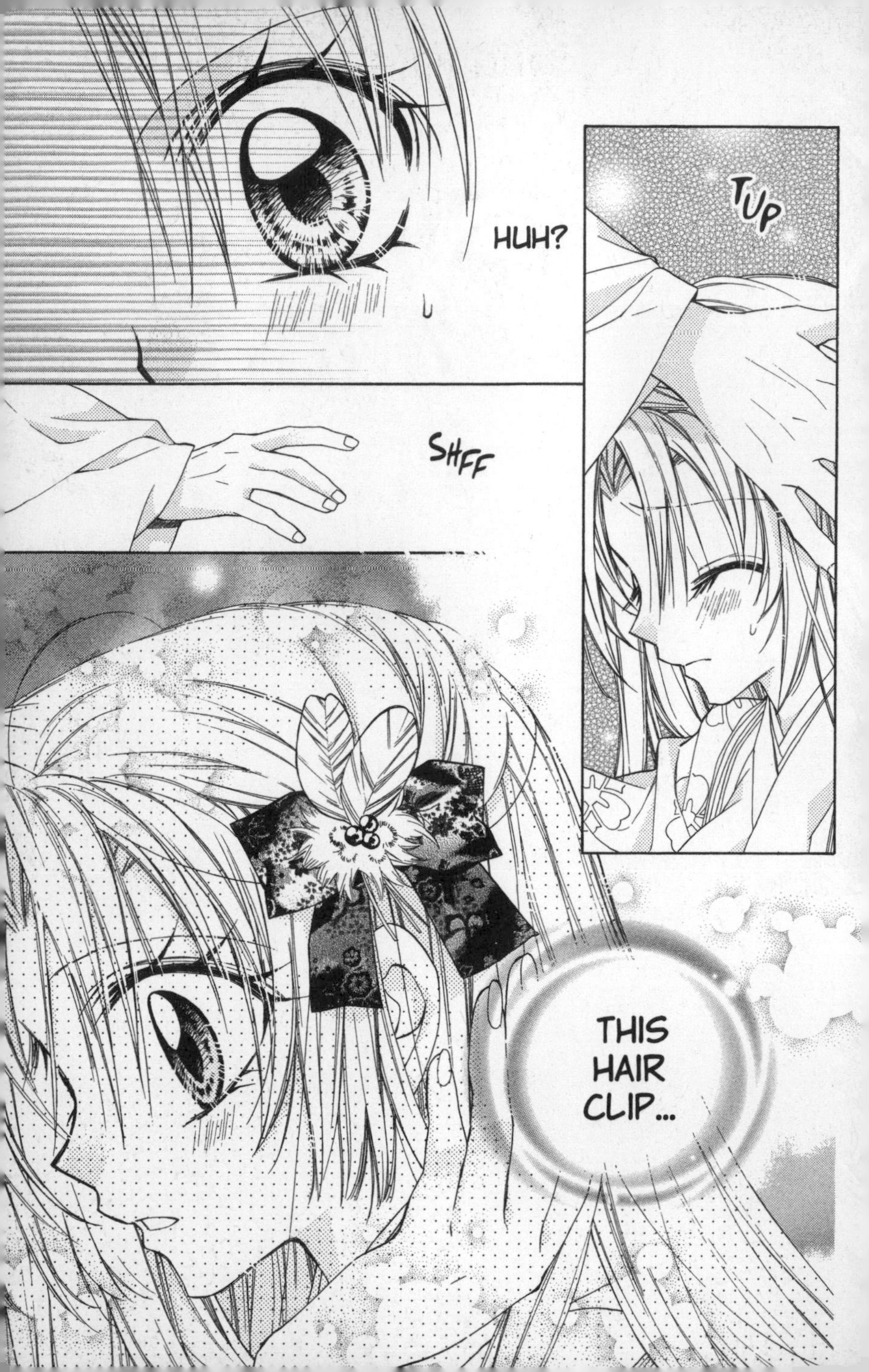
TUP
HUH?
SHFF
THIS HAIR CLIP...

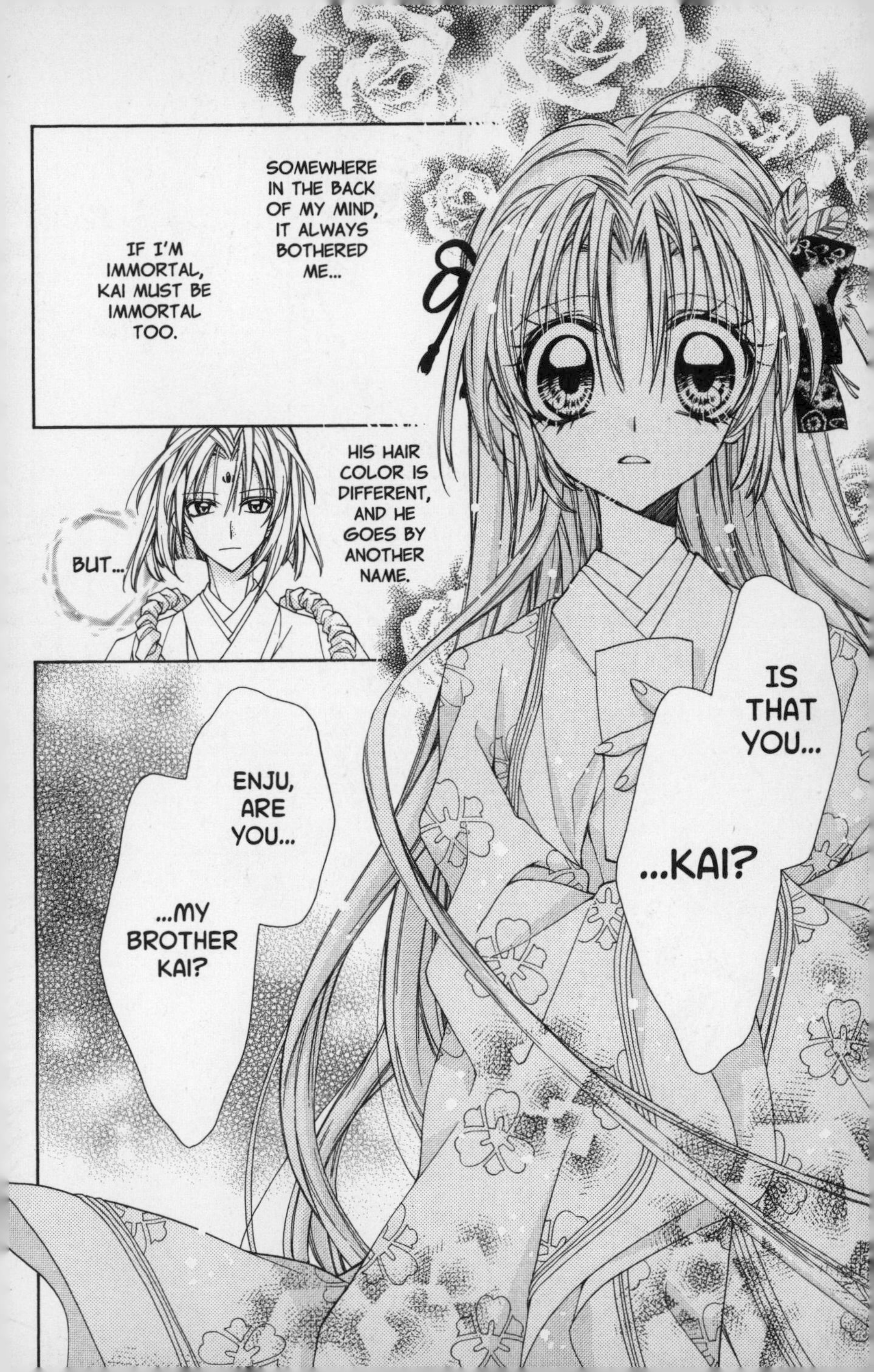
IS THAT YOU...
...KAI?
SOMEWHERE IN THE BACK OF MY MIND, IT ALWAYS BOTHERED ME...
IF I'M IMMORTAL, KAI MUST BE IMMORTAL TOO.
HIS HAIR COLOR IS DIFFERENT, AND HE GOES BY ANOTHER NAME.
BUT...
ENJU, ARE YOU...
...MY BROTHER KAI?

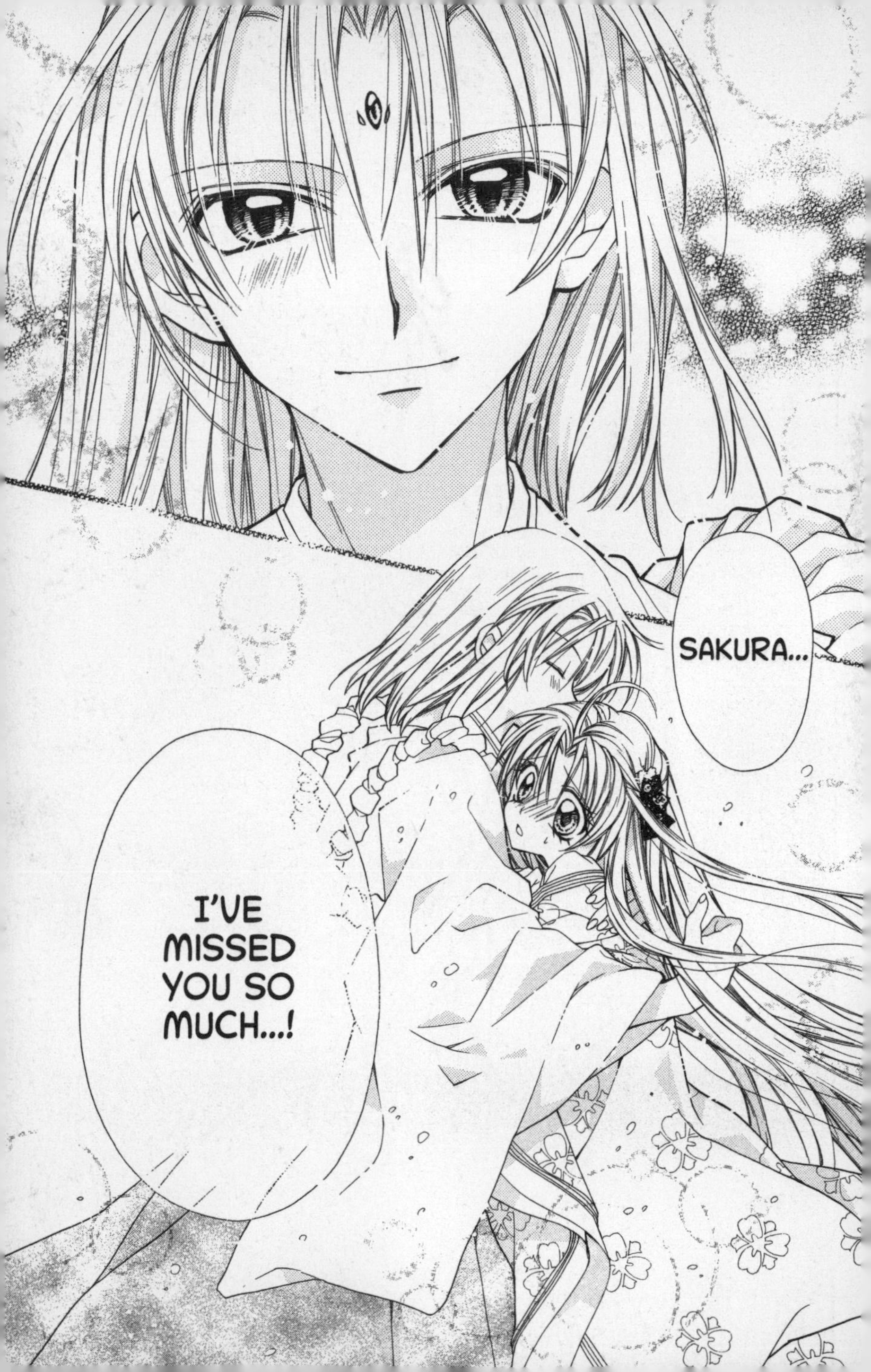
SAKURA...
I'VE MISSED YOU SO MUCH...!

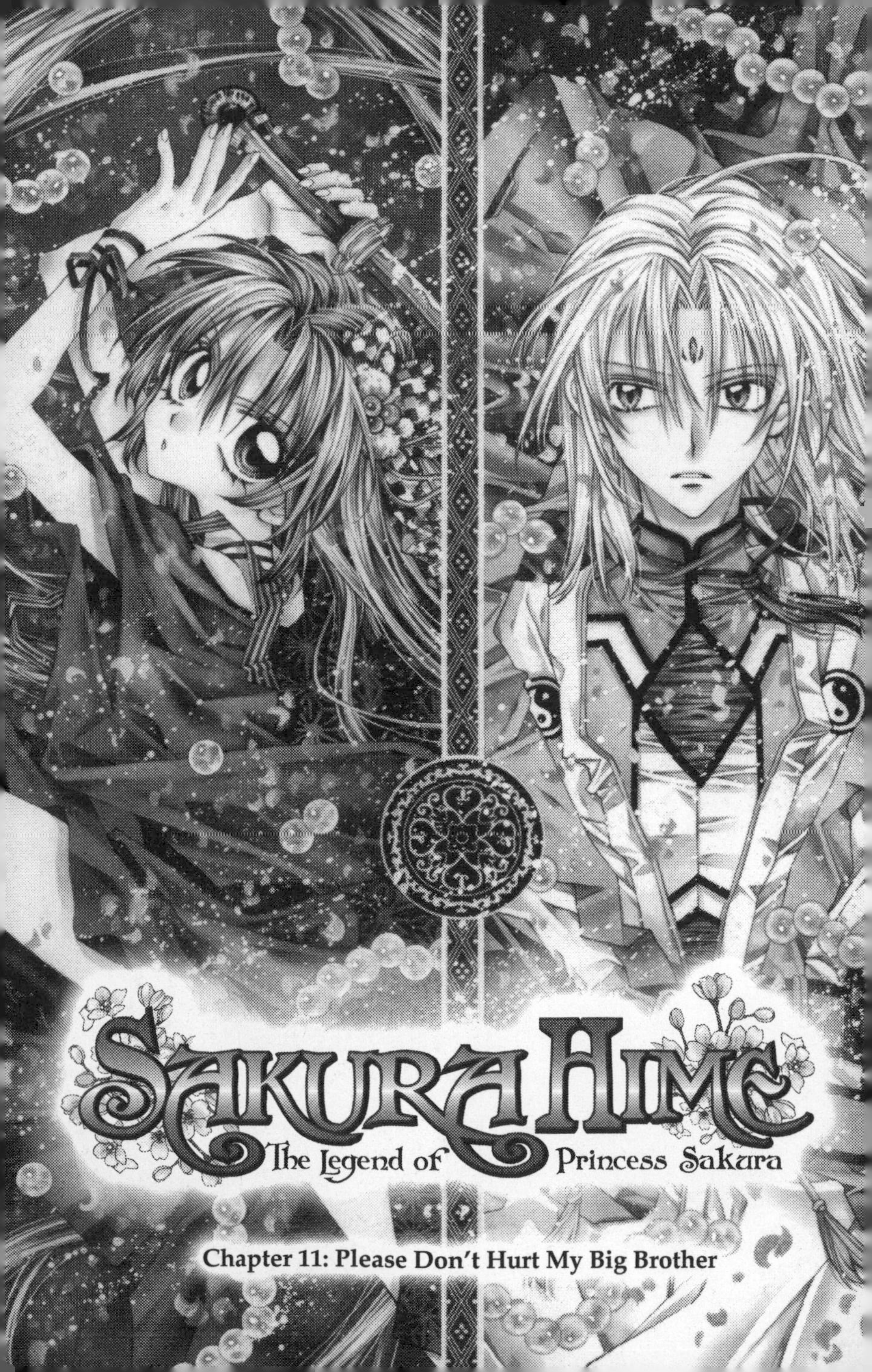
Sakura Hime
The Legend of Princess Sakura
Chapter 11: Please Don't Hurt My Big Brother

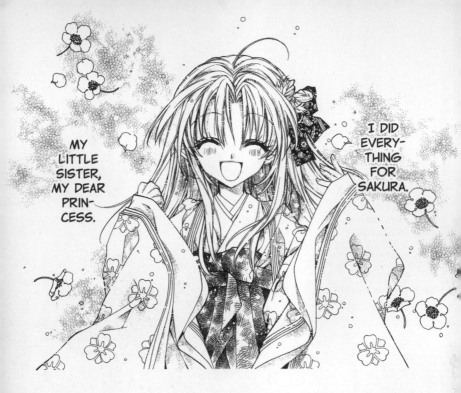

I DID EVERY-THING FOR SAKURA.
MY LITTLE SISTER, MY DEAR PRIN-CESS.

Chapter 11: Please Don't Hurt My Big Brother Lead-in Overwhelming love bares its fangs tonight.

※ I'm giving away the story.

Several chapter titles happen to be lines right out of *Sakura Hime*. The pages with the chapter titles are sent to the printer before I work on the storyboard, so I'm always worried if the chapter title will fit the final version.
I use text from the story when I'm certain the chapter will center on that very line. This chapter focuses on...how Enju is deeply hurt.

I felt as if I was suffocating while I worked on the water chamber scene, even when I did the storyboard.
It was a challenging chapter for me as a mangaka.
Like Enju said, there is a part of him that has gone insane. So something about him isn't right.
I wonder if that's how people would turn out after dying and being revived many times?

The only thing that has not changed is his love for Sakura. Kai always knew that he and Sakura were from the moon. That probably made him care for Sakura all the more as there was no one else he could call a friend apart from her.
You'll learn more about the people from the moon (the four new characters you see at the end + Enju) in the next chapter.
To be continued in volume 4! Thank you very much. ♪

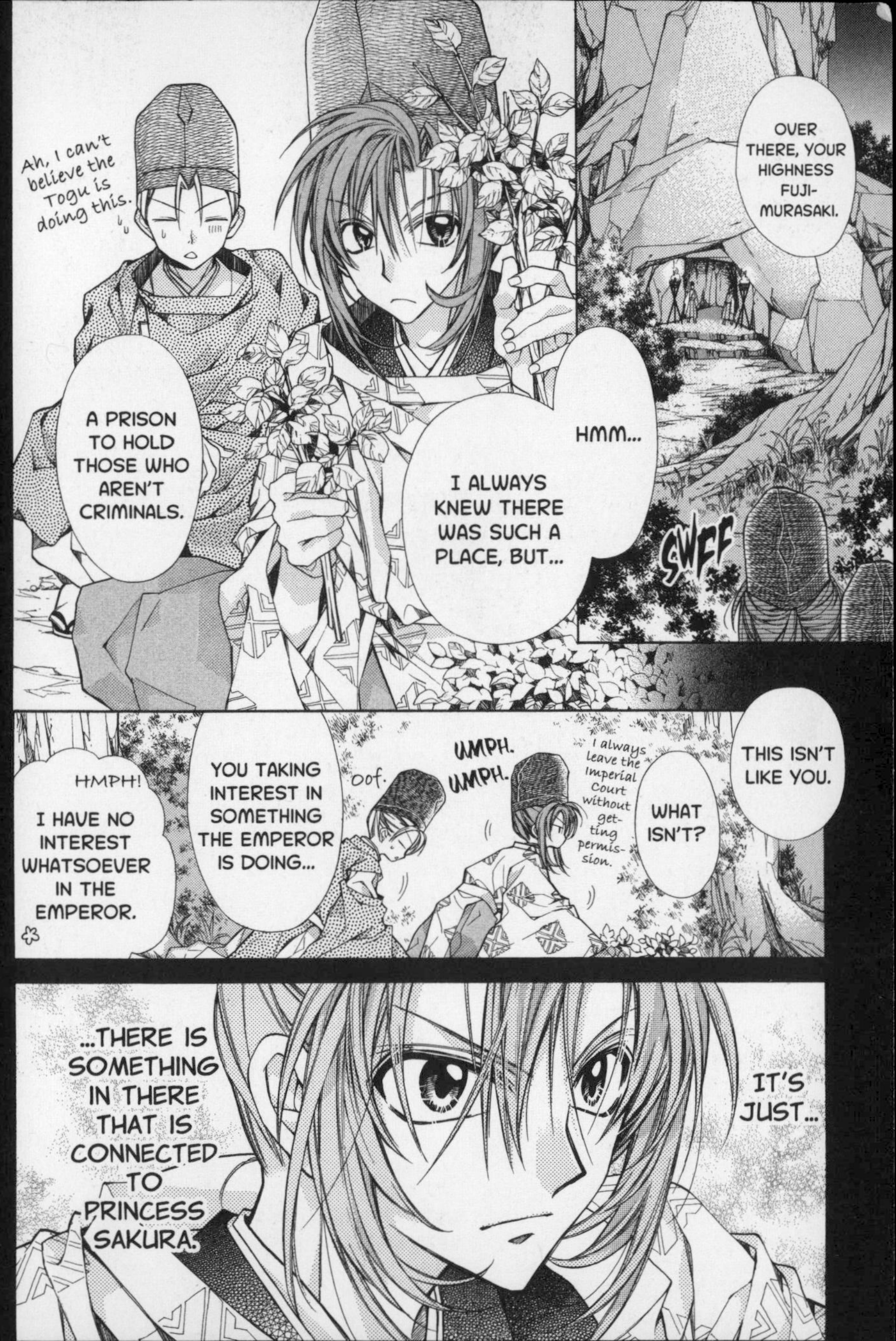
OVER THERE, YOUR HIGHNESS FUJI-MURASAKI.
SWFF
HMM...
I ALWAYS KNEW THERE WAS SUCH A PLACE, BUT...
A PRISON TO HOLD THOSE WHO AREN'T CRIMINALS.
Ah, I can't believe the Togu is doing this.
THIS ISN'T LIKE YOU.
WHAT ISN'T?
I always leave the Imperial Court without getting permission.
UMPH. UMPH.
Oof.
YOU TAKING INTEREST IN SOMETHING THE EMPEROR IS DOING...
HMPH!
I HAVE NO INTEREST WHATSOEVER IN THE EMPEROR.
IT'S JUST...
...THERE IS SOMETHING IN THERE THAT IS CONNECTED TO PRINCESS SAKURA.

Germany Diary 3

By the way, *Mistress Fortune* had been published in a hurry to make it in time for this event. Everybody knew my face after the autograph session, so afterward in the corridor I was bombarded with "Please give me your autograph...!" I was so popular. (laugh)

I had some free time on my hands, so I signed autographs in the corridor for about an hour, but there'd be people sitting along the side of the corridor who'd suddenly stand up, and three out of ten would pull out my art book from their bags and line up to get it signed! Wow! There were so many people who knew about me! I kept signing autographs and forgot I was covered in sweat from all the excitement! (I signed a special autograph card for the people who attended the autograph session, but I signed manga and whatnot here.) I even had...

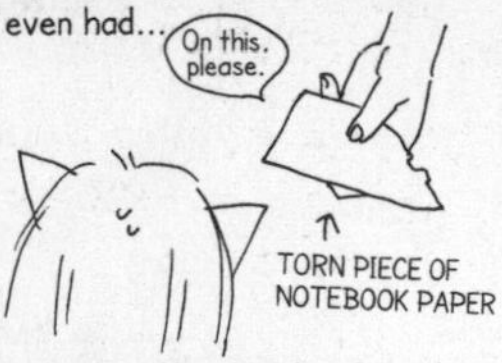
On this, please.
TORN PIECE OF NOTEBOOK PAPER

...something like this, but I tried to do everything I could. I think I signed autographs for 50-70 people?

I continued to give autographs and take photographs with people who came over to talk to me on the second day too. (I don't usually have a lot of time in Japan, so I can't do things like that.) And when my name was called out at the closing ceremony and I went out onto the stage, I received much greater applause than at the opening ceremony...

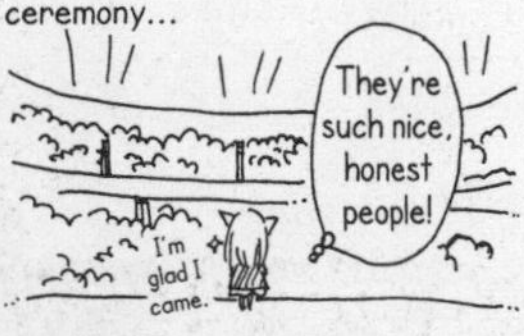
They're such nice, honest people!
I'm glad I came.

That's what I thought.

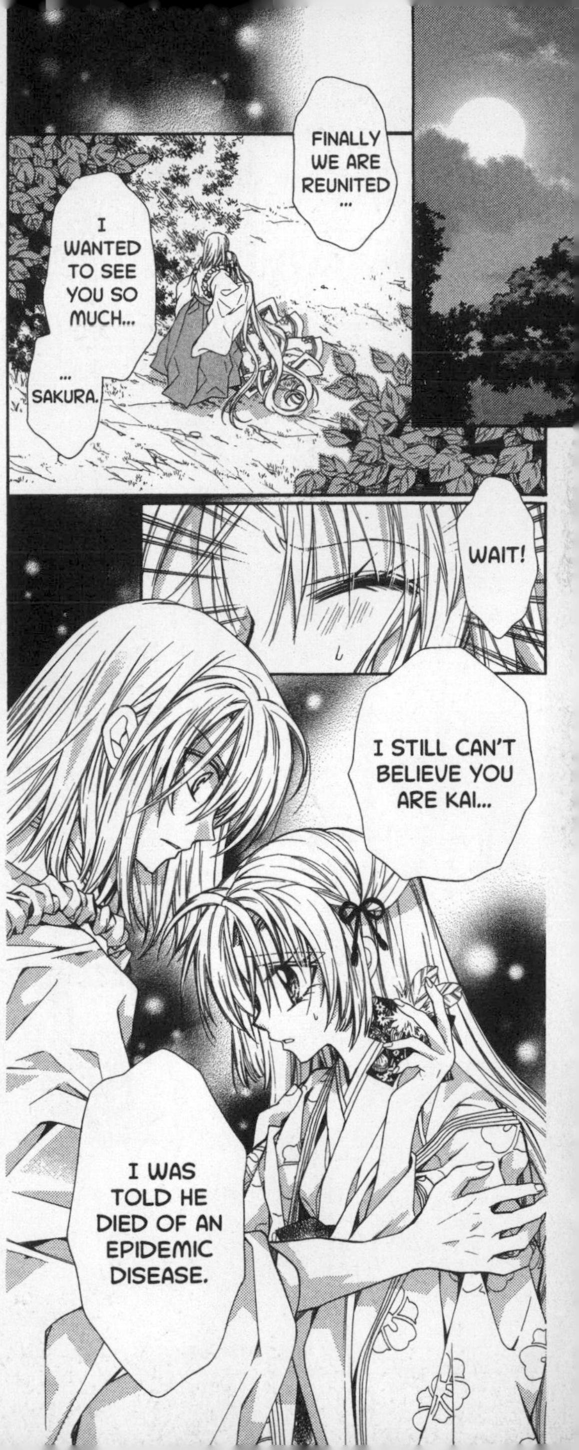
FINALLY WE ARE REUNITED ...
I WANTED TO SEE YOU SO MUCH...
... SAKURA.
WAIT!
I STILL CAN'T BELIEVE YOU ARE KAI...
I WAS TOLD HE DIED OF AN EPIDEMIC DISEASE.

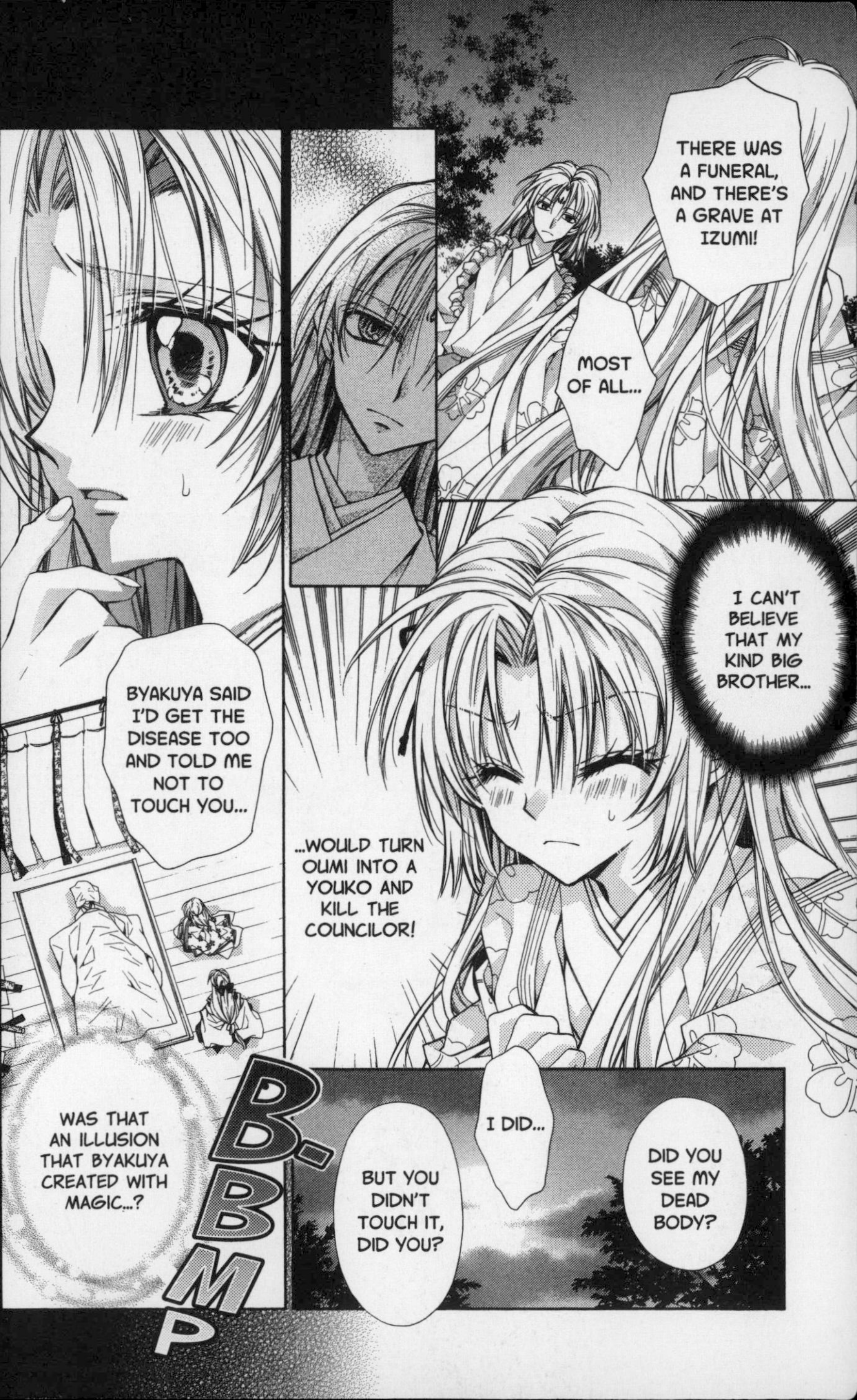
THERE WAS A FUNERAL, AND THERE'S A GRAVE AT IZUMI!
MOST OF ALL...
I CAN'T BELIEVE THAT MY KIND BIG BROTHER...
...WOULD TURN OUMI INTO A YOUKO AND KILL THE COUNCILOR!
DID YOU SEE MY DEAD BODY?
I DID...
BUT YOU DIDN'T TOUCH IT, DID YOU?
BYAKUYA SAID I'D GET THE DISEASE TOO AND TOLD ME NOT TO TOUCH YOU...
B-BMP
WAS THAT AN ILLUSION THAT BYAKUYA CREATED WITH MAGIC...?

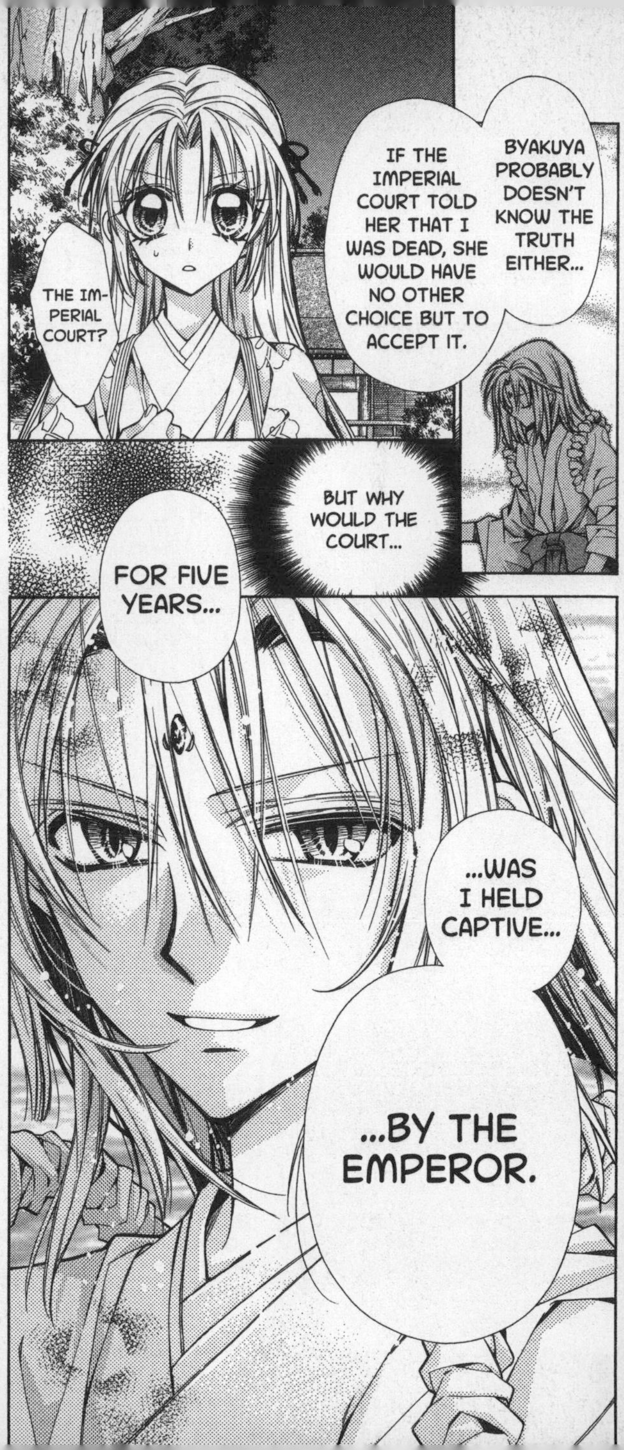
BYAKUYA PROBABLY DOESN'T KNOW THE TRUTH EITHER...
IF THE IMPERIAL COURT TOLD HER THAT I WAS DEAD, SHE WOULD HAVE NO OTHER CHOICE BUT TO ACCEPT IT.
THE IMPERIAL COURT?
BUT WHY WOULD THE COURT...
FOR FIVE YEARS...
...WAS I HELD CAPTIVE...
...BY THE EMPEROR.

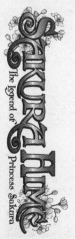

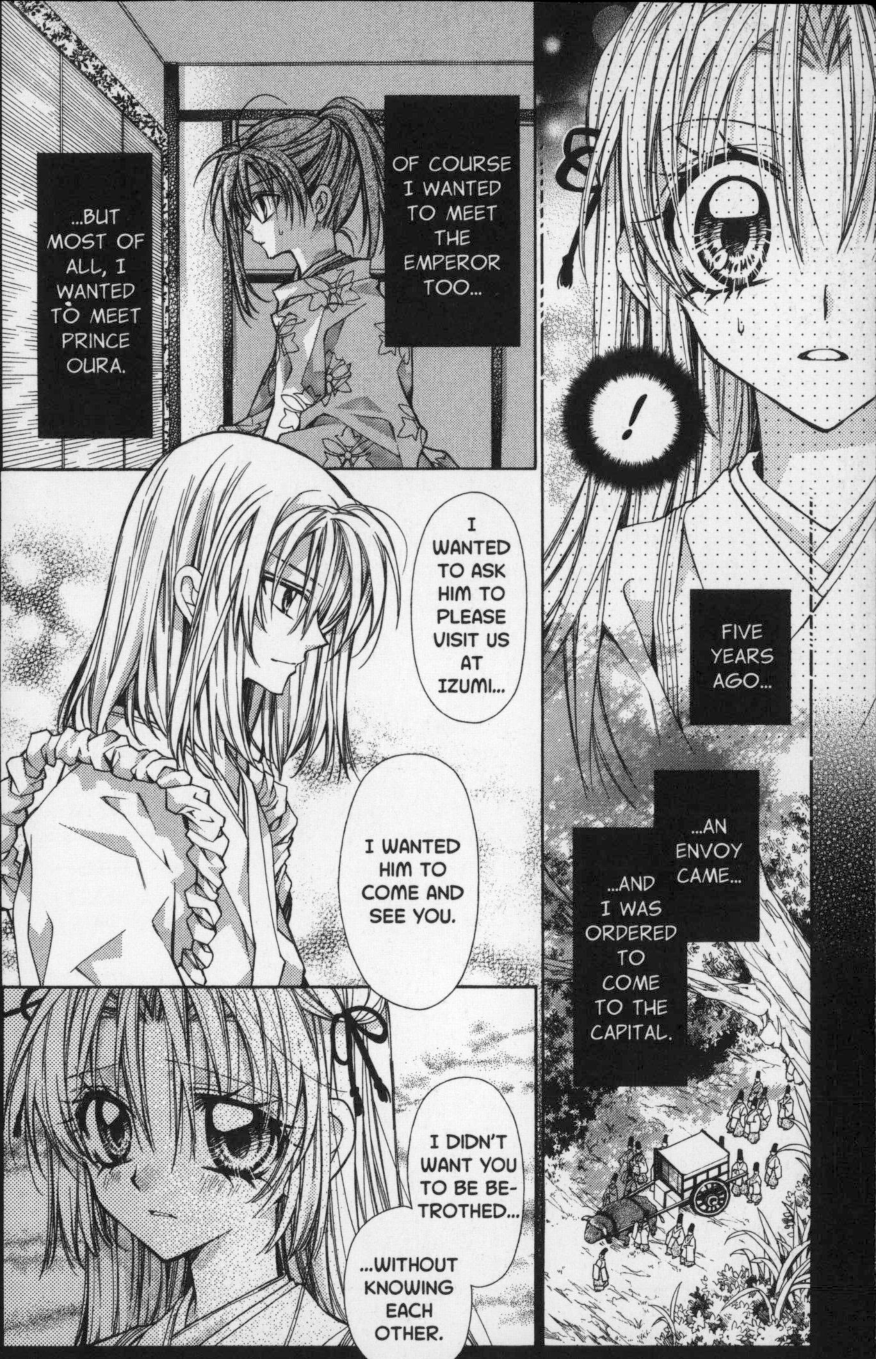
!
FIVE YEARS AGO...
...AN ENVOY CAME...
...AND I WAS ORDERED TO COME TO THE CAPITAL.
OF COURSE I WANTED TO MEET THE EMPEROR TOO...
...BUT MOST OF ALL, I WANTED TO MEET PRINCE OURA.
I WANTED TO ASK HIM TO PLEASE VISIT US AT IZUMI...
I WANTED HIM TO COME AND SEE YOU.
I DIDN'T WANT YOU TO BE BE-TROTHED...
...WITHOUT KNOWING EACH OTHER.

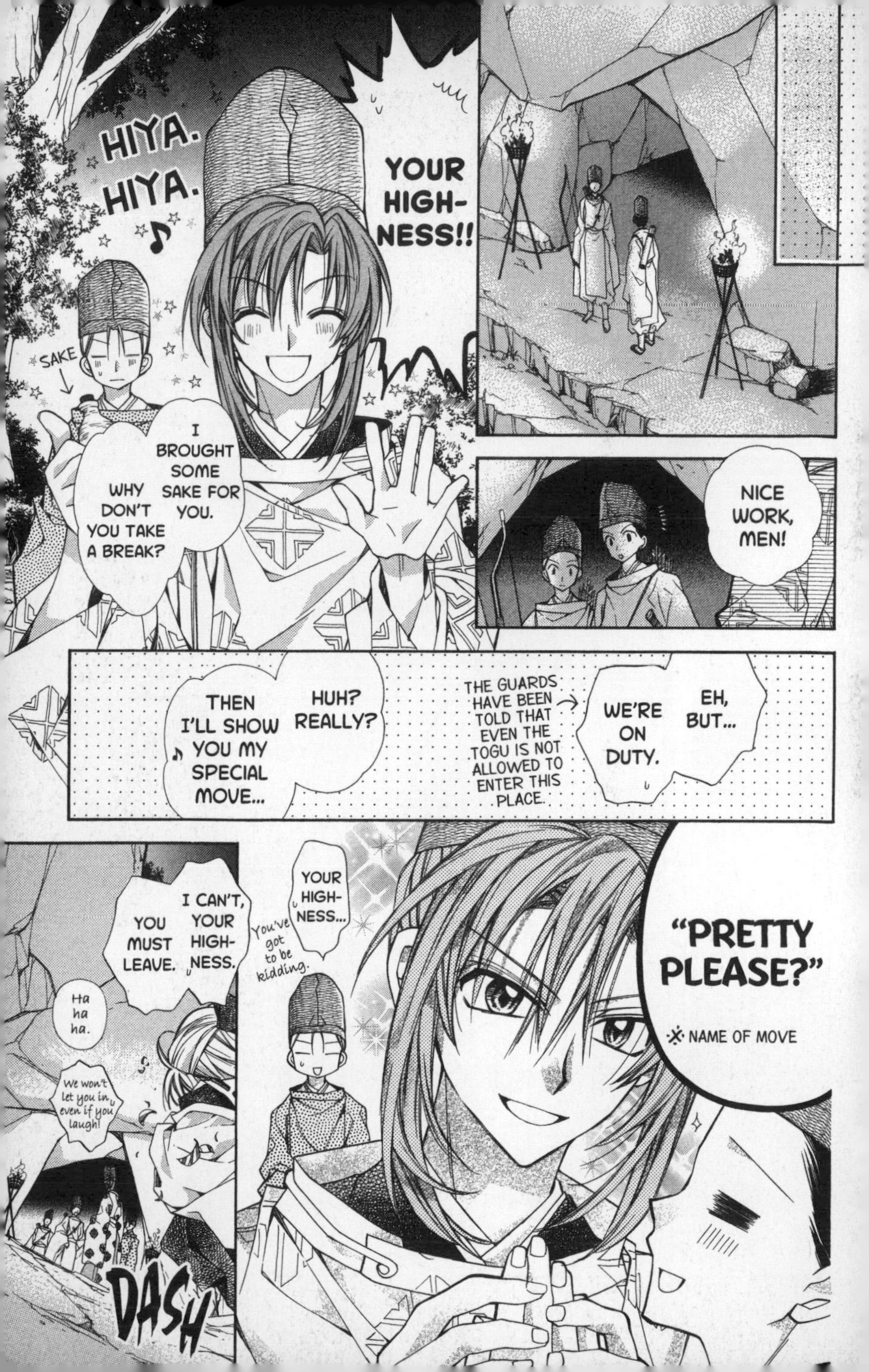
NICE WORK, MEN!
YOUR HIGHNESS!!
HIYA. HIYA. ♪
SAKE
I BROUGHT SOME SAKE FOR YOU. WHY DON'T YOU TAKE A BREAK?
EH, BUT... WE'RE ON DUTY.
THE GUARDS HAVE BEEN TOLD THAT EVEN THE TOGU IS NOT ALLOWED TO ENTER THIS PLACE.
HUH? REALLY?
THEN I'LL SHOW YOU MY SPECIAL MOVE... ♪
"PRETTY PLEASE?"
※NAME OF MOVE
YOUR HIGHNESS...
You've got to be kidding.
I CAN'T, YOUR HIGHNESS. YOU MUST LEAVE.
Ha ha ha.
We won't let you in even if you laugh!
DASH

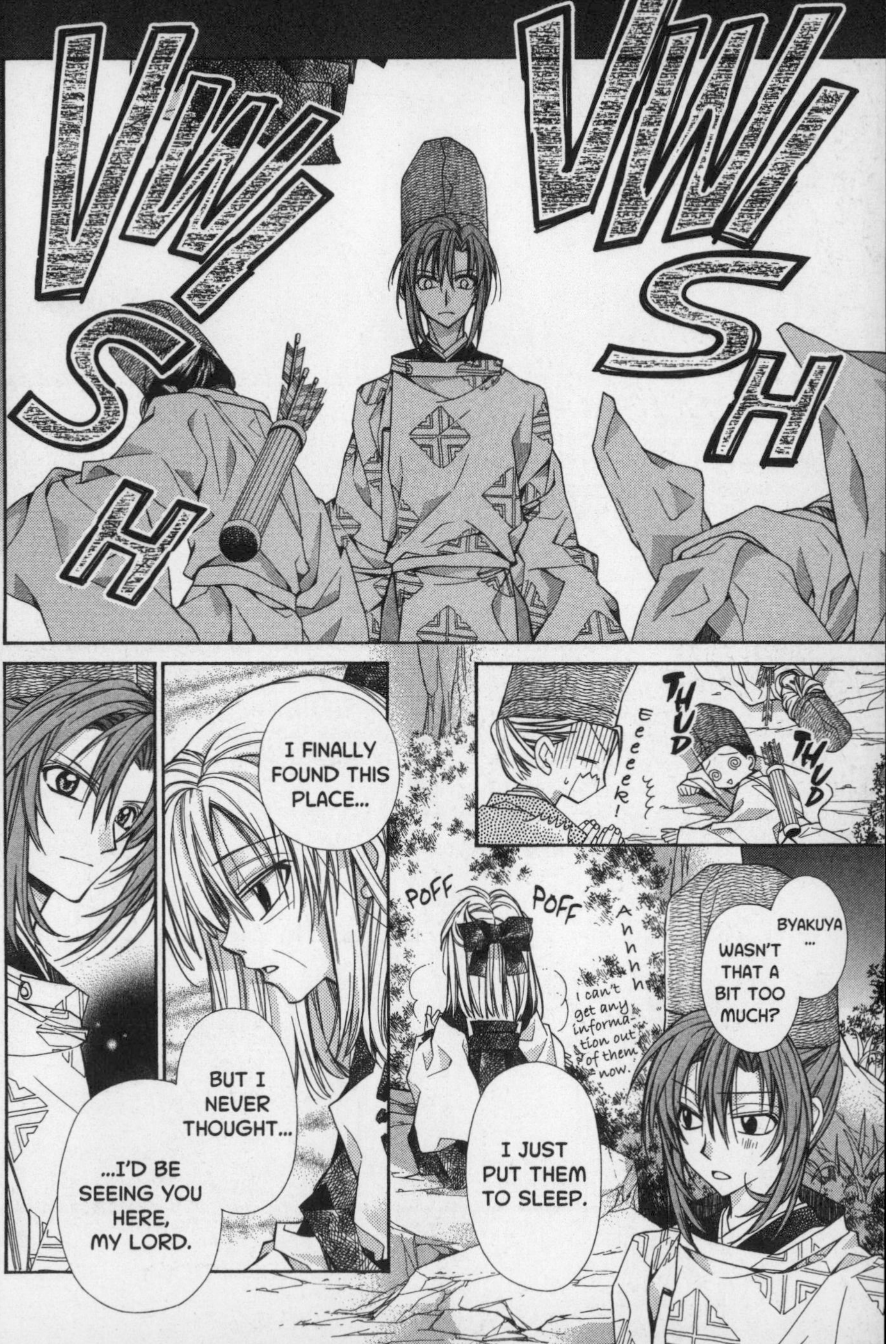
VWISH
VWISH
THUD
Eeeeek!
THUD
BYAKUYA... WASN'T THAT A BIT TOO MUCH?
POFF
POFF
Ahhhh
I can't get any information out of them now.
I JUST PUT THEM TO SLEEP.
I FINALLY FOUND THIS PLACE...
BUT I NEVER THOUGHT...
...I'D BE SEEING YOU HERE, MY LORD.

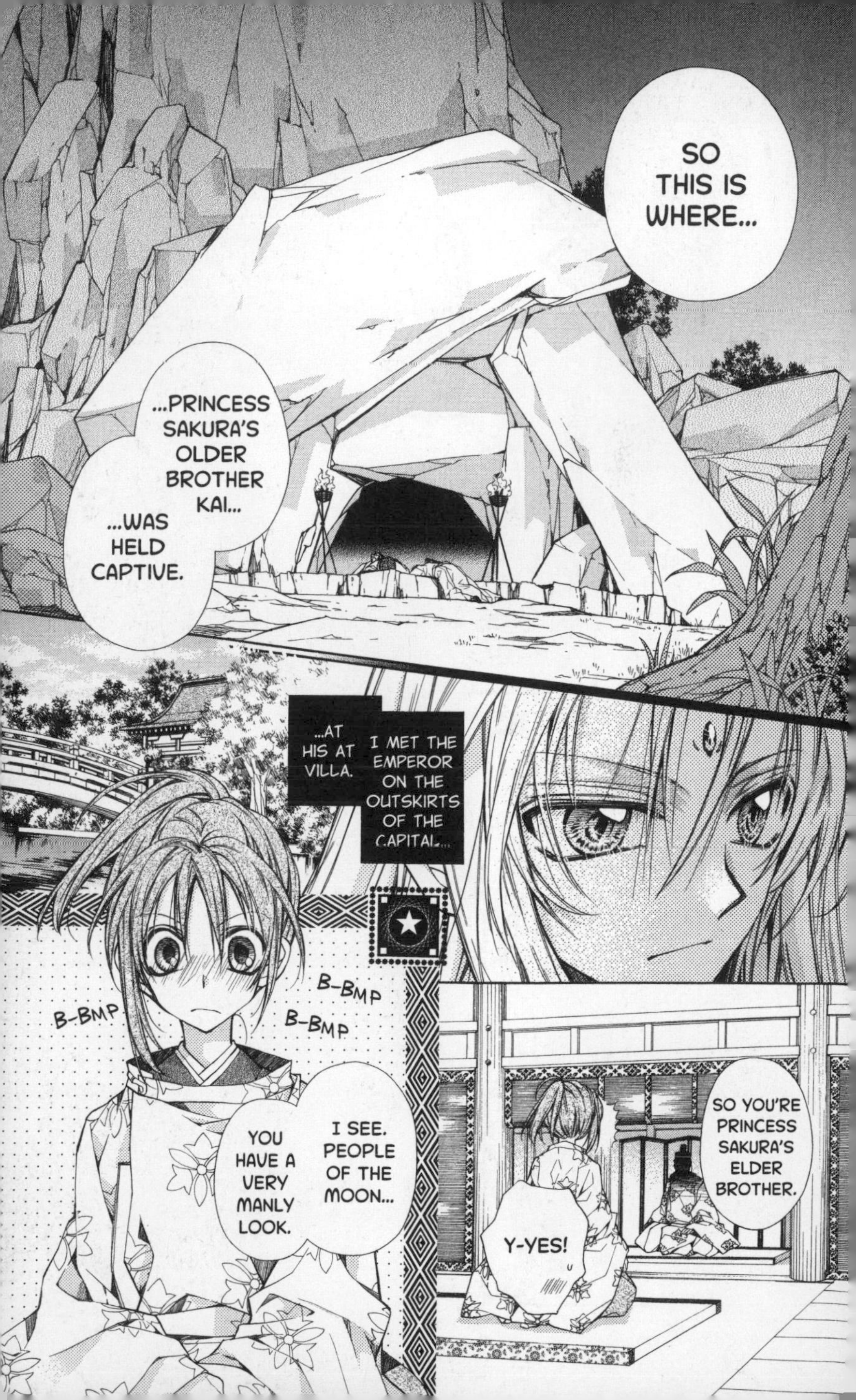
SO THIS IS WHERE...
...PRINCESS SAKURA'S OLDER BROTHER KAI...
...WAS HELD CAPTIVE.
I MET THE EMPEROR ON THE OUTSKIRTS OF THE CAPITAL...
...AT HIS AT VILLA.
SO YOU'RE PRINCESS SAKURA'S ELDER BROTHER.
Y-YES!
I SEE. PEOPLE OF THE MOON...
YOU HAVE A VERY MANLY LOOK.
B-BMP
B-BMP
B-BMP

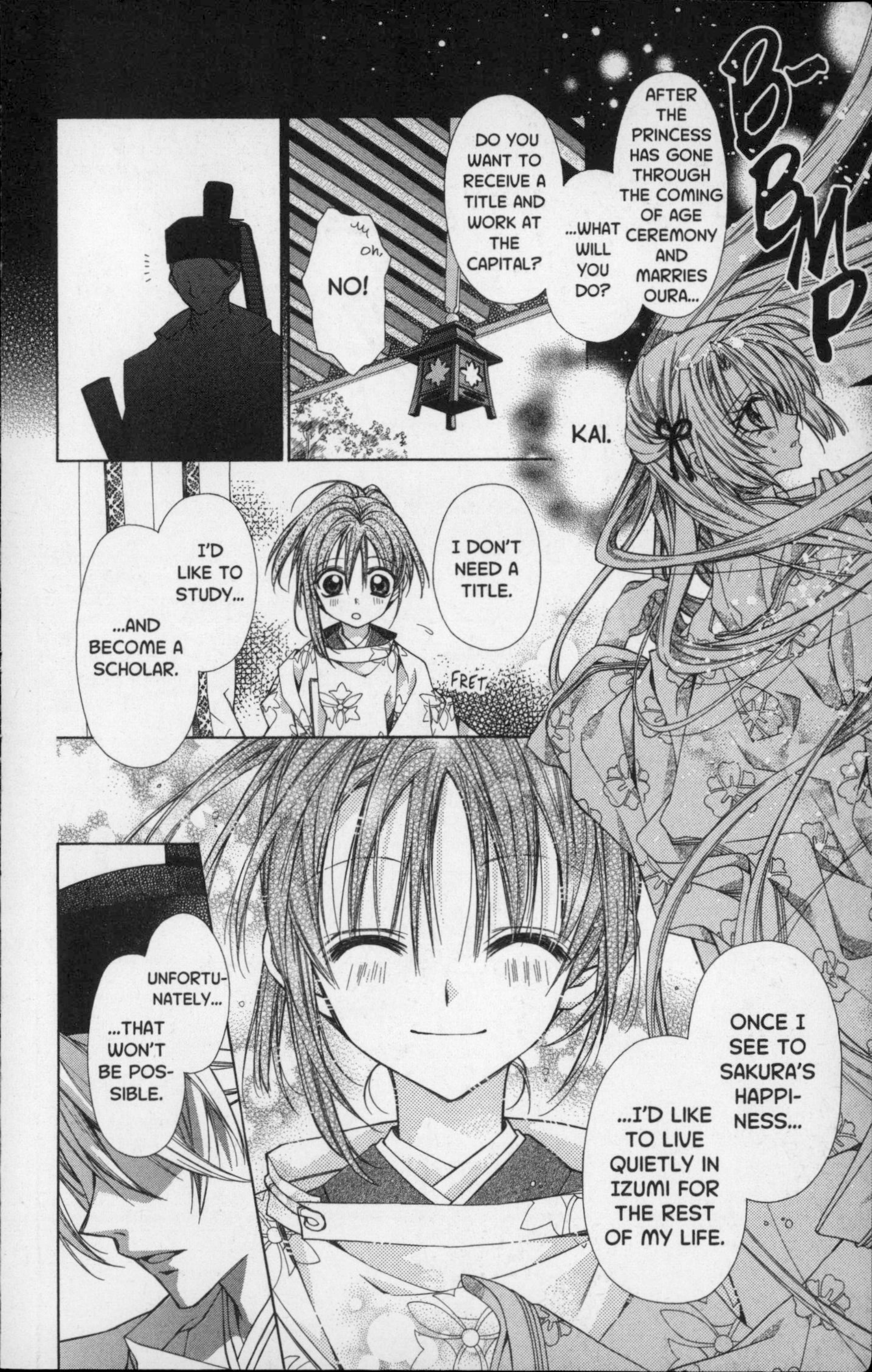
B-BMP
AFTER THE PRINCESS HAS GONE THROUGH THE COMING OF AGE CEREMONY AND MARRIES OURA...
...WHAT WILL YOU DO?
DO YOU WANT TO RECEIVE A TITLE AND WORK AT THE CAPITAL?
Oh, NO!
KAI.
I DON'T NEED A TITLE.
FRET
I'D LIKE TO STUDY...
...AND BECOME A SCHOLAR.
ONCE I SEE TO SAKURA'S HAPPINESS...
...I'D LIKE TO LIVE QUIETLY IN IZUMI FOR THE REST OF MY LIFE.
UNFORTUNATELY...
...THAT WON'T BE POSSIBLE.

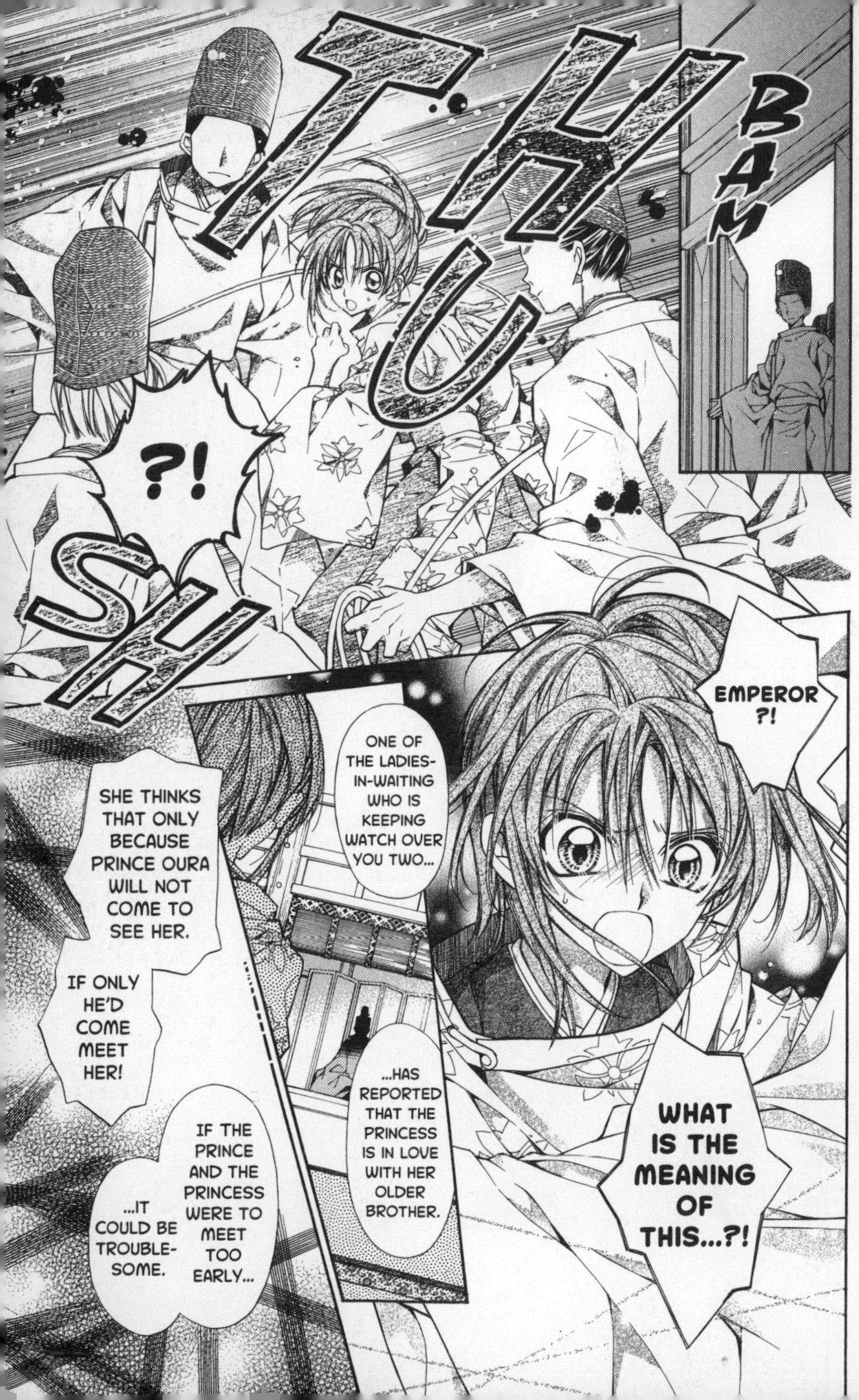
BAM
THUSH
?!
EMPEROR ?!
WHAT IS THE MEANING OF THIS...?!
ONE OF THE LADIES-IN-WAITING WHO IS KEEPING WATCH OVER YOU TWO...
...HAS REPORTED THAT THE PRINCESS IS IN LOVE WITH HER OLDER BROTHER.
SHE THINKS THAT ONLY BECAUSE PRINCE OURA WILL NOT COME TO SEE HER.
IF ONLY HE'D COME MEET HER!
IF THE PRINCE AND THE PRINCESS WERE TO MEET TOO EARLY...
...IT COULD BE TROUBLE-SOME.

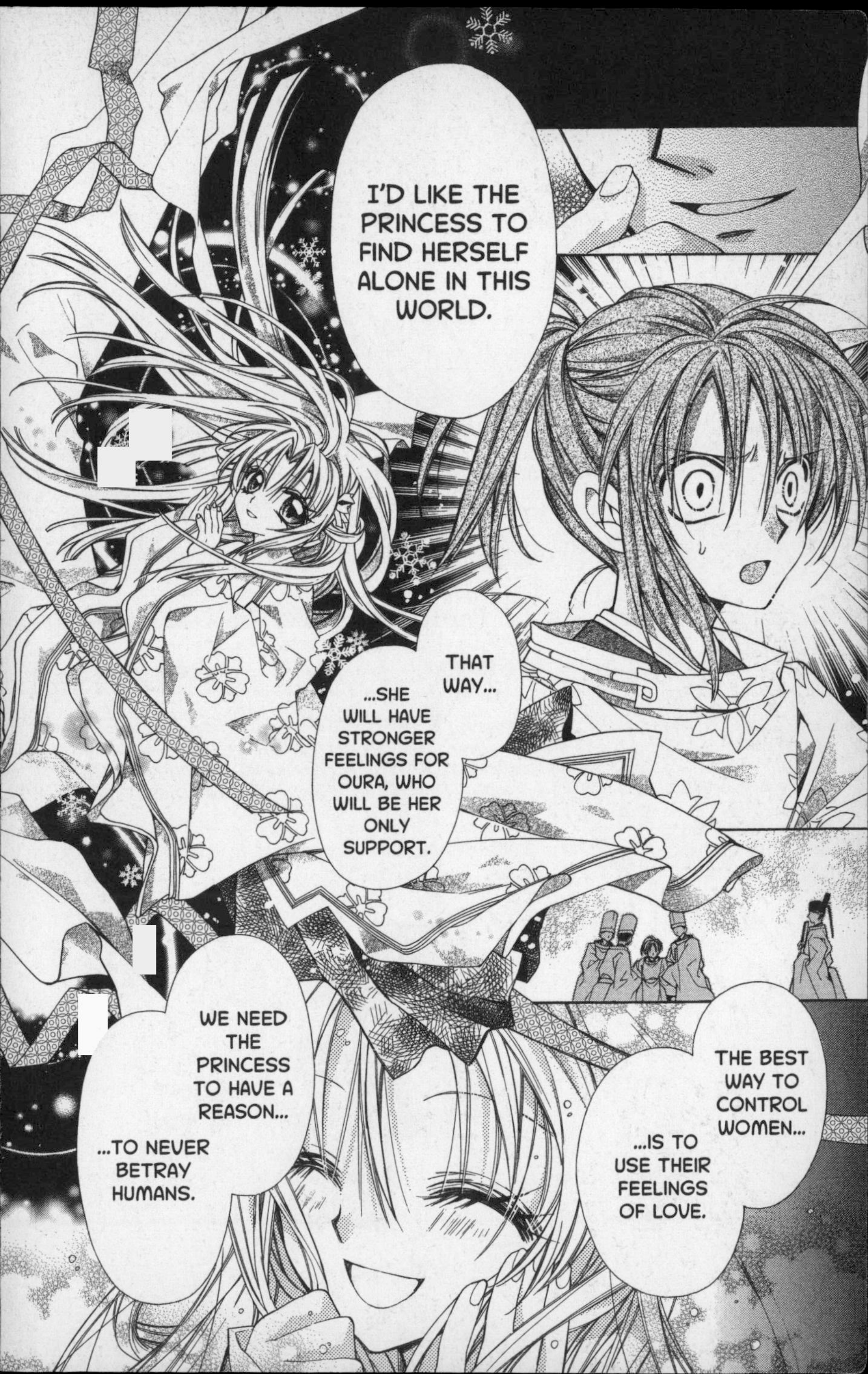
I'D LIKE THE PRINCESS TO FIND HERSELF ALONE IN THIS WORLD.
THAT WAY...
...SHE WILL HAVE STRONGER FEELINGS FOR OURA, WHO WILL BE HER ONLY SUPPORT.
THE BEST WAY TO CONTROL WOMEN...
...IS TO USE THEIR FEELINGS OF LOVE.
WE NEED THE PRINCESS TO HAVE A REASON...
...TO NEVER BETRAY HUMANS.

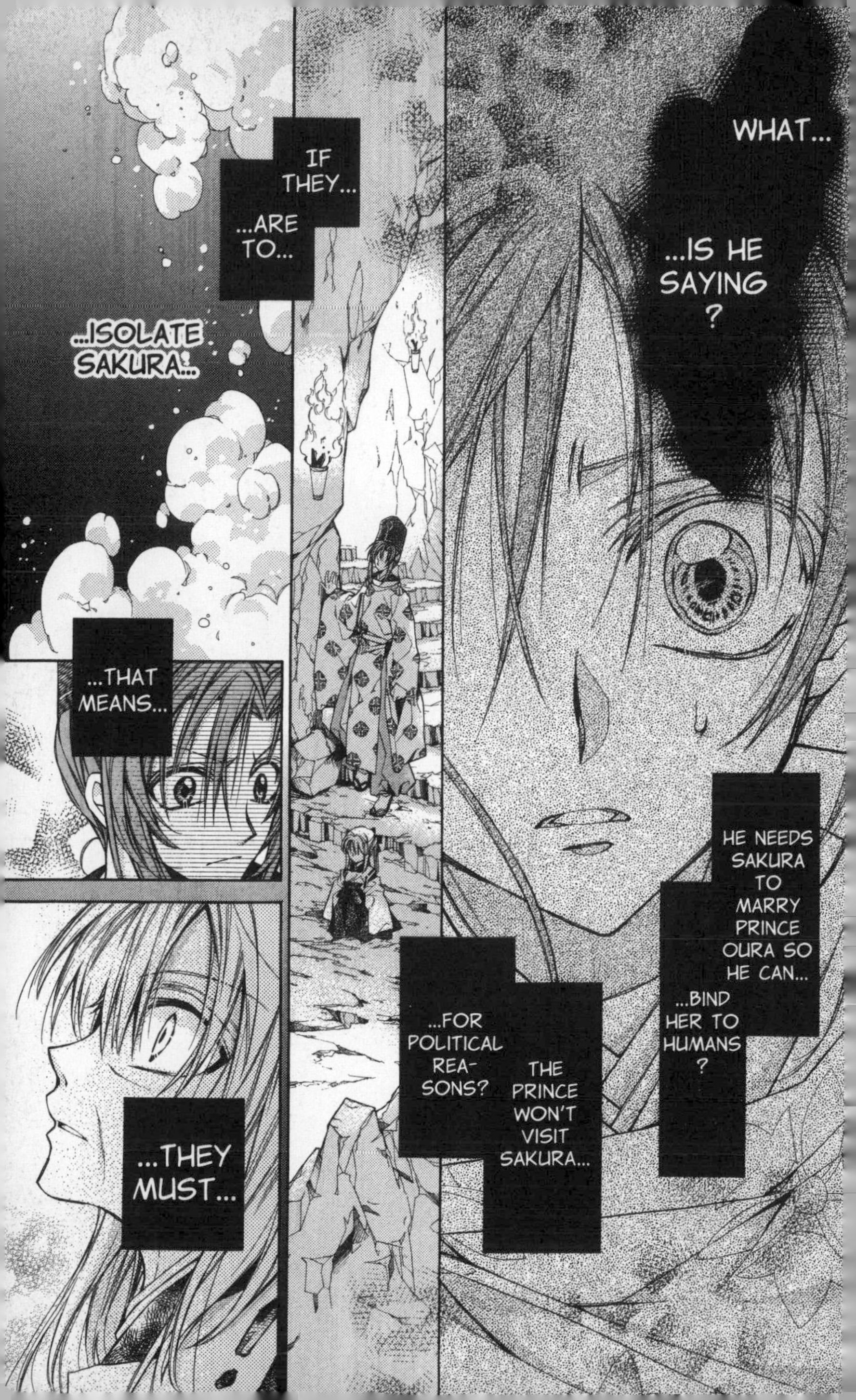
WHAT...
...IS HE SAYING?
HE NEEDS SAKURA TO MARRY PRINCE OURA SO HE CAN...
...BIND HER TO HUMANS?
THE PRINCE WON'T VISIT SAKURA...
...FOR POLITICAL REA-SONS?
IF THEY...
...ARE TO...
...ISOLATE SAKURA...
...THAT MEANS...
...THEY MUST...

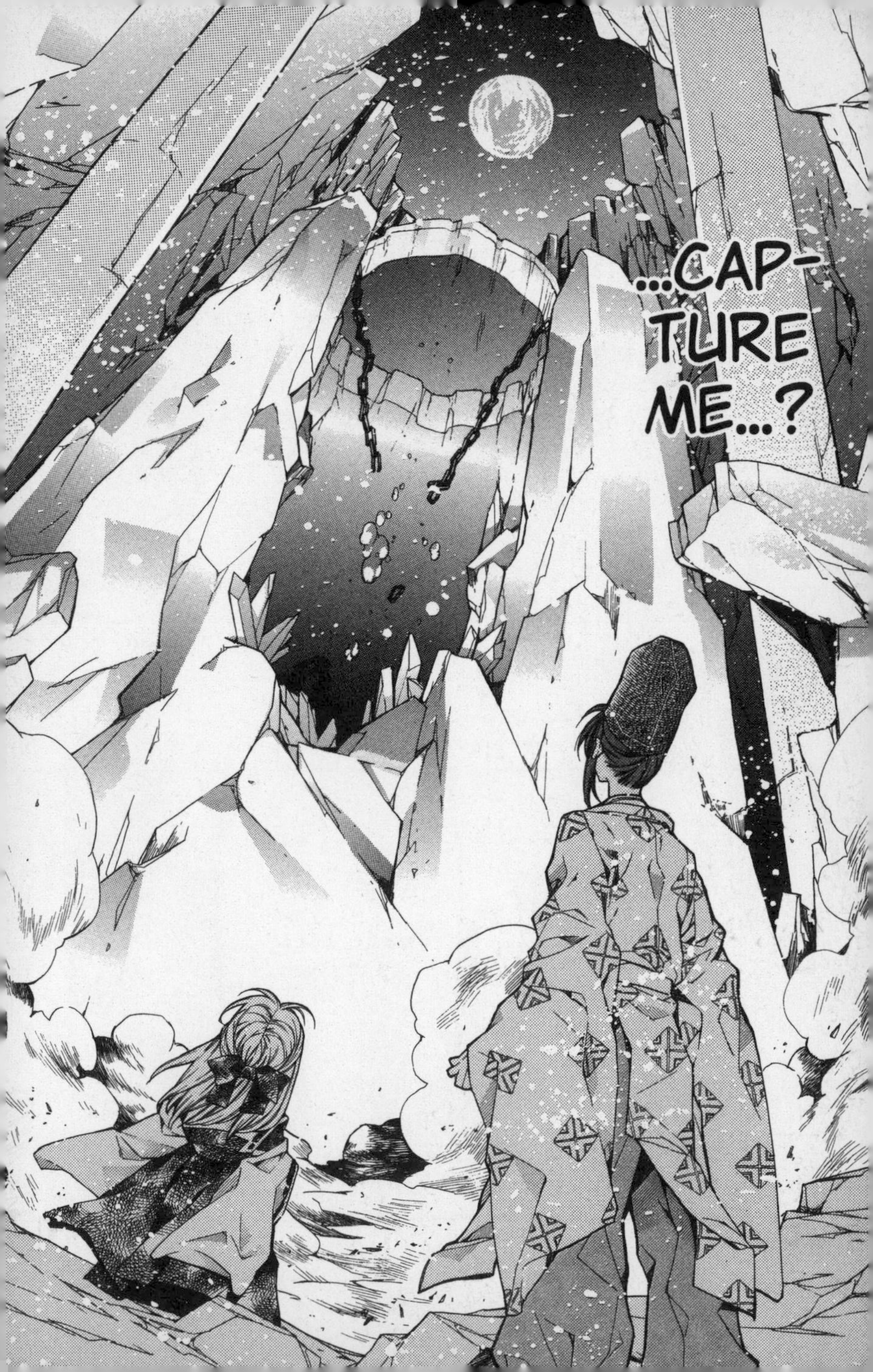
...CAP-
TURE
ME...?

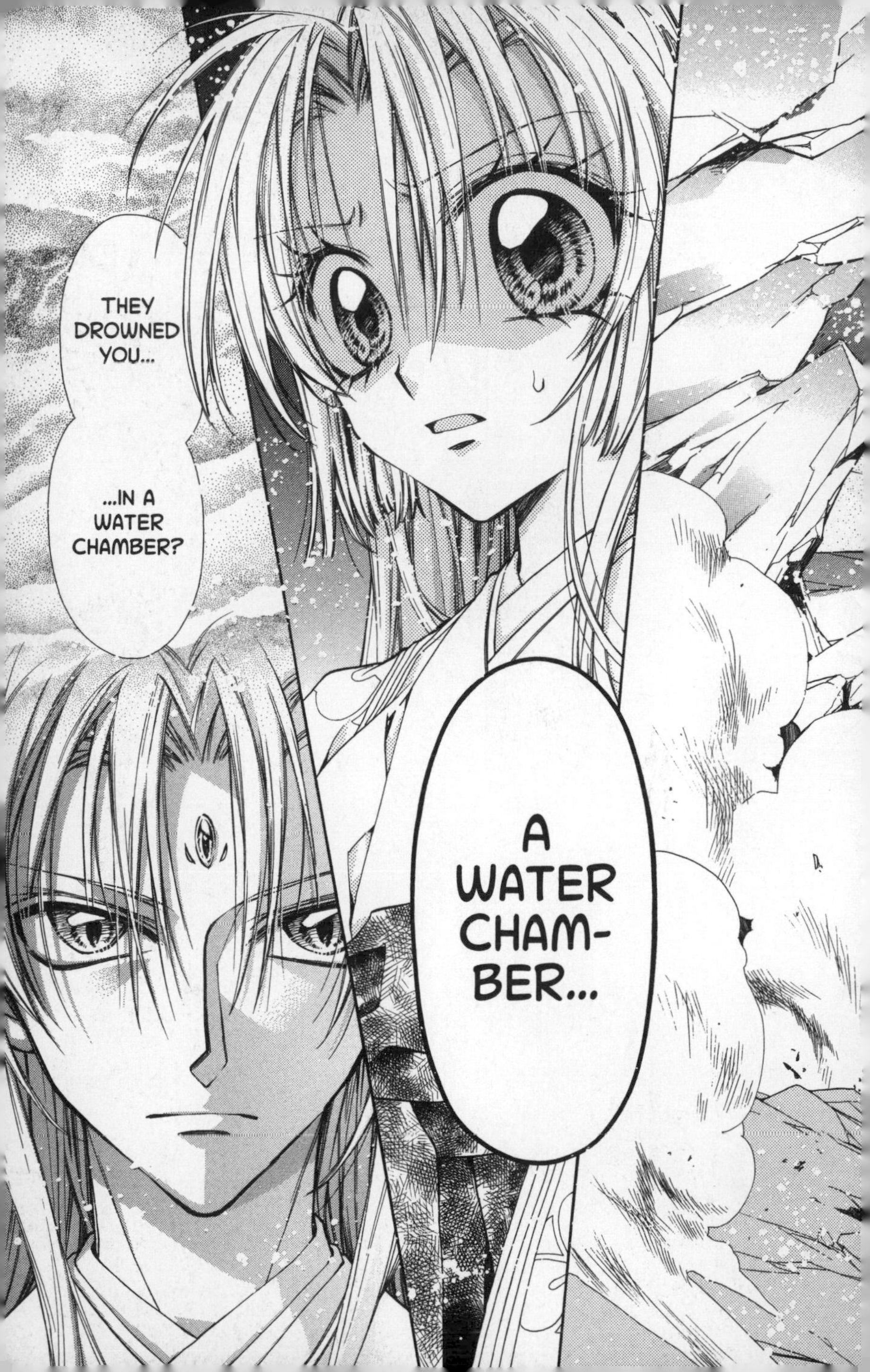
A WATER CHAM-BER...
THEY DROWNED YOU...
...IN A WATER CHAMBER?

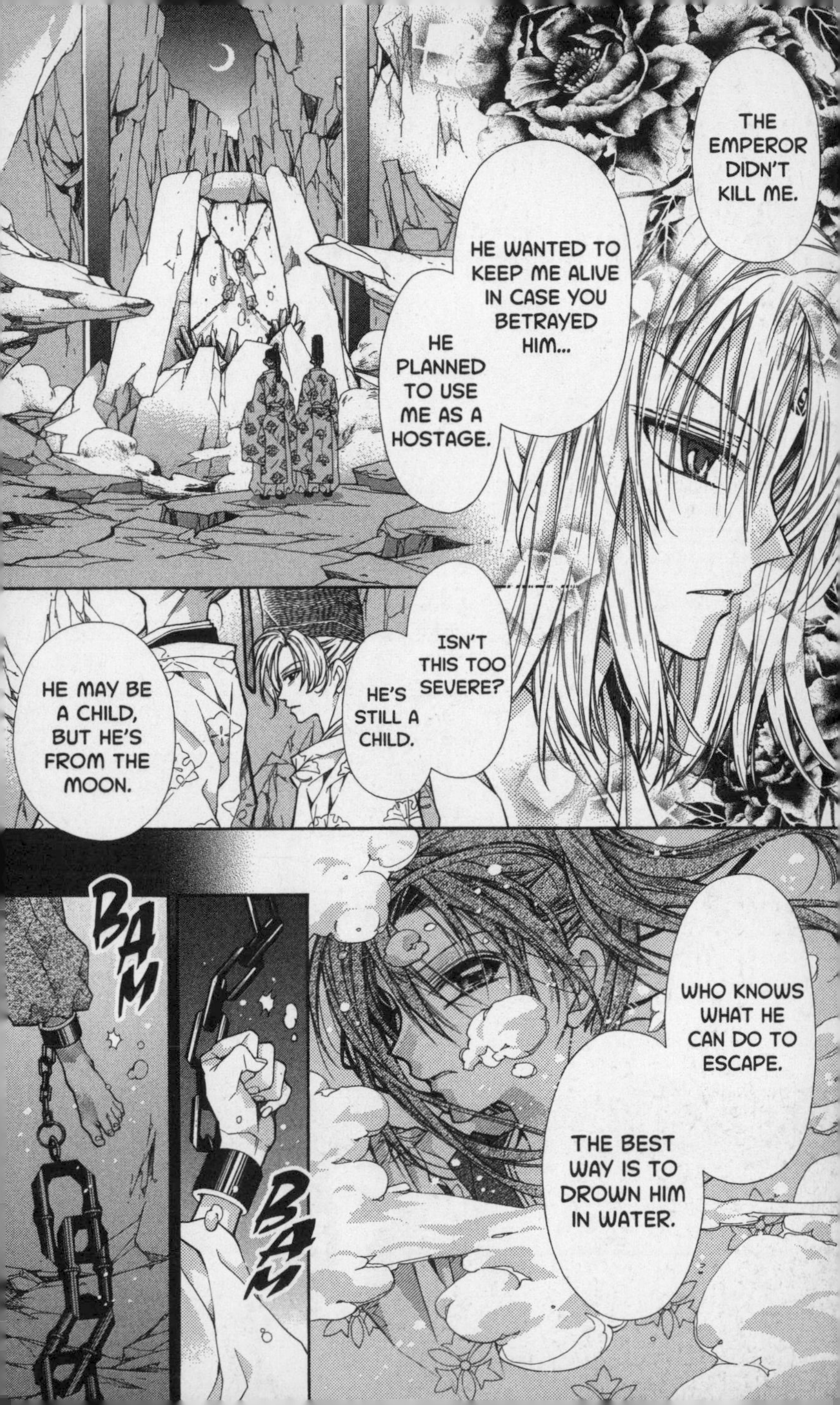
THE EMPEROR DIDN'T KILL ME.
HE WANTED TO KEEP ME ALIVE IN CASE YOU BETRAYED HIM...
HE PLANNED TO USE ME AS A HOSTAGE.
ISN'T THIS TOO SEVERE?
HE'S STILL A CHILD.
HE MAY BE A CHILD, BUT HE'S FROM THE MOON.
WHO KNOWS WHAT HE CAN DO TO ESCAPE.
THE BEST WAY IS TO DROWN HIM IN WATER.
BAM
BAM

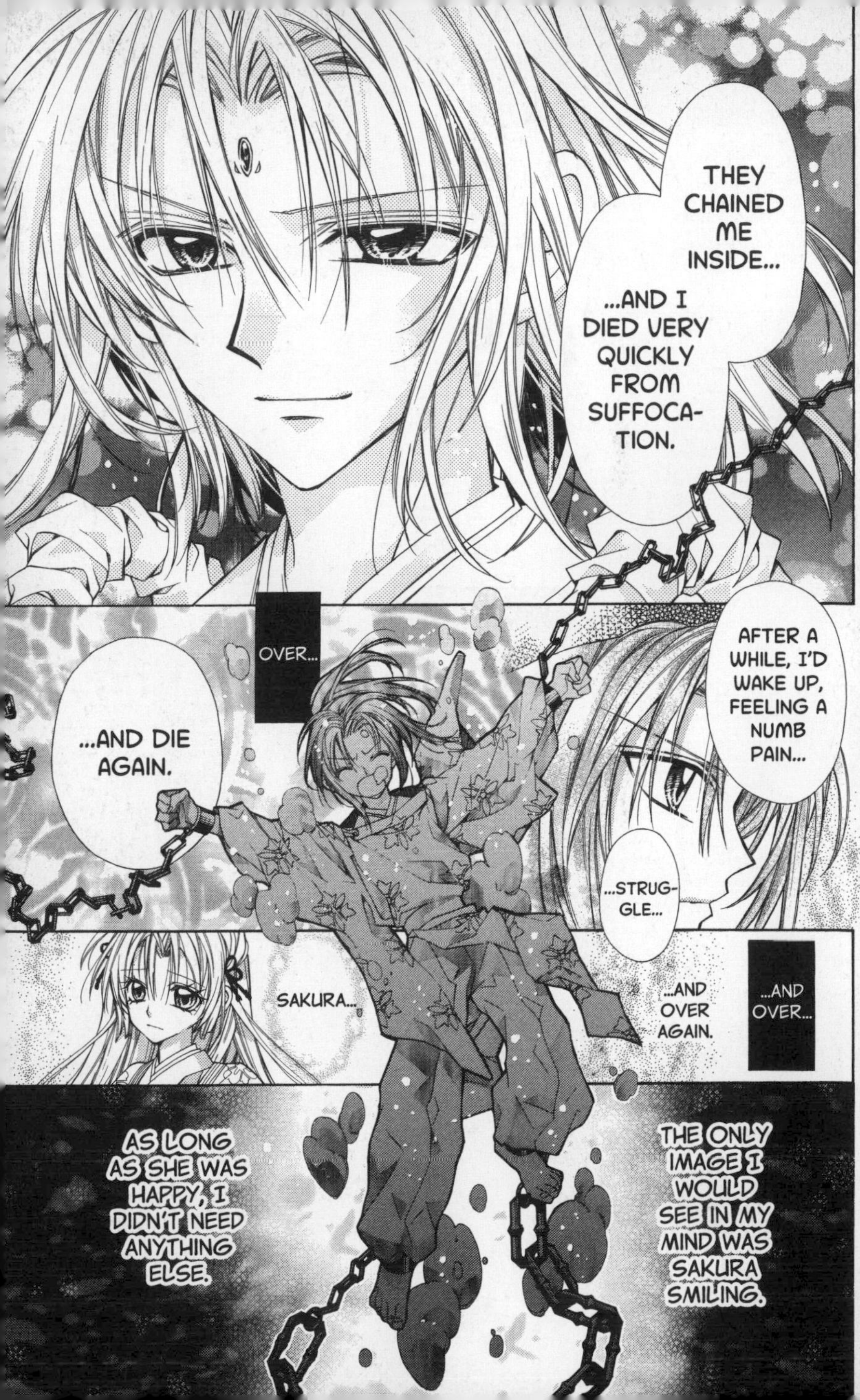
THEY CHAINED ME INSIDE...
...AND I DIED VERY QUICKLY FROM SUFFOCA-TION.
AFTER A WHILE, I'D WAKE UP, FEELING A NUMB PAIN...
...STRUG-GLE...
...AND DIE AGAIN.
OVER...
...AND OVER...
...AND OVER AGAIN.
SAKURA...
THE ONLY IMAGE I WOULD SEE IN MY MIND WAS SAKURA SMILING.
AS LONG AS SHE WAS HAPPY, I DIDN'T NEED ANYTHING ELSE.

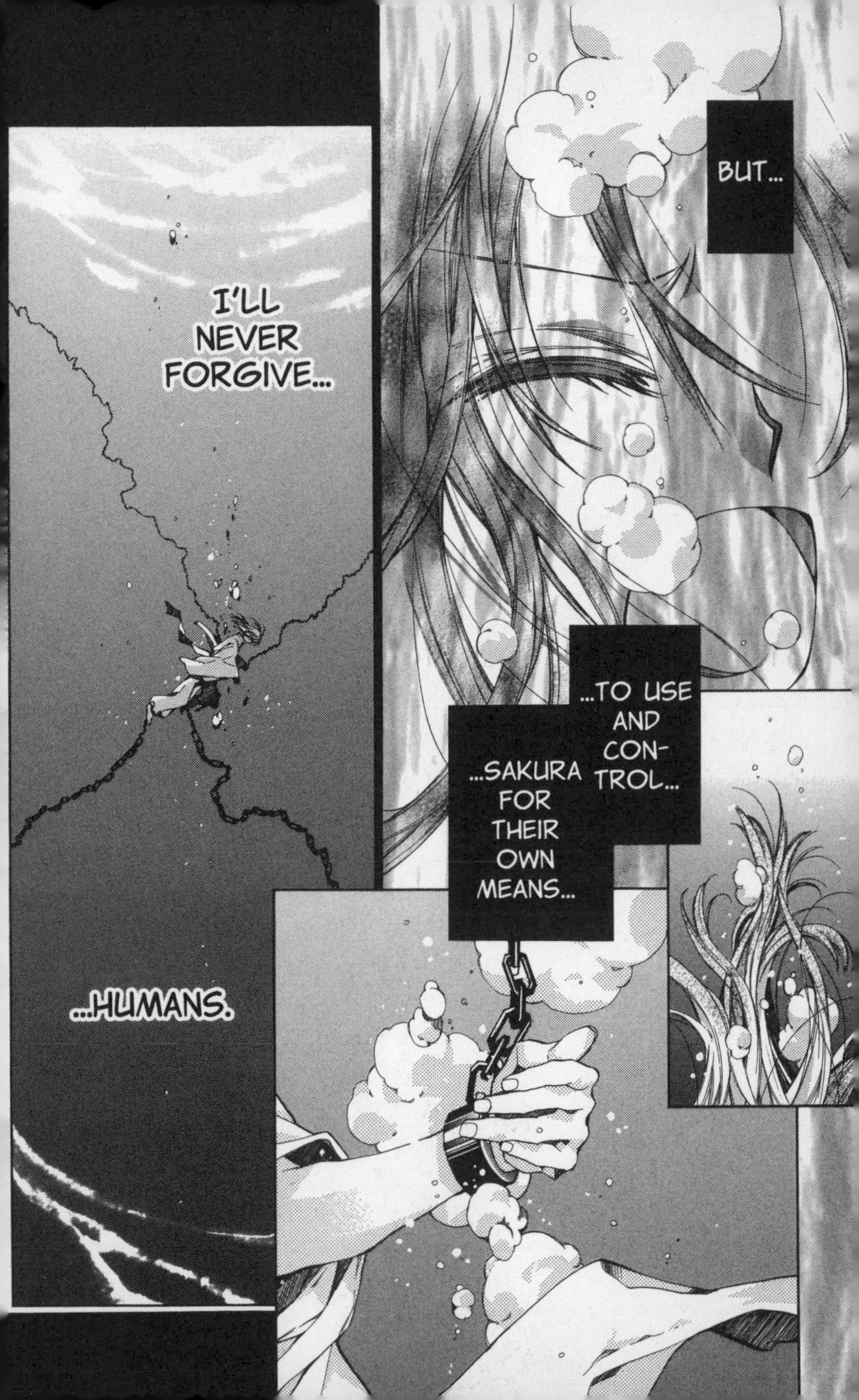
BUT...
...TO USE AND CON-TROL...
...SAKURA FOR THEIR OWN MEANS...
I'LL NEVER FORGIVE...
...HUMANS.

Germany Diary 4 ✿

Let me be a little serious now. As a mangaka, it is rather shocking to see my autographs being sold at auctions and the like. (It's that kind of job, so I know it can't be stopped, but...)
Whenever people ask me for an autograph, I feel very happy, but I can also tell who the sellers are. It creates a complex atmosphere when people come ask me for my autograph, to be honest. (Please don't worry; I can tell who my real fans are. ♥)
And like I wrote above, I feel that I don't really have any privacy as long as I'm in this job, and I can't do anything about my illustrations and autographs being sold. I'd rather sign autographs for all my fans around the world so that nobody will have to consider buying them for a high price in the auctions.

That is why I'd like to give out autographs to people on every possible occasion.

In Germany I was really happy to see people being genuinely happy when I was signing autographs.

If I have the opportunity to go to Germany again, I'd like to bring a little something for the people who attend the autograph sessions. I'd be more than willing to give autographs, do handshakes, and take pictures as long as we don't cause too much trouble for the other attendees.
Really, I'll do anything if it's something I can do for you!

So please invite me again.

My dream is to have an autograph session in Korea!

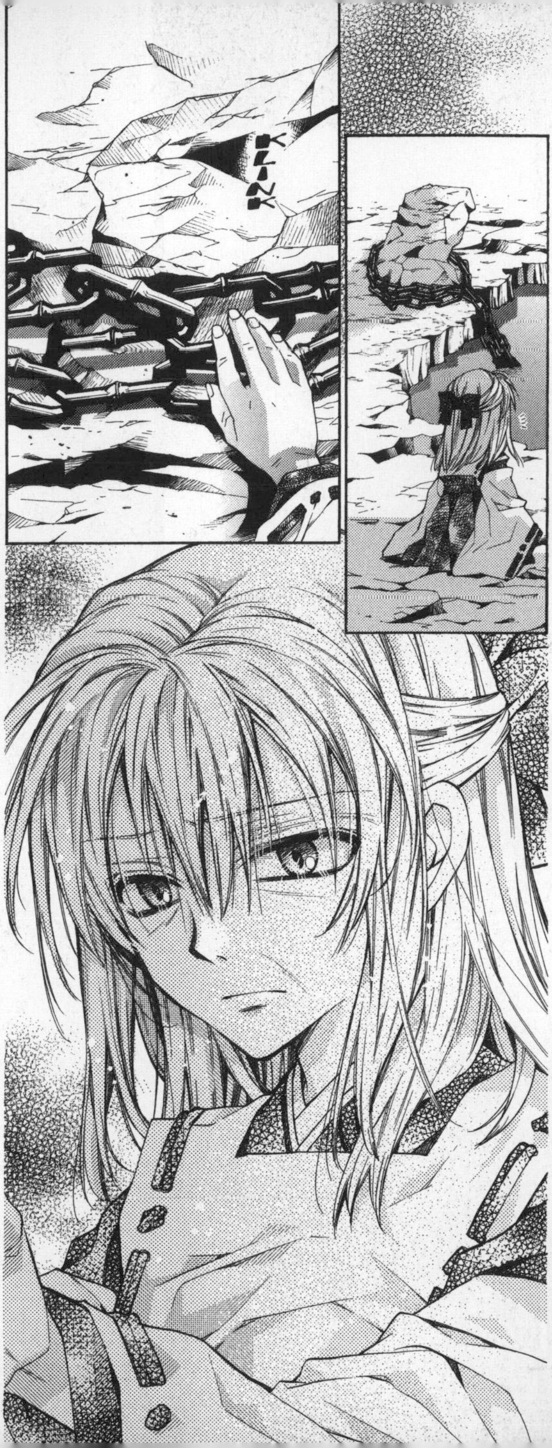
KLINK

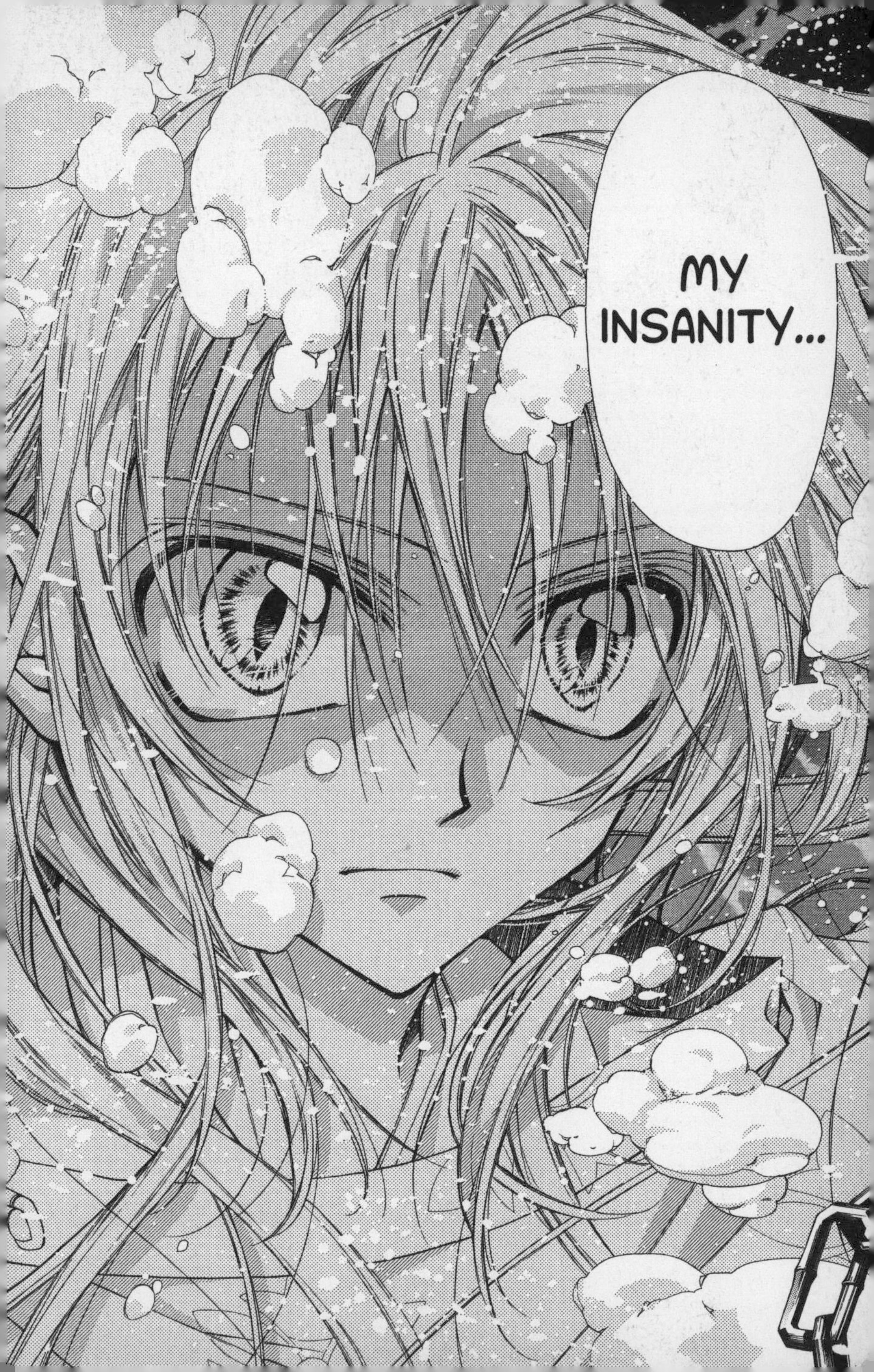
MY INSANITY...

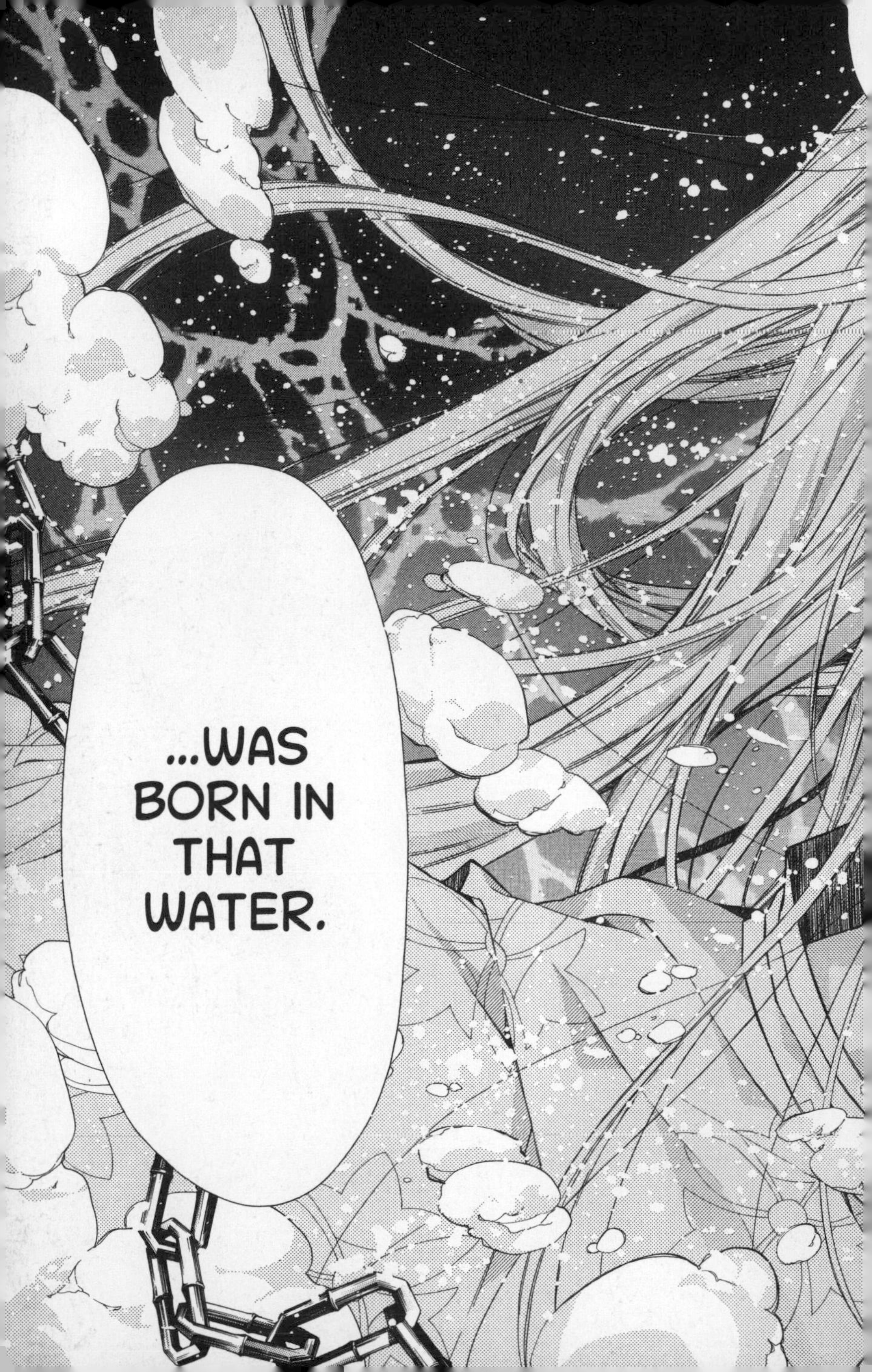
...WAS BORN IN THAT WATER.

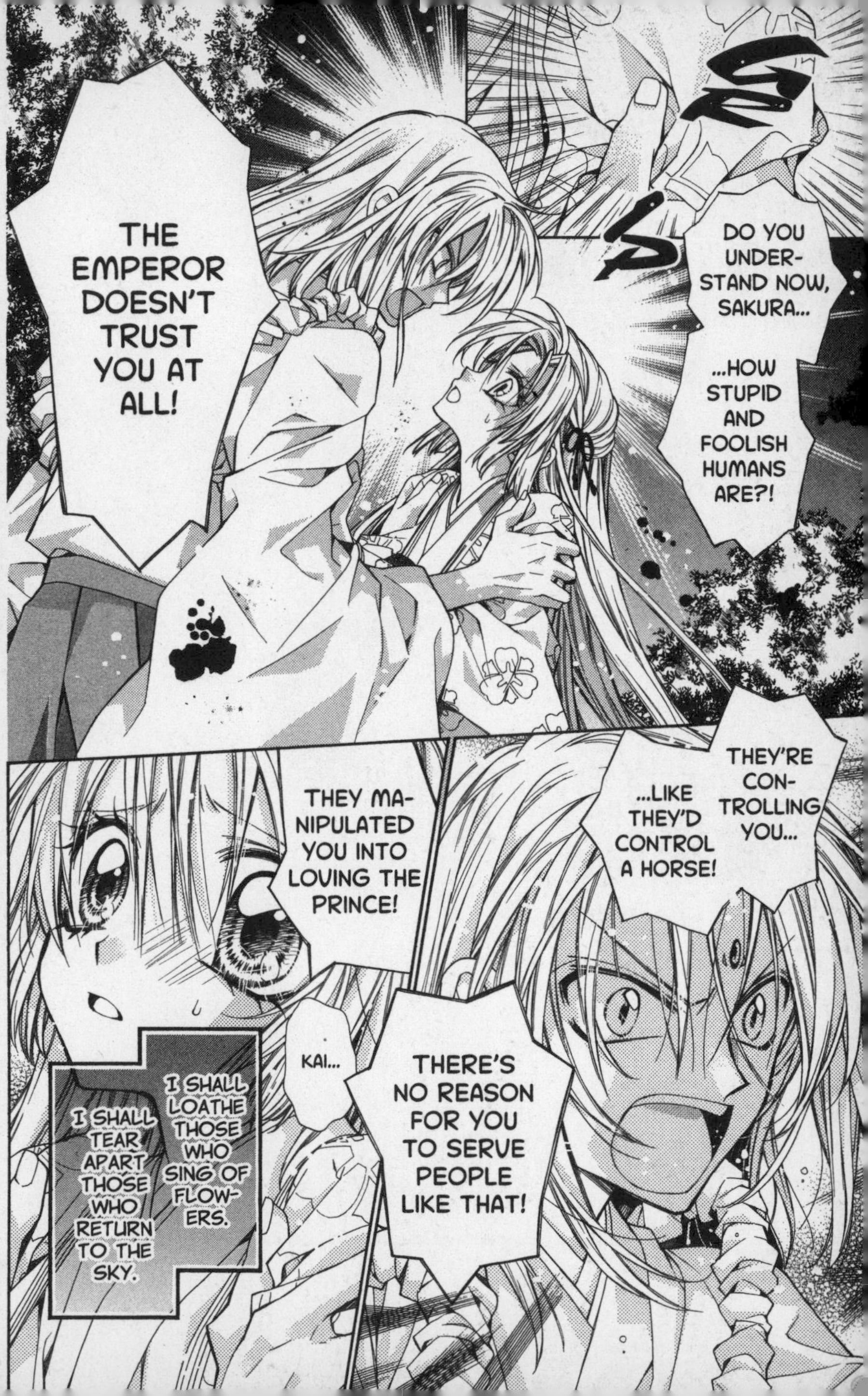
DO YOU UNDERSTAND NOW, SAKURA...
...HOW STUPID AND FOOLISH HUMANS ARE?!
THE EMPEROR DOESN'T TRUST YOU AT ALL!
THEY'RE CONTROLLING YOU...
...LIKE THEY'D CONTROL A HORSE!
THERE'S NO REASON FOR YOU TO SERVE PEOPLE LIKE THAT!
THEY MANIPULATED YOU INTO LOVING THE PRINCE!
KAI...
I SHALL LOATHE THOSE WHO SING OF FLOWERS.
I SHALL TEAR APART THOSE WHO RETURN TO THE SKY.

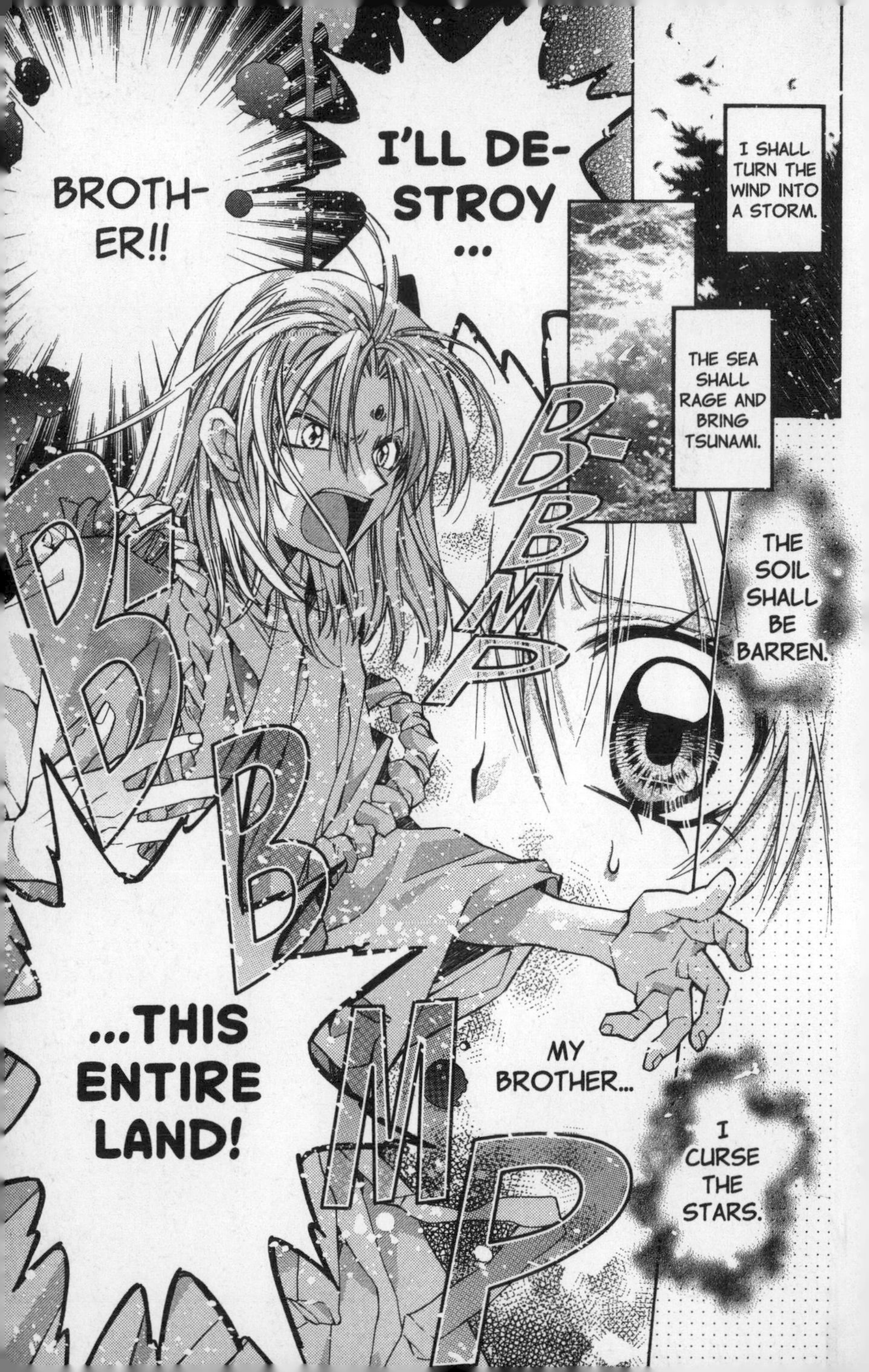
I SHALL TURN THE WIND INTO A STORM.
THE SEA SHALL RAGE AND BRING TSUNAMI.
I'LL DE-STROY ...
BROTH-ER!!
B-BBMP
THE SOIL SHALL BE BARREN.
MY BROTHER...
I CURSE THE STARS.
BBMP
...THIS ENTIRE LAND!

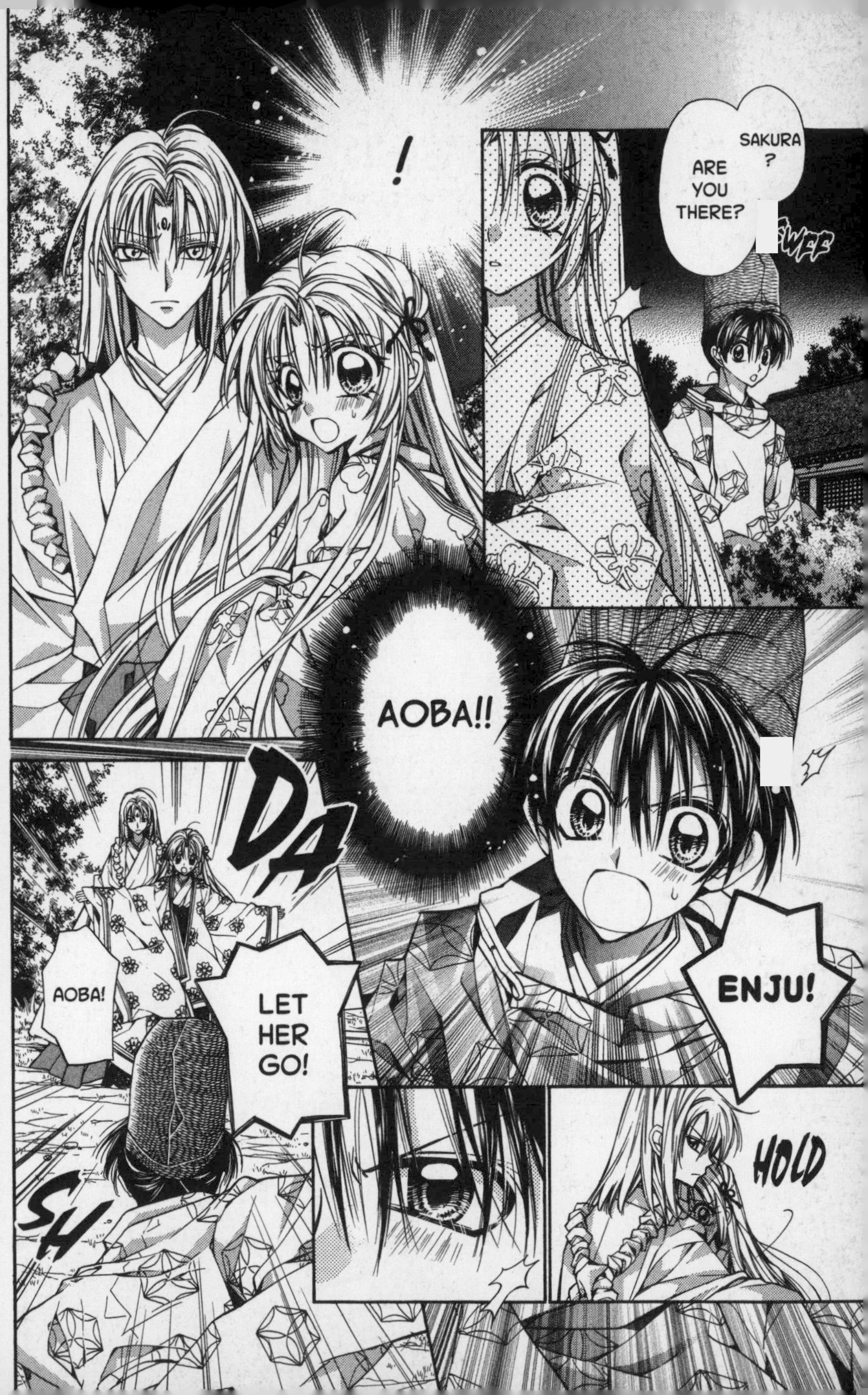
SAKURA? ARE YOU THERE?
SWEF
!
AOBA!!
ENJU!
DA
LET HER GO!
AOBA!
SH
HOLD

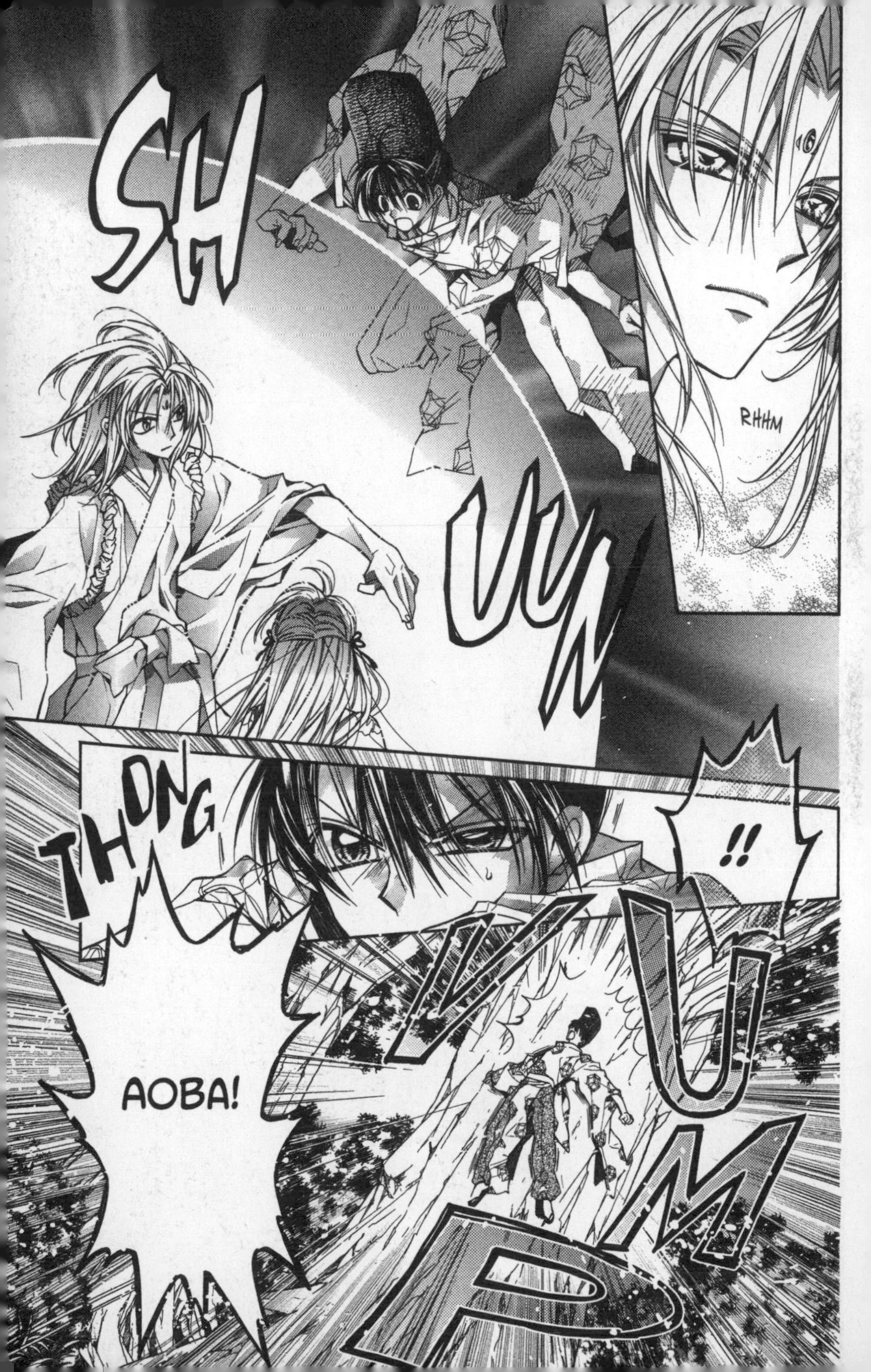
RHHM
SH
UYN
THONG
!!
VUMP
AOBA!

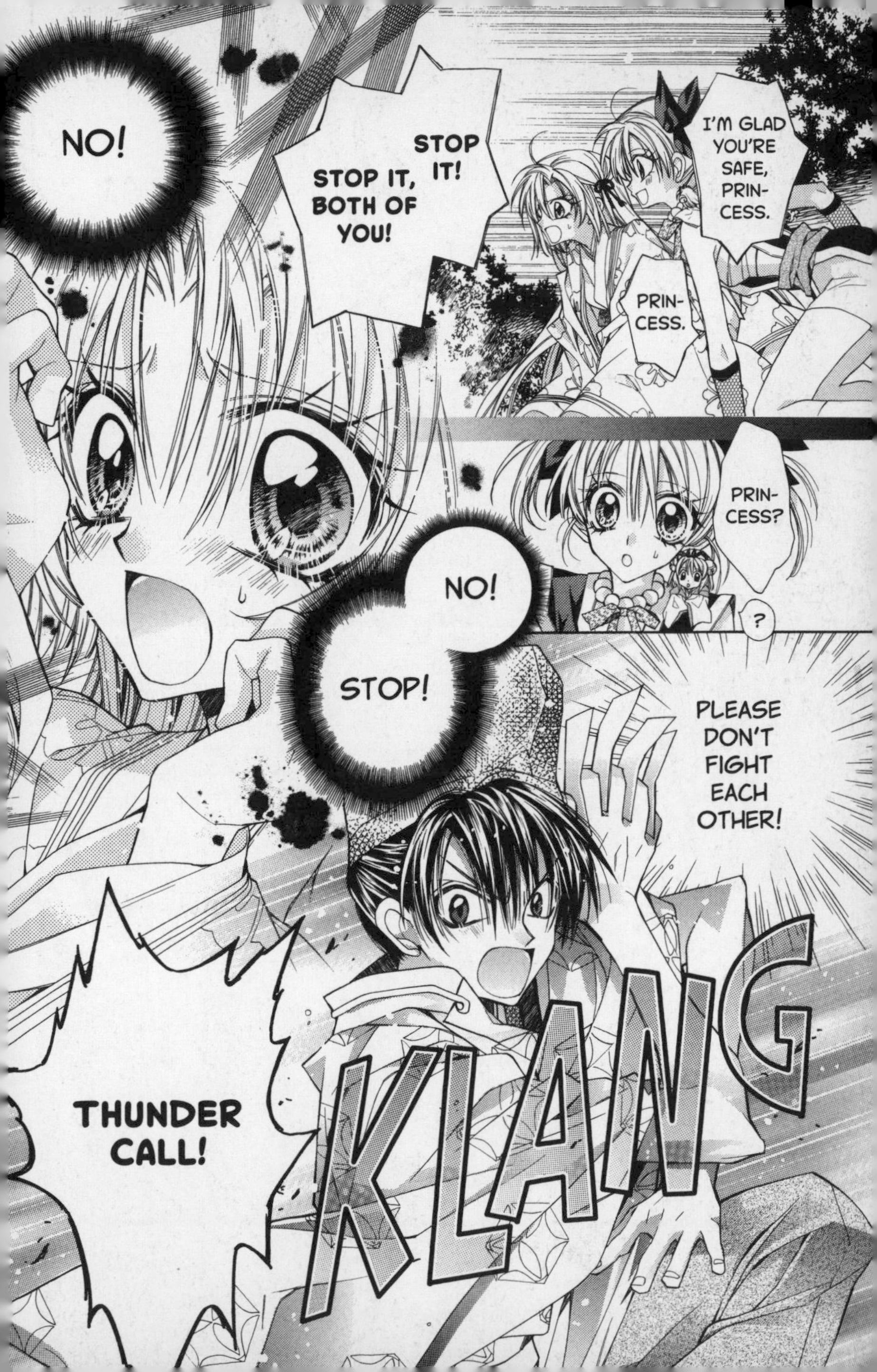
I'M GLAD YOU'RE SAFE, PRINCESS.
PRINCESS.
PRINCESS?
?
STOP IT!
STOP IT, BOTH OF YOU!
NO!
NO!
STOP!
PLEASE DON'T FIGHT EACH OTHER!
KLANG
THUNDER CALL!

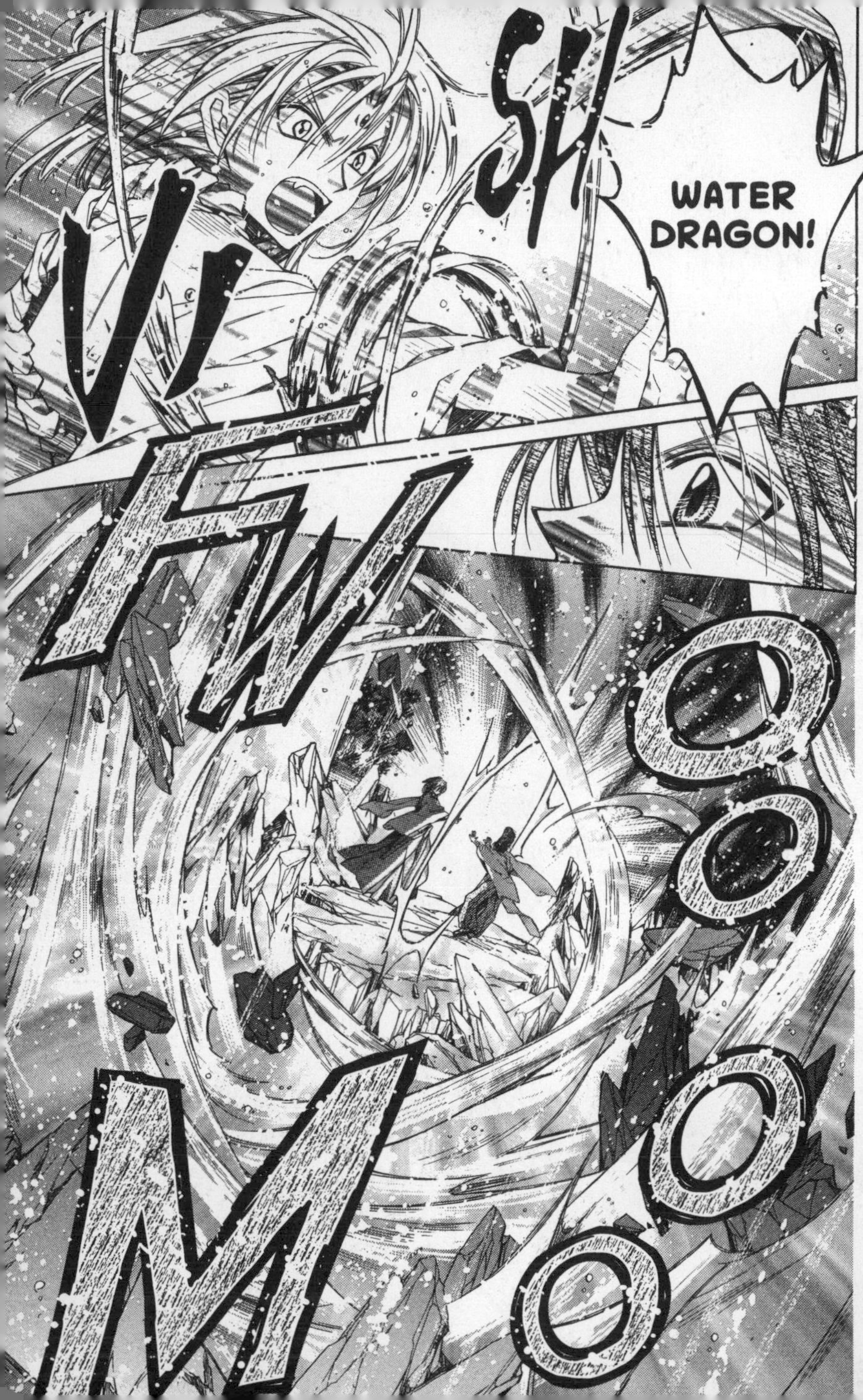
WATER
DRAGON!

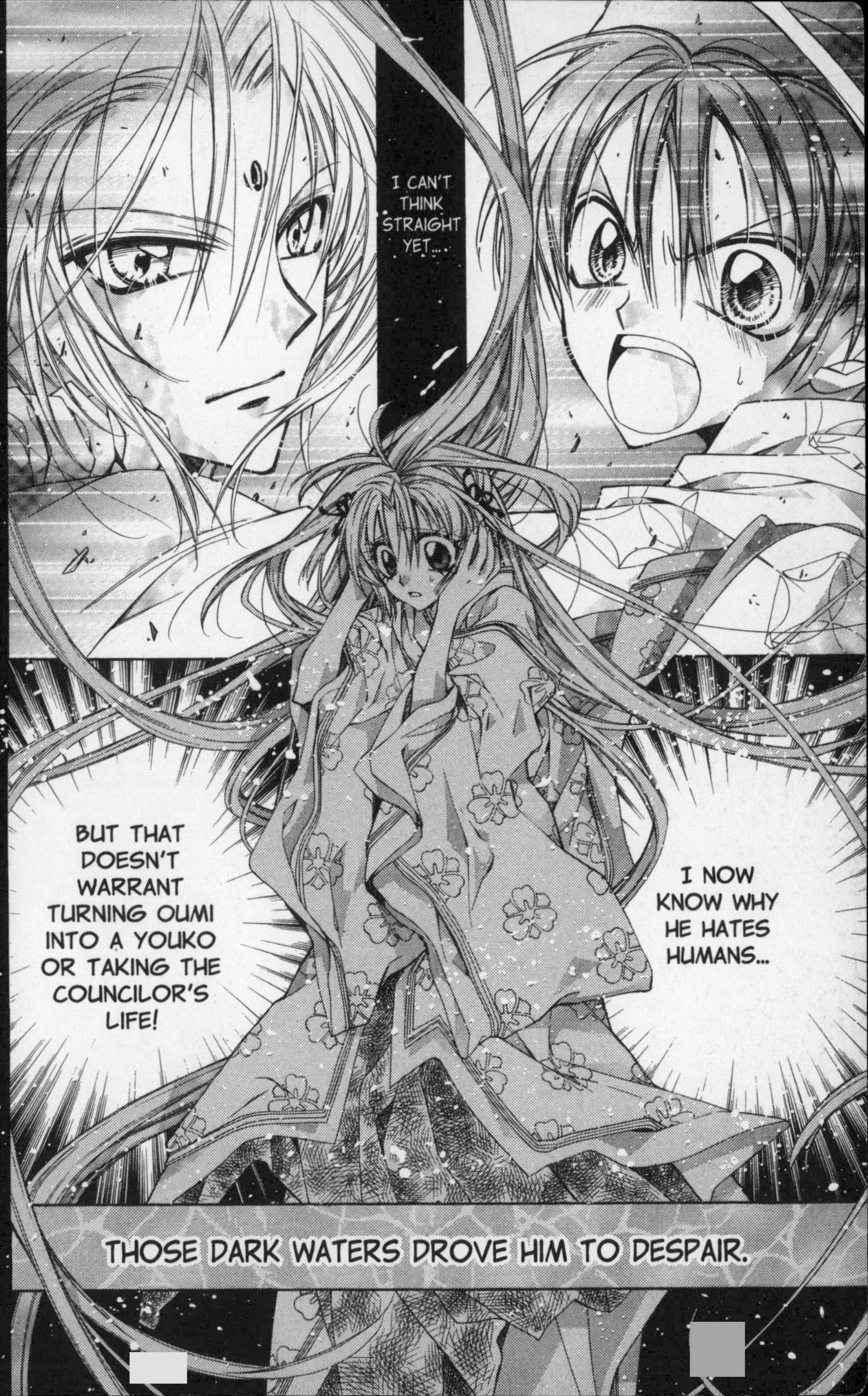

I CAN'T THINK STRAIGHT YET...
I NOW KNOW WHY HE HATES HUMANS...
BUT THAT DOESN'T WARRANT TURNING OUMI INTO A YOUKO OR TAKING THE COUNCILOR'S LIFE!
THOSE DARK WATERS DROVE HIM TO DESPAIR.

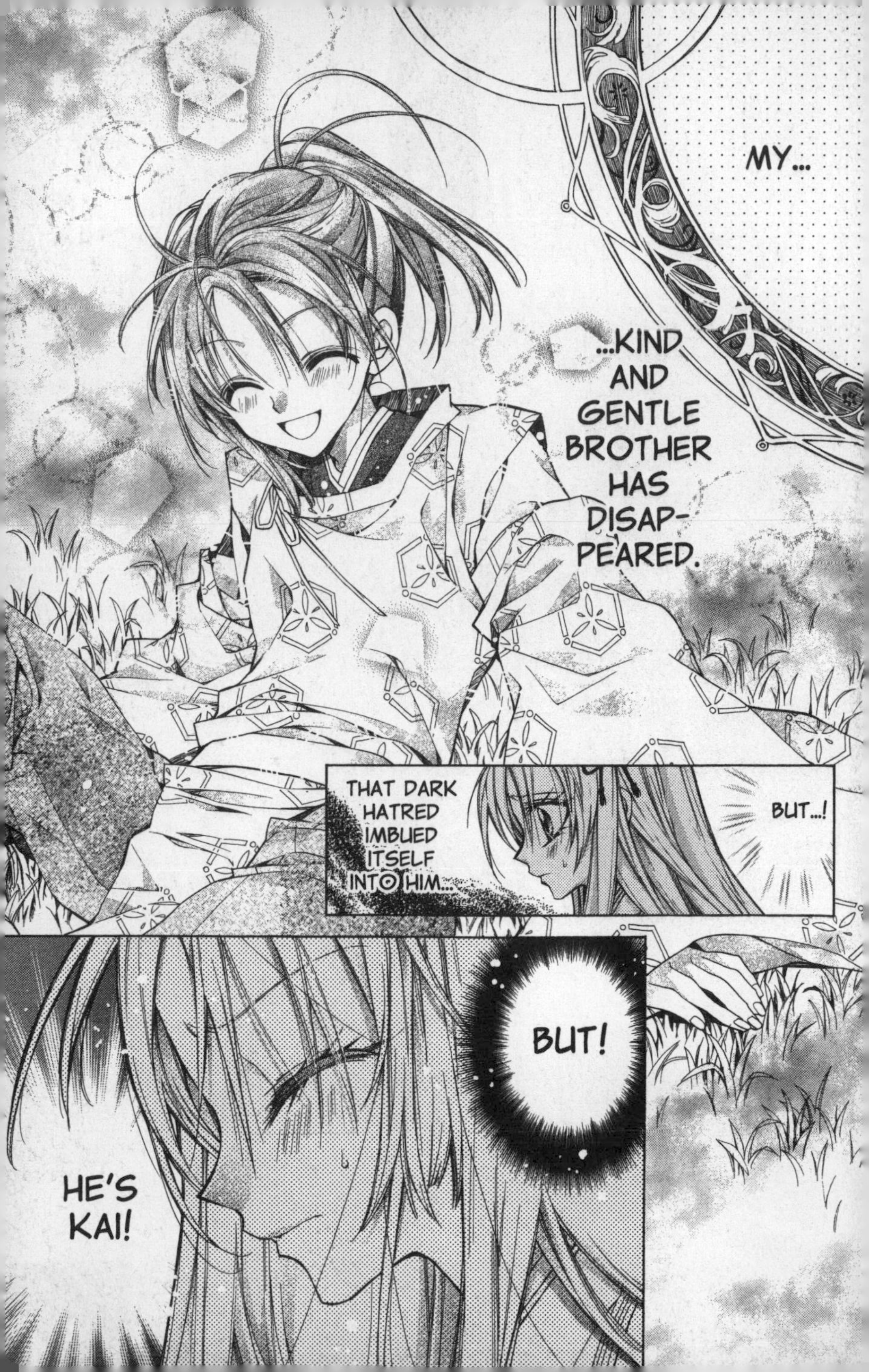
MY...
...KIND AND GENTLE BROTHER HAS DISAP-PEARED.
BUT...!
THAT DARK HATRED IMBUED ITSELF INTO HIM...
BUT!
HE'S KAI!

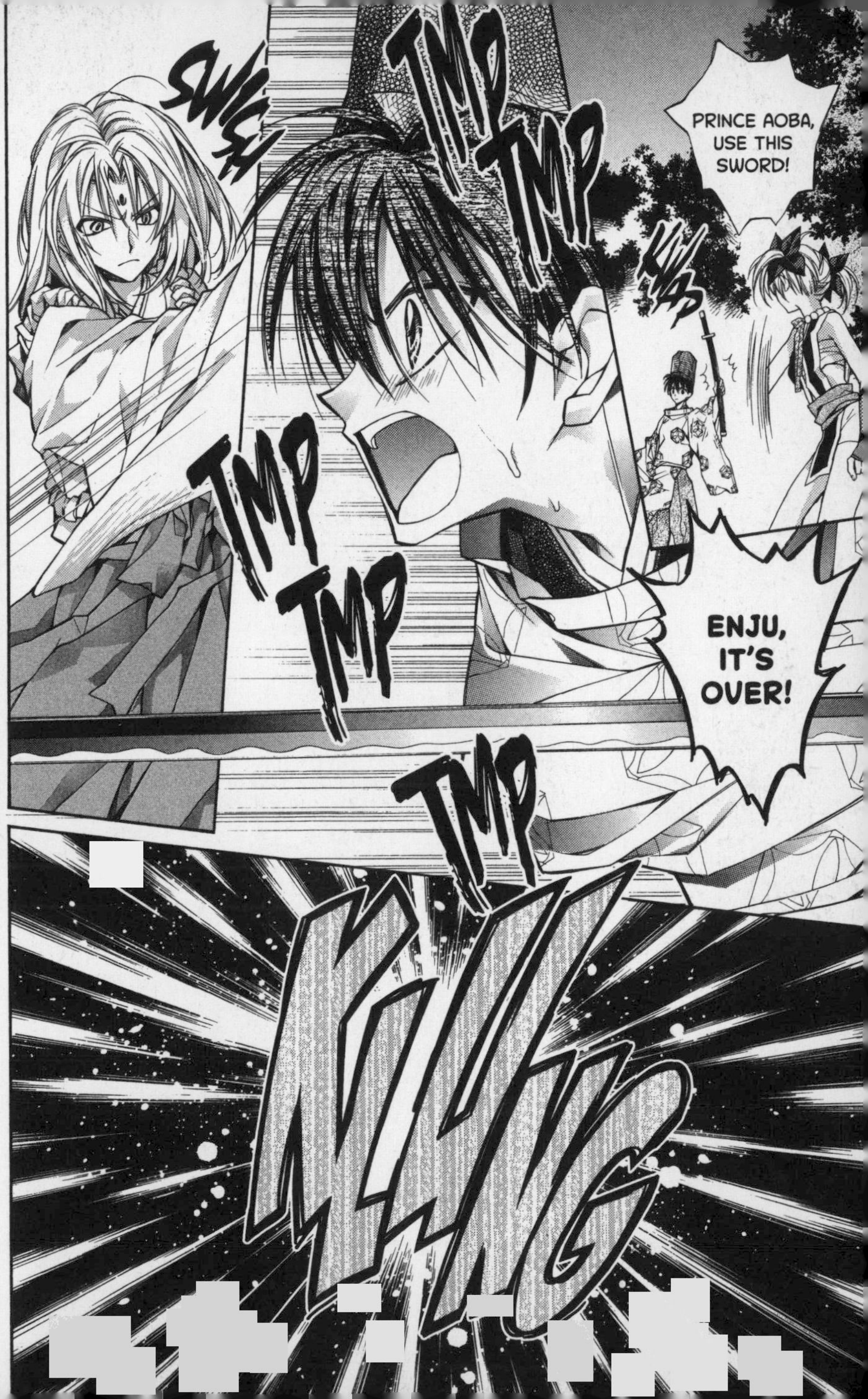
PRINCE AOBA, USE THIS SWORD!
TMP TMP
ENJU, IT'S OVER!
TMP TMP
TMP

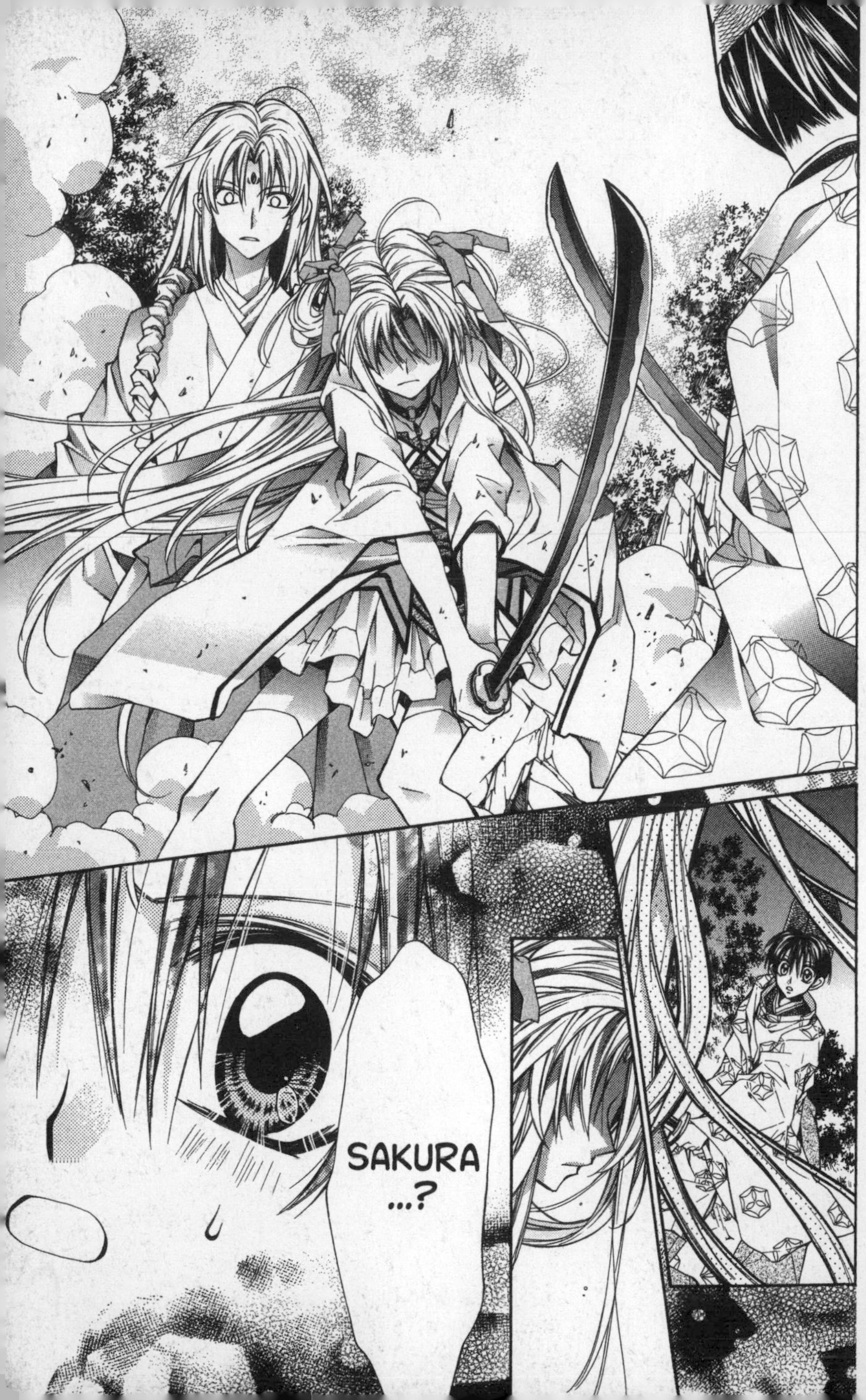
SAKURA ...?

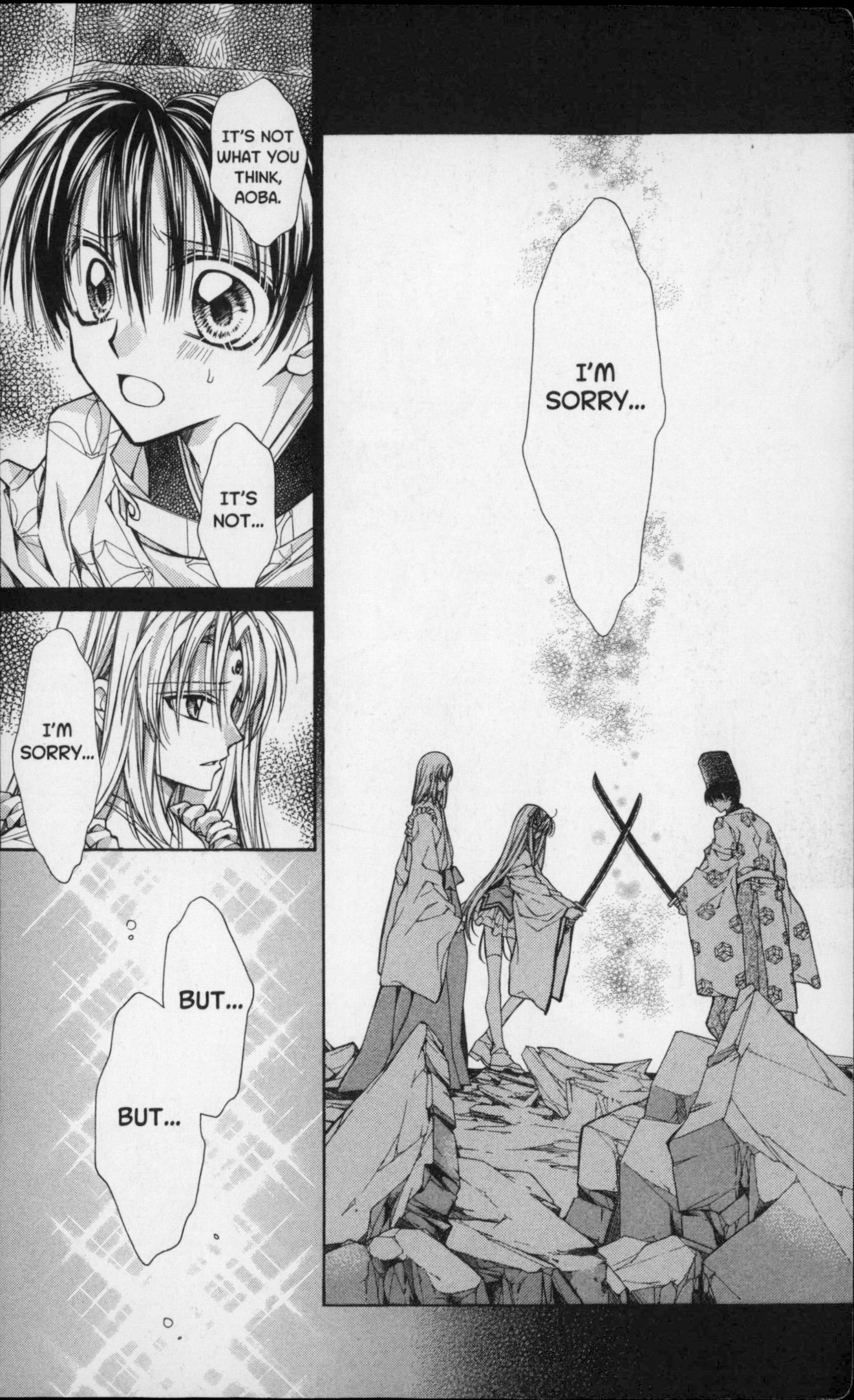
I'M SORRY...
IT'S NOT WHAT YOU THINK, AOBA.
IT'S NOT...
I'M SORRY...
BUT...
BUT...

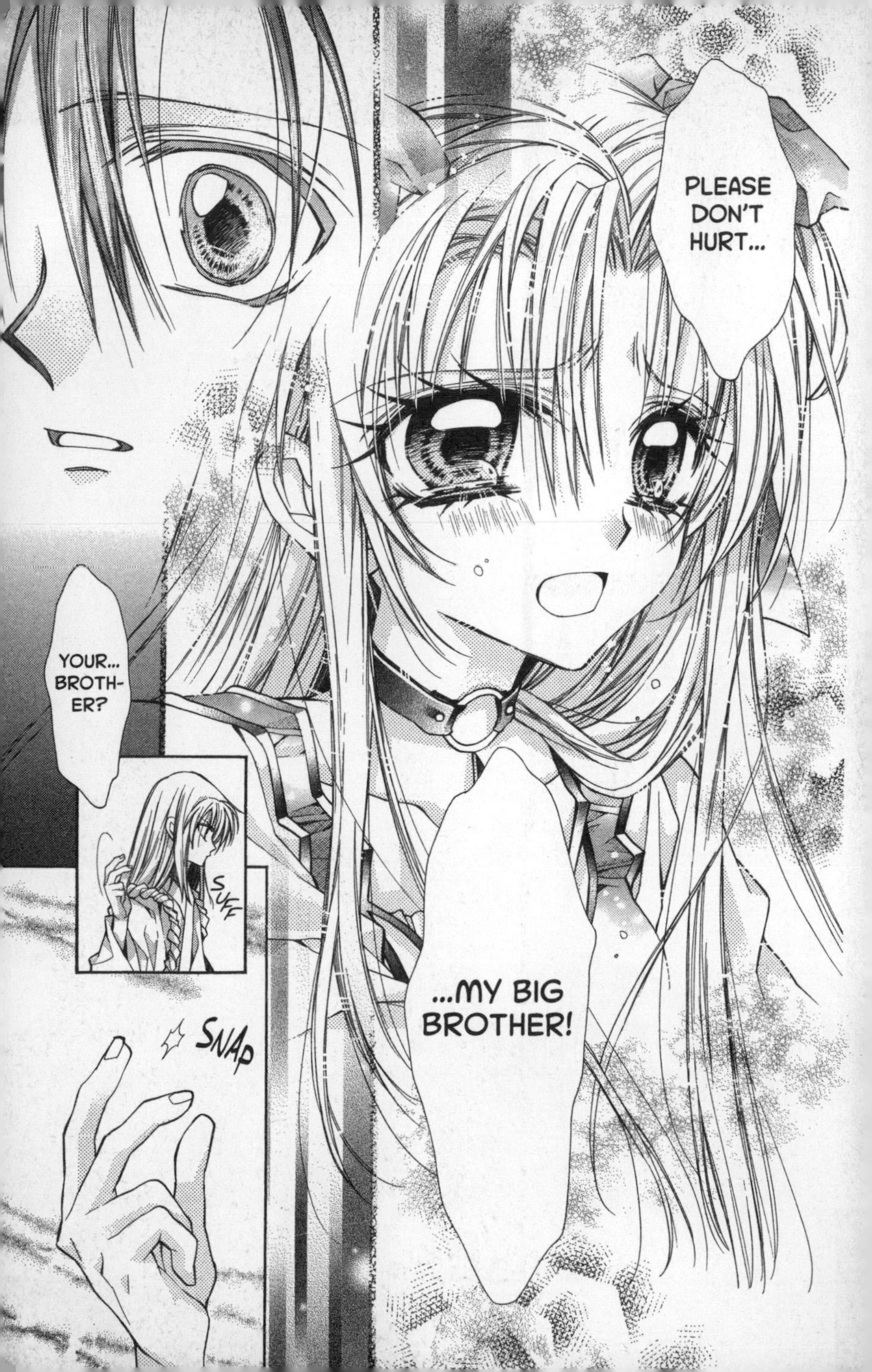
PLEASE DON'T HURT...
...MY BIG BROTHER!
YOUR... BROTHER?
SNIFF
SNAP

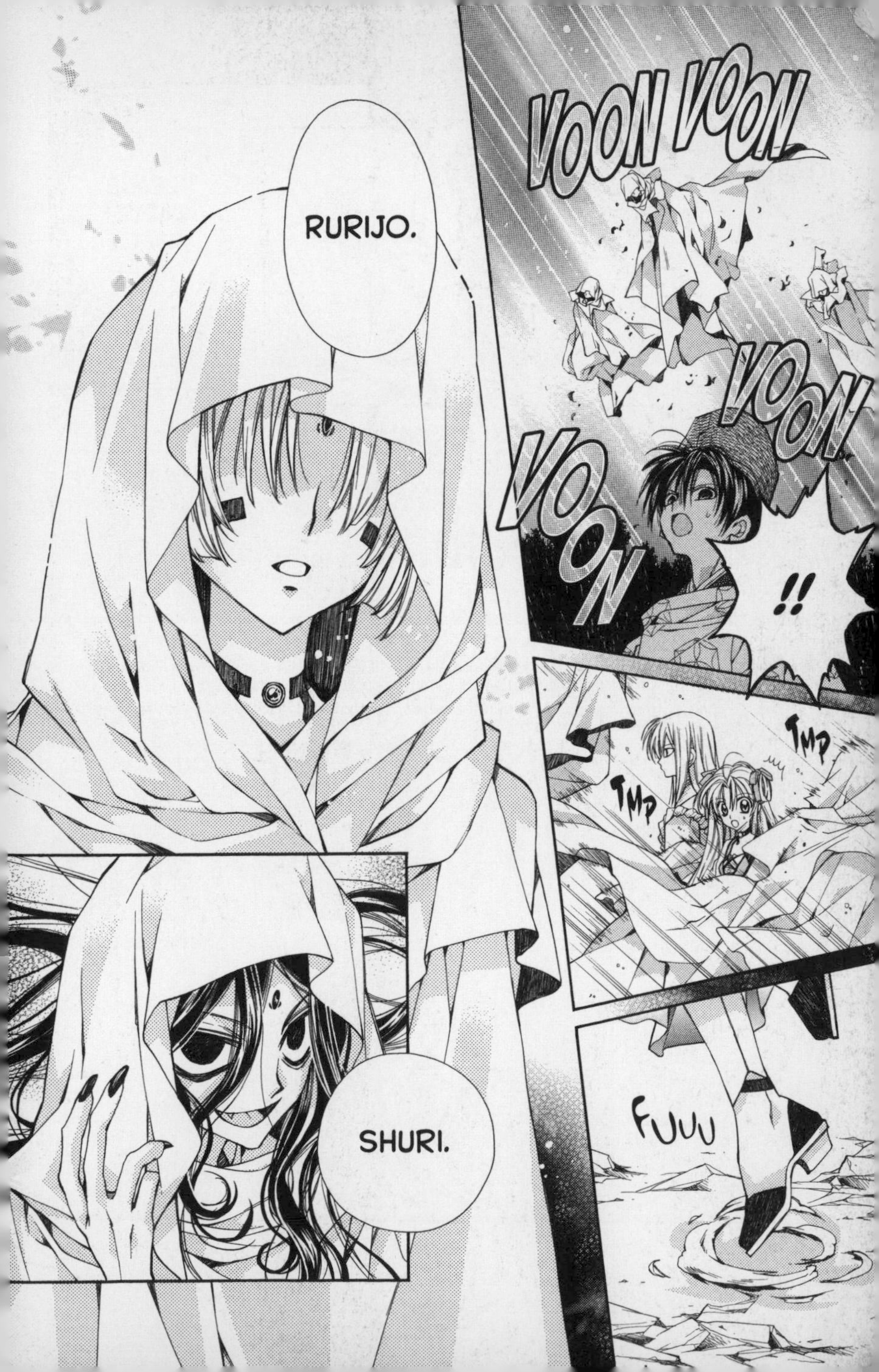
VOON VOON
VOON
VOON
!!
TMP
TMP
FUUU
RURIJO.
SHURI.

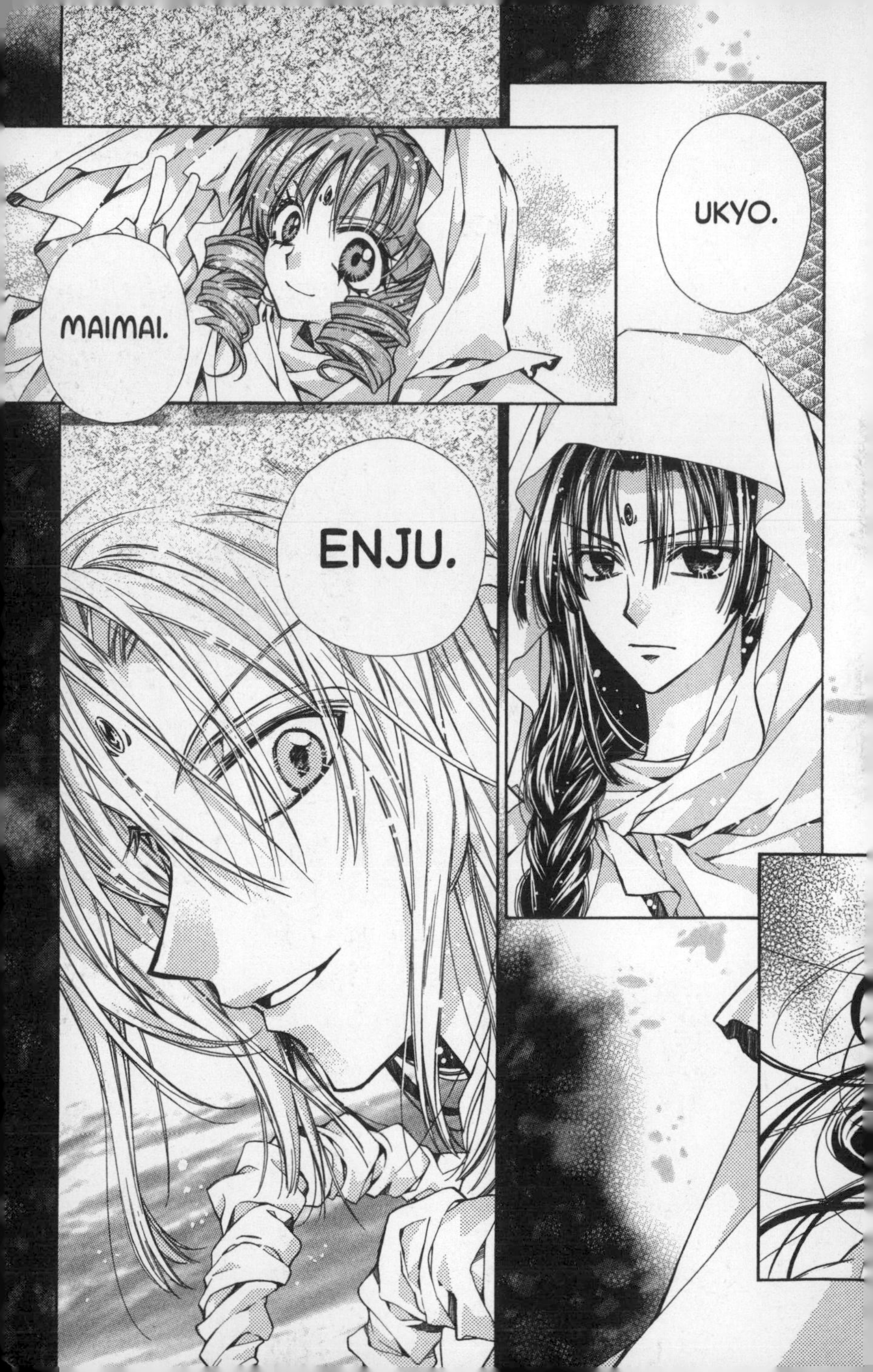
UKYO.
MAIMAI.
ENJU.

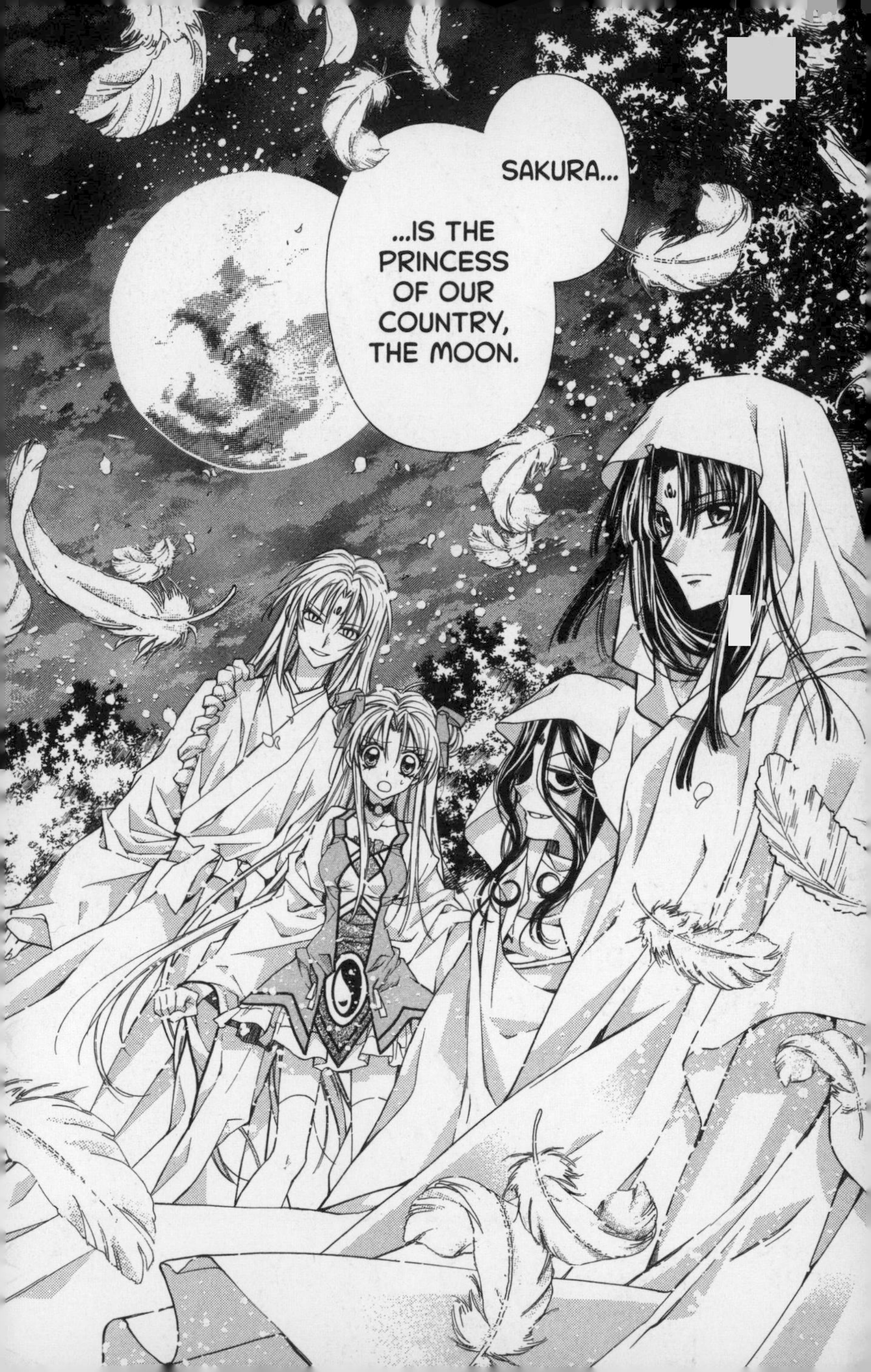
SAKURA...
...IS THE PRINCESS OF OUR COUNTRY, THE MOON.

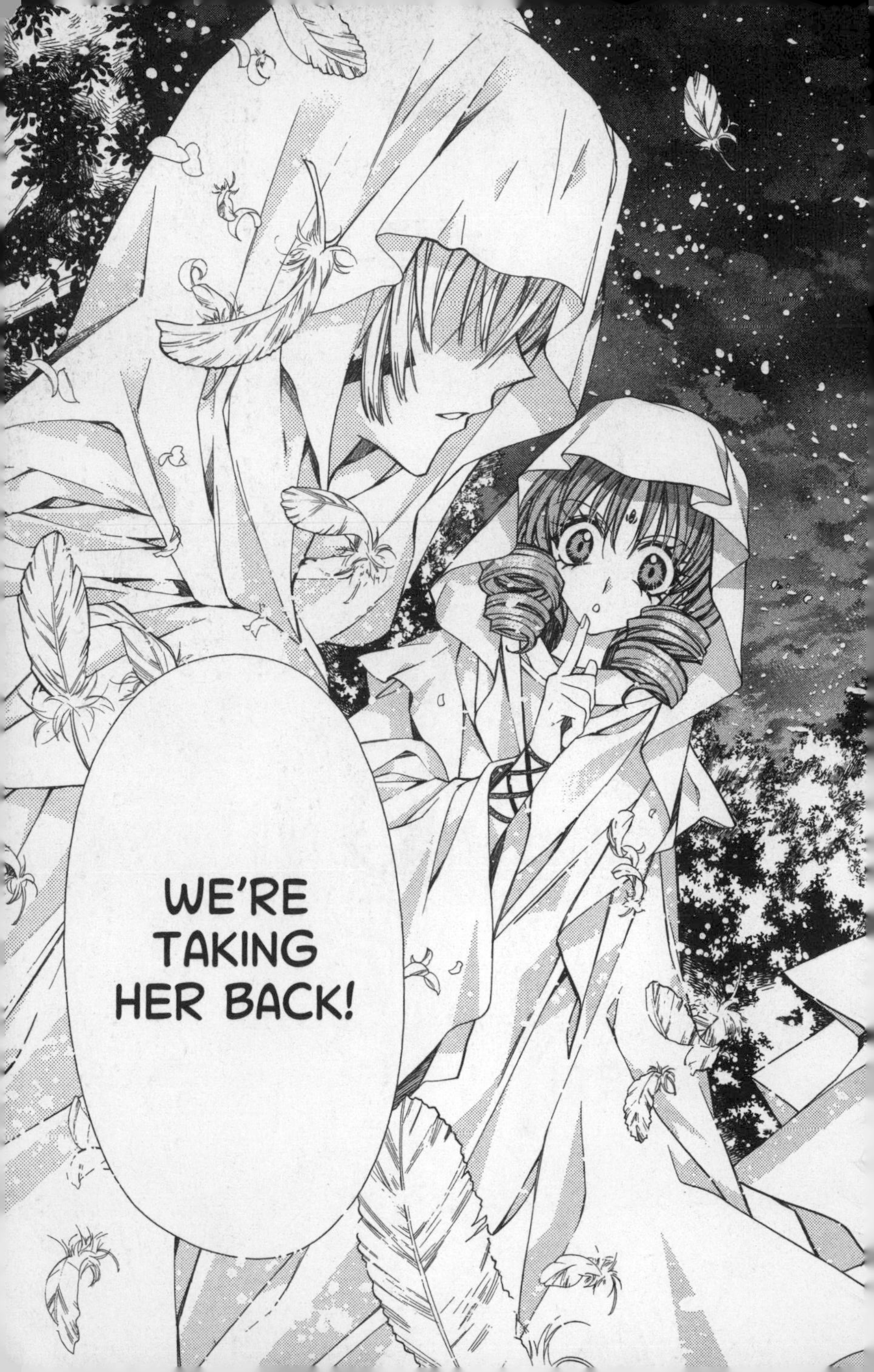
WE'RE TAKING HER BACK!

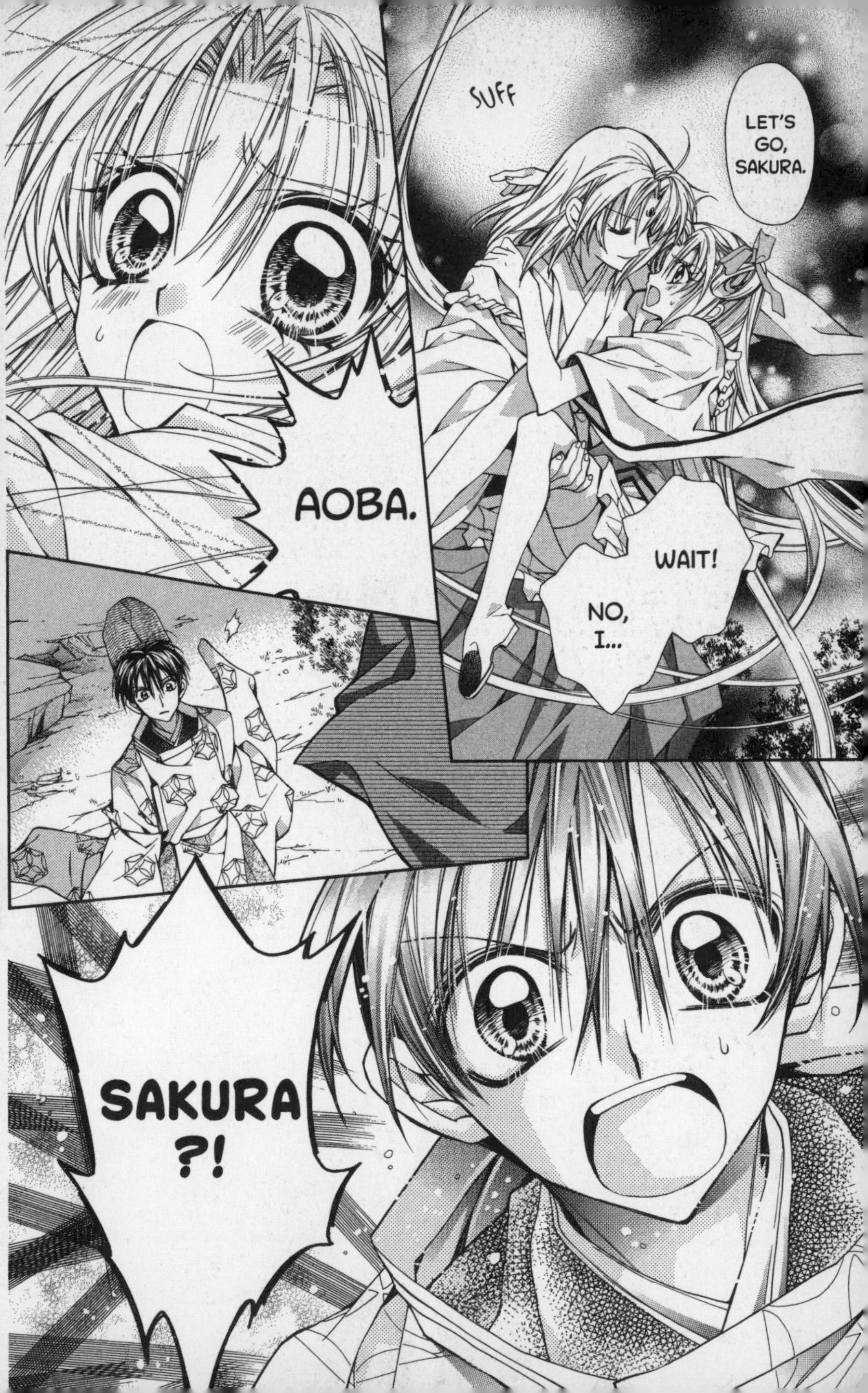
SUFF
LET'S GO, SAKURA.
WAIT!
NO, I...
AOBA.
SAKURA ?!

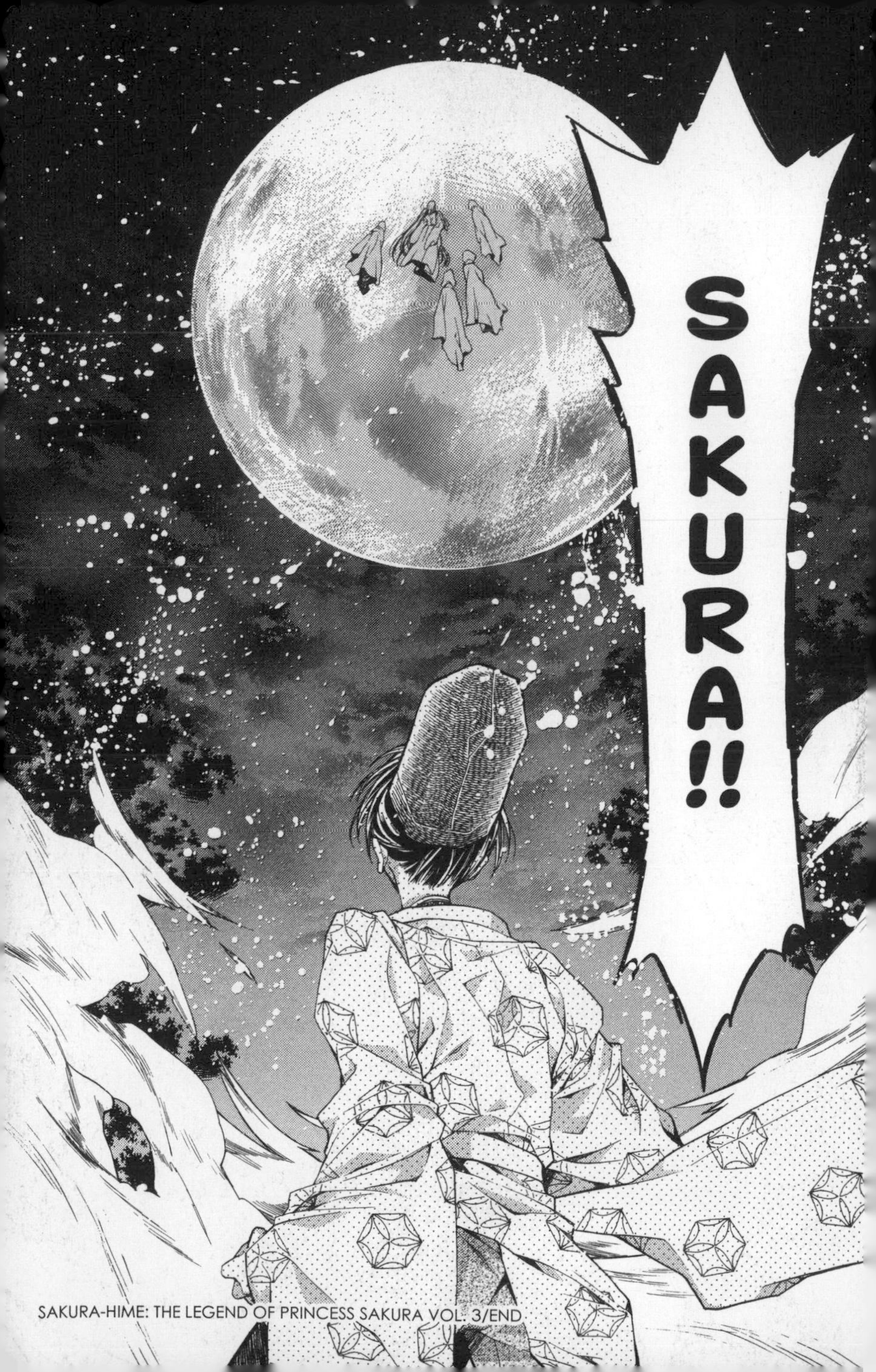

SAKURA-HIME: THE LEGEND OF PRINCESS SAKURA VOL. 3/END

SAKURA HIME
The Legend of Princess Sakura

BONUS FUNNIES

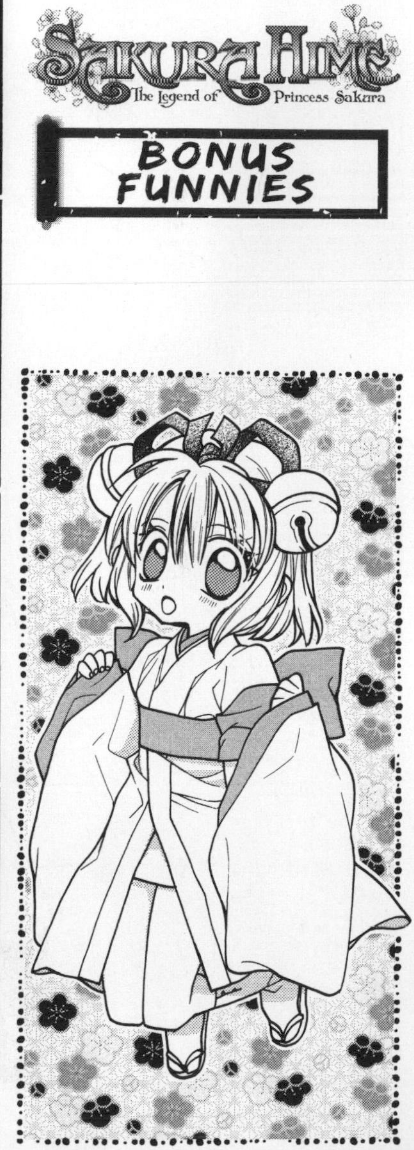

From Chapter 8

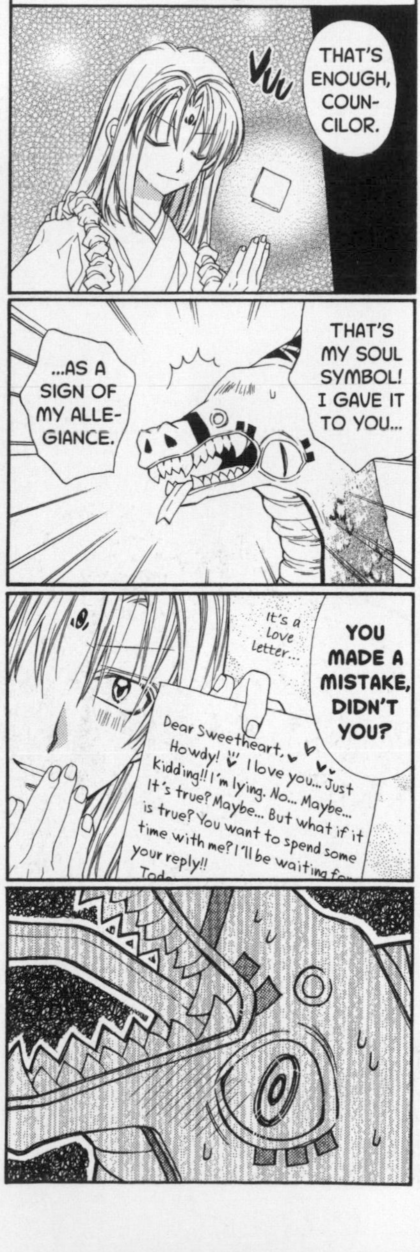
THAT'S ENOUGH, COUN-CILOR.
VUU
THAT'S MY SOUL SYMBOL! I GAVE IT TO YOU...
...AS A SIGN OF MY ALLE-GIANCE.
YOU MADE A MISTAKE, DIDN'T YOU?
It's a love letter...
Dear Sweetheart, Howdy! I love you... Just Kidding!! I'm lying. No... Maybe... It's true? Maybe... But what if it is true? You want to spend some time with me? I'll be waiting fo your reply!!

It Hurts

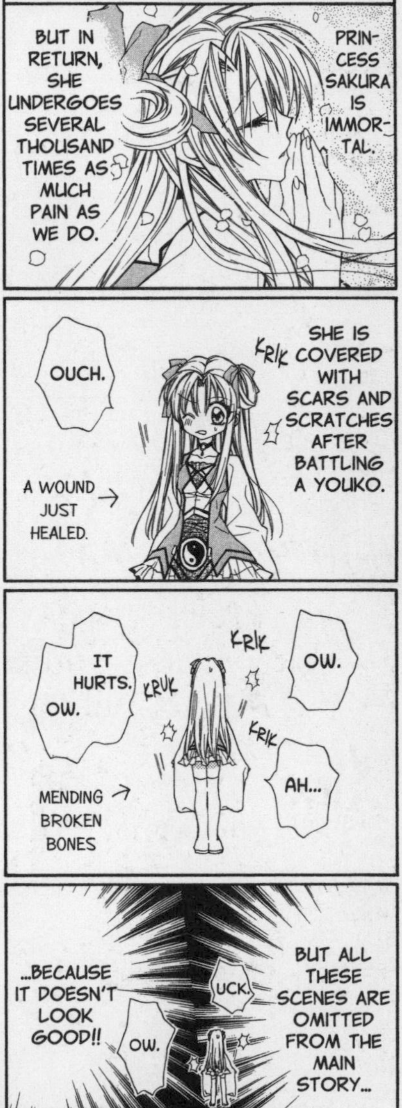
PRINCESS SAKURA IS IMMORTAL.
BUT IN RETURN, SHE UNDERGOES SEVERAL THOUSAND TIMES AS MUCH PAIN AS WE DO.
SHE IS COVERED WITH SCARS AND SCRATCHES AFTER BATTLING A YOUKO.
KRIK
OUCH.
A WOUND JUST HEALED.
OW.
KRIK
IT HURTS.
OW.
KRUK
KRIK
AH...
MENDING BROKEN BONES
BUT ALL THESE SCENES ARE OMITTED FROM THE MAIN STORY...
UCK.
...BECAUSE IT DOESN'T LOOK GOOD!!
OW.

Hold Me Tight

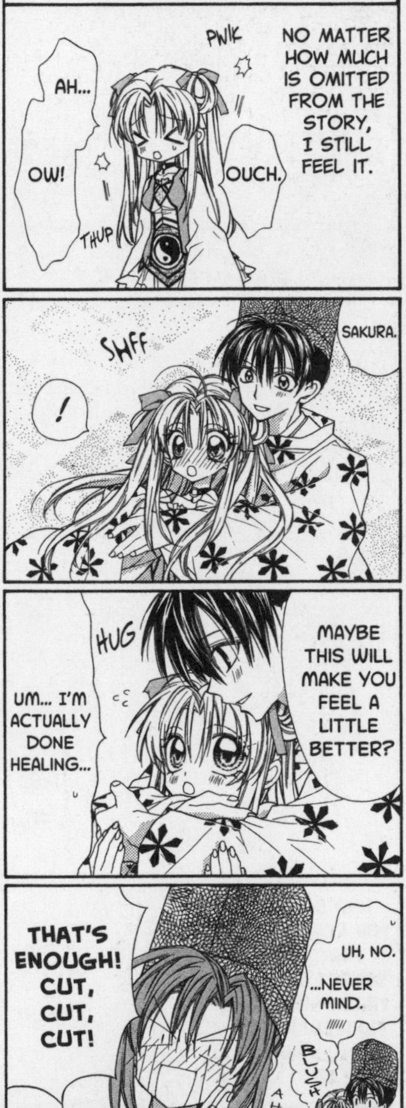
NO MATTER HOW MUCH IS OMITTED FROM THE STORY, I STILL FEEL IT.
PWIK
OUCH.
AH...
OW!
THUP
SAKURA.
SHFF
!
MAYBE THIS WILL MAKE YOU FEEL A LITTLE BETTER?
HUG
UM... I'M ACTUALLY DONE HEALING...
UH, NO.
...NEVER MIND.
BLUSH
AHHHH
THAT'S ENOUGH! CUT, CUT, CUT!

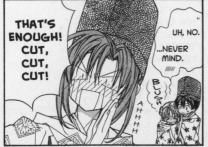

Easygoing Togu

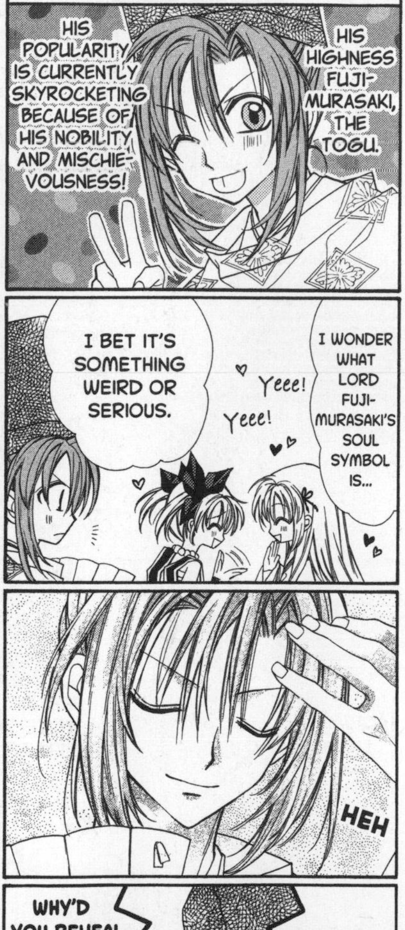
HIS HIGHNESS FUJI-MURASAKI, THE TOGU.
HIS POPULARITY IS CURRENTLY SKYROCKETING BECAUSE OF HIS NOBILITY AND MISCHIEVOUSNESS!
I WONDER WHAT LORD FUJI-MURASAKI'S SOUL SYMBOL IS...
Yeee!
Yeee!
I BET IT'S SOMETHING WEIRD OR SERIOUS.
HEH
MY SOUL SYMBOL IS "GREED"!
欲
WHY'D YOU REVEAL THAT SECRET IN THE BONUS FUNNIES?! AND I KNEW IT'D BE SOMETHING WEIRD!

Kiss Me, Hayate

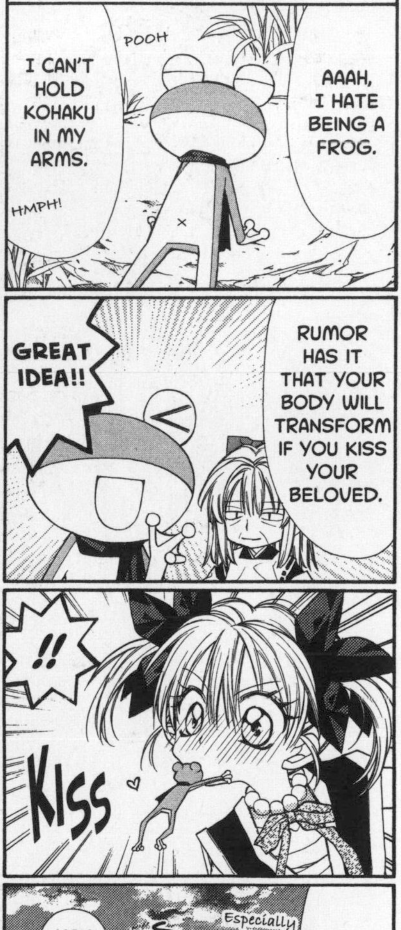
AAAH, I HATE BEING A FROG.
POOH
I CAN'T HOLD KOHAKU IN MY ARMS.
HMPH!
RUMOR HAS IT THAT YOUR BODY WILL TRANSFORM IF YOU KISS YOUR BELOVED.
GREAT IDEA!!
!!
KISS
SEE, YOU TRANSFORMED, DIDN'T YOU?
Especially your face.
SSSST
YOU GOT THAT RIGHT.
But I'm happy.

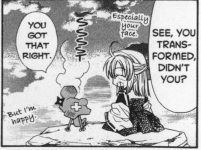

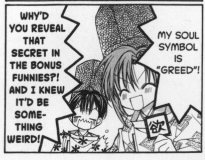

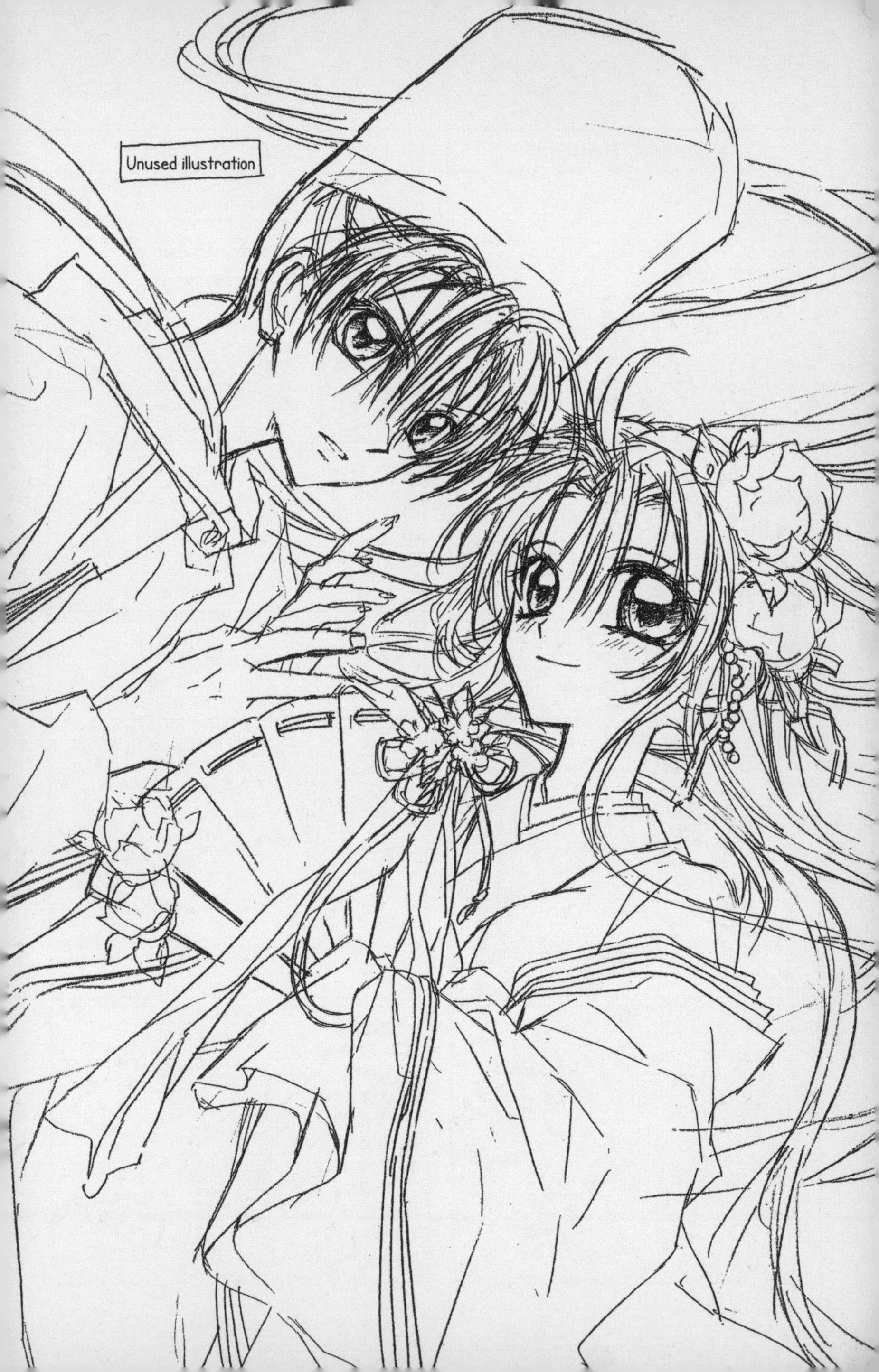

Unused illustration

Rough draft of the title page illustration for chapter 11.

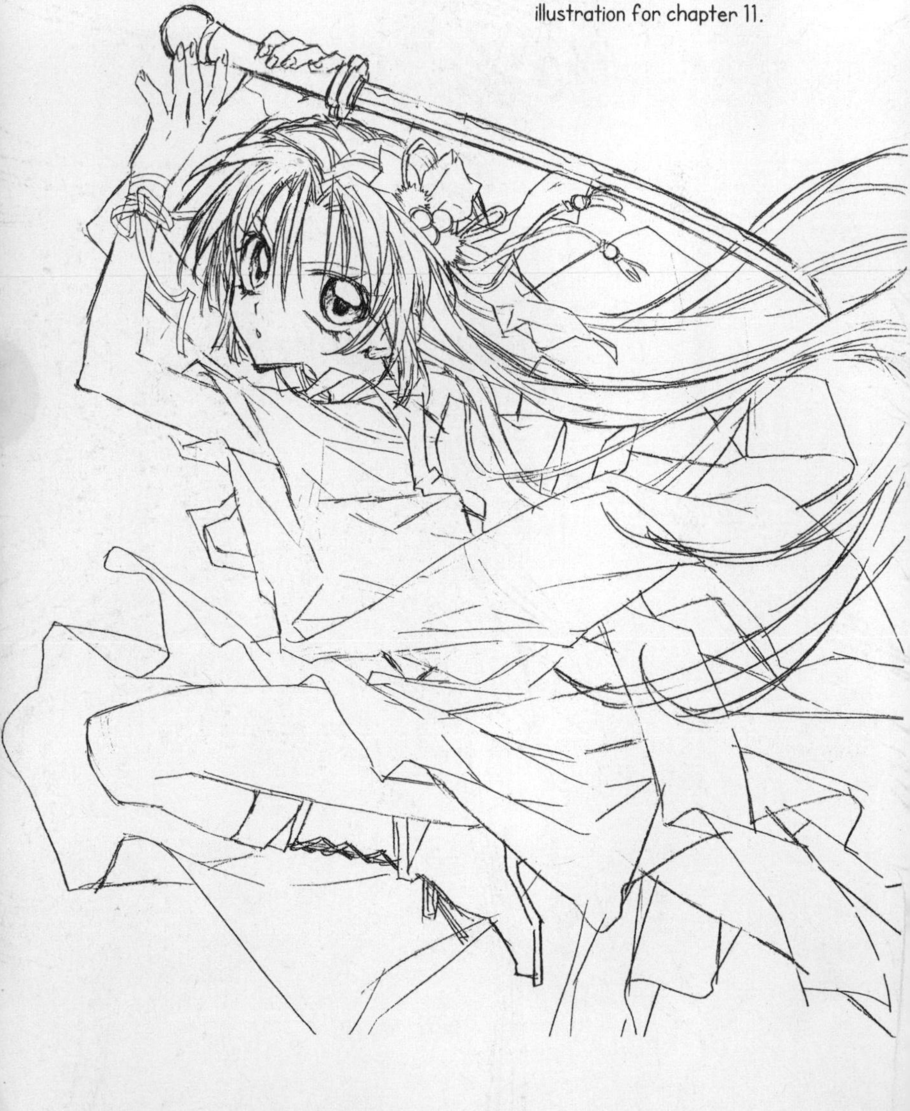

ARINA TANEMURA

The real story begins this volume. Most of the characters have made their appearances too. The character who will most likely become my favorite has appeared as well. (Do you know who it is?) My head is completely filled with *Sakura Hime* right now! It's rather serious, so sometimes I feel rather depressed about working on it, but I promise you that I'll commit myself to Sakura and the others with a positive attitude as much as possible!

Please feel free to tell me who your favorite characters are.

Arina Tanemura began her manga career in 1996 when her short stories debuted in *Ribon* magazine. She gained fame with the 1997 publication of *I·O·N*, and ever since her debut Tanemura has been a major force in shojo manga with popular series *Kamikaze Kaito Jeanne*, *Time Stranger Kyoko*, *Full Moon*, and *The Gentlemen's Alliance†*. Both *Kamikaze Kaito Jeanne* and *Full Moon* have been adapted into animated TV series.

Sakura Hime: The Legend of Princess Sakura
Volume 3
Shojo Beat Edition

STORY AND ART BY
Arina Tanemura

Translation & Adaptation/Tetsuichiro Miyaki
Touch-up Art & Lettering/Inori Fukuda Trant
Design/Sam Elzway
Editor/Nancy Thistlethwaite

SAKURA-HIME KADEN © 2008 by Arina Tanemura
All rights reserved.
First published in Japan in 2008 by SHUEISHA Inc., Tokyo.
English translation rights arranged by SHUEISHA Inc.

Printed in the U.S.A.

Published by VIZ Media, LLC
P.O. Box 77010
San Francisco, CA 94107

10 9 8 7 6 5 4 3 2 1
First printing, August 2011

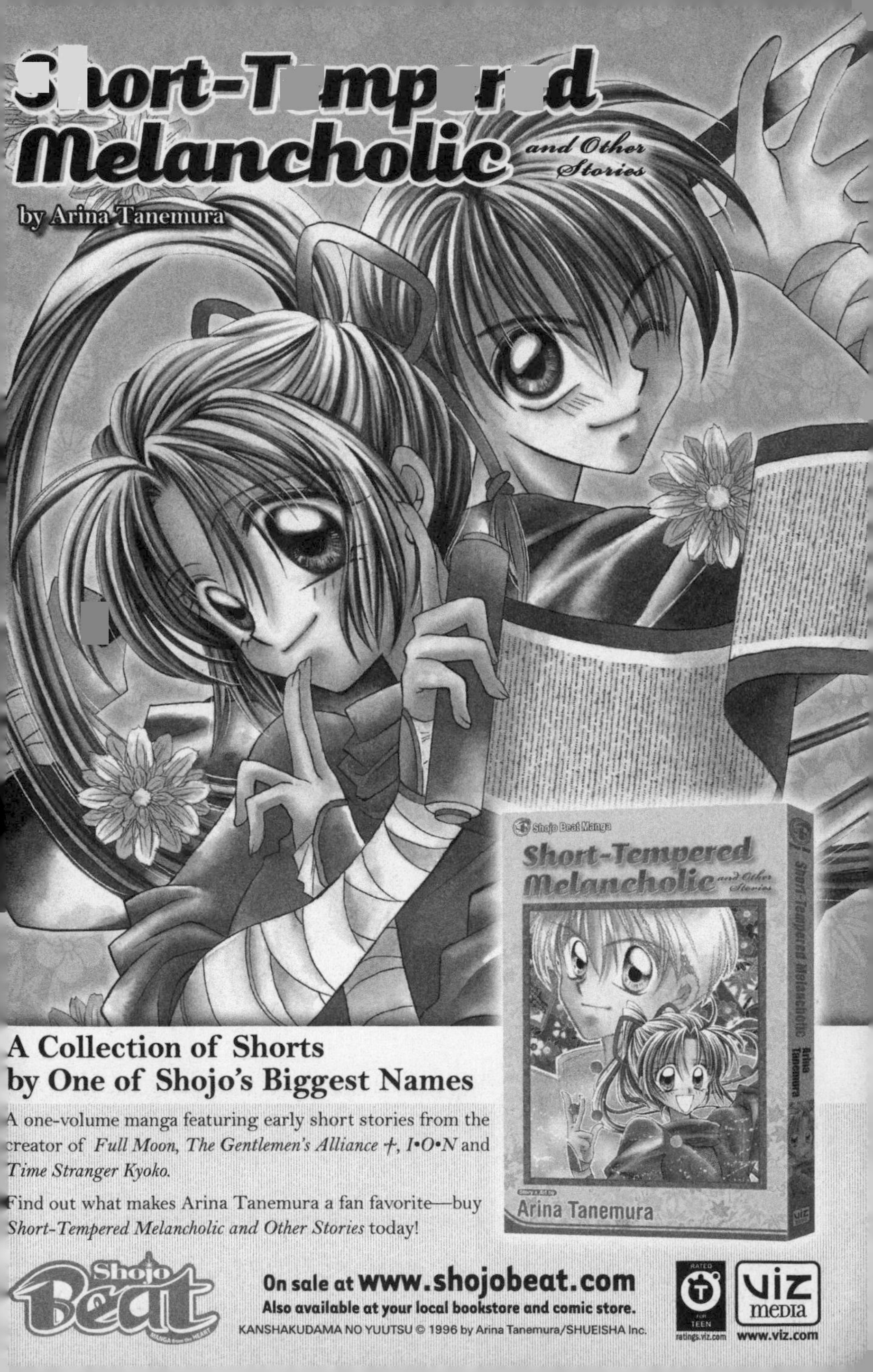
Short-Tempered Melancholic and Other Stories
by Arina Tanemura
Shojo Beat Manga
Short-Tempered Melancholic and Other Stories
Short-Tempered Melancholic Arina Tanemura
Story & Art by
Arina Tanemura
A Collection of Shorts
by One of Shojo's Biggest Names
A one-volume manga featuring early short stories from the creator of *Full Moon, The Gentlemen's Alliance †, I•O•N* and *Time Stranger Kyoko.*
Find out what makes Arina Tanemura a fan favorite—buy *Short-Tempered Melancholic and Other Stories* today!
Shojo Beat
MANGA from the HEART
On sale at www.shojobeat.com
Also available at your local bookstore and comic store.
KANSHAKUDAMA NO YUUTSU © 1996 by Arina Tanemura/SHUEISHA Inc.
RATED T FOR TEEN
ratings.viz.com
VIZ media
www.viz.com

Art book featuring 216 pages of beautiful color images personally selected by Tanemura

Read where Mitsuki's pop dreams began in the manga—all 7 volumes now available

Complete your collection with the anime, now on DVD

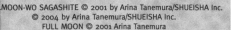

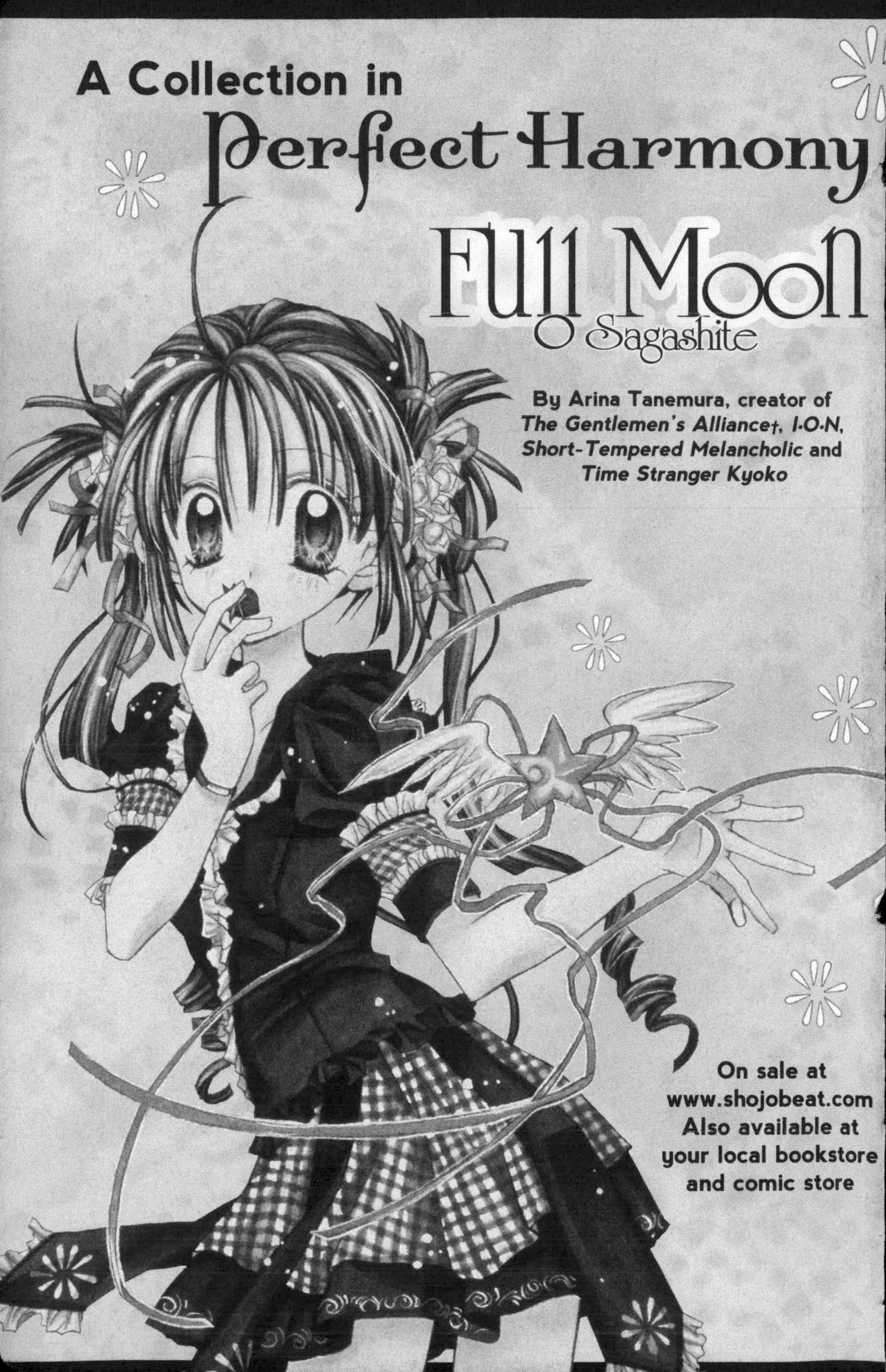
A Collection in
Perfect Harmony
Full Moon
O Sagashite
By Arina Tanemura, creator of
The Gentlemen's Alliance†, I·O·N, Short-Tempered Melancholic and *Time Stranger Kyoko*
On sale at
www.shojobeat.com
Also available at
your local bookstore
and comic store

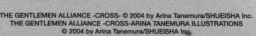

WELCOME to Imperial Academy: a private school where trying to become SUPERIOR can make you feel INFERIOR!

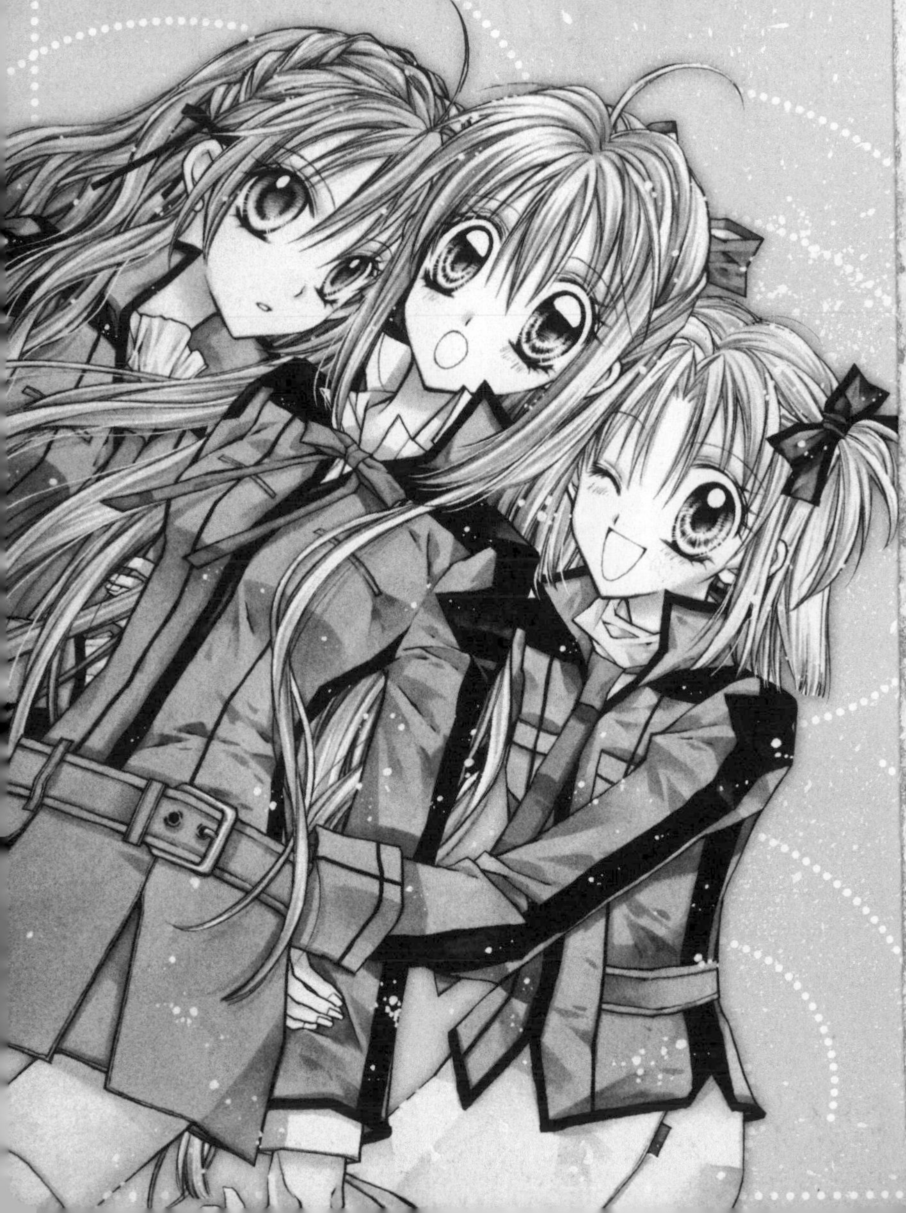

The World's Greatest Manga Now available on your iPad

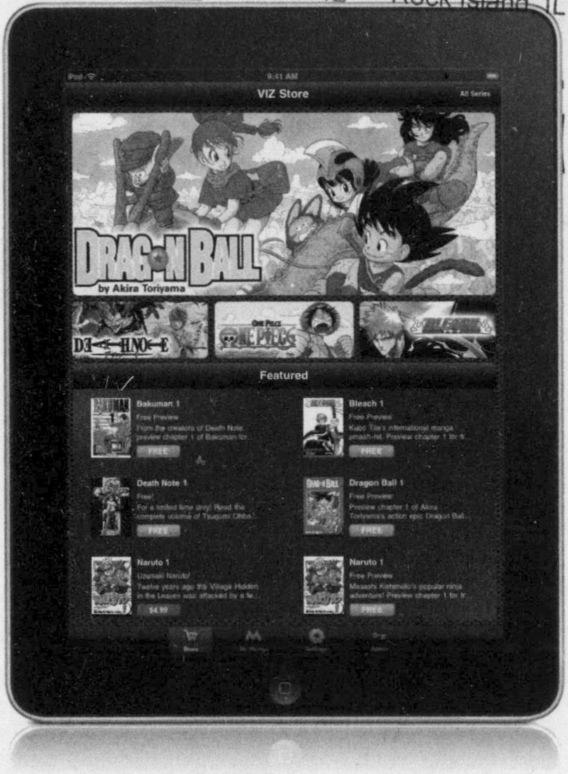
VIZ Store
All Series
DRAGON BALL
by Akira Toriyama
DEATH NOTE
ONE PIECE
Featured
Bakuman 1
FREE
Bleach 1
FREE
Death Note 1
FREE
Dragon Ball 1
FREE
Naruto 1
$4.99
Naruto 1
FREE

Full of FREE previews and tons of new manga for you to explore

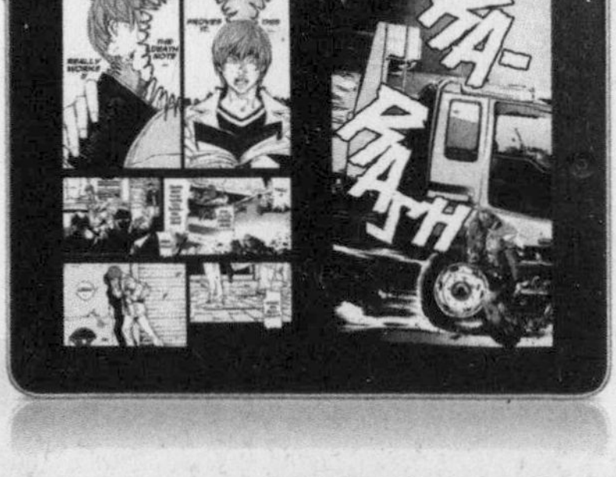
KA-BLASH

From legendary manga like *Dragon Ball* to *Bakuman。*, the newest series from the creators of *Death Note*, the best manga in the world is now available on the iPad through the official VIZ Manga app.

- Free App
- New content weekly
- Free chapter 1 previews